Instructor's Resource Guide

Organizational Behavior
Ninth Edition

John R. Schermerhorn
Ohio University

James G. Hunt
Texas Tech University

Richard N. Osborn
Wayne State University

Prepared by
Michael McCuddy
Valparaiso University

John Wiley & Sons, Inc.

To order books or for customer service call 1-800-CALL-WILEY (225-5945).

ISBN 0-471-71350-3

Printed in the United States of America.

10 9 8 7 6 5 4 3 2 1

Printed and bound by Malloy Lithographing, Inc.

CONTENTS

Chapter 13: Information and Communication 211

Chapter 14: Decision Making 225

Chapter 15: Conflict and Negotiation 243

Chapter 16: Change, Innovation, and Stress 261

Chapter 17: Organizing for Performance 279

Chapter 18: Organization Design for Strategic Competency

299

Chapter 19: Organizational Culture and Development

317

Unit 2, Part 1 — The OB Skills Workbook
The Jossey-Bass/Pfeiffer Classroom Collection

333

Unit 2, Part 2 — The OB Skills Workbook
Cases for Critical Thinking   **341**

Unit 2, Part 3 — The OB Skills Workbook
Cross-Functional Integrative Case — Trilogy Software:
High-Performance Company of the Future?   **381**

Unit 2, Part 4 — The OB Skills Workbook
Experiential Exercises   **385**

Unit 2, Part 5 — *The OB Skills Workbook*
Self-Assessment Inventories   **423**

Unit 3 — **Sample Course Outlines**   **437**

Unit 4 — **Student and Instructor Resources**   **439**

Unit 5 — **Organizational Behavior Lecture Launcher Videos**   **451**

PREFACE

This *Instructor's Resource Guide* has been designed for use with ***ORGANIZATIONAL BEHAVIOR*** *ninth edition*, written by John R. Schermerhorn, Jr., James G. Hunt, and Richard N. Osborn. The ***Instructor's Resource Guide*** contains five units of material. Unit 1 pertains directly to the textbook chapters — chapters 1 through 19 in this unit parallel the 19 chapters of ***ORGANIZATIONAL BEHAVIOR*** *ninth edition*. Unit 2 contains information and instructional guidance regarding the various components of *The OB Skills Workbook* that is located at the back of the textbook. Unit 3 contains sample course outlines. Unit 4 provides resources that will be useful to students and/or instructors. Unit 5, which was supplied by Joan R. Rentsch, provides information regarding the "Organizational Behavior Lecture Launcher Videos."

My goal in writing this ***Instructor's Resource Guide*** has been to develop instructional support materials that are both useful and user friendly. I hope these materials serve you well in your efforts within the teaching/learning enterprise.

Michael K. McCuddy
Valparaiso University
November 2004

Chapter 1
INTRODUCING ORGANIZATIONAL BEHAVIOR

STUDY QUESTIONS

1.	What is organizational behavior and why is it important?
2.	What are organizations like as work settings?
3.	What is the nature of managerial work?
4.	How do we learn about organizational behavior?

LEARNING OBJECTIVES

After completing this chapter students should be able to:

1.	Discuss the meaning of the term "organizational behavior" and describe why an understanding of organizational behavior is important.
2.	Describe the scientific foundations of organizational behavior and the trends that are influencing organizational behavior.
3.	Describe what an organization is and the context in which an organization operates.
4.	Discuss the nature of managerial work and describe the four functions of management.
5.	Discuss the three sets of roles that managers perform on a daily basis, the mind-sets that contribute to managerial success, and the skills that managers use in fulfilling their responsibilities.
6.	Define "individual learning" and "organizational learning," and explain the role of experiential learning in organizational behavior.

MATERIAL IN *THE OB SKILLS WORKBOOK* SUPPORTING THE CHAPTER

Case for Critical Thinking	Case 1: Drexler's Bar-B-Que
Experiential Exercises	Exercise 1: My Best Manager Exercise 2: Graffiti Needs Exercise 3: My Best Job
Self-Assessments	Assessment 1: Managerial Assumptions Assessment 2: A 21st Century Manager

CHAPTER OVERVIEW

This chapter provides an introduction to the field of organizational behavior. Organizational behavior is important because virtually everyone works with other people in some organized capacity, whether for monetary gain or voluntarily. An understanding of the principles of organizational behavior will not only help people to become better employees and managers, but will also help people become more astute observers of the organizational world, in general, and the business world, in particular.

The chapter begins by defining organizational behavior, discussing its scientific foundations, and identifying contemporary workplace trends that are being reflected in organizational behavior theories, concepts, and applications. The chapter then describes organizations as work settings. The meaning of "organization" is examined and put in the context of several important concepts, including: the organization's purpose, mission and strategy; the environment and stakeholders; organizational culture and diversity; and organizational effectiveness.

Next, the nature of managerial work is described. Emphasis is placed on the manager's role in fostering two key results: task performance and job satisfaction, and how the managerial functions of planning, organizing, directing, and controlling contribute to achieving these results. In addition, this section of the chapter discusses typical managerial activities; the interpersonal, informational, and decisional roles that managers assume; the different mind-sets that are important for successful managerial work; and the technical, human, and conceptual skills that managers utilize. The chapter concludes with a discussion of individual learning and organizational learning, placing emphasis on experiential learning within the context of organizational behavior.

CHAPTER OUTLINE

I.   **Study Question 1: What is organizational behavior and why is it important?**
    A. What is organizational behavior?
    B. Scientific foundations of organizational behavior
    C. Shifting paradigms of organizational behavior

II. **Study Question 2: What are organizations like as work settings?**
    A. Organizational purpose, mission, and strategy
    B. Organizational environments and stakeholders
    C. Organizational cultures and diversity
    D. Organizational effectiveness

III. **Study Question 3: What is the nature of managerial work?**
    A. The management process
    B. The nature of managerial work
    C. Managerial roles, networks, and mind-sets
    D. Managerial skills and competencies

IV. **Study Question 4: How do we learn about organizational behavior?**
    A. Learning and experience
    B. Learning guide to *Organizational Behavior 9/E*

CHAPTER LECTURE NOTES

I.   **Introduction to the Chapter 1 Lecture.**

    A.   Study questions for Chapter 1. (See *PowerPoint Slide 2* for Chapter 1.)

        1.   What is organizational behavior and why is it important?

        2.   What are organizations like as work settings?

        3.   What is the nature of managerial work?

        4.   How do we learn about organizational behavior?

    B.   The lecture material for Chapter 1 is organized around the study questions.

        1.   Point out to the students that the text's "Chapter At A Glance" identifies the key topics contained in the chapter and links them to the appropriate study questions.

    C.   The chapter opens by making the assertion that "people are an organization's most important assets" and then cites the case of Malden Mills to support this argument.

II.   **Study Question 1: What is organizational behavior and why is it important?**

    A.   Background on organizational behavior.

        1.   Success in any work setting depends on the following (see *PowerPoint Slide 3* for Chapter 1):

            a.   A respect for people.

            b.   An understanding of human behavior in complex organizational systems.

            c.   Individual commitment to flexibility, creativity, and learning.

            d.   Individual willingness to change with the challenges of the times.

        2.   The institutions of society and the people who make them work are challenged to do the following (see *PowerPoint Slide 4* for Chapter 1):

            a.   Simultaneously achieve high performance and high quality of life.

            b.   Embrace ethics and social responsibility as core values.

            c.   Respect the vast potential of demographic and cultural diversity among people.

            d.   Recognize the impact of globalization on daily living and organizational competitiveness.

B. What is organizational behavior? (See *PowerPoint Slide 5* for Chapter 1.)

    1. <u>**Organizational behavior**</u> (OB) is the study of human behavior in organizations.

    2. Organizational behavior is a multidisciplinary field devoted to understanding individual and group behavior, interpersonal processes, and organizational dynamics.

C. Scientific foundations and organizational behavior.

    1. Organizational behavior is an interdisciplinary body of knowledge with strong ties to the behavioral sciences of psychology, sociology, anthropology, and the allied social sciences such as economics and political science.

    2. Organizational behavior uses scientific methods to develop and empirically test generalizations about behavior in organizations.

    3. *Figure 1.1* from the textbook identifies the research methodologies that are commonly used in organizational behavior. (See *PowerPoint Slide 6* for Chapter 1.)

    4. Scientific thinking is important to OB researchers and scholars for the following reasons (see *PowerPoint Slide 7* for Chapter 1):

        a. The process of data collection is controlled and systematic.

        b. Proposed explanations are carefully tested.

        c. Only explanations that can be scientifically verified are accepted.

    5. Organizational behavior focuses on applications that can make a real difference in how organizations and people in them perform.

    6. Organizational behavior uses contingency thinking in its search for ways to improve organizational outcomes. (See *PowerPoint Slide 8* for Chapter 1.)

        a. The <u>**contingency approach**</u> tries to identify how different situations can be best understood and handled.

        b. Important contingency variables include environment, technology, tasks, structure, and people.

LECTURE ENHANCEMENT

Ask students to describe examples of management practices that may work well in one organization, but poorly in another.

D. Shifting paradigms of organizational behavior.

1. Progressive workplaces today look and act very differently from those of the past.

2. Intense global competition, job migration due to outsourcing and offshoring, highly interdependent national economies, constantly emerging computer and information technologies, new forms of organizations, and shifting population demographics are now part of the norm for businesses.

3. Trends occurring in modern workplaces include the following (see *PowerPoint Slide 9* for Chapter 1):

   a. Commitment to ethical behavior.

   b. Importance of human capital.

   c. Demise of "command and control."

   d. Emphasis on teamwork.

   e. Pervasive influence of information technology.

   f. Respect for new workforce expectations.

   g. Changing definition of "jobs" and "career."

LECTURE ENHANCEMENT

Conduct a brainstorming session with students to identify recent examples of each of the preceding workplace trends. After generating a sufficient number of examples, focus class discussion on the implications of these examples for managerial and leadership activities.

III. **Study Question 2: What organizations like as work settings?**

A. Organizations defined.

1. An **organization** is a collection of people working together in a division of labor to achieve a common purpose. (See *PowerPoint Slide 10* for Chapter 1.)

B. Organizational purpose, mission, and strategy.

1. The core purpose of an organization is the creation of goods and services for customers. (See *PowerPoint Slide 11* for Chapter 1.)

2. *Missions* and *mission statements* focus the attention of organizational members and external constituents on the core purpose. (See *PowerPoint Slide 11* for Chapter 1.)

    a. Mission statements are written to communicate the following to employees, customers, and other audiences:

        (i) A clear sense of the domain in which the organization's products and services fit.

        (ii) A vision and sense of future aspirations.

3. Given a sense of purpose and a vision, organizations pursue strategies to accomplish them. (See *PowerPoint Slide 12* for Chapter 1.)

    a. A **strategy** is a comprehensive plan that guides organizations to operate in ways that allow them to outperform their competitors.

    b. Strategic management responsibilities include both the formulation of strategies and their successful implementation.

    c. Knowledge of organizational behavior is essential to effectively implement strategies.

LECTURE ENHANCEMENT

Describe your college's or university's mission and strategy to the students. Explain how the strategy is implemented.

C. Organizational environments and stakeholders.

1. *Figure 1.2* from the textbook characterizes organizations as dynamic **open systems** that obtain resource inputs from the environment and transform them into finished goods or services that are returned to the environment as outputs. (See *PowerPoint Slide 13* for Chapter 1.)

2. The complex environment or organizations contains a variety of stakeholders.

3. **Stakeholders** are the people, groups, and institutions that are affected by and thus have an interest or "stake" in an organization's performance. (See *PowerPoint Slide 14* for Chapter 1.)

    a. Customers, owners, employees, suppliers, regulators, and local communities are the key stakeholders of most organizations.

    b. The interests of multiple stakeholders are sometimes conflicting.

    c. Executive leadership often becomes a task of finding the right balance among multiple stakeholder expectations.

D. Organizational culture and diversity. (See *PowerPoint Slide 15* for Chapter 1.)

   1. **Organizational culture** refers to the shared beliefs and values that influence the behavior of organizational members.

   2. Organizations with positive cultures have a high-performance orientation, emphasize teamwork, encourage risk taking, and emphasize innovation.

   3. Positive organizational cultures have an underlying respect for people and **workforce diversity** (*i.e.*, the presence of differences based on gender, race and ethnicity, age, able-bodiedness, and sexual orientation).

   4. Success in the contemporary business world rests in part on **valuing diversity**, which refers to managing and working with others in full respect for their individual differences.

E. Organizational effectiveness.

   1. **Organizational effectiveness** is a measure of how well organizations perform as open systems, using their resources to achieve high performance results.

   2. Approaches to organizational effectiveness. (See *PowerPoint Slide 16* for Chapter 1.)

      a. The *systems resource approach* focuses on inputs and defines effectiveness in terms of success in acquiring needed resources from the organization's external environment.

      b. The *internal process approach* focuses on the transformation process and defines effectiveness in terms of how efficiently resources are utilized to produce goods and/or services.

      c. The *goal approach* focuses on outputs and defines effectiveness in terms of achieving key operating objectives.

      d. The *strategic contingencies approach* analyzes the impact of the organization on key stakeholders and their interests.

   3. Organizational effectiveness can be evaluated longitudinally and the performance emphasis can vary as conditions change and new challenges arise. (See *PowerPoint Slide 17* for Chapter 1.)

      a. In the short run, emphasis is placed on goal accomplishment, resource utilization, and stakeholder satisfaction.

      b. In the intermediate run, emphasis is placed on the organization's ability to adapt to changing environmental conditions and its ability to develop people and systems to meet new challenges.

c. In the long run, emphasis is placed on survival under conditions of environmental uncertainty.

LECTURE ENHANCEMENT

Divide students into small groups to brainstorm on appropriate short-term, medium-term, and long-term criteria for evaluating the effectiveness of a college/university. Have a spokesperson from each group report out to the entire class.

IV. **Study Question 3: What is the nature of managerial work?**

A. Background on managerial work. (See *PowerPoint Slide 18* for Chapter 1.)

1. **Managers** are individuals who perform jobs that involve directly supporting the work efforts of other people.

2. In the new workplace, managers fulfill their responsibilities through "helping" and "supporting" rather than through traditional notions of "directing" and "controlling."

B. The management process.

1. An **effective manager** is one whose organizational unit, group, or team consistently achieves its goals while members remain capable, committed, and enthusiastic. (See *PowerPoint Slide 19* for Chapter 1.)

2. This definition focuses on two key results in a manager's daily work: task performance and job satisfaction. (See *PowerPoint Slide 19* for Chapter 1.)

a. **Task performance** refers to the quality and quantity of the work produced or the services provided by the work unit as a whole.

b. **Job satisfaction** refers to how people feel about their work and the work setting.

3. The jobs of managers and team leaders can be described by the four functions of management, as shown in *Figure 1.3* from the textbook. (See *PowerPoint Slide 20* for Chapter 1.) These four functions are as follows:

a. **Planning** — defining goals, setting specific performance objectives, and identifying the actions needed to achieve them.

b. **Organizing** — creating work structures and systems, and arranging resources to accomplish goals and objectives.

c. **Leading** — instilling enthusiasm by communicating with others, motivating them to work hard, and maintaining good interpersonal relations.

d. **Controlling** — ensuring that things go well by monitoring performance and taking corrective action as necessary.

LECTURE ENHANCEMENT

Divide students into discussion groups of five to six members. Have each group select a different campus organization to analyze. Each group should explore how planning, organizing, leading, and controlling are exhibited in the chosen campus organization.

C. The nature of managerial work.

1. Anyone who serves as a manager or team leader assumes a position of unique responsibility for work that is accomplished largely through the efforts of one or more other people.

2. The managerial job can be described in the following terms (see ***PowerPoint Slide 21*** for Chapter 1):

   a. Managers work long hours.

   b. Managers are busy people.

   c. Managers are often interrupted.

   d. Managerial work is fragmented and variable.

   e. Managers work mostly with other people.

   f. Managers spend a lot of time communicating.

LECTURE ENHANCEMENT

Poll the class in order to identify students with managerial experience. Have three of these students describe their "normal" workday.

D. Managerial roles, networks, and mind-sets.

1. Based on the work of Henry Mintzberg, ***Figure 1.4*** from the textbook identifies the various interpersonal, informational, and decisional roles of effective managers. (See ***PowerPoint Slide 22*** for Chapter 1.)

   a. Interpersonal roles involve working directly with other people and include the roles of figurehead, leader, and liaison.

      b.   Informational roles involve exchanging information with other people and include the roles of monitor, disseminator, and spokesperson.

      c.   Decisional roles involve making decisions that affect other people and include the roles of entrepreneur, disturbance handler, resource allocator, and negotiator.

LECTURE ENHANCEMENT

Have students draw on their work, educational, athletic team, or other extracurricular experiences to identify examples of how people in managerial and leadership positions enact the various interpersonal, informational, and decisional roles.

---

    2.   Good interpersonal relationships are essential to success in the interpersonal, informational, and decisional roles, and in all managerial work.

    3.   Managers and team leaders need to develop and maintain good working relations with a wide variety of people, inside and outside the organization.

    4.   Managers must seek out and work with other people in task networks and social networks.

    5.   A **managerial mind-set** is an attitude or frame of mind that opens up new vistas.

    6.   Mind-sets that are important for successful managerial work include the following (see *PowerPoint Slide 23* for Chapter 1):

      a.   The reflective mind-set deals with being able to manage one's self.

      b.   The analytic mind-set deals with managing organizational operations and decisions.

      c.   The worldly mind-set deals with managing in a global context.

      d.   The collaborative mind-set deals with managing relationships.

      e.   The action mind-set deals with managing change.

    7.   All five mind-sets must work together.

  E. Managerial skills and competencies.

    1.   A *skill* is an ability to translate knowledge into action that results in a desired performance. (See *PowerPoint Slide 24* for Chapter 1.)

    2.   Robert Katz divides essential managerial skills in three categories: technical, human, and conceptual. (See *PowerPoint Slide 24* for Chapter 1.)

a. A **technical skill** is the ability to perform specialized tasks.

b. A **human skill** is the ability to work well with other people.

    (i) **Emotional intelligence** (EI) is the ability to understand and deal with emotions.

    (ii) EI is an important area of human skills that includes self-awareness, self-regulation, motivation, empathy, and social skill.

LECTURE ENHANCEMENT

Have the students spend eight to ten minutes of class time writing a brief self-assessment essay regarding the extent to which they perceive themselves as having developed each the above components of emotional intelligence. Have the students, who are willing to do so, contribute their examples as you discuss the components of emotional intelligence.

---

c. A **conceptual skill** is the ability to analyze and solve complex and interrelated problems.

3. Technical skills are more important at entry levels of management and conceptual skills are more important for senior executives. Human skills, which are strongly grounded in the foundations of organizational behavior, are important across all managerial levels.

LECTURE ENHANCEMENT

Have students discuss the roles that technical skills, human skills, and conceptual skills play in their professors' performance of their jobs. Then have the students think of their own educational pursuits as a job. What roles do technical skills, human skills, and conceptual skills play in the students' performance of their jobs?

V.   **Study Question 4: How do we learn about organizational behavior?**

A. Background on learning about organizational behavior. (See *PowerPoint Slide 25* for Chapter 1.)

1. **Learning** is an enduring change in behavior that results from experience.

2. The modern knowledge-based economy places a premium on learning by both organizations and individuals.

3. **Organizational learning** is the process of acquiring knowledge and utilizing information to adapt successfully to changing circumstances.

B. Learning and experience.

1. *Figure 1.5* from the textbook shows how the content and activities of a typical organizational behavior course fit together as part of an experiential learning cycle that begins with initial experience and progresses sequentially through reflection, theory building, and experimentation. (See *PowerPoint Slide 26* for Chapter 1.)

2. *Life-long learning* refers to the need to learn from day-to-day work experiences, conversations with colleagues and friends, counseling and advice from mentors, success models, training seminars and workshops, and the information available in the popular press and mass media.

C. Learning guide to *Organizational Behavior 9/E*.

1. *Figure 1.6* from the textbook shows that "organizational behavior is a knowledge base" "that helps people work together" "to improve the performance of organizations." (See *PowerPoint Slide 27* for Chapter 1.)

VI. Study summary for Chapter 1.

A. Point out to the students that the text's "Chapter 1 Study Guide" recaps the key theories, concepts, and ideas in the chapter in relation to the appropriate study questions.

CHAPTER STUDY GUIDE

Study Question 1: What is organizational behavior and why is it important?

- Organizational behavior is the study of individuals and groups in organizations.
- OB is an applied discipline based on scientific methods that uses a contingency approach, recognizing that management practices must fit the situation.
- Dramatic changes signal the emergence of a new workplace with high-technology, global competition, demanding customers, high-performance systems, and concerns for ethical behavior and social responsibility.

Study Question 2: What are organizations like as work settings?

- An organization is a collection of people working together in a division of labor for a common purpose — to produce goods or services for society.
- As open systems, organizations interact with their environments to obtain resources that are transformed into outputs returned to the environment for consumption.
- The resources of organizations are material — such as technology, capital, and information, as well as human — the people who do the required work.
- Organizations pursue strategies that facilitate the accomplishment of purpose and mission; the field of OB is an important foundation for effective strategy implementation.
- Key stakeholders in the external environments of organizations include customers, owners, suppliers, regulators, local communities, and employees.

- The organizational culture is the internal "personality" of the organization, including the beliefs and values that are shared by members.
- Positive organizational cultures place a high value on inclusiveness of all members, showing respect for all aspects of workforce diversity.
- Organizational effectiveness can be measured from different perspectives, including the systems resource, internal process, goal, and strategic constituencies approaches.

Study Question 3: What is the nature of managerial work?

- Managers in the new workplace are expected to act more like "coaches" and "facilitators" than as "bosses" and "controllers."
- An effective manager is one whose work unit, team, or group accomplishes high levels of performance that are sustainable over the long term by enthusiastic workers.
- The four functions of management are (1) planning — to set direction, (2) organizing — to assemble resources and systems, (3) leading — to create workforce enthusiasm, and (4) controlling — to ensure desired results.
- Managers fulfill a variety of interpersonal, informational, and decisional roles while working with networks of people both within and outside of the organization.
- Managers should understand and be comfortable with five mind-sets that guide and activate their work: collaborative, action, reflective, worldly, and analytic.
- Managerial performance is based on a combination of essential technical, human, and conceptual skills.

Study Question 4: How do we learn about organizational behavior?

- Learning is an enduring change in behavior that results from experience.
- Organization learning is the process of acquiring knowledge and utilizing information to adapt successfully to changing circumstances.
- Many organizational behavior courses use multiple methods and approaches that take advantage of the experiential learning cycle.
- True learning about organizational behavior involves more than just reading a textbook; it requires a commitment to continuous and lifelong learning from one's work and everyday experiences.

KEY TERMS

Conceptual skill: the ability to analyze and solve complex and interrelated problems.
Contingency approach: an approach to management that tries to identify how different situations can be best understood and handled.
Controlling: ensuring that things go well by monitoring performance and taking corrective action as necessary.
Effective manager: a manager whose organizational unit, group, or team consistently achieves its goals while members remain capable, committed, and enthusiastic.
Emotional intelligence: the ability to understand and deal with emotions.
Human skill: the ability to work well with other people.
Job satisfaction: how people feel about their work and the work setting.
Leading: instilling enthusiasm by communicating with others, motivating them to work hard, and maintaining good interpersonal relations.
Learning: an enduring change in behavior that results from experience.

Managerial mind-set: an attitude or frame of mind that opens up new vistas.

Managers: individuals who perform jobs that involve directly supporting the work efforts of other people.

Open system: a system that obtains resource inputs from the environment and transforms them into finished goods or services that are returned to the environment as outputs.

Organizational behavior: the study of human behavior in organizations.

Organizational culture: the shared beliefs and values that influence the behavior of organizational members.

Organizational effectiveness: how well organizations perform as open systems, using their resources to achieve high performance results.

Organizational learning: the process of acquiring knowledge and utilizing information to adapt successfully to changing circumstances.

Organizations: collections of people working together in a division of labor to achieve a common purpose.

Organizing: creating work structures and systems, and arranging resources to accomplish goals and objectives.

Planning: defining goals, setting specific performance objectives, and identifying the actions needed to achieve them.

Stakeholders: the people, groups, and institutions that are affected by and thus have an interest or "stake" in an organization's performance.

Strategy: a comprehensive plan that guides organizations to operate in ways that allow them to outperform their competitors.

Task performance: the quality and quantity of the work produced or the services provided by the work unit as a whole.

Technical skill: the ability to perform specialized tasks.

Workforce diversity: the presence of differences based on gender, race and ethnicity, age, able-bodiedness, and sexual orientation.

Chapter 2
CURRENT ISSUES IN ORGANIZATIONAL BEHAVIOR

STUDY QUESTIONS

1.	What is a high-performance organization?
2.	What is multiculturalism, and how can workforce diversity be managed?
3.	How do ethics and social responsibility influence human behavior in organizations?
4.	What are key OB transitions in the new workplace?

LEARNING OBJECTIVES

After completing this chapter students should be able to:

1.	Define what is meant by the term "high-performance organization" and describe the key characteristics of high-performance organizations.
2.	Explain the importance of stakeholders, value creation, total quality management, continuous improvement, human capital, empowerment, and organizational learning for high-performance organizations.
3.	Define workforce diversity, multiculturalism, and inclusivity; and describe their implications for organizations.
4.	Discuss important diversity issues and challenges, and describe the characteristics of diversity-mature individuals and organizations.
5.	Define ethical behavior, explain the nature of moral management and ethics mindfulness, and describe four different views of ethical behavior.
6.	Discuss the nature of ethical dilemmas and common rationalizations for unethical behavior.
7.	Describe the implications of organizational social responsibility.
8.	Discuss important organizational behavior transitions that are occurring in the new workplace.

MATERIAL IN *THE OB SKILLS WORKBOOK* SUPPORTING THE CHAPTER

Case for Critical Thinking	Case 2: The Panera Bread Case — Not By Bread Alone
Experiential Exercises	Exercise 3: My Best Job
	Exercise 4: What Do You Value in Work?
	Exercise 5: My Asset Base
Self-Assessments	Assessment 2: 21st Century Manager
	Assessment 3: Turbulence Tolerance Test

CHAPTER OVERVIEW

This chapter focuses on current issues in organizational behavior. The chapter begins by discussing the nature of high-performance organizations, giving attention to identifying their key characteristics. Several concepts that are relevant to an understanding of high-performance organizations are then introduced. These concepts include stakeholders, value creation, total quality management, continuous improvement, various aspects of human capital and empowerment, and organizational learning and high-performance cultures.

The chapter continues with a discussion of multiculturalism and workforce diversity. After defining relevant key terms, attention is focused on describing important diversity issues and challenges. Then the discussion turns to managing diversity, with particular emphasis being placed on the nature of diversity-mature managers and organizations.

Next, the chapter explores the very important issues of ethics and social responsibility in organizations. Emphasis is placed on the nature of ethical behavior; immoral, amoral, and moral models of management; ethics mindfulness; the utilitarian, individualism, moral-rights and justice views of ethical behavior; the nature of ethical dilemmas; common rationalizations for unethical behavior; and the nature of organizational social responsibility.

The chapter concludes with a discussion of some important organizational behavior transitions that are occurring in the new workplace. This section examines the nature of corporate governance, ethics leadership, and personal integrity; as well as the nature of quality of work life and related concepts such as empowerment, trust, performance-based rewards, responsiveness, and work-life balance. Also addressed are the concept of positive organizational behavior and the core capacities around which it is built, important concerns regarding globalization, and the roles that personal management and self-monitoring play in successful careers in the contemporary workplace.

CHAPTER OUTLINE

I. **Study Question 1: What is a high-performance organization?**
    A. Stakeholders, value creation, and customer satisfaction
    B. Human capital and empowerment
    C. Learning and high performance cultures

II. **Study Question 2: What is multiculturalism, and how can workforce diversity be managed?**
    A. Multiculturalism and inclusivity
    B. Diversity issues and challenges
    C. Managing diversity

III. **Study Question 3: How do ethics and social responsibility influence human behavior in organizations?**
    A. Moral management and ethics mindfulness
    B. Ways of thinking about ethical behavior
    C. Ethics failures and dilemmas
    D. Organizational social responsibilities

IV. **Study Question 4: What are key OB transitions in the new workplace?**

    A. Corporate governance and ethics leadership

    B. Quality of work life and positive organizational behavior

    C. Globalization, job migration and organizational transformations

    D. Personal management and career planning

CHAPTER LECTURE NOTES

I. **Introduction to the Chapter 2 Lecture.**

    A. Study questions for Chapter 2. (See *PowerPoint Slide 2* for Chapter 2.)

        1. What is a high-performance organization?

        2. What is multiculturalism, and how can workforce diversity be managed?

        3. How do ethics and social responsibility influence human behavior in organizations?

        4. What are key OB transitions in the new workplace?

    B. The lecture material for Chapter 2 is organized around the study questions.

        1. Point out to the students that the text's "Chapter At A Glance" identifies the key topics contained in the chapter and links them to the appropriate study questions.

    C. The chapter opens with a description of the changing conditions that bring about the need for high-performance organizations and the crucial role that human resources play in attaining high performance.

II. **Study Question 1: What is a high-performance organization?**

    A. An introduction to the concept of high-performance organizations.

        1. Creating high-performance organizations is an important means by which businesses can respond the varied challenges of the 21st century global economy.

        2. A **high-performance organization** is intentionally designed to bring out the best in people and thereby produce sustainable organizational results while creating a high quality-of-work-life environment.

        3. Key characteristics of high-performance organizations include the following (see *PowerPoint Slide 3* for Chapter 2):

            a. High-performance organizations value people as assets, respect diversity, and empower all members to fully use their talents.

            b. High-performance organizations mobilize self-directed work teams to build synergies from the members' talents.

      c.   High-performance organizations use cutting-edge information and production technologies to achieve success.

      d.   High-performance organizations thrive on learning and have norms and cultures that encourage knowledge sharing and enable members to experience continuous growth and development.

      e.   High-performance organizations are achievement-oriented, sensitive to the external environment, focused on total quality management, and provide exceptional customer service.

LECTURE ENHANCEMENT

Divide the class into groups of four or five students. Have each group select an organization with which they are reasonably familiar. Then using the above list of key characteristics of high-performance organizations, have each group assess the extent to which the chosen organization possesses each characteristic.

  B. Stakeholders, value creation and customer satisfaction.

      1. **Stakeholders** are the individuals, groups, and other organizations affected by an organization's performance. (See *PowerPoint Slide 4* for Chapter 2).

      2. The interests of stakeholders can be described in terms of the organization's multiple responsibilities for **value creation**, which is the extent to which an organization satisfies the needs of strategic constituencies. (See *PowerPoint Slide 4* for Chapter 2).

      3. The needs of strategic constituencies may overlap and potentially conflict with each other.

      4. As shown in *Figure 2.1* from the textbook, the upside-down pyramid view of organizations focuses attention on value creation for customers and clients by placing them at the top of the organization and giving them primary importance. (See *PowerPoint Slide 5* for Chapter 2.)

      5. **Total quality management** involves management being dedicated to ensuring that an organization and all its members are committed to high quality, continuous improvement, and customer satisfaction. (See *PowerPoint Slide 6* for Chapter 2.)

         a. *Quality* means that customers' needs are met and that all tasks are done right the first time.

         b. **Continuous improvement** is the belief that all workplace activities should be continually subjected to two questions: Is it necessary? If so, can it be done better?

C. Human capital and empowerment.

1. The essential foundation for long-term performance success is **human capital**, which refers to the economic value of people with job-relevant abilities, knowledge, ideas, energies, and commitments. (See *PowerPoint Slide 7* for Chapter 2.)

2. **Knowledge workers** are people whose minds rather than physical capabilities create value for the organization. (See *PowerPoint Slide 7* for Chapter 2.)

3. Through knowledge workers, human capital become **intellectual capital** — the performance potential of the expertise, competencies, creativity, and commitment within an organization's workforce. (See *PowerPoint Slide 7* for Chapter 2.)

4. Intellectual capital is unlocked through **empowerment**, which allows people, individually and in groups, to use their talents and knowledge to make decisions that affect their work. (See *PowerPoint Slide 8* for Chapter 2.)

5. **Social capital**, which refers to the performance potential represented in the relationships maintained among people at work, provides an important means for mobilizing the value of people as human assets. (See *PowerPoint Slide 8* for Chapter 2.)

D. Learning and high-performance cultures.

1. Uncertainty highlights the importance of organizational learning. (See *PowerPoint Slide 9* for Chapter 2.)

2. High-performance organizations are designed for organizational learning. (See *PowerPoint Slide 9* for Chapter 2.)

3. A *learning organization* has a strong and positive culture that values human capital and invigorates learning for performance enhancement. (See *PowerPoint Slide 9* for Chapter 2.)

    a. *Organizational culture* is a system of shared beliefs and values that influences the behavior of organization members.

    b. High-performance organizational cultures provide members with a clear vision of the organization's purpose and goals, encourage positive behavior that supports those goals, and discourages dysfunctional behaviors.

LECTURE ENHANCEMENT

Have the students describe the culture of an organization to which they belong. Campus organizations, athletic teams, past or present employers, etc. can be used. How would that organization "stack up" as a learning organization with a strong and positive culture?

---

    c. *Figure 2.2* from the text identifies an approach for describing cultures as less effective (*i.e.*, passive/defensive or aggressive/defensive) or more effective (*i.e.*, constructive). (See *PowerPoint Slide 10* for Chapter 2.)

        (i) In a passive/defensive culture, members tend to act defensively in their working relationships, seeking to protect their security.

        (ii) In an aggressive/defensive culture, members tend to act forcefully in their working relationships to protect their status and position.

        (iii) In a constructive culture, members are encouraged to work together in ways that meet higher order human needs.

        (iv) A constructive culture is most closely associated with the high-performance organization.

III.   **Study Question 2: What is multiculturalism, and how can workforce diversity be managed?**

A. **Workforce diversity** describes differences among people with respect to age, race, ethnicity, gender, physical ability, and sexual orientation. Diversity includes all people, and positive organizational cultures tap the talents, ideas, and creative potential of all organization members. (See *PowerPoint Slide 11* for Chapter 2.)

B. Multiculturalism and inclusivity.

    1. Workforce diversity is a major characteristic of contemporary American society.

    2. **Multiculturalism** refers to pluralism and respect for diversity and individual differences in the workplace. (See *PowerPoint Slide 11* for Chapter 2.)

    3. **Inclusivity** is the degree to which the organization's culture respects and values diversity, and is open to anyone who can perform a job, regardless of his or her diversity attributes. (See *PowerPoint Slide 11* for Chapter 2.)

C. Diversity issues and challenges.

    1. Unequal distribution of differences across organizational levels or across work functions can significantly influence operations and relationships within an organization.

    2. Diversity biases in the workplace include the following (see *PowerPoint Slide 12* for Chapter 2):

        a. *Prejudice*, which is the holding of negative, irrational opinions and attitudes regarding members of diverse populations.

        b. *Discrimination*, which actively disadvantages someone by treating them unfairly and denying then the full benefits of organizational membership.

c. The *glass ceiling effect*, which is an invisible barrier in some organizations that prevents the advancement of women and minorities.

   (i) *Figure 2.3* from the text depicts the operation of the glass ceiling. (See *PowerPoint Slide 13* for Chapter 2.)

   (ii) The dominant culture of white males holds most top positions, is present at all levels, and is included in entry-level hiring.

   (iii) The minority cultures consisting of women, people of color, and other minorities hold few top positions, are distributed in lower to middle levels, and are included in entry-level hiring.

d. *Sexual harassment* refers to unwanted sexual advances, requests for sexual favors, and other sexually laced communications.

e. Verbal abuse often occurs in the form of cultural jokes.

f. Pay discrimination against women and minorities remains an issue in American society.

D. Managing diversity.

1. Managing diversity refers to developing a work environment and organizational culture that allows all organization members to reach their full potential. (See *PowerPoint Slide 14* for Chapter 2.)

2. Managing diversity can be guided by addressing the following questions (see *PowerPoint Slide 14* for Chapter 2):

   a. What do I as a manager need to do to ensure the effective and efficient utilization of employees in pursuit of the corporate mission?

   b. What are the implications of diversity for the way I manage?

3. Positive answers by managers throughout the organization to the following questions signifies a diversity mature organization:

   a. Do you accept personal responsibility for improving your performance?

   b. Do you accept personal responsibility for improving your organization's performance?

   c. Do you understand yourself and your organization?

   d. Do you understand important diversity concepts?

   e. Do you make decisions involving differences based on ability to meet job requirements?

    f.   Do you understand that diversity is complex and accompanied by tensions?

    g.   Are you able to cope with complexity and tensions in addressing diversity?

    h.   Are you willing to challenge the ways things are?

    i.   Are you willing to learn continuously?

LECTURE ENHANCEMENT

Have each student answer the above questions regarding his or her involvement in some organization. Subsequent to answering the questions, hold a general class discussion regarding how diversity mature the class members are and what would need to be done to achieve a greater level of diversity maturity.

---

4.   Diversity-mature individuals are the basic buildings blocks of diversity-mature organizations.

5.   Well-managed workforce diversity increases human capital. (See *PowerPoint Slide 14* for Chapter 2.)

6.   A diverse workforce is also aligned with the needs and expectations of a diverse customer and supplier base.

IV.   **Study Question 3: How do ethics and social responsibility influence human behavior in organizations?**

    A.   Basic background on ethics. (See *PowerPoint Slide 15* for Chapter 2.)

        1.   <u>**Ethical behavior**</u> is behavior that is accepted as morally "good" or "right" as opposed to "bad" or "wrong" in the context of a particular setting.

        2.   The public demands that people in organizations act according to high moral standards.

    B.   Moral management and ethics mindfulness.

        1.   *Immoral managers* do not subscribe to any ethical principles; they make decisions and take actions that generate the best personal advantage. (See *PowerPoint Slide 16* for Chapter 2.)

        2.   *Amoral managers* fail to consider the ethics associated with any decision or action; the question of ethics is simply not on the amoral manager's "radar screen." (See *PowerPoint Slide 16* for Chapter 2.)

        3.   *Moral managers* incorporate ethical principles and goals into their personal behavior. (See *PowerPoint Slide 16* for Chapter 2.)

LECTURE ENHANCEMENT

Ask students for examples of immoral managers, amoral managers, and moral managers. Have them discuss the potential implications of each type for the employing organization as well as for the managers themselves.

---

4. *Figure 2.4* from the textbook shows that an organization's "ethics center of gravity" can be moved positively through moral leadership or negatively through amoral leadership. (See *PowerPoint Slide 17* for Chapter 2.)

5. **Ethics mindfulness** refers to an enriched awareness that causes one to behave with an ethical consciousness from one decision or behavioral event to another.

   a. According to this concept, the moral manager or moral leader always acts as an ethical role model.

C. Ways of thinking about ethical behavior:

   1. **Utilitarian view** — ethical behavior is that which delivers the greatest good to the greatest number of people. (See *PowerPoint Slide 18* for Chapter 2.)

   2. **Individualism view** — ethical behavior is that which best serves long-term self-interests. (See *PowerPoint Slide 18* for Chapter 2.)

   3. **Moral-rights view** — ethical behavior is that which respects and protects the fundamental rights of all human beings. (See *PowerPoint Slide 18* for Chapter 2.)

   4. **Justice view** — ethical behavior is that which is fair and impartial in the treatment of all people. (See *PowerPoint Slide 18* for Chapter 2.)

      a. **Procedural justice** — the degree to which the rules and procedures specified by policies are properly followed in all cases. (See *PowerPoint Slide 19* for Chapter 2.)

      b. **Distributive justice** — the degree to which people are treated the same under a policy, regardless of individual characteristics based on ethnicity, race, gender, age, or other demographic criteria. (See *PowerPoint Slide 19* for Chapter 2.)

      c. **Interactional justice** — the degree to which people affected by a decision are treated with dignity and respect. (See *PowerPoint Slide 19* for Chapter for Chapter 2.)

LECTURE ENHANCEMENT

Ask students for examples of each of the above views of ethical behavior. These can be either hypothetical examples or situations they have encountered in their own lives. Ask them to indicate which view they think is the most useful in business, and why. Also ask them to indicate which view they think is the most useful in their personal lives, and why. Compare and contrast the two sets of answers, exploring he nature and reasons for any differences in the two sets.

D. Ethics failures and dilemmas.

1. An **ethical dilemma** occurs when someone must choose whether or not to pursue a course of action that, although offering the potential of personal or organizational benefit or both, may be considered unethical. (See *PowerPoint Slide 20* for Chapter 2.)

2. Ethical dilemmas commonly involve honesty in communications and contracts, gifts and entertainment, kickbacks, pricing practices, and employee terminations.

3. Common rationalizations for ethical misconduct include the following (See *PowerPoint Slide 21* for Chapter 2.):

   a. Pretending the behavior in not really unethical or illegal.

   b. Excusing the behavior as being in the organization's or one's own best interest.

   c. Assuming the behavior is acceptable because no one is expected to find out about it.

   d. Assuming that superiors will provide protection and support if anything goes wrong.

4. Personal values that emphasize honesty, fairness, integrity, and self-respect provide ethical anchors that help people to make correct decisions.

5. Ethics codes and ethics training also help organization members to make ethical decisions and act ethically.

E. Organizational social responsibilities. (See *PowerPoint Slide 22* for Chapter 2.)

1. **Social responsibility** is the obligation of organizations to act in ethical and moral ways as institutions of the broader society.

2. Managers and leaders should commit organizations to actions that are consistent with both high performance and corporate social responsibility.

3. A <u>**whistleblower**</u> is someone within an organization who exposes the wrongdoings of others in order to preserve high ethical standards.

V. **Study Question 4: What are key OB transitions in the new workplace?**

A. Corporate governance and ethics leadership. (See *PowerPoint Slides 23 and 24* for Chapter 2.)

   1. Society expects and demands ethical decisions and actions from businesses and other social institutions. The passage of the Sarbanes-Oxley Act of 2002 is but one manifestation of this.

   2. There has been reemerging interest in <u>**corporate governance**</u> — the active oversight of management decisions, corporate strategy, and financial reporting by boards of directors.

   3. There are renewed calls for <u>**ethics leadership**</u>, which refers to business and organizational decisions being made with high moral standards that meet the ethical test of being "good" and not "bad," and of being "right" and not "wrong."

      a. Ethics leadership is based on a foundation of personal <u>**integrity**</u> — acting in ways that are always honest, credible, and consistent in putting one's values into practice.

B. Quality of work life and positive organizational behavior.

   1. <u>**Quality of work life**</u> refers to the overall quality of human experience in the workplace. (See *PowerPoint Slide 25* for Chapter 2.)

      a. An organization's commitment to quality of work life is an important value within organizational behavior.

      b. McGregor's Theory X and Theory Y assumptions about human behavior are highly relevant to the issue of quality of work life. Specifically, Theory Y provides the theoretical underpinnings for the following contemporary quality of work life concepts:

         (i) *Empowerment* — involving people from all levels of responsibility in decision making.

         (ii) *Trust* — redesigning jobs, systems, and structures to give people more personal discretion in their work.

         (iii) *Performance-based rewards* — building reward systems that are fair, relevant, and consistent, while contingent on work performance.

         (iv) *Responsiveness* — making the work setting more pleasant and supportive of individual needs and family responsibilities.

(v) <u>**Work-life balance**</u> — making sure that the demands of the job are a reasonable fit with one's personal life and nonwork responsibilities.

LECTURE ENHANCEMENT

Break the class into groups of four or five students. Assign each group one of the above quality of work life concepts, and have them come of with several examples to illustrate the application of that particular concept.

---

    2.   Positive organizational behavior focuses on practices that value human capacities and encourage their full utilization. (See ***PowerPoint Slide 26*** for Chapter 2.)

        a.   Fred Luthans defines positive organizational behavior as "the study and application of positively oriented human resource strengths and psychological capacities that can be measured, developed, and effectively managed for performance improvement in today's workplace."

        b.   Positive organizational behavior is based on the following core capacities:

           (i) Confidence — the belief in one's ability to achieve success on a task.

           (ii) Hope — the belief in one's capacity to set goals and make plans for their achievement.

           (iii) Optimism — helping people to avoid pessimism and become more self-confident in experiencing and creating positive outcomes.

           (iv) Resilience — the capacity for positive adaptation.

  C. Globalization, job migration, and organizational transformations. (See ***PowerPoint Slides 27*** and ***28*** for Chapter 2.)

    1.   <u>**Globalization**</u> refers to the worldwide interdependence of resource flows, product markets, and business competition that characterize the new economy.

    2.   Job migration and global outsourcing affect the competitiveness of nations.

        a.   <u>**Job migration**</u> is the shifting of jobs from one nation to another.

        b.   <u>**Global outsourcing**</u> involves employers cutting back on domestic jobs and replacing them with contract workers in other nations.

        c.   Job migration and global outsourcing have contributed to <u>**organizational transformation**</u> wherein businesses, government institutions, and nonprofit organizations react to globalization by redesigning themselves for high performance in a changed world.

D. Personal management and career planning.

    1. **Shamrock organizations** are firms that operate with a core group of permanent workers supplemented by outside contractors and part-time workers. More and more companies are relying more heavily on contract and part-time workers; consequently, today's college graduates must be prepared to succeed in those domains. (See *PowerPoint Slide 29* for Chapter 2.)

    2. Personal management and self-monitoring are essential skills for achieving success in today's challenging career setting. (See *PowerPoint Slide 30* for Chapter 2.)

        a. **Personal management** is the ability to understand one's self individually and in the social context, to exercise initiative, to accept responsibility for accomplishments, to work well with others, and to continually learn from experience in the quest for self-improvement.

        b. **Self-monitoring** refers to a person making the effort to observe and reflect on his/her own behavior, and act in ways that adapt to best fit the needs of the situation.

VI. **Study summary for Chapter 2.**

A. Point out to the students that the text's "Chapter 2 Study Guide" recaps the key theories, concepts, and ideas in the chapter in relation to the appropriate study questions.

CHAPTER STUDY GUIDE

Study Question 1: What is a high-performance organization?

- A high-performance organization is designed to bring out the best in people and achieve sustained high performance while creating high quality-of-work-life environments.
- The key components of HPOs include valuing people as human assets, mobilizing synergy from teams, utilizing appropriate technology, focusing on learning, and being customer driven.
- Customer-driven organizations that focus on customer service and product quality as foundations of competitive advantage can be viewed as upside-down pyramids where workers operate in ways directly affecting customers and managers directly support the workers.
- Total quality management deals with meeting the customers' needs, making sure all tasks are done right the first time, and emphasizing continuous improvement.
- Human capital in the form of productive potential of people is a foundation for HPOs; both intellectual capital (the intellect and talents of people) and social capital (the value or working relationships) are major contributors to human capital.
- In organizations with strong and positive cultures, members behave with shared norms and beliefs that support high-performance goals.

Study Question 2: What is multiculturalism, and how can workforce diversity be managed?

- Multicultural organizations operate with a commitment to pluralism and respect for diversity and individual differences.
- A key aspect to multiculturalism is inclusivity, the degree to which the culture respects and values diversity and is open to anyone who can perform a job, regardless of their diversity attributers.
- Diversity bias in organizations includes prejudice, in the form of negative attitudes, and discrimination — active disenfranchisement of minorities from rights or organizational membership.
- Challenges faced by diverse populations in the workplace include sexual harassment, pay discrimination, job discrimination, and the glass ceiling effect — a hidden barrier that limits advancement by women and minorities.
- Managing diversity is the process of developing a work environment that is fully inclusive and allows everyone to reach his or her full work potential.

Study Question 3: How do ethics and social responsibility influence human behavior in organizations?

- Ethical behavior is that which is morally "good" and "right" instead of "bad" or "wrong."
- Managers and people in organizations may be amoral — prone to unintentional ethical lapses; immoral — intentionally pursuing unethical courses of actions; or moral — consistently acting according to ethics principles.
- Ethics leaders can create a virtuous shift in the ethics center of gravity of organizations and help members to develop ethics mindfulness as an "enriched awareness" that causes one to behave with an ethical consciousness from one decision or behavioral event to another.
- Ways of thinking about an ethical behavior include the utilitarian, individualism, moral-rights, and justice views.
- The workplace is a source of possible ethical dilemmas in which someone must decide whether or not to pursue a course of action that, although offering the potential for personal or organizational benefit or both, may be considered potentially unethical.
- Managers report that their ethical dilemmas often involve conflicts with superiors, customers, and subordinates over such matters as dishonesty in advertising and communications as well as pressure from their bosses to do unethical things.
- Common rationalizations for unethical behavior include believing the behavior is not illegal, is in everyone's best interests, will never be noticed, or will be supported by the organization.
- Corporate social responsibility is an obligation of the organization to act in ways that serve both its own interests and the interests of its many external publics, often called stakeholders.
- Whistleblowers actively expose wrongdoing in organizations and help further the obligations of organizations and their members to act in ethical ways.

Study Question 4: What are key OB transitions in the new workplace?

- In the wake of major ethics scandals, there is a renewed emphasis in our society on corporate governance — the active oversight of management decisions, corporate strategy, and financial reporting by boards of directors.

- There are corresponding expectations for more ethics leadership, whereby business and organizational decisions are made with high moral standards, and for leaders to act with greater integrity by always being honest, credible, and consistent in putting values into practice.
- A historical value underlying the field of OB has been a commitment to fully valuing and respecting people as human beings and to building high quality-of-work-life environments for them.
- Positive organizational behavior is a new development that directs managerial attention toward nurturing confidence, hope, optimism, and resiliency as positive states that build individual performance capacities.
- The forces of globalization are bringing increased interdependencies among nations and economies as customer markets and resource flows create intense business competition.
- Job migration through global outsourcing of manufacturing and white-collar jobs is one of the areas of current concern and controversy; it is associated with organization transformations including workforce reductions, new structures, and creative use of technology in the quest for greater operating efficiencies.
- The new economy and organizational transformations are resulting in changes to the traditional notion of a career and employer-employee relationships; more people today are working as independent contractors rather than full-time employees.
- To sustain career success in our challenging times, everyone must engage in personal management to continually learn and improve from experiences and to build skill portfolios that are always up to date and valuable to employers challenged by the intense competition and opportunities of the information age.

KEY TERMS

Continuous improvement: the belief that all workplace activities should be continually subjected to two questions: Is it necessary? If so, can it be done better?

Corporate governance: the active oversight of management decisions, corporate strategy, and financial reporting by boards of directors.

Distributive justice: the degree to which people are treated the same under a policy, regardless of individual characteristics based on ethnicity, race, gender, age, or other demographic criteria.

Empowerment: a philosophy that allows people, individually and in groups, to use their talents and knowledge to make decisions that affect their work.

Ethical behavior: behavior that is accepted as morally "good" and "right" as opposed to "bad" or "wrong" in the context of a particular setting.

Ethical dilemma: occurs when someone must choose whether or not to pursue a course of action that, although offering the potential of personal or organizational benefit or both, may be considered unethical.

Ethics leadership: refers to business and organizational decisions being made with high moral standards that meet the ethical test of being "good" and not "bad," and of being "right" and not "wrong."

Ethics mindfulness: refers to an enriched awareness that causes one to behave with an ethical consciousness from one decision or behavioral event to another.

Globalization: the worldwide interdependence of resource flows, product markets, and business competition that characterize the new economy.

Global outsourcing: involves employers cutting back on domestic jobs and replacing them with contract workers in other nations.

High-performance organization: an organization that is intentionally designed to bring out the best in people and thereby produce sustainable organizational results while creating a high quality-of-work-life environment.

Human capital: the economic value of people with job-relevant abilities, knowledge, ideas, energies, and commitments.

Inclusivity: the degree to which the organization's culture respects and values diversity, and is open to anyone who can perform a job, regardless of his or her diversity attributes.

Individualism view of ethics: ethical behavior is that which best serves long-term self-interests.

Integrity: acting in ways that are always honest and credible and consistent in putting one's values into practices.

Intellectual capital: the performance potential of the expertise, competencies, creativity, and commitment within an organization's workforce.

Interactional justice: the degree to which people affected by a decision are treated with dignity and respect.

Job migration: the shifting of jobs from one nation to another.

Justice view of ethics: ethical behavior is that which is fair and impartial in the treatment of all people.

Knowledge workers: people whose minds rather than physical capabilities create value for the organization.

Moral-rights view of ethics: ethical behavior is that which respects and protects the fundamental rights of all human beings.

Multiculturalism: pluralism and respect for diversity and individual differences in the workplace.

Organizational transformation: businesses, government institutions, and nonprofit organizations react to globalization by redesigning themselves for high performance in a changed world.

Personal management: the ability to understand one's self individually and in the social context, to exercise initiative, to accept responsibility for accomplishments, to work well with others, and to continually learn from experience in the quest for self-improvement.

Procedural justice: the degree to which the rules and procedures specified by policies are properly followed in all cases.

Quality of work life: the overall quality of human experience in the workplace.

Self-monitoring: refers to a person making the effort to observe and reflect on his/her own behavior, and act in ways that adapt to best fit the needs of the situation.

Shamrock organizations: firms that operate with a core group of permanent workers supplemented by outside contractors and part-time workers.

Social capital: the performance potential represented in the relationships maintained among people at work.

Social responsibility: the obligation of organizations to act in ethical and moral ways as institutions of the broader society.

Stakeholders: the individuals, groups, and other organizations affected by an organization's performance.

Total quality management: a management philosophy that involves management being dedicated to ensuring that an organization and all its members are committed to high quality, continuous improvement, and customer satisfaction.

Utilitarian view of ethics: ethical behavior is that which delivers the greatest good to greatest number of people.

Value creation: the extent to which an organization satisfies the needs of strategic constituencies.

Whistleblower: someone within an organization who exposes the wrongdoings of others in order to preserve high ethical standards.

Workforce diversity: differences among people with respect to age, race, ethnicity, gender, physical ability, and sexual orientation.

Work-life balance: making sure that the demands of the job are a reasonable fit with one's personal life and nonwork responsibilities.

Chapter 3
ORGANIZATIONAL BEHAVIOR ACROSS CULTURES

STUDY QUESTIONS

1.	Why is globalization significant for organizational behavior?
2.	What is culture and how can we understand cultural differences?
3.	How does cultural diversity affect people at work?
4.	What is a global view of organizational learning?

LEARNING OBJECTIVES

After completing this chapter students should be able to:

1.	Define "globalization" and describe the various forces that influence globalization.
2.	Explain why domestic self-sufficiency is no longer viable for nations or businesses.
3.	Describe the role of regional economic alliances in the globalization of business.
4.	Discuss the issues of outsourcing, offshoring, and job migration, and describe the characteristics of a global manager.
5.	Provide an overview of the popular dimensions of culture, including language, time orientation, use of space, and religion.
6.	Describe how a working knowledge of Geert Hofstede's five dimensions of national culture can help a global manager do his or her job more effectively.
7.	Discuss Fons Trompenaars's descriptions of major culture differences in how people relate to other individuals, time, and the environment.
8.	Describe the nature and impacts of multinational corporations, and the challenges encountered by these organizations and their employees.
9.	Discuss cross-cultural ethical differences.
10.	Discuss global organizational learning and the transferability of management theories and practices around the world.

MATERIAL IN *THE OB SKILLS WORKBOOK* SUPPORTING THE CHAPTER

Case for Critical Thinking	Case 3: Crossing Borders
Experiential Exercises	Exercise 6: Expatriate Assignments
	Exercise 7: Cultural Cues
	Exercise 8: Prejudice in Our Lives
Self-Assessments	Assessment 4: Global Readiness Index
	Assessment 5: Personal Values

CHAPTER OVERVIEW

This chapter focuses on the topic of organizational behavior and globalization. The chapter begins by examining the global context of organizational behavior. Globalization is defined and the various forces that foster globalization are identified. Given the rapid spread of globalization in many industries, domestic self-sufficiency is no longer a viable option for nations or businesses. To reinforce this point the chapter provide several examples, many of which focus on regional economic alliances. The increased importance of outsourcing, offshoring, and job migration within the global context are examined as well. The first section of the chapter concludes with a discussion of the nature and attributes of global managers.

The next section of the chapter provides a lively discussion of cultures and cross-cultural understanding. Geert Hofstede's five dimensions of national culture are introduced along with Fons Trompenaars model of the major cultural differences in how people handle relationships with others, their attitudes toward time, and their attitudes toward the environment.

The chapter then examines cultural diversity, focusing on the nature and impacts of multinational corporations, the challenges created by multicultural workforces, and the challenges faced by expatriates. An important consideration of cross-cultural diversity occurs in the form of differences in ethical behavior among the nations and cultures of the world. Special consideration is given to the concepts of cultural relativism and ethical absolutism.

The chapter concludes with a discussion of organizational learning in the global context, making the point that people from different cultures and parts of the world can learn much from each other. This section of the chapter also examines the universality of management theories and best practices around the globe.

CHAPTER OUTLINE

I. **Study Question 1: Why is globalization significant for organizational behavior?**
   A. Forces of globalization
   B. Global regional economic alliances
   C. Global outsourcing and offshoring
   D. Global managers

II. **Study Question 2: What is culture and how can we understand cultural differences?**
   A. Popular dimensions of culture
   B. Values and national cultures
   C. Understanding cultural differences

III. **Study Question 3: How does cultural diversity affect people at work?**
   A. Multinational employers
   B. Multicultural workforces and expatriates
   C. Ethical behavior across cultures

IV. **Study Question 4: What is a global view of organizational learning?**
   A. Are management theories universal?
   B. Best practices around the world

CHAPTER LECTURE NOTES

I.   **Introduction to the Chapter 3 Lecture.**

    A. Study questions for Chapter 3. (See *PowerPoint Slide 2* for Chapter 3.)

        1. Why is globalization significant for organizational behavior?

        2. What is culture and how can we understand cultural differences?

        3. How does cultural diversity affect people at work?

        4. What is a global view on organizational learning?

    B. The lecture material for Chapter 3 is organized around the study questions.

        1. Point out to the students that the text's "Chapter At A Glance" identifies the key topics contained in the chapter and links them to the appropriate study questions.

    C. The chapter opens with a description of Wal-Mart's experience in expanding its operations to the international arena. Lessons regarding understanding of and sensitivity to the local culture are highlighted.

LECTURE ENHANCEMENT

Prior to discussing this chapter in class, have each student find a recent newspaper or magazine article that relates to globalization issues. Articles can easily be found in business publications such as *The Wall Street Journal, Business Week, Fortune*, and *Forbes,* as well as many other publications such as the "Money" section of *USA Today,* or popular magazines such as *Time* and *Newsweek.* Each student should be prepared to discuss his/her article in class. Choose several students to talk about the key ideas in their selected articles, and ask the entire class to help identify how these ideas relate to the challenges of globalization.

II.   **Study Question 1: Why is globalization significant for organizational behavior?**

    A. Forces of globalization.

        1. Most organization today must achieve high performance in the context of a competitive and complex global environment. (See *PowerPoint Slide 3* for Chapter 3.)

        2. **Globalization** refers to the complex economic networks of international competition, resource suppliers, and product markets. (See *PowerPoint Slide 3* for Chapter 3.)

        3. Forces of globalization. (See *PowerPoint Slide 4* for Chapter 3.)

      a. The rapid growth in information technology and electronic communication has heightened the average person's awareness of the global economy.

      b. Valuable skills and investments easily move from country to country.

      c. Cultural diversity is increasing among the populations of many nations.

      d. Immigration is having profound implications for many nations.

      e. Job migration among nations is increasing.

      f. Employers have greater needs to deal with **multicultural workforces** that draw workers from nontraditional labor sources and from ethnic backgrounds representing all corners of the globe.

4. Domestic self-sufficiency is no longer a viable option for nations or businesses.

B. Global regional economic alliances. (See *PowerPoint Slide 5* for Chapter 3.)

    1. One impact of globalization is the emergence of regional economic alliances.

    2. The European Union (EU).

      a. The European Union is a regional economic alliance wherein member countries have entered into agreements to eliminate border controls and trade barriers, create uniform technical product standards, open government procurement contracts, and unify financial regulations.

      b. The European Union is moving forward with its agendas of political, economic, and monetary union among member countries.

    3. North American Free Trade Agreement (NAFTA).

      a. The EU's counterpart in North America, the North American Free Trade Agreement, links the economies and customer markets of Canada, the United States, and Mexico in freer trade.

      b. Efforts are underway to create additional economic alliances throughout the Americas.

    4. Similar regional economic partnerships are being forged in other parts of the globe as well, including the Asia-Pacific Economic Co-operation Forum (APEC) and efforts in Africa.

LECTURE ENHANCEMENT

Divide the class into small discussion groups. Assign each group one of the following four geographic regions: Europe, the Americas, Asia and the Pacific Rim, or Africa. Have the groups spend 10-12 minutes identifying the potential challenges and opportunities that these areas face in the context of the global economy. Have each group report out to the entire class with a brief summary of its key discussion points.

    C. Global outsourcing and offfshoring.

        1. **Outsourcing** is the contracting out of work rather than accomplishing it with a full-time permanent workforce. (See *PowerPoint Slide 6* for Chapter 3.)

        2. **Offshoring** — a form of outsourcing — involves contracting out work to persons in other countries. (See *PowerPoint Slide 6* for Chapter 3.)

        3. Through offshoring, employers reduce costs by taking advantage of foreign labor with equivalent or better skills and at a fraction of the cost of domestic labor.

        4. **Job migration** — the movement of jobs from one location or country to another — is major controversy associated with the growing use of offshoring. (See *PowerPoint Slide 6* for Chapter 3.)

        5. Outsourcing, offshoring, and job migration will continue to be a permanent part of the global competitive environment of business.

LECTURE ENHANCEMENT

To illustrate the widespread impact outsourcing, offshoring, and job migration in the global economy, ask the student's where their shoes, clothes, and watches were manufactured. Have the student's physically check the labels on those items.

---

        6. Growing global commitment to total quality is facilitating job migration.

            a. *ISO* is a global quality designation that reflects the quality standards set by the International Standards Organization in Geneva, Switzerland.

            b. ISO certification is considered to be a "must have" designation by companies seeking to do business as total quality "world class" manufacturers.

            c. Because of the ISO commitment, it is becoming much easier to outsource contracts and engage in offshoring.

    D. Global managers. (See *PowerPoint Slide 7* for Chapter 3.)

1. Globalization requires a new breed of manager known as the **global manager** — someone who knows how to conduct business in multiple countries and is culturally adaptable and often multilingual.

2. A global manager thinks with a worldview; appreciates diverse beliefs, values, behaviors, and practices; and is able to map strategy in the global context.

3. Global managers have a global attitude, which is the willingness to embrace good ideas without regard to their origin.

4. The global dimensions in business and management, though pervasive, provide many challenges that can be overcome only with a "global mind-set" of cultural adaptability, patience, flexibility, and tolerance.

III.   **Study Question 2: What is culture and how can we understand cultural differences?**

A.   Background on culture. (See *PowerPoint Slide 8* for Chapter 3.)

1. **Culture** is the learned, shared way of doing things in a particular society.

2. Geert Hofstede refers to culture as the "software of the mind."

3. Since culture is shared among people, it helps to define the boundaries between different groups and affects how their members relate to one another.

4. **Cultural intelligence** describes a person's ability to identify, understand, and act with sensitivity and effectiveness in cross-cultural situations.

B.   Popular Dimensions of Culture

1. The popular dimensions of culture — such as language, time orientation, use of space, and religion — reflect the things that are most apparent to people when they travel abroad.

2. Language. (See *PowerPoint Slide 9* for Chapter 3.)

   a. Perhaps the most conspicuous aspect of culture is language.

   b. The *Whorfian hypothesis* considers language to be a major determinant of peoples' thinking.

   c. Vocabulary and structure of a language reflect the history of a society and can also reveal how members relate to the environment.

3. Differences in the ways cultures use language.

   (i) **Low-context cultures** are very explicit in using the spoken and written word.

(ii) **High-context cultures** use words to convey only a limited part of the message.

(iii) Many Asian and Middle Eastern cultures are considered high context whereas most Western cultures are low context.

4. Time orientation. (See *PowerPoint Slide 10* for Chapter 3.)

   a. In a **polychronic culture** people hold a circular or cyclical view of time that does not create pressure for immediate action or performance, and consequently people emphasize the present and often do more than one thing at a time.

   b. In a **monochronic culture** people have a linear view of time that creates pressure for action and performance and results in people tending to give complete attention to each activity.

5. Use of space. (See *PowerPoint Slide 11* for Chapter 3.)

   a. *Proxemics*, the study of how people use space to communicate, reveals important cultural differences.

   b. The preference for personal space varies from culture to culture.

   c. In some cultures, often polychronic ones, space is organized in such a way that many activities can be carried out simultaneously.

6. Religion. (See *PowerPoint Slide 12* for Chapter 3.)

   a. Religion is also a major element of culture and can be one of its more visible manifestations.

   b. Religion can have significant effects on codes of ethics, moral behavior, and economic activities.

LECTURE ENHANCEMENT

If any of your students have lived or traveled abroad, ask them to describe their experiences and what they learned about different cultures.

C. Values and national cultures.

1. A framework offered by Geert Hofstede helps in understanding how value differences across national cultures can influence human behavior at work. (See *PowerPoint Slide 13* for Chapter 3.)

2. The five dimensions of national culture in Hofstede's framework are as follows (see *PowerPoint Slide 13* for Chapter 3 for a summary listing of the five dimensions):

   a. Power distance. (See *PowerPoint Slide 14* for Chapter 3.)

      (i) <u>**Power distance**</u> is the willingness of a culture to accept status and power differences among its members.

      (ii) It reflects the degree to which people are likely to respect hierarchy and rank in organizations.

      (iii) Indonesia is considered a high-power distance culture, whereas Sweden is considered a relatively low-power distance culture.

   b. Uncertainty avoidance. (See *PowerPoint Slide 15* for Chapter 3.)

      (i) <u>**Uncertainty avoidance**</u> is a cultural tendency toward discomfort with risk and ambiguity.

      (ii) It reflects the degree to which people are likely to prefer structured or unstructured organizational situations.

      (iii) France is considered a high-uncertainty avoidance culture, whereas Hong Kong is considered a low-uncertainty avoidance culture.

   c. Individualism-collectivism. (See *PowerPoint Slide 16* for Chapter 3.)

      (i) <u>**Individualism-collectivism**</u> is the tendency of a culture to emphasize individual versus group interests.

      (ii) It reflects the degree to which people are likely to prefer working as individuals or working together in groups.

      (iii) The United States is a highly individualistic culture, whereas Mexico is a more collectivistic one.

   d. Masculinity-femininity. (See *PowerPoint Slide 17* for Chapter 3.)

      (i) <u>**Masculinity-femininity**</u> is the tendency of a culture to value stereotypical masculine or feminine traits.

      (ii) It reflects the degree to which organizations emphasize competition and assertiveness versus interpersonal sensitivity and concerns for relationships.

      (iii) Japan is considered a very masculine culture, whereas Thailand is considered a more feminine culture.

e.   Long-term/short-term orientation. (See *PowerPoint Slide 18* for Chapter 3.)

(i)   **Long-term/short-term orientation** is the tendency of a culture to emphasize values associated with the future, such as thrift and persistence, versus values that focus largely on the present.

(ii) It reflects the degree to which people and organizations adopt long-term or short-term performance horizons.

(iii) South Korea is high on long-term orientation, whereas the United States is a more short-term-oriented country.

3.   The five dimensions of Hofstede's cultural framework are interrelated; consequently, national cultures may best understood in terms of cluster maps that combine multiple dimensions. *Figure 3.1* from the textbook provides an example of a cluster map for the dimensions of individualism-collectivism and power distance. (See *PowerPoint Slide 19* for Chapter 3.)

LECTURE ENHANCEMENT

Focus again on the students who, in the previous *Lecture Enhancement* activity, identified themselves as having lived or traveled abroad. Ask them to identify the nation(s) and attempt, on the basis of their experiences, to characterize those nations in terms of Hofstede's dimensions of culture. If enough nations are represented, a comparative analysis could be fruitful. Also compare these nations to the United States.

D.   Understanding cultural differences.

1.   Knowing one's own culture helps guard against two problems that arise in international dealings: parochialism and ethnocentrism. (See *PowerPoint Slide 20* for Chapter 3.)

a.   *Parochialism* involves assuming that the ways of one's own culture are the only ways of doing things.

b.   **Ethnocentrism** involves assuming that the ways of one's own culture are the best ways of doing things.

2.   A framework developed by Fons Trompenaars offers a useful vantage point for understanding and dealing with cultural differences.

3.   Trompenaars distinguishes among cultures on the basis of how people handle relationships with other people, attitudes toward time, and attitudes toward the environment.

4.   Cultural differences based on in how people handle relationships with other people are illustrated in *Figure 3.2* from the textbook. (See *PowerPoint Slide 21* for Chapter 3.) These orientations are as follows:

    a. *Universalism* versus *particularism* — relative emphasis on rules and consistency, or on relationships and flexibility. (See *PowerPoint Slide 22* for Chapter 3.)

    b. *Individualism* versus *collectivism* — relative emphasis on individual freedom and responsibility, or on group interests and consensus. (See *PowerPoint Slide 22* for Chapter 3.)

    c. *Neutral* versus *affective* — relative emphasis on objectivity and detachment, or on emotion and expressed feelings. (See *PowerPoint Slide 23* for Chapter 3.)

    d. *Specific* versus *diffuse* — relative emphasis on focused and narrow involvement, or on involvement with the whole person. (See *PowerPoint Slide 23* for Chapter 3.)

    e. *Achievement* versus *prescription* — relative emphasis on performance-based and earned status, or on ascribed status. (See *PowerPoint Slide 24* for Chapter 3.)

5. Cultural differences based on attitudes toward time. (See *PowerPoint Slide 25* for Chapter 3.)

    a. *Sequential* view of time — time is a passing series of events.

    b. *Synchronic* view of time — time consists of an interrelated past, present, and future.

6. Cultural differences based on attitudes toward the environment. (See *PowerPoint Slide 26* for Chapter 3.)

    a. *Inner-directed culture* — people tend to view themselves as separate from nature and believe they can control it.

    b. *Outer-directed culture* — people tend to view themselves as part of nature and believe they go along with it.

LECTURE ENHANCEMENT

Linking back to the previous *Lecture Enhancement*, ask the students to characterize those nations in terms of Fons Trompenaars's description of systematic cultural differences with respect to the ways in which people handle their relationships, their attitudes toward time, and their attitudes toward the environment.

IV.   **Study Question 3: How does cultural diversity affect people at work?**

    A. Multinational employers.

       1. A **multinational corporation** (MNC) is a business firm that has extensive international operations in more than one foreign country. (See *PowerPoint Slide 27* for Chapter 3.)

       2. A truly global corporation operates with a total worldview and does not have allegiance to any one national "home." (See *PowerPoint Slide 27* for Chapter 3.)

       3. MNCs have enormous economic power and impact. (See *PowerPoint Slide 27* for Chapter 3.)

       4. MNCs bring both benefits and potential controversies to the host countries in which they operate. (See *PowerPoint Slide 27* for Chapter 3.)

LECTURE ENHANCEMENT

An easy way to get students involved in a discussion at this point is to ask them to provide examples of MNCs. Students are able to quickly generate a long list of MNCs. Engage the students in some discussion of where these firms have their operations and what types of products or services they provide.

---

       5. *Maquiladoras* refer to foreign-owned plants operating in Mexico, which assemble imported parts and ship finished products to the United States.

         a. The benefits of maquiladoras include the following:

           (i) Inexpensive labor for the foreign operators.

           (ii) Industrial development for Mexico.

           (iii) Reduced unemployment in the Mexican workforce.

           (iv) Increased foreign exchange earnings for Mexico.

         b. The disadvantages of maquiladoras include the following:

           (i) Stress on housing and public services in Mexican border towns.

           (ii) Inequities in the way Mexican workers are treated relative to their foreign counterparts.

           (iii) The environmental impact of pollution from the industrial sites.

    B. Multicultural workforces and expatriates.

1. Styles of leadership, motivation, decision making, planning, organizing, leading, and controlling vary from country to country. (See *PowerPoint Slide 28* for Chapter 3.)

2. The challenges of managing across cultures are not limited to international operations.

   a. **Domestic multiculturalism** describes cultural diversity within a given national population.

3. **Expatriates** are people who work and live abroad for extended periods of time. (See *PowerPoint Slide 28* for Chapter 3.)

4. Since expatriate workers can be very costly for employers, progressive companies will maximize the potential of expatriate performance by engaging in a variety supportive activities. (See *PowerPoint Slide 28* for Chapter 3.)

5. *Figure 3.3* from the textbook illustrates the phases of a typical expatriate international career cycle. (See *PowerPoint Slide 29* for Chapter 3.)

   a. To adequately deal with initial assignment shock, pre-departure support and counseling in the recruitment, selection, and orientation processes is essential.

   b. An important part of the international career cycle concerns the expatriate's adjustment to the foreign country. The expatriate undergoes the following three phases of adjustment to the new country:

      (i) In the *tourist stage*, the expatriate enjoys discovering the new culture.

      (ii) In the *disillusionment stage*, the expatriate's mood is dampened as difficulties become more evident. Typical problems include conversing well in the local language and obtaining personal products and food supplies of preference.

      (iii) In the *culture shock stage*, the expatriate's mood often hits bottom as confusion, disorientation, and frustration set in regarding the ways of the local culture and living in the foreign environment.

   c. If culture shock is handled well, the expatriate is assimilated into the foreign culture and is able to perform effectively.

   d. If culture shock is not handled well, cultural assimilation problems and poor performance result.

   e. Reentry shock can occur after the expatriate assignment ends and the employee returns to the home country.

C. Ethical behavior across cultures. (See *PowerPoint Slide 30* for Chapter 3.)

1.   In the international arena, special ethical challenges arise as a result of cultural diversity and the variation in governments and legal systems that characterize our world.

2.   Prominent current cross-cultural ethical issues include corruption and bribery in international business practices, poor working conditions and the employment of child and prison labor in some countries, and the role of international business in supporting repressive governments that fail to protect and respect basic human rights.

3.   In the United States, the Foreign Corrupt Practices Act of 1977 makes it illegal for firms to engage in corrupt practices overseas.

4.   <u>Sweatshops</u> refer to organizations that force workers to labor under adverse conditions that may include long workdays, unsafe conditions, and even the use of child labor.

   a.   A variety of advocacy groups are now active in campaigning against sweatshops, and a number of well-recognized firms have been the targets of their attention.

LECTURE ENHANCEMENT

The Institute for Global Ethics is an independent, nonprofit, organization dedicated to elevating public awareness and promoting the discussion of ethics in a global context. The site provides links to a variety of ethics related material and is available at <u>http://www.globalethics.org/</u>.

---

5.   The influence of culture on ethical behavior.

   a.   *Figure 3.4* from the textbook describes the extremes of cultural relativism and ethical absolutism in international business ethics. (See *PowerPoint Slide 31* for Chapter 3.)

   b.   <u>Cultural relativism</u> is the position that there is no universal right way to behave and that ethical behavior is determined by its cultural context.

   c.   <u>Ethical absolutism</u> is the universalistic assumption that there is a single moral standard that fits all situations, regardless of culture and national location.

LECTURE ENHANCEMENT

Have the students debate cultural relativism (there is no universal right way to behave and that ethical behavior is determined by its cultural context) and ethical absolutism (the universalistic assumption that a single moral standard applies to all cultures). Apply these concepts to the events of 9/11/01.

---

    d. Thomas Donaldson, a business ethicist, provides the following advice regarding the debate between cultural relativism and ethical absolutism (see *PowerPoint Slide 32* for Chapter 3):

        (i) Multinational businesses should adopt core or threshold values to guide behavior in ways that respect and protect fundamental human rights in any situation.

        (ii) Beyond the threshold, there is room to adapt and tailor actions in ways that respect the traditions, foundations, and needs of different cultures.

V.   **Study Question 4: What is a global view on organizational learning?**

    A. Background on organizational learning. (See *PowerPoint Slide 33* for Chapter 3.)

        1. In Chapter 1, *organizational learning* was described as the process of acquiring the knowledge necessary to adapt to a changing environment.

        2. **Global organizational learning** is the ability to gather from the world at large the knowledge required for long-term organizational adaptation.

    B. Are management theories universal? (See *PowerPoint Slide 34* for Chapter 3.)

        1. According to Geert Hofstede, management theories are universal, at least not without careful consideration of cultural influences.

        2. Culture can influence both the development of a theory or concept and its application.

        3. Concepts such as merit pay and job enrichment work well in individualistic cultures but not necessarily in collectivistic cultures.

    C. Best practices around the world. (See *PowerPoint Slide 35* for Chapter 3.)

        1. An appropriate goal in global organizational learning is to identify the "best practices" found around the world.

        2. Potential benchmarks of excellence for high-performance organizations can be discovered anywhere in the world.

3. Global organizational learning is evident in workplace themes such as the value of teams and workgroups, consensus decision making, employee involvement, flatter structures, and strong corporate cultures.

4. As the field or organizational behavior continues to mature in its global research and understanding, we will all benefit from an expanding knowledge base that is enriched by cultural diversity.

VI.   Study summary for Chapter 3.

A. Point out to the students that the text's "Chapter 3 Study Guide" recaps the key theories, concepts, and ideas in the chapter in relation to the appropriate study questions.

CHAPTER STUDY GUIDE

Study Question 1: Why is globalization significant for organizational behavior?

- Globalization, with its complex worldwide economic networks of business competition, resource supplies, and product markets, is having a major impact on businesses, employers, and workforces around the world.
- Nations in Europe, North America, and Asia are forming regional trade agreements, such as the EU, NAFTA, and PEC, to gain economic strength in the highly competitive global economy.
- More and more organizations, large and small, do an increasing amount of business abroad; more and more local employers are foreign owned, in whole or in part; the domestic workforce is becoming multicultural and more diverse.
- One of the important trends today is increasing use by businesses of global resourcing, or offshoring, with the result that many jobs previously performed by domestic workers are migrating to foreign countries.
- All organizations need global managers with the special interests and talents needed to excel in international work and cross-cultural relationships.

Study Question 2: What is culture and how can we understand cultural differences?

- Culture is the learned and shared way of doing things in a society; it represents deeply ingrained influences on the way people from different societies think, behave, and solve problems.
- Popular dimensions of culture include observable differences in language, time orientation, use of space, and religion.
- Hofstede's five national culture dimensions are power distance, individualism-collectivism, uncertainty avoidance, masculinity-femininity, and long-term/short-term orientation.
- Trompenaars's framework for understanding cultural differences focuses on relationships among people, attitudes toward time, and attitudes toward the environment.
- Cross-cultural awareness requires a clear understanding of one's own culture and the ability to overcome the limits of parochialism and ethnocentrism.

Study Question 3: How does cultural diversity affect people at work?

- Among multinational corporations (MNCs), truly global businesses operate with a worldwide scope; the largest of the world's MNCs are powerful forces in the global economy.
- Multiculturalism in the domestic workforce requires everyone to work well with people of different cultural backgrounds.
- Expatriate employees who work abroad for extended periods of time face special challenges, including possible adjustment problems abroad and reentry problems upon returning home.
- The international dimensions of business create unique and challenging ethical challenges; ethical behavior across cultures can be viewed from the perspectives of cultural relativism and absolutism.

Study Question 4: What is a global view on organizational learning?

- A global view on learning about OB seeks to understand the best practices from around the world, with due sensitivity to cultural differences.
- Management concepts and theories must always be considered relative to the cultures in which they are developed and applied.
- Interest in Japanese management practices continues, with the traditional focus on long-term employment, emphasis on teams, quality commitment, careful career development, and consensus decision making.
- Global learning will increasingly move beyond North America, Europe, and Japan to include best practices anywhere in the world.

KEY TERMS

Cultural intelligence: describes a person's ability to identify, understand, and act with sensitivity and effectiveness in cross-cultural situations.

Cultural relativism: the position that there is no universal right way to behave and that ethical behavior is determined by its cultural context.

Culture: the learned, shared way of doing things in a particular society.

Domestic multiculturalism: cultural diversity within a given national population.

Ethical absolutism: the universalistic assumption that there is a single moral standard that fits all situations, regardless of culture and national location.

Ethnocentrism: involves assuming that the ways of one's own culture are the best ways of doing things.

Expatriates: people who work and live abroad for extended periods of time.

Globalization: the complex economic networks of international competition, resource suppliers, and product markets.

Global manager: a manager who knows how to conduct business in multiple countries and is culturally adaptable and often multilingual.

Global organizational learning: the ability to gather from the world at large the knowledge required for long-term organizational adaptation.

High-context culture: a culture that uses words to convey only a limited part of the message.

Individualism-collectivism: the tendency of a culture to emphasize individual versus group interests.

Job migration: the movement of jobs from one location or country to another.

Long-term/short-term orientation: the tendency of a culture to emphasize values associated with the future, such as thrift and persistence, versus values that focus largely on the present.

Low-context culture: a culture that is very explicit in using the spoken and written word.

Masculinity-femininity: the tendency of a culture to value stereotypical masculine or feminine traits.

Monochronic culture: a culture in which people have a linear view of time that creates pressure for action and performance and results in people tending to give complete attention to each activity.

Multicultural workforces: draw workers from nontraditional labor sources and from ethnic backgrounds representing all corners of the globe.

Multinational corporation: a business firm that has extensive international operations in more than one foreign country.

Offshoring: a form of outsourcing that involves contracting out work to persons in other countries.

Outsourcing: the contracting out of work rather than accomplishing it within a full-time permanent workforce.

Polychronic culture: a culture in which people hold a circular or cyclical view of time that does not create pressure for immediate action or performance, and consequently people emphasize the present and often do more than one thing at a time.

Power distance: the willingness of a culture to accept status and power differences among its members.

Sweatshops: organizations that force workers to labor under adverse conditions that may include long workdays, unsafe conditions, and even the use of child labor.

Uncertainty avoidance: a cultural tendency toward discomfort with risk and ambiguity.

Chapter 4
DIVERSITY AND INDIVIDUAL DIFFERENCES

STUDY QUESTIONS

1.	What is personality?
2.	How do personalities differ?
3.	What are value and attitude differences among individuals, and why are they important?
4.	What are individual differences and how are they related to workforce diversity?

LEARNING OBJECTIVES

After completing this chapter students should be able to:

1.	Explain personality and personality traits, how personality develops, and how personality is related to the self-concept.
2.	Describe the nature and implications of the "Big Five" personality traits, social traits, personal conception traits, and emotional adjustment traits.
3.	Discuss the nature and importance of values in the workplace, and describe different types of values classifications.
4.	Describe the nature of attitudes, discuss their implications for organizational behavior, and explain the roles of cognitive consistency and cognitive dissonance in attitudes.
5.	Explain the nature and interconnections of workforce diversity, stereotyping, and equal employment opportunity.
6.	Describe individual differences in the workforce from the perspectives of demographic characteristics and abilities/aptitudes.
7.	Explain the challenges associated of managing diversity and individual differences.

MATERIAL IN *THE OB SKILLS WORKBOOK* SUPPORTING THE CHAPTER

Case for Critical Thinking	Case 4: Never on a Sunday
Experiential Exercise	Exercise 8: Prejudice in our Lives
Self-Assessment	Assessment 5: Personal Values

CHAPTER OVERVIEW

This chapter focuses on the important and timely topic of diversity and individual differences in the workplace. The chapter begins with a discussion of personality, personality traits, and the self-concept. The "Big Five" personality traits — extraversion, agreeableness, conscientiousness, emotional stability, and openness to experience — are introduced and discussed, as are various social, personal conception, and emotional adjustment traits. The social traits focus on problem-solving styles, whereas the personal conception traits include locus of control, authoritarianism/dogmatism, Machiavellianism, and self-monitoring. The emotional adjustment traits reflect the Type A and Type B orientations.

The chapter then transitions to a discussion of values and attitudes. The difference between terminal and instrumental values is explained and discussed. Six categories of human values and four types of workplace values are described. The nature and components of attitudes are addressed next, with attention being given to workplace attitudes and cognitive dissonance.

The chapter concludes with a discussion of individual differences and diversity, giving attention to workforce diversity; stereotyping; equal employment opportunity; important demographic characteristics in the workforce, including gender, age, able-bodiedness, race and ethnicity; and aptitude and ability. The challenges associated with managing diversity and individual differences are also explored.

CHAPTER OUTLINE

I.   **Study Question 1: What is personality?**
    A. What is personality?
    B. Personality and development
    C. Personality and the self-concept

II.   **Study Question 2: How do personalities differ?**
    A. Big Five personality traits
    B. Social traits
    C. Personal conception traits
    D. Emotional adjustment traits

III.   **Study Question 3: What are value and attitude differences among individuals, and why are they important?**
    A. Values
    B. Attitudes

IV.   **Study Question 4: What are individual differences and how are they related to workforce diversity?**
    A. Equal employment opportunities
    B. Demography and individual differences
    C. Aptitude and ability
    D. Managing diversity and individual differences

CHAPTER LECTURE NOTES

I.   **Introduction to the Chapter 4 Lecture.**

    A. Study questions for Chapter 4. (See *PowerPoint Slide 2* for Chapter 4.)

1. What is personality?

2. How do personalities differ?

3. What are value and attitude differences among individuals, and why are they important?

4. What are individual differences and how are they related to workforce diversity?

B. The lecture material for Chapter 4 is organized around the study questions.

1. Point out to the students that the text's "Chapter At A Glance" identifies the key topics contained in the chapter and links them to the appropriate study questions.

C. The chapter opens with a description of a Hispanic woman's use of Bank of America's telebanking system. This description is used to make the point that diversity is everywhere with customers and employees, and that diversity brings into focus important OB concepts regarding personality, values, and attitudes.

II.   **Study Question 1: What is personality?**

A. What is personality? (See *PowerPoint Slide 3* for Chapter 4.)

1. **Personality** represents the overall profile or combination of characteristics that capture the unique nature of a person as that person reacts and interacts with others.

2. Personality combines a set of physical and mental characteristics that reflect how a person looks, thinks, acts, and feels.

3. An understanding of personality contributes to an understanding of organizational behavior in that predictable relationships are expected between people's personalities and their behaviors.

B. Personality and development.

1. *Figure 4.1* in the textbook shows the two forces — heredity and environment — that act together to determine an individual's personality. (See *PowerPoint Slide 4* for Chapter 4.)

   a. *Heredity* consists of those factors that are determined at conception, including physical characteristics, gender, and personality factors.

   b. *Environment* consists of cultural, social, and situational factors.

2. Heredity sets the limits on just how much personality characteristics can be developed; environment determines development within these limits. There is about a 50-50 heredity environment split. (See *PowerPoint Slide 5* for Chapter 4.)

a. Cultural values and norms play a substantial role in the development of personality.

b. Social factors include family life, religion, and many kinds of formal and informal groups.

c. Situational factors reflect the opportunities or constraints imposed by the context in which one operates.

3. **Developmental approaches** are systematic models of ways in which personality develops across time.

a. *Figure 4.2* from the text shows how personality develops over time from immaturity to maturity. (See **PowerPoint Slide 6** for Chapter 4.) Chris Argyris, who developed the immaturity-maturity continuum, believes that many organizations treat mature adults as if they were still immature, which in turn creates many problems in bringing out the best in employees.

LECTURE ENHANCEMENT

Using *Figure 4.2* as a point of reference, have students analyze an organization of their choosing in terms of terms of whether employees are treated as mature or immature individuals. Discuss the implications of this treatment.

C. Personality and the self-concept.

1. **Personality dynamics** refer to the ways in which an individual integrates and organizes social traits, values and motives, personal conceptions, and emotional adjustments.

2. The **self-concept** is the view individuals have of themselves as physical, social, and spiritual or moral beings. (See **PowerPoint Slide 7** for Chapter 4.)

3. Two aspects of the self-concept are self-esteem and self-efficacy.

a. *Self-esteem* is a belief about one's own worth based on an overall self-evaluation.

b. *Self-efficacy* is an individual's belief about the likelihood of successfully completing a specific task.

LECTURE ENHANCEMENT

Discuss the following: How could an organization affect an individual's self-concept? Explain the effect of self-esteem and self-efficacy upon individual performance.

III. **Study Question 2: How do personalities differ?**

A. Big Five personality traits.

   1. *Personality traits* are enduring characteristics describing an individual's behavior.

   2. The Big Five personality dimensions have been distilled from extensive lists of specific personality traits. The *Big Five traits* are the following (see ***PowerPoint Slide 8*** for Chapter 4):

      a. Extraversion — being outgoing, sociable, assertive.

      b. Agreeableness — being good-natured, trusting, cooperative.

      c. Conscientiousness — being responsible, dependable, persistent.

      d. Emotional stability — being unworried, secure, relaxed.

      e. Openness to experience — being imaginative, curious, broad-minded.

B. Social traits.

   1. **Social traits** are surface-level traits that reflect the way a person appears to others when interacting in various social settings. (See ***PowerPoint Slide 9*** for Chapter 4.)

   2. Problem-solving style, based on the work of Carl Jung, is one important social trait. See ***PowerPoint Slide 9*** for Chapter 4.)

   3. *Problem-solving style* reflects the way a person goes about gathering and evaluating information in solving problems and making decisions. (See ***PowerPoint Slide 9*** for Chapter 4.)

      a. Information gathering involves getting and organizing data for use. Styles of information-gathering vary from sensation to intuitive. (See ***PowerPoint Slide 10*** for Chapter 4.)

         (i) Sensation-type individuals prefer routine and order and emphasize well-defined details in gathering information; they would rather work with known facts than look for possibilities.

         (ii) Intuitive-type individuals like new problems, dislike routine, and would rather look for possibilities than work with facts.

      b. Information evaluation involves making judgments about how to deal with information once it has been collected. Styles of information evaluation vary from an emphasis on feeling to an emphasis on thinking. (See ***PowerPoint Slide 11*** for Chapter 4.)

(i) Feeling-type individuals are oriented toward conformity and try to accommodate themselves to other people; they try to avoid problems that may result in disagreements.

(ii) Thinking-type individuals use reason and intellect to deal with problems and downplay emotions.

4. When the information gathering and information evaluation dimensions are combined, four basic problem-solving styles result: sensation-feeling (SF), intuitive-feeling (IF), sensation-thinking (ST), and intuitive-thinking (IT). *Figure 4.3* from the textbook summarizes these four problem-solving styles. (See *PowerPoint Slide 12* for Chapter 4.)

LECTURE ENHANCEMENT

Using *Figure 4.3* as a point of departure, have each student identify the problem-solving style that seems to best describe him or her. Then, in groups of four or five, have the students share their analyses and discuss how their different problem-solving styles might affect their ability to work together on a major project.

---

5. Problem-solving styles are most frequently measured with the (typically 100-item) Myers-Briggs Type Indicator (MBTI).

C. Personal conception traits.

1. *Personal conception traits* represent the way individuals tend to think about their social and physical setting as well as their major benefits and personal orientation concerning a range of issues. (See *PowerPoint Slide 13* for Chapter 4.)

2. Personal conception traits include locus of control, authoritarianism and dogmatism, Machiavellianism, and self-monitoring. (See *PowerPoint Slide 13* for Chapter 4.)

3. Locus of control. (See *PowerPoint Slide 14* for Chapter 4.)

a. *Locus of control* refers to the extent to which a person feels able to control his or her own life.

b. *Externals* are more extraverted in their interpersonal relationships and are more oriented toward the world around them.

c. *Internals* tend to be more introverted and are more oriented towards their own feelings and ideas.

    d. *Figure 4.4* in the textbook describes how internals differ from externals regarding information processing; job satisfaction; performance; self-control, risk, and anxiety; motivation, expectancies, and results; and response to others. (See *PowerPoint Slide 15* for Chapter 4.)

LECTURE ENHANCEMENT

Using *Figure 4.4* as a point of departure, have each student identify his or her internal/external locus of control orientation regarding information processing; job satisfaction; performance; self-control, risk, and anxiety; motivation, expectancies, and results; and response to others.

---

    4. Authoritarianism/dogmatism. (See *PowerPoint Slide 16* for Chapter 4.)

        a. Both "authoritarianism" and "dogmatism" deal with the rigidity of a person's beliefs.

        b. A person high in **authoritarianism** tends to adhere rigidly to conventional values and to obey recognized authority. This person is concerned with toughness and power and opposes the use of subjective feelings.

        c. An individual high in **dogmatism** sees the world as a threatening place. This person regards legitimate authority as absolute and accepts or rejects others according to how much they agree with accepted authority.

        d. Highly authoritarian individuals are so susceptible to authority that in their eagerness to comply they may behave unethically.

    5. Machiavellianism.

        a. The *Machiavellian personality* views and manipulates others purely for personal gain.

        b. A *high-Mach personality* approaches situations logically and thoughtfully and is even capable of lying to achieve personal goals; is rarely swayed by loyalty, friendships, past promises, or the opinions of others; is skilled at influencing others; tries to exploit loosely structured situations; and performs in a perfunctory manner in highly structured situations. (See *PowerPoint Slide 17* for Chapter 4.)

        c. A *low-Mach personality* accepts direction imposed by others in loosely structured situations; works hard to do well in highly structured situations; is guided more strongly by ethical considerations; and is less likely to lie or cheat. (See *PowerPoint Slide 18* for Chapter 4.)

    6. Self-monitoring. (See *PowerPoint Slide 19* for Chapter 4.)

a. **Self-monitoring** reflects a person's ability to adjust his or her behavior to external or situational (environmental) factors.

b. *High self-monitoring individuals* are sensitive to external cues and tend to behave differently in different situations. High self-monitors can present a very different appearance from their true self.

c. In contrast, *low self-monitors*, like their low-Mach counterparts, aren't able to disguise their behaviors — "what you see is what you get."

D. Emotional adjustment traits. (See *PowerPoint Slide 20* for Chapter 4.)

   1. **Emotional adjustment traits** measure how much an individual experiences emotional distress or displays unacceptable acts.

   2. A frequently encountered emotional adjustment trait that is especially important for OB is the Type A/Type B orientation.

      a. Individuals with a **Type A orientation** are characterized by impatience, desire for achievement, and perfectionism.

      b. Individuals with a **Type B orientation** are characterized by as being more easy going and less competitive than Type A.

LECTURE ENHANCEMENT

As an outside assignment, have students write an essay describing themselves in terms of the Big Five personality traits, social traits, personal conception traits, and emotional adjustment traits that were discussed above. Also have them describe how their personality profile (in terms of these various dimensions) seems to influence their behavior.

IV. **Study Question 3: What are value and attitude differences among individuals, and why are they important?**

A. Values

   1. **Values** are broad preferences concerning appropriate courses of action or outcomes. (See *PowerPoint Slide 21* for Chapter 4.)

   2. Values influence attitudes and behavior. (See *PowerPoint Slide 21* for Chapter 4.)

   3. The **sources and types of values** include parents, friends, teachers, and external reference groups, all of which can influence individual values. (See *PowerPoint Slide 21* for Chapter 4.)

4. Peoples' values develop as a product of the learning and experiences they encounter in the cultural setting in which they live. (See *PowerPoint Slide 21* for Chapter 4.)

5. Milton Rokeach's values classification.
   a. <u>**Terminal values**</u> reflect a person's preferences concerning the "ends" to be achieved.

   b. <u>**Instrumental values**</u> reflect a person's beliefs about the means for achieving desired ends.

   c. *Figure 4.5* from the text provides numerous examples of terminal values and instrumental values. (See *PowerPoint Slide 22* for Chapter 4.)

LECTURE ENHANCEMENT

Using *Figure 4.5* as a point of departure, have each student identify the five most important terminal values and the five most important instrumental values for him or her. Divide the class into small groups to discuss the implications of their selected sets of values for how they might work together on a long-term group project.

---

6. Gordon Allport's values classification. (See *PowerPoint Slide 23* for Chapter 4.)

   a. Theoretical — interest in the discovery of truth through reasoning and systematic thinking.

   b. Economic — interest in usefulness and practicality, including the accumulation of wealth.

   c. Aesthetic — interest in beauty, form, and artistic harmony.

   d. Social — interest in people and love as a human relationship.

   e. Political — interest in gaining power and influencing other people.

   f. Religious — interest in unity and in understanding the cosmos as a whole.

7. Rokeach's and Allport's values classifications have had a major impact on the values literature, but they were not specifically designed for people in a work setting. Maglino and associates have developed a values classification that is targeted toward people in the workplace.

8. Values classification of Maglino and associates. (See *PowerPoint Slide 24* for Chapter 4.)

   a. Achievement — getting things done and working hard to accomplish difficult things in life.

b. Helping and concern for others — being concerned with other people and helping others.

c. Honesty — telling the truth and doing what you feel is right.

d. Fairness — being impartial and doing what is fair for all concerned.

9. **Value congruence** occurs when individuals express positive feelings upon encountering others who exhibit values similar to their own. When values differ, or are incongruent, conflicts over such things as goals and the means to achieve them may result.

10. There is a movement away from values such as duty, honesty, responsibility, economic incentives, organizational loyalty, and work-related identity; and a movement toward values such as meaningful work, pursuit of leisure, personal identity, and self-fulfillment.

B. Attitudes.

1. Attitudes are influenced by values and are acquired from the same sources as values. (See *PowerPoint Slide 25* for Chapter 4.)

2. Attitudes are more specific and less stable than values. (See *PowerPoint Slide 25* for Chapter 4.)

3. An **attitude** is a predisposition to respond in a positive or negative way to someone or something in one's environment. (See *PowerPoint Slide 25* for Chapter 4.)

LECTURE ENHANCEMENT

Break the class in small groups and have the group members discuss their attitudes toward: work, leisure, education, group work, social responsibility, corporate ethics, individual ethics, making money, etc.

---

4. *Figure 4.6* in the textbook shows how beliefs and values create feelings that influence intended behavior. (See *PowerPoint Slide 26* for Chapter 4.)

a. Beliefs and values represent the **cognitive component** of an attitude (*i.e.*, the beliefs, opinions, knowledge, or information a person possesses).

(i) **Beliefs** represent ideas about someone or something and the conclusions people draw about them.

b. The **affective component** of an attitude is a specific feeling regarding the personal impact of the antecedents.

      c.   The **behavioral component** of an attitude is an intention to behave in a certain way based on the individual's specific feelings.

  5.   Relationships between attitudes and behavior. (See *PowerPoint Slide 27* for Chapter 4.)

      a.   The more specific attitudes and behavior are, the stronger the relationship between them.

      b.   Lack of freedom to follow through on behavioral intent weakens the relationship between attitudes and behavior.

      c.   Experience with a given attitude strengthens the relationship between attitudes and behavior.

  6.   Attitudes and cognitive consistency.

  7.   **Cognitive dissonance** describes a state of inconsistency between an individual's attitude and behavior. (See *PowerPoint Slide 28* for Chapter 4.)

      a.   Cognitive dissonance can be reduced in the following ways: changing the underlying attitude, changing future behavior, or developing new ways of explaining or rationalizing the inconsistency. (See *PowerPoint Slide 28* for Chapter 4.)

      b.   Choices regarding cognitive dissonance reduction methods are influenced by the degree of a person's perceived control over the situation and the magnitude of the rewards involved. (See *PowerPoint Slide 29* for Chapter 4.)

V.   **Study Question 4: What are individual differences and how are they related to workforce diversity?**

  A.   Background on workforce diversity and individual differences. (See *PowerPoint Slides 30* and *31* for Chapter 4.)

      1.   **Workforce diversity** refers to the presence of individual human characteristics that make people different from one another.

LECTURE ENHANCEMENT

Solicit input from the students regarding examples of workplace diversity that they have encountered.

---

      2.   The challenge is how to manage workforce diversity in a way that both respects the individual's unique perspectives and contributions and promotes a shared sense of organization vision and identity.

3. As workforce diversity increases, the possibility of stereotyping and discrimination increases.

4. **Stereotyping** occurs when one thinks of an individual as belonging to a group or category and the characteristics commonly associated with the group or category are assigned to the individual in question.

5. **Demographic characteristics** are the background variables (*e.g.*, age and gender) that help shape what a person becomes over time.

   a. Demographic characteristics may serve as the basis of stereotypes.

LECTURE ENHANCEMENT

Have students assume that they are employers who are preparing to hire an individual for an important management position. The two finalists are both females. One is 53 years old, and the other is 25 years old. Instruct the students to identify stereotypes that they might have concerning these two individuals, and the impact of these stereotypes on the hiring decision.

B. Equal employment opportunity. (See *PowerPoint Slide 32* for Chapter 4.)

1. *Equal employment opportunity* involves both workplace nondiscrimination and affirmative action.

2. Employment decisions are nondiscriminatory when there is no intent to exclude or disadvantage legally protected groups.

3. *Affirmative action* is a set of remedial actions designed to compensate for proven discrimination or to correct for statistical imbalances in the labor force.

4. Federal, state and provincial, and local laws, as well as numerous court cases, legally drive affirmative action.

LECTURE ENHANCEMENT

Is there any conflict between equal employment opportunity and affirmative action? Have students debate this question.

C. Demography and individual differences.

1. **Demographic characteristics** are the background characteristics that help shape what a person becomes. (See *PowerPoint Slide 33* for Chapter 4.)

2. Demographic characteristics may be thought of in both current terms and historical terms.

3. Demographic characteristics of special interest from equal employment opportunity and workplace diversity considerations include gender, age, able-bodiedness, race, and ethnicity. (See *PowerPoint Slide 33* for Chapter 4.)

4. Gender.

   a. Men and women show no consistent differences in their problem-solving abilities, analytical skills, competitive drive, motivation, learning ability, or sociability. (See *PowerPoint Slide 34* for Chapter 4.)

   b. Women, as compared to men, are reported to be more conforming, to have lower expectations of success, and tend to be absent more frequently. (See *PowerPoint Slide 35* for Chapter 4.)

   c. Women leaders tend to be more democratic and less autocratic than men leaders. (See *PowerPoint Slide 35* for Chapter 4.)

   d. Prejudice toward female leaders can occur as a result of conflict between gender role and leader role requirements.

   e. The outlook for women's leadership participation is promising.

LECTURE ENHANCEMENT

Working Woman magazine (see http://www.workingwomanmag.com) is a periodical designed specifically to provide information and resources of interest to women in the workforce. The magazine provides a lot of information that may be of interest to students.

---

5. Age. (See *PowerPoint Slide 36* for Chapter 4.)

   a. The research findings concerning age are particularly important given the aging of the workforce. People 50 years old and older are expected to increase by 50 percent between 2000 and 2010.

   b. Older workers are more susceptible to being stereotyped as inflexible and undesirable in other ways.

   c. Age discrimination lawsuits are increasingly common in the United States.

   d. Small businesses tend to value older workers for their experience, stability, and low turnover.

   e. More experienced workers, who are usually older, tend to perform well and have low absence rates and relatively low turnover.

6. Able-bodiedness. (See *PowerPoint Slide 37* for Chapter 4.)

a. Even though recent studies report that disabled workers do their jobs as well, or better than, nondisabled workers, nearly three quarters of severely disabled persons are reported to be unemployed.

LECTURE ENHANCEMENT

Ask the students to identify stereotypes, and the validity of those stereotypes, that would explain the high rate of unemployment among the disabled.

---

b. Almost 80 percent of those with disabilities say they want to work.

c. More firms are expected to give serious consideration to hiring disabled workers.

7. Racial and ethnic groups. (See *PowerPoint Slide 38* for Chapter 4.)

a. Racial and ethnic groups reflect the broad spectrum of employees of differing ethnicities or races who make up an ever-increasing portion of the new workforce.

b. Of particular significance in the American workplace is the diversity reflected in an increasing proportion of African Americans, Asian Americans and Hispanic Americans in the workforce.

c. The potential for stereotypes and discrimination to adversely affect the career opportunities and progress for members of minority groups must be recognized.

d. Employment decisions based on demographic differences are allowable under Title VII of the Civil Rights Act if they can be justified as bona fide occupational qualifications (BFOQs) reasonable to normal business operations, but race cannot be one of these BFOQs.

8. Important lessons regarding demographic differences. (See *PowerPoint Slide 39* for Chapter 4.)

a. Respect and deal with the needs and concerns of people with different demographics.

b. Avoid linking demographics to stereotypes.

c. Demography is not a good indicator of individual-job fits.

D. Aptitude and ability. (See *PowerPoint Slide 40* for Chapter 4.)

1. **Aptitude** represents a person's capability of learning something.

2. **Ability** reflects a person's existing capacity to perform the various tasks needed for a given job and includes both relevant knowledge and skills.

3. Aptitudes are potential abilities; whereas abilities are the knowledge and skills than an individual currently possesses.

4. Aptitudes and abilities are important considerations for a manager when initially hiring or selecting candidates for a job.

LECTURE ENHANCEMENT

Ask the students to identify their own aptitudes and abilities. Discuss with them the aptitudes and abilities that seem to be critical for effective entry into the workforce, and have them compare their own aptitudes and abilities to the critical ones revealed during the discussion.

E. Managing diversity and individual differences.

1. The concept of managing diversity in organizations emphasizes appreciation of differences in creating a setting where everyone feels valued and accepted.

2. Progressive organizations undertake programs that are intended to actively address diversity issues and to make diversity an essential component of operating activities.

VI.   Study summary for Chapter 4.

A. Point out to the students that the text's "Chapter 4 Study Guide" recaps the key theories, concepts, and ideas in the chapter in relation to the appropriate study questions.

CHAPTER STUDY GUIDE

Study Question 1: What is personality?

- Personality captures the overall profile, or combination of characteristics, that represents the unique nature of an individual as that individual interacts with others.
- Personality is determined by both heredity and environment; across all personality characteristics, the mix of heredity and environment is about 50-50.

Study Question 2: How do personalities differ?

- The Big Five personality traits consist of extraversion, agreeableness, conscientiousness, emotional stability, and openness to experience.
- A useful personality framework consists of social traits, personal conception traits, emotional adjustment traits, and personality dynamics, where each category represents one or more personality dimensions.

- Personality characteristics are important because of their predictable interplay with an individual's behavior. Along with demographics and aptitude/ability differences, personality characteristics must be matched to organizations and jobs.

Study Question 3: What are value and attitude differences among individuals, and why are they important?

- Values are broad preferences concerning courses of action or outcomes.
- Rokeach divides values into 18 terminal values (preferences concerning ends) and 18 instrumental values (values concerning means).
- Allport and his associates identify six value categories, ranging from theoretical to religious.
- Maglino and his associates classify values into achievement, helping and concern for others, honesty, and fairness.
- There have been societal changes in value patterns away from economic and organizational loyalty and toward meaningful work and self-fulfillment.
- Attitudes are a predisposition to respond positively or negatively to someone or something in one's environment; they are influenced by values but are more specific.
- Individuals desire consistency between their attitudes and their behaviors.
- Values and attitudes are important because they indicate predispositions toward behaviors.
- Along with demographics, aptitude/ability, and personality differences, values and attitudes need to be matched to organizations and jobs.

Study Question 4: What are individual differences and how are they related to workforce diversity?

- Workforce diversity is the mix of gender, race and ethnicity, age, and able-bodiedness in the workforce.
- Workforces in the Untied States, Canada, and Europe are becoming more diverse, and valuing and managing such diversity is becoming increasingly more important to enhance organizational competitiveness and provide individual development.
- Demographic differences are background characteristics that help shape what a person has become.
- Gender, age, race and ethnicity, and able-bodiedness are particularly important demographic characteristics.
- The use of demographic differences in employment is covered by a series of federal, state/provincial, and local laws outlawing discrimination.
- Demographic differences can be the basis for inappropriate stereotyping that can influence workplace decisions and behaviors.
- Aptitude is a person's capability of learning something.
- Ability is a person's existing capacity to perform the various tasks needed for a given job.
- Aptitudes are potential abilities.
- Both mental and physical aptitudes and abilities are used in matching individuals to organizations and jobs.
- Managing diversity and individual differences involves striving for a match among the firm, specific jobs, and the people recruited, hired, and developed, while recognizing an increasingly diverse workforce.

- Increasing workforce diversity is provided by equal employment opportunity, through nondiscrimination and affirmative action; ethical considerations; local, national, and global competitive pressures; and a projected change in the nature of the workforce.
- Firms now use a wide variety of practices in managing workforce diversity; for example, interactive networks, recruitment, education, development, promotion, pay, and assessment.

KEY TERMS

Ability: reflects a person's existing capacity to perform the various tasks needed for a given job and includes both relevant knowledge and skills.

Affective component: a specific feeling regarding the personal impact of the antecedents of an attitude.

Aptitude: represents a person's capability of learning something.

Attitude: a predisposition to respond in a positive or negative way to someone or something in one's environment.

Authoritarianism: a tendency to adhere rigidly to conventional values and to obey recognized authority.

Behavioral component: an intention to behave in a certain way based on the individual's specific feelings.

Beliefs: represent ideas about someone or something and the conclusions people draw about them.

Cognitive component: the beliefs, opinions, knowledge, or information a person possesses.

Cognitive dissonance: a state of inconsistency between an individual's attitude and behavior.

Demographic characteristics: the background variables (*e.g.*, age, gender) that help shape what a person becomes over time.

Developmental approaches: systematic models of ways in which personality develops across time.

Dogmatism: a tendency to regard legitimate authority as absolute and to accept or reject others according to how much they agree with accepted authority.

Emotional adjustment traits: measure how much an individual experiences emotional distress or displays unacceptable acts.

Instrumental values: reflect a person's beliefs about the means for achieving desired ends.

Personality: represents the overall profile or combination of characteristics that capture the unique nature of a person as that person reacts and interacts with others.

Personality dynamics: refer to the ways in which an individual integrates and organizes social traits, values and motives, personal conceptions, and emotional adjustments.

Self-concept: the view individuals have of themselves as physical, social, and spiritual or moral beings.

Self-monitoring: reflects a person's ability to adjust his or her behavior to external or situational (environmental) factors.

Social traits: surface-level traits that reflect the way a person appears to others when interacting in various social settings.

Sources and types of values: Parents, friends, teachers, and external reference groups can all influence individual values.

Stereotyping: occurs when one thinks of an individual as belonging to a group or category, and the characteristics commonly associated with the group or category are assigned to the individual in question.

Terminal values: reflect a person's preferences concerning the "ends" to be achieved.

Type A orientation: people who are characterized by impatience, desire for achievement, and perfectionism.

Type B orientation: people who are characterized as more easy going and less competitive than Type A individuals.

Value congruence: occurs when individuals express positive feelings upon encountering others who exhibit values similar to their own.

Values: broad preferences concerning appropriate courses of action or outcomes.

Workforce diversity: refers to the presence of individual human characteristics that make people different from one another.

Chapter 5
PERCEPTION AND ATTRIBUTION

STUDY QUESTIONS

1.	What is the perception process?
2.	What are common perceptual distortions?
3.	How can perceptions be managed?
4.	What is attribution theory?

LEARNING OBJECTIVES

After completing this chapter students should be able to:

1.	Describe the perceptual process, focusing on the factors that influence the process and the stages of the process.
2.	Discuss the common perceptual distortions, including stereotypes or prototypes, halo effects, selective perception, projection, contrast effects, and self-fulfilling prophecies.
3.	Explain the roles of impression management and distortion management in managing perceptions.
4.	Discuss the nature of attribution theory, explain why attributions are important for managers and other organization members, and describe two basic attribution errors.
5.	Describe some of the cultural aspects of attribution theory.

MATERIAL IN *THE OB SKILLS WORKBOOK* SUPPORTING THE CHAPTER

Cases for Critical Thinking	Case 5: MAGREC, Inc.
Experiential Exercises	Exercise 9: How We View Differences
	Exercise 10: Alligator River Story
Self-Assessment	Assessment 6: Intolerance for Ambiguity

CHAPTER OVERVIEW

This chapter focuses on perception and attribution. The chapter begins with a discussion of the perceptual process and the factors that influence that process. The roles of the perceiver, the setting, and the perceived in the perceptual process are discussed. The specific stages of the perceptual process — attention and selection, organization, interpretation, and retrieval — are examined. The chapter then moves on to review common perceptual distortions, including stereotypes or prototypes, halo effects, selective perception, projection, contrast effects, and self-fulfilling prophecies. This section should be of particular interest to your students because it is easy to see these distortions at work in our own lives and in the lives of others. The first half of the chapter concludes with a discussion of managing perceptions, with emphasis being placed on impression management and distortion management.

The second half of the chapter focuses on attribution theory, which is an insightful approach to understanding human behavior. The nature and importance of attributions are explored and two attribution errors — the fundamental attribution error and the self-serving bias — are discussed. The chapter concludes with a discussion of cultural effects on the attribution process.

CHAPTER OUTLINE

I.   **Study Question 1: What is the perception process?**
      A. Factors influencing perception
      B. Stages of the perceptual process
      C. Response to the perceptual process

II.   **Study Question 2: What are common perceptual distortions?**
      A. Stereotypes or prototypes
      B. Halo effects
      C. Selective perception
      D. Projection
      E. Contrast effects
      F. Self-fulfilling prophecies

III.   **Study Question 3: How can perceptions be managed?**
      A. Impression Management
      B. Distortion Management

IV.   **Study Question 4: What is attribution theory?**
      A. Importance of attributions
      B. Attribution errors
      C. Attributions across cultures

CHAPTER LECTURE NOTES

I.   **Introduction to the Chapter 5 Lecture.**

      A. Study questions for Chapter 5. (See ***PowerPoint Slide 2*** for Chapter 5.)

          1. What is the perception process?

          2. What are common perceptual distortions?

          3. How can perceptions be managed?

          4. What is attribution theory?

B. The lecture material for Chapter 5 is organized around the study questions.

   1. Point out to the students that the text's "Chapter At A Glance" identifies the key topics contained in the chapter and links them to the appropriate study questions.

C. The chapter opens with a description of the differing perceptions that are associated with the city of Dallas, Texas.

II.   Study Question 1: What is the perception process?

A. Introduction

   1. **Perception** is the process through which people select, organize, interpret, retrieve, and respond to information from their environment. (See ***PowerPoint Slide 3*** for Chapter 5.)

   2. Through perception, people process information inputs into responses involving feeling and action. The quality or accuracy of a person's perceptions, therefore, has a major impact on his or her responses to a given situation. (See ***PowerPoint Slide 3*** for Chapter 5.)

   3. ***Figure 5.1*** from the textbook shows how the perceptions of the performance appraisal interview differ between managers and subordinates. (See ***PowerPoint Slide 4*** for Chapter 5.)

LECTURE ENHANCEMENT

To generate an interesting, and perhaps quite animated, discussion of differing perceptions of the same situation, ask students to describe how they perceive one or more of the following situations:

- Cutting costs by sending American jobs overseas.
- Downsizing of companies.
- Providing organizationally funded fringe benefits to same sex partners.
- Restricting trade with nations that are known for human rights abuses.
- Peer evaluations of performance.
- Self-management practices in businesses.
- Drug testing in the workplace.
- Electronic surveillance of employees.

B. Factors influencing the perceptual process.

   1. The factors that contribute to perceptual differences and the perceptual process among people at work are summarized in ***Figure 5.2*** in the textbook (see ***PowerPoint Slide 5*** for Chapter 5).

   2. The factors include characteristics of the perceiver, the setting, and the perceived.

    a. The *perceiver* — a person's past experiences, needs or motives, personality, and values and attitudes may all influence the perceptual process

    b. The *setting* — the physical, social, and organizational context of the perceptual setting also can influence the perceptual process.

    c. The *perceived* — characteristics of the perceived person, object, or event, such as contrast, intensity, figure-ground separation, size, motion, and repetition or novelty, are also important in the perceptual process.

C. Stages of the perceptual process.

  1. *Figure 5.4* from the textbook depicts the four stages of the perceptual process in relation to the factors that influence perception (*i.e.*, the perceiver, the setting, and the perceived) and the feeling/thinking actions that result from perception. (See *PowerPoint Slide 6* for Chapter 5.)

  2. Stage 1 of the perceptual process: *information attention and selection*. Our senses are constantly bombarded with so much information that if we don't screen it, we quickly become incapacitated with information overload. (See *PowerPoint Slide 7* for Chapter 5.)

    a. Selective screening lets in only a tiny portion of all the information available.

    b. Selective screening can occur through controlled processing, which reflects a conscious decision regarding what information to pay attention to and what to ignore.

    c. Selective screening can also occur without the perceiver's conscious awareness.

LECTURE ENHANCEMENT

In order to illustrate selective screening, while in the middle of your lecture for the day insert a sentence stating that the next exam or paper has been cancelled. Discuss the students' reaction.

---

  3. Stage 2 of the perceptual process: *information organization*. Even though selective screening takes place in the attention stage, it is still necessary to find ways to organize the information efficiently. This is accomplished through the use of schemas. (See *PowerPoint Slide 8* for Chapter 5.)

    a. **Schemas** are cognitive frameworks that represent organized knowledge about a given concept or stimulus developed through experience.

    b. A self schema contains information about a person's own appearance, behavior, and personality.

      c.   Person schemas refer to the way individuals sort others into categories, such as types or groups, in terms of similar perceived features.

         (i)   A prototype, or stereotype, is often used to represent person schemas. A prototype is an abstract set of features commonly associated with members of that category. Once the prototype is formed, it is stored in long-term memory; it is retrieved when it is needed for a comparison of how well a person matches the prototype's feature.

      d.   A script schema is a knowledge framework that describes the appropriate sequence of events in a given situation.

      e.   Person-in situation schemas combine schemas built around persons (self and person schemas) and events (script schemas).

4.   Stage 3 of the perceptual process: *information interpretation.* Once one's attention has been drawn to certain stimuli and this information has been grouped or organized, reasons behind the actions need to be uncovered since people interpret information differently or make different attributions about what they have perceived. (See ***PowerPoint Slide 9*** for Chapter 5.)

5.   Stage 4 of the perceptual process: *information retrieval.* Stages 1 through 3 form part of a person's memory and contribute to the information stored there. In Stage 4, this stored information must be retrieved if it is to be used. (See ***PowerPoint Slide 10*** for Chapter 5.)

D. Response to the perceptual process.

1.   Organizational behavior responses to the perceptual process include thoughts, feelings, and actions.

III.   Study Question 2: What are common perceptual distortions?

A. ***Figure 5.5*** from the textbook identifies the common perceptual distortions that influence the various stages of the perceptual process. (See ***PowerPoint Slide 11*** for Chapter 5.) These perceptual distortions include the following: stereotype/prototype, halo effect, selective perception, projection, self-fulfilling prophecy, and contrast effects.

B. Stereotypes and prototypes. (See ***PowerPoint Slide 12*** for Chapter 5.)

1.   Stereotypes, or prototypes, are useful ways of combining information in order to deal with information overload, but they can cause inaccuracies in retrieving information and can obscure individual differences.

2.   Stereotypes are most likely to occur in the organization stage of perception.

3.   Both managers and employees need to be sensitive to stereotypes and their potential impact.

LECTURE ENHANCEMENT

Are all stereotypes inaccurate? Are stereotypes ever useful? Have students discuss and debate these questions.

    C.   Halo effects. (See *PowerPoint Slide 13* for Chapter 5.)

        1.   A **halo effect** occurs when one attribute of a person or situation is used to develop an overall impression of the individual or situation.

        2.   Halo effects are most likely to occur in the organization stage of perception.

        3.   Halo effects are particularly important in the performance appraisal process because they can influence a manager's evaluations of subordinates' work performance.

LECTURE ENHANCEMENT

Many students work while attending college. Encourage students to identify examples of the halo effect where they work or in the classroom.

    D.   Selective perception. (See *PowerPoint Slide 14* for Chapter 5.)

        1.   **Selective perception** is the tendency to single out for attention those aspects of a situation or person that are consistent with one's existing beliefs, values, and needs.

        2.   Selective perception is strongest in the attention stage of the perceptual process.

        3.   According to research results, selective perception is more important at some times than at others. Managers should be aware of this characteristic and determine, by gathering additional opinions, whether or not situations, events, or individuals are being selectively perceived.

LECTURE ENHANCEMENT

Have students to identify examples of the selective perception that they have encountered at work or in the classroom.

    E.   Projection. (See *PowerPoint Slide 15* for Chapter 5.)

        1.   **Projection** is the assignment of one's personal attributes to other individuals.

2. Projection is especially likely to occur in the interpretation stage or perception.

3. Projection can be controlled through a high degree of self-awareness and empathy.

LECTURE ENHANCEMENT

Discuss the idea that as cultural diversity increases in the workplace, projection is often inappropriate.

F. Contrast effects. (See *PowerPoint Slide 16* for Chapter 5.)

1. **Contrast effects** occur when an individual's characteristics are contrasted with those of others recently encountered who rank higher or lower on the same characteristics.

2. Both managers and employees need to be aware of the possible perceptual distortion the contrast effect may create in many work settings.

LECTURE ENHANCEMENT

Have students to identify examples of the contrast effect that they have experienced or witnessed at work or in the classroom.

G. Self-fulfilling prophecy. (See *PowerPoint Slide 17* for Chapter 5.)

1. The **self-fulfilling prophecy** is the tendency to create or find in another situation or individual that which you expected to find in the first place.

2. The self-fulfilling prophecy is sometimes referred to as the "Pygmalion effect."

3. The self-fulfilling prophecy can have both positive and negative results for managers in that subordinates are likely to "perform up to" or "perform down to" the expectations managers set for them.

LECTURE ENHANCEMENT

Have the students provide examples of how the self-fulfilling prophecy works in the classroom.

IV.   **Study Question 3: How can perceptions be managed?**

A. Impression management.

1. Impression management is a person's systematic attempt to behave in ways that will create and maintain desired impressions in the eyes of others. (See *PowerPoint Slide 18* for Chapter 5.)

2. Impression management is influenced by such activities as associating with the "right people," doing favors to gain approval, flattering others to make oneself look better, taking credit for a favorable event, apologizing for a negative event while seeking a pardon, agreeing with the opinions of others, downplaying the severity of a negative event, and doing favors for others.

3. Successful managers use impression management to enhance their own images and are sensitive to other people's use of impression management. (See *PowerPoint Slide 18* for Chapter 5.)

LECTURE ENHANCEMENT

Impression management can be extremely powerful as students make the transition from high school to the college atmosphere. Have students provide examples of how they managed impressions in making this transition.

B. Distortion Management. (See *PowerPoint Slide 19* for Chapter 5.)

1. During the attention and selection stage, managers should be alert to balancing automatic and controlled information processing. Most managerial responsibilities will involve controlled processing.

2. Managers should broaden their schemas at the organizing stage.

3. Managers should be attuned to attributions at the interpretation stage.

V. **Study Question 4: What is attribution theory?**

A. Background on attribution theory and the importance of attributions.

1. **Attribution theory** aids in perceptual interpretation by focusing on how people attempt to do the following (see *PowerPoint Slide 20* for Chapter 5):

   a. Understand the cause(s) of a certain event.

   b. Assess responsibility for the outcomes of the event.

   c. Evaluate the personal qualities of the people involved in the event.

2. Attribution theory is concerned with the question of whether one's behavior has been internally or externally caused. Internal causes are believed to under an individual's control, whereas external causes are seen as outside a person's control.

3. Three factors influence whether a person's behavior is attributed to internal or external causes. These factors are: distinctiveness, consensus, and consistency. (See ***PowerPoint Slide 21*** for Chapter 5.)

   a. *Distinctiveness* considers how consistent a person's behavior is across different situations.

   b. *Consensus* takes into account how likely all those facing a similar situation are to respond in the same way.

   c. *Consistency* concerns whether an individual responds the same way across time.

B. Attribution errors.

   1. The **fundamental attribution error** is the tendency to underestimate the influence of situational factors and to overestimate the influence of personal factors in evaluating someone else's behavior. (See ***PowerPoint Slide 22*** for Chapter 5.)

   2. A **self-serving bias** is the tendency to deny personal responsibility for performance problems but to accept personal responsibility for performance success. (See ***PowerPoint Slide 23*** for Chapter 5.)

LECTURE ENHANCEMENT

Students can probably relate to the self-serving bias. Have students provide examples of this bias that they have observed.

C. Attributions Across Cultures

   1. Research on the self-serving bias and fundamental attribution error has been done in cultures outside the United States with unexpected results.

   2. Differing cultural values appear to play a role in attributions of internal and external causes. Certain cultures, such as the United States, tend to overemphasize internal causes and underestimate external causes.

   3. Perceptions and attributions can be managed effectively by doing the following (see ***PowerPoint Slide 24*** for Chapter 5):

   a. Be self-aware.

   b. Seek a wide range of differing information.

   c. Try to see a situation as others would.

d. Be aware of different kinds of schemas.

e. Be aware of perceptual distortions.

f. Be aware of self and impression management.

g. Be aware of attribution theory implications.

VI.   Study summary for Chapter 5.

A. Point out to the students that the text's "Chapter 5 Study Guide" recaps the key theories, concepts, and ideas in the chapter in relation to the appropriate study questions.

CHAPTER STUDY GUIDE

Study Question 1: What is the perception process?

- Individuals use the perceptual process to pay attention to and to select, organize, interpret, and retrieve information from the world around them.
- The perceptual process involves the perceiver, the setting, and the perceived.
- Responses to the perceptual process involve thinking and feeling and action classifications.

Study Question 2: What are common perceptual distortions?

- Stereotypes or prototypes: an abstract set of features commonly associated with members of a given category.
- Halo effects: one attribute of a person or situation is used to develop an overall impression of the person or situation.
- Selective perception: the tendency to single out for attention those aspects of a situation or person that reinforce or emerge and are consistent with existing beliefs, values, and needs.
- Projection: assignments of personal attributes to other individuals.
- Contrast effects: when an individual's characteristics are contrasted with those of others recently encountered who rank higher or lower on the same characteristics.

Study Question 3: How can perceptions be managed?

- Managing perception involves:
- Impression management of the self and others.
- Managing the information attention and selection stages.
- Managing the information organizing stage.
- Managing the information interpretation stage.
- Managing the information storage and retrieval stage.
- Being sensitive to effects of the common perceptual distortions.

Study Question 4: What is attribution theory?

- Attribution theory involves emphasis on the interpretation stage of the perceptual process and consideration of whether individuals' behaviors result primarily from external causes or from causes internal to the individuals.
- Three factors influence an external or internal causal attribution — distinctiveness, consensus, and consistency.
- Two errors influencing an external or internal causal attribution are the fundamental attribution error and self-serving bias.
- Attributions can be managed by recognizing a typical overemphasis on internal causes of behavior and an underemphasis on external causes.
- An overemphasis on internal causes tends to lead to failure, to employees having accompanying disciplinary actions or negative performance evaluations, and the like.
- An underemphasis on external causes tends to lead to a lack of workplace support.

KEY TERMS

Attribution theory: an aid to perceptual interpretation that attempts to understand the cause(s) of an event, assess responsibility for outcomes of the event, and assess the personal qualities of the people involved in the event.

Contrast effects: a perceptual distortion that occurs when an individual's characteristics are contrasted with those of others recently encountered who rank higher or lower on the same characteristics.

Fundamental attribution error: the tendency to underestimate the influence of situational factors and to overestimate the influence of personal factors in evaluating someone else's behavior.

Halo effect: a perceptual distortion that occurs when one attribute of a person or situation is used to develop an overall impression of the individual or situation.

Perception: the process through which people select, organize, interpret, retrieve, and respond to information from their environment.

Projection: a perceptual distortion involving the assignment of one's personal attributes to other individuals.

Schema: a cognitive framework that represents organized knowledge about a given concept or stimulus developed through experience.

Selective perception: a perceptual distortion involving the tendency to single out for attention those aspects of a situation or person that are consistent with one's existing beliefs, values, and needs.

Self-fulfilling prophecy: a perceptual distortion involving the tendency to create or find in another situation or individual that which you expected to find in the first place.

Self-serving bias: the tendency to deny personal responsibility for performance problems but to accept personal responsibility for performance success.

Chapter 6
MOTIVATION THEORIES

STUDY QUESTIONS

1.	What is motivation?
2.	What do the content theories suggest about individual needs and motivation?
3.	What do the process theories suggest about individual motivation?
4.	What are reinforcement theories and how are they linked to motivation?

LEARNING OBJECTIVES

After completing this chapter students should be able to:

1.	Define "motivation" and explain the vital role of motivation in business organizations.
2.	Discuss the differences among content theory, process theory, and reinforcement theory
3.	Describe the needs addressed by each of the content theories of motivation, and explain how those needs are expected to influence behavior.
4.	Discuss the focus of equity theory and the influence that perceived inequity can have on workplace behavior.
5.	Describe the variables in the expectancy model of motivation, explain how those variables influence work motivation, and discuss the managerial implications of trying to influence these variables.
6.	Discuss reinforcement theory and the different types of reinforcement (or behavioral management) strategies.
7.	Discuss key ethical issues regarding reinforcement theory and its application.

MATERIAL IN *THE OB SKILLS WORKBOOK* SUPPORTING THE CHAPTER

Case for Critical Thinking	Case 6: It Isn't Fair
Experiential Exercises	Exercise 11: Teamwork & Motivation
	Exercise 12: The Downside of Punishment
Self-Assessment	Assessment 7: Two Factor Profile

CHAPTER OVERVIEW

This chapter provides a reasonable review of employee motivation and reinforcement in the workplace. The chapter begins by defining the term "motivation" and introducing the content, process, and reinforcement perspectives on employee motivation and workplace behavior. The issue of motivation across cultures is then raised, and the point is made that the chapter focuses on theories developed on the basis of the North American experience. The content theories of motivation discussed in the chapter include Maslow's hierarchy of needs theory, Alderfer's ERG theory, McClelland's acquired needs theory, and Herzberg's two-factor theory. The discussion of process theories focuses on Adam's equity theory and Vroom's expectancy theory. The material on reinforcement theory focuses on the application of operant conditioning principles to the workplace, with attention being given to different behavioral management strategies — including positive reinforcement, negative reinforcement, punishment, and extinction. Ethical issues regarding reinforcement theory and its application are also explored.

CHAPTER OUTLINE

I.   **Study Question 1: What is motivation?**
   A. Content, process, and reinforcement theories
   B. Motivation across cultures

II.   **Study Question 2: What do the content theories suggest about individual needs and motivation?**
   A. Hierarchy of needs theory
   B. ERG theory
   C. Acquired needs theory
   D. Two-factor theory

III.   **Study Question 3: What do the process theories suggest about individual motivation?**
   A. Equity theory
   B. Expectancy theory

IV.   **Study Question 4: What are reinforcement theories and how are they linked to motivation?**
   A. Classical and operant conditioning
   B. Reinforcement strategies
   C. Ethics and reinforcement

CHAPTER LECTURE NOTES

I.   **Introduction to the Chapter 6 Lecture.**

   A. Study questions for Chapter 6. (See ***PowerPoint Slide 2*** for Chapter 6.)

      1. What is motivation?

      2. What do content theories suggest about individual needs and motivation?

      3. What do the process theories suggest about individual motivation?

      4. What are reinforcement theories and how are they linked to motivation?

   B. The lecture material for Chapter 6 is organized around the study questions.

1. Point out to the students that the text's "Chapter At A Glance" identifies the key topics contained in the chapter and links them to the appropriate study questions.

C. The chapter opens with a description of different approaches that are being used to motivate students to earn money for college by earning good grades in middle and high school.

II. **Study Question 1: What is motivation?**

A. **Motivation** refers to forces within an individual that account for the level, direction, and persistence of effort expended at work. (See ***PowerPoint Slide 3*** for Chapter 6.)

1. *Direction* refers to an individual's choice when presented with a number of possible alternatives (*e.g.*, whether to exert effort toward product quality or toward product quantity).

2. *Level* refers to the amount of effort a person puts forth (*e.g.*, a lot or a little).

3. *Persistence* refers to the length of time a person sticks with a given action (*e.g.*, to try to achieve product quantity and give up when it is found difficult to attain).

B. Content, process, and reinforcement theories.

1. The theories of motivation can be divided into the following three broad categories (see ***PowerPoint Slide 4*** for Chapter 6):

    a. **Content theories** focus on profiling the different physiological and psychological needs that people seek to fulfill.

    b. **Process theories** focus on the thought or cognitive processes that take place within the minds of people and influence their behavior.

    c. **Reinforcement theories** emphasize the process of controlling an individual's behavior by manipulating its consequences.

C. Motivation across cultures.

1. Motivation is a key concern in firms around the globe. However, North American theories (and these are the only ones discussed in this chapter) are subject to cultural limitations.

2. The determinants of motivation and the best ways to deal with it are likely to vary considerably across Asia, South America, Eastern Europe, and Africa.

III. **Study Question 2: What do the content theories suggest about individual needs and motivation?**

A. Background on content theories. (See ***PowerPoint Slide 5*** for Chapter 6.)

1. Content theories suggest that motivation results from the individual's attempts to satisfy needs.

2. The content theories proposed by Abraham Maslow, Clayton Alderfer, David McClelland, and Frederick Herzberg are presented in this chapter.

3. Each content theory offers a slightly different view of the needs individuals may bring with them to work.

B. Hierarchy of needs theory.

1. Abraham Maslow's **hierarchy of needs theory**, as shown in *Figure 6.1* in the textbook, identifies five distinct levels of individual needs: from self-actualization and esteem at the top, to social, safety, and physiological at the bottom. (See *PowerPoint Slide 6* for Chapter 6.)

   a. **Lower order needs** include physiological, safety, and social needs.

   b. **Higher order needs** include esteem and self-actualization.

2. Maslow assumes that some needs are more important than others and must be satisfied before the other needs can serve as motivators.

3. Maslow's view is quite popular in U.S. firms because it appears easily implemented. Research does not support the existence of a precise five-step hierarchy of needs. The needs more likely operate in a flexible hierarchy.

LECTURE ENHANCEMENT

You can generate discussion by asking students to identify the types of rewards that could be used to satisfy the various needs.

C. ERG theory.

1. Clayton Alderfer's ERG theory differs from Maslow's theory in three basic respects.

2. **ERG theory** collapses Maslow's five need categories into three: existence needs, relatedness needs, and growth needs. (See *PowerPoint Slide 7* for Chapter 6.)

   a. **Existence needs** are the desires for physiological and material well-being.

   b. **Relatedness needs** refer to the desire for satisfying interpersonal relationships.

   c. **Growth needs** refer to the desire for continued personal growth and development.

3. Whereas Maslow's theory argues that individuals progress up the "needs" hierarchy, ERG theory emphasizes a unique frustration-regression component wherein an already satisfied need can be activated when a higher need level cannot be satisfied.

4. Unlike Maslow's theory, ERG theory contends that more than one need may be activated at the same time.

5. The supporting evidence on ERG theory is encouraging, particularly with regard to the frustration-regression component.

D. Acquired needs theory.

1. Using the Thematic Apperception Test (TAT), David McClelland identified three needs that he believed are important for understanding human behavior: need for achievement, need for affiliation, and need for power. (See *PowerPoint Slide 8* for Chapter 6.)

    a. **Need for achievement** (nAch) is the desire to do something better or more efficiently, to solve problems, or to master complex tasks.

    b. **Need for affiliation** (nAff) is the desire to establish and maintain friendly and warm relations with others.

    c. **Need for power** (nPower) is the desire to control others, to influence their behavior, or to be responsible for others.

LECTURE ENHANCEMENT

McClelland uses a Thematic Apperception Test (TAT) to measure the strengths of the needs for achievement, power, and affiliation. The Thematic Apperception Test (TAT) is based on need interpretations of descriptions of various stimulus situations. To help students understand how this works, describe the following scenario:

In one case, McClelland tested three executives using a photograph that showed a man sitting down and looking at family photos arranged on his work desk. One executive wrote of an engineer who was daydreaming about a family outing scheduled for the next day (nAff). Another described a designer who had picked up an idea for a new gadget from remarks made by his family (nPow). The third saw an engineer who was intently working on a bridge-stress problem that he seemed sure to solve because of his confident look (nAch).

---

2. McClelland posits that these three needs are acquired over time, as a result of life experiences.

3. Managers should create work environments that are responsive to the respective need profiles.

    a. People with high nAch will prefer individual responsibilities, challenging goals, and performance feedback.

    b. People with high nAff like interpersonal relationships and opportunities for communication.

    c. People with high nPow seek influence over others and like attention and recognition.

ENHANCEMENT

Which occupations would be best suited for individuals with a high need for achievement? For individuals with a high need for affiliation? For individuals with a high need for power? Matching the motivational needs of the individual with the situation is important not only for the employer, but also for the individual.

    E. Two-factor theory.

        1. As shown in *Figure 6.2* from the text, Frederick Herzberg's **two-factor theory** focuses on two sets of factors — one set identifies sources of job dissatisfaction (hygienes) and the other set identifies sources of job satisfaction (motivators). (See *PowerPoint Slide 9* for Chapter 6.)

ENHANCEMENT

For those students who have held jobs, ask them to identify work situations where they experienced satisfaction and work situations where they experienced dissatisfaction. For those students who have not held any jobs, have them identify educational situations where they have experienced satisfaction or dissatisfaction. Have the students share their examples while you record them on the chalkboard, whiteboard, or a flipchart. After all the examples have been recorded, have the class compare the satisfying and dissatisfying situations to Herzberg's hygiene factors and satisfier factors.

---

        2. **Hygiene factors** are sources of job dissatisfaction that are associated with the job context or work setting. Hygiene factors relate more to the environment in which people work and include organizational policies, quality of supervision, working conditions, base wage or salary, relationships with peers, relationships with subordinates, status, and security.

        3. **Motivator factors** are sources of satisfaction that are associated with job content — what people actually do in their work. Motivator factors include achievement, recognition, work itself, responsibility, advancement, and growth.

4. According to two-factor theory, job satisfaction and job dissatisfaction are totally separate dimensions. Therefore, improving a hygiene factor will not make people satisfied with their work; it will only prevent them from being dissatisfied. People will be satisfied only by improving the motivator factors.

5. Two-factor theory is difficult to confirm through empirical research.

IV. **Study Question 3: What do the process theories suggest about individual motivation?**

A. Introduction to process theories. (See *PowerPoint Slide 10* for Chapter 6.)

1. Content theories focus on ways of improving motivation by dealing with activated or deprived needs, whereas process theories focus on the thought processes through which people choose among alternative courses of action.

2. The chapter focuses on two process theories: equity theory and expectancy theory.

B. Equity Theory

1. Stacy Adam's **equity theory** posits that people will gauge the fairness of their work outcomes relative to others, and will act to eliminate any felt inequity in the rewards they receive for their work. (See *PowerPoint Slide 11* for Chapter 6.)

2. Felt *negative inequity* exists when an individual feels that he or she has received relatively less than others have in proportion to work inputs. (See *PowerPoint Slide 11* for Chapter 6.)

3. Felt *positive inequity* exists when an individual feels that he or she has received relatively more than others have. (See *PowerPoint Slide 11* for Chapter 6.)

LECTURE ENHANCEMENT

Ask students to think about a job they have held or currently hold. Next, ask them if they feel they were rewarded fairly. Many are likely to say that they were not paid enough, or that the work was not challenging enough. Be sure to ask them how they responded to the inequity. In nearly all cases, students will indicate that they exhibited one of the responses to perceived inequity that are listed below.

---

4. When either feeling exists, the individual will likely engage in one or more of the following behaviors to restore a sense of equity. (See *PowerPoint Slide 12* for Chapter 6.)

a. Change work inputs.

b. Change the outcomes (rewards) received.

      c. Leave the situation.

      d. Change the comparison person.

      e. Psychologically distort the comparisons.

      f. Take actions to change the inputs or outputs of the comparison person.

5. Coping methods for dealing with equity comparisons include the following (see *PowerPoint Slide 13* for Chapter 6):

      a. Recognize that equity comparisons are inevitable in the workplace.

      b. Anticipate felt negative inequities when rewards are given.

      c. Communicate clear evaluations for any rewards given.

      d. Communicate an appraisal of performance on which the reward is based.

      e. Communicate comparison points that are appropriate in the situation.

6. Research indicates that people who feel they are overpaid (perceived positive inequity) increase the quantity or quality of their work, whereas those who feel they are underpaid (perceived negative inequity) decrease the quantity or quality of their work.

C. Expectancy Theory

1. Victor Vroom's **expectancy theory** posits that motivation is a result of a rational calculation reflecting the degree to which a person believes that effort will yield acceptable performance, performance will be rewarded, and the value of the rewards is highly positive.

2. As shown in *Figure 6.3* of the textbook, the three beliefs of expectancy theory are identified as expectancy, instrumentality, and valence. (See *PowerPoint Slide 14* for Chapter 6.)

      a. **Expectancy** is the probability assigned by an individual that a given level of achieved task performance will follow work effort.

      b. **Instrumentality** is the probability assigned by the individual that a given level of achieved task performance will lead to various work outcomes.

      c. **Valence** is the value attached by the individual to various work outcomes.

3. Expectancy, instrumentality, and valence combine multiplicatively to determine the level of motivation (Motivation = E x I x V). Thus, for a given outcome to have a strong, positive motivational impact, expectancy and instrumentality must be high and valence must be highly positive. (See *PowerPoint Slide 15* for Chapter 6.)

LECTURE ENHANCEMENT

A useful way to help students understand the multiplier effect of expectancy theory is to relate it to their own academic experiences. Ask students to think about their motivation in their various classes. Do they believe that if they work hard, they will be able to achieve a high level of performance (expectancy)? If they succeed in performing well, do they expect to be rewarded with a high grade (instrumentality)? Finally, do they value a high grade (valence)? If the answer to any of these questions is "no," their motivation will suffer.

---

4. Expectancy logic argues that a manger must try to intervene actively in work situations to maximize work expectancies, instrumentalities, and valences that support organizational objectives.

5. Expectancy theory has received substantial support although some details of the theory — such as the multiplier effect — are still subject to debate. In exploring outcomes, researchers have also differentiated between been **extrinsic rewards** (*i.e.*, positively valued work outcomes given to the individual by some other person) and **intrinsic rewards** (*i.e.*, positively valued work outcomes that the individual receives directly as a result of task performance). (See *PowerPoint Slide 16* for Chapter 6.)

ENHANCEMENT

A nice way to involve students in the discussion of work-related rewards is to ask them to identify as many different types of rewards as possible that managers can use to motivate subordinates. While students are typically able to quickly list a large variety of rewards, they also usually overlook some more subtle rewards such as an enriched job or training opportunities. You may want to wrap up this discussion by presenting the following table and complimenting the students on the number of rewards they named.

Intrinsic Rewards:	**Extrinsic Rewards:**
Participation in decision making	Performance bonuses
Increased responsibility	Overtime and holiday premiums
Opportunities for personal growth	Profit sharing
Greater job freedom and discretion	Stock options
More interesting work	Impressive titles
Diversity of activities	Preferred work assignments
Training opportunities	Praise and recognition

---

6. Guidelines for the distribution of extrinsic rewards include the following (see *PowerPoint Slides 17* and *18* for Chapter 6):

    a. Clearly identify the desired behaviors.

    b. Maintain an inventory of rewards that have the potential to serve as positive reinforcers.

    c. Recognize individual differences in the rewards that will have a positive value for each person.

    d. Let each person know exactly what must be done to receive a desirable reward; set clear target antecedents and give performance feedback.

    e. Allocate rewards contingently and immediately upon the appearance of the desired behaviors.

    f. Allocate rewards wisely in terms of scheduling the delivery of positive reinforcement.

V. **Study Question 4: What are reinforcement theories and how are they related to motivation?**

A. Introduction to reinforcement theory. (See *PowerPoint Slide 19* for Chapter 6.)

    1. **Reinforcement** is the administration of a consequence as a result of behavior.

    2. Managing reinforcement properly can change the direction, level, and persistence of an individual's behavior.

B. Classical and operant conditioning.

    1. *Figure 6.4* from the text briefly describes the fundamental nature of classical conditioning and operant conditioning and identifies the difference between them. (See *PowerPoint Slide 20* for Chapter 6.)

    2. **Classical conditioning** is a form of learning through association that involves the manipulation of stimuli to influence behavior. Learning occurs by pairing a natural **stimulus** (*i.e.*, something that incites action and draws forth a response) with a neutral stimulus. Through this pairing, the neutral stimulus becomes a conditioned stimulus that is capable of eliciting a response in the same manner as the natural stimulus.

    3. **Operant conditioning**, popularized by B.F. Skinner, is the process of controlling behavior by manipulating its consequences.

    4. Classical and operant conditioning differ in two important ways.

        a. First, control in operant conditioning is via manipulation of consequences.

b. Second, operant conditioning calls for examining the antecedent (*i.e.*, the condition leading up to or "cueing" behavior), the behavior, and consequences of the behavior.

5. Behavior is influenced by manipulating its consequences, and the basis for this manipulation is E.L. Thorndike's Law of Effect.

6. The **law of effect** states that behavior that results in a pleasant outcome is likely to be repeated while behavior that results in an unpleasant outcome is not likely to be repeated. Practical use of the law of effect relies heavily on extrinsic rewards. (See *PowerPoint Slide 21* for Chapter 6.) *Figure 6.5* from the textbook provides examples of extrinsic rewards that can be used by managers. (See *PowerPoint Slide 22* for Chapter 6.)

C. Reinforcement strategies.

1. **Organizational behavior modification (OB Mod)** is the systematic reinforcement of desirable work behavior and the non-reinforcement or punishment of unwanted work behavior. (See *PowerPoint Slide 23* for Chapter 6.)

2. OB Mod utilizes four basic strategies: positive reinforcement, negative reinforcement (or avoidance), punishment, and extinction. (See *PowerPoint Slide 23* for Chapter 6.)

3. Positive reinforcement.

a. **Positive reinforcement** is the administration of positive consequences that tend to increase the likelihood of repeating the desired behavior in a similar setting. (See *PowerPoint Slide 24* for Chapter 6.)

(i) Rewards are not necessarily positive reinforcers.

(ii) A reward is a positive reinforcer only if the behavior improves.

b. The **law of contingent reinforcement** indicates that, for a reward to have maximum reinforcing value, it must be delivered only if the desired behavior is exhibited. (See *PowerPoint Slide 25* for Chapter 6.)

c. The **law of immediate reinforcement** states that the more immediate the delivery of a reward after the occurrence of a desired behavior, the greater the reinforcing effect. (See *PowerPoint Slide 25* for Chapter 6.)

d. **Shaping** is the creation of a new behavior by the positive reinforcement of successive approximations to the desired behavior.

e. Positive reinforcement can be given according to either continuous or intermittent schedules. (See *PowerPoint Slide 26* for Chapter 6.)

        (i) <u>**Continuous reinforcement**</u> administers a reward each time a desired behavior occurs.

        (ii) <u>**Intermittent reinforcement**</u> rewards behavior only periodically.

        (iii) *Figure 6.6* in the textbook depicts the following four types of intermittent reinforcement schedules (see *PowerPoint Slide 27* for Chapter 6):

           1. Fixed interval schedules provide rewards at the first appearance of a behavior after a given time has elapsed.

           2. Fixed ratio schedules result in a reward each time a certain number of behaviors have occurred.

           3. A variable interval schedule rewards behavior at random times.

           4. A variable ratio schedule rewards behavior after a random number of occurrences.

4. Negative reinforcement (avoidance). (See *PowerPoint Slide 28* for Chapter 6.)

    a. <u>**Negative reinforcement**</u> is the withdrawal of negative consequences, which tends to increase the likelihood of repeating the behavior in a similar setting.

    b. The strategy is also sometimes called avoidance because its intent is for the person to avoid the negative consequences by performing the desired behavior.

5. Punishment.

    a. <u>**Punishment**</u> is the administration of negative consequences or the withdrawal of positive consequences that tend to reduce the likelihood of repeating the behavior in similar settings. (See *PowerPoint Slide 29* for Chapter 6.)

    b. Punishment that is justifiably administered for poor performance leads to enhanced performance without a significant effect on job satisfaction. (See *PowerPoint Slide 30* for Chapter 6.)

    c. Punishment that is viewed by workers as being arbitrary and capricious leads to low performance and low satisfaction. (See *PowerPoint Slide 30* for Chapter 6.)

    d. Punishment may be offset or overridden by positive reinforcement from another source. (See *PowerPoint Slide 30* for Chapter 6.)

LECTURE ENHANCEMENT

Tampa Electric uses punishment in an interesting way. The company gives an oral reminder to employees who come in late, mistreat a colleague, or do a sloppy job. Next comes a written reminder. Then a paid day off is scheduled — it's called a "decision-making leave day." After this day off employees must agree orally or in writing that they will be on their best behavior for the next year. This is an all-or-nothing chance to reform; employees who don't shape up are terminated. Since the process is documented, it's perfectly legal.

---

      6.   Extinction. (See ***PowerPoint Slide 31*** for Chapter 6.)

            a.   **Extinction** refers to the withdrawal of the reinforcing consequences for a given behavior.

            b.   Extinction is intended to weaken and eliminate undesired behavior that has been reinforced previously.

            c.   The behavior is not <u>unlearned</u>; it simply is not exhibited.

            d.   The behavior will reappear if it is reinforced again.

      7.   Summary of strategies.

            a.   ***Figure 6.7*** in the textbook summarizes and illustrates the use of each OB Mod strategy. (See ***PowerPoint Slide 32*** for Chapter 6.)

            b.   All of the OB Mod strategies are designed to direct work behavior toward practices desired by management.

            c.   The OB Mod strategies may be used in combination as well as independently.

LECTURE ENHANCEMENT

To reinforce the learning of the different operant conditioning strategies, have students identify examples from their work, educational, and/or personal experiences that illustrate positive reinforcement, negative reinforcement, punishment, or extinction. On the board, a flipchart, or overhead projector, draw the chart shown below this box. In that chart, fill in the positive reinforcement, negative reinforcement, punishment, and extinction cells with the students' examples. Select some examples from each cell and have the students discuss how their behavior was influenced by these consequences. Did the behavior increase in frequency, or did it decrease?

	Pleasant Consequence	Unpleasant Consequence
Presentation of the Consequence	Positive Reinforcement	Punishment
Removal of the Consequence	Negative Reinforcement	Extinction

D. Ethics and reinforcement.

   1. The effective use of reinforcement strategies can help manage human behavior at work.

   2. Managerial use of OB Mod is not without criticism, including the lack of scientific research designs in some instances, the potential value dilemmas associated with using reinforcement to influence human behavior at work, and the potential abuse of managerial power.

   3. Key ethical questions include the following (see *PowerPoint Slide 33* for Chapter 6):

      a. Is improved performance really due to reinforcement?

      b. Is the use of reinforcement demeaning and dehumanizing?

      c. Will managers abuse their power by exerting external control over behavior?

      d. How can we ensure that the manipulation of consequences is done in a positive and constructive fashion?

VI. **Study summary for Chapter 6.**

   A. Point out to the students that the text's "Chapter 6 Study Guide" recaps the key theories, concepts, and ideas in the chapter in relation to the appropriate study questions.

CHAPTER STUDY GUIDE

Study Question 1: What is motivation?

- Motivation is an internal force that accounts for the level, direction, and persistence of effort expended at work.
- Content theories — including the work of Maslow, Alderfer, McClelland, and Herzberg — focus on locating individual needs that influence behavior in the workplace.
- Process theories, such as equity and expectancy theory, examine the thought processes that affect decisions about alternative courses of action by people at work.
- Reinforcement theories emphasize the means through which the process of controlling an individual's behavior by manipulating its consequences takes place. They focus on observable aspects rather than what is inside an employee's head.

- One should be sensitive to the fact that motivation is important to firms across the globe; however, specific aspects may vary across different cultures.

Study Question 2: What do the content theories suggest about individual needs and motivation?

- Maslow's hierarchy of needs theory views human needs as activated in a five-step hierarchy ranging from physiological (lowest), to safety, to social, to esteem, to self-actualization (highest).
- Alderfer's ERG theory collapses the five needs into three: existence, relatedness, and growth; it maintains that more than one need can be activated at a time.
- McClelland's acquired needs theory focuses on the needs for achievement, affiliation, and power, and it views needs as developed over time through experience and training.
- Herzberg's two-factor theory links job satisfaction to motivator factors, such as responsibility and challenge, associated with job content.
- Herzberg's two-factor theory links job dissatisfaction to hygiene factors, such as pay and working conditions, associated with job context.

Study Question 3: What do the process theories suggest about individual motivation?

- Equity theory points out that social comparisons take place when people receive rewards and that any felt inequity will motivate them to try to restore a sense of perceived equity.
- When felt inequity is negative — that is, when the individual feels unfairly treated — he or she may decide to work less hard in the future or to quit a job.
- Vroom's expectancy theory describes motivation as a function of an individual's beliefs concerning effort-performance relationships (expectancy), work-outcome relationships (instrumentality), and the desirability of various work outcomes (valence).
- Expectancy theory states that Motivation = Expectancy x Instrumentality x Valence, and argues that managers should make each factor positive in order to ensure high levels of motivation.

Study Question 4: What are reinforcement theories and how are they linked to motivation?

- The foundation of reinforcement is the law of effect, which states that behavior will be repeated or extinguished depending on whether the consequences are positive or negative.
- Positive reinforcement is the administration of positive consequences that tend to increase the likelihood of a person's repeating a behavior in similar settings.
- Positive reinforcement should be contingent and immediate, and it can be scheduled continuously or intermittently, depending on resources and desired outcomes.
- Negative reinforcement (avoidance) is used to encourage desirable behavior through the withdrawal of negative consequences for previously undesirable behavior.
- Punishment is the administration of negative consequences or the withdrawal of positive consequences, which tends to reduce the likelihood of repeating an undesirable behavior in similar settings.
- Extinction is the withdrawal of reinforcing consequences for a given behavior.

KEY TERMS

Classical conditioning: a form of learning through association that involves the manipulation of stimuli to influence behavior. Learning occurs by pairing a natural stimulus with a neutral stimulus.

Content theories: focus on profiling the different physiological and psychological needs that people seek to fulfill.

Continuous reinforcement: administers a reward each time a desired behavior occurs.

Equity theory: posits that people will gauge the fairness of their work outcomes relative to others, and will act to eliminate any felt inequity in the rewards they receive for their work.

ERG theory: collapses Maslow's five need categories into three: existence needs, relatedness needs, and growth needs.

Existence needs: in Alderfer's ERG theory, the desires for physiological and material well-being.

Expectancy: the probability assigned by an individual that a given level of achieved task performance will follow work effort.

Expectancy theory: posits that motivation is a result of a rational calculation reflecting the degree to which a person believes that (1) effort will yield acceptable performance, (2) performance will be rewarded, and (3) the value of the rewards is highly positive.

Extinction: the withdrawal of the reinforcing consequences for a given behavior.

Extrinsic rewards: positively valued work outcomes given to the individual by some other person.

Growth needs: in Alderfer's ERG theory, the desire for continued personal growth and development.

Hierarchy of needs theory: a content theory of motivation that identifies five distinct levels of individual needs: from self-actualization and esteem at the top, to social, safety, and physiological at the bottom.

Higher order needs: the esteem and self-actualization needs of Maslow's need hierarchy.

Hygiene factors: sources of job dissatisfaction that are associated with the job context or work setting.

Instrumentality: the probability assigned by the individual that a given level of achieved task performance will lead to various work outcomes.

Intermittent reinforcement: rewards behavior only periodically.

Intrinsic rewards: positively valued work outcomes that the individual receives directly as a result of task performance

Law of contingent reinforcement: for a reward to have maximum reinforcing value, it must be delivered only if the desired behavior is exhibited.

Law of effect: behavior that results in a pleasant outcome is likely to be repeated while behavior that results in an unpleasant outcome is not likely to be repeated.

Law of immediate reinforcement: the more immediate the delivery of a reward after the occurrence of a desired behavior, the greater the reinforcing effect.

Lower order needs: the physiological, safety, and social needs of Maslow's need hierarchy.

Motivation: forces within an individual that account for the level, direction, and persistence of effort expended at work.

Motivator factors: sources of satisfaction that are associated with job content — what people actually do in their work.

Need for achievement: the desire to do something better or more efficiently, to solve problems, or to master complex tasks.

Need for affiliation: the desire to establish and maintain friendly and warm relations with others.

Need for power: the desire to control others, to influence their behavior, or to be responsible for others.

Negative reinforcement: the withdrawal of negative consequences, which tends to increase the likelihood of repeating the behavior in a similar setting.

Operant conditioning: the process of controlling behavior by manipulating its consequences.

Organizational behavior modification (OB Mod): the systematic reinforcement of desirable work behavior and the non-reinforcement or punishment of unwanted work behavior.

Positive reinforcement: the administration of positive consequences that tend to increase the likelihood of repeating the desired behavior in a similar setting.

Process theories: focus on the thought or cognitive processes that take place within the minds of people and influence their behavior.

Punishment: the administration of negative consequences or the withdrawal of positive consequences that tend to reduce the likelihood of repeating the behavior in similar settings.

Reinforcement: the administration of a consequence as a result of behavior.

Reinforcement theories: emphasize the process of controlling an individual's behavior by manipulating its consequences.

Relatedness needs: in Alderfer's ERG theory, the desire for satisfying interpersonal relationships.

Shaping: the more immediate the delivery of a reward after the occurrence of a desired behavior, the greater the reinforcing effect.

Stimulus: something that incites action and draws forth a response.

Two-factor theory: focuses on two sets of factors — one set identifies sources of job dissatisfaction (hygienes) and the other set identifies sources of job satisfaction (motivators).

Valence: the value attached by the individual to various work outcomes.

Chapter 7
MOTIVATION AND JOB DESIGN

STUDY QUESTIONS

1.	How are motivation, job satisfaction, and performance related?
2.	What are job-design approaches?
3.	What are the keys to designing motivating jobs?
4.	How are technology and job design related?
5.	What alternative work arrangements are used today?

LEARNING OBJECTIVES

After completing this chapter students should be able to:

1.	Describe the concept of job satisfaction and discuss the potential relationships between job satisfaction and work performance.
2.	Describe the integrated model of motivation.
3.	Describe the concept of job design and basic alternatives for designing jobs, including scientific management, job enlargement, job rotation, and job enrichment.
4.	Discuss the components of the job characteristics model, how those components are related, and how managers can influence them..
5.	Discuss the social information processing theory of job design and its implications.
6.	Discuss the role of technology in job design, including automation and robotics, flexible manufacturing systems, electronic offices, and workflow and processing reengineering.
7.	Discuss the growing importance of alternative work arrangements for American workers, including compressed workweeks, flexible working hours, job sharing, work at home and the virtual office, and part-time work.

MATERIAL IN *THE OB SKILLS WORKBOOK* SUPPORTING THE CHAPTER

Case for Critical Thinking	Case 8: I'm Not in Kansas Anymore
Experiential Exercises	Exercise 14: Tinkertoys
	Exercise 15: Job Design Preferences
	Exercise 16: My Fantasy Job
	Exercise 17: Motivation by Job Enrichment
Self-Assessment	Assessment 8: Are You Cosmopolitan?

CHAPTER OVERVIEW

Building on the content, process, and reinforcement theories discussed in Chapter 6, the initial section of Chapter 7 focuses on the relationships among motivation, job satisfaction, and work performance. The nature of job satisfaction is described, three alternative views of the linkage between satisfaction and performance are offered, and an integrated model of the individual motivation to work is presented. This model incorporates key components of the content, process, and reinforcement theories.

The chapter then shift to a discussion of alternative job design approaches. After defining job design and pointing out that the "best job design" is the one that meets a given organization's requirements for high performance, this section of the chapter describes the scientific management, job enlargement, job rotation, and job enrichment approaches to achieving a "good job design." The chapter then turns to a description of the job characteristics model and the social information processing model of job design. The section concludes with a discussion of the managerial and global implication of enriching jobs.

The next section of the chapter focuses on technology and job design, giving emphasis to the roles played by automation and robotics, flexible manufacturing systems, electronic offices, and workflow and processing reengineering in designing and redesigning jobs in the modern workplace. The chapter concludes with a discussion of alternative work arrangements, including compressed workweeks, flexible working hours, job sharing, work at home and the virtual office, and part-time work. Progressive companies are using these alternative work arrangements to reshape existing schedules of work hours to better meet the needs of employees.

CHAPTER OUTLINE

I. **Study Question 1: How are motivation, job satisfaction, and performance related?**
   A. Job satisfaction
   B. Job satisfaction and performance
   C. Integrating the motivation theories

II. **Study Question 2: What are job-design approaches?**
   A. Scientific management
   B. Job enlargement and job rotation
   C. Job enrichment

III. **Study Question 3: What are the keys to designing motivating jobs?**
   A. Job characteristics model
   B. Social information processing
   C. Managerial and global implications

IV. **Study Question 4: How are technology and job design related?**
   A. Automation and robotics
   B. Flexible manufacturing systems
   C. Electronic offices
   D. Workflow and process reengineering

V. **Study Question 5: What alternative work arrangements are used today?**
   A. Compressed workweeks

B. Flexible working hours
C. Job sharing
D. Work at home and the virtual office
E. Part-time work

CHAPTER LECTURE NOTES

I. **Introduction to the Chapter 7 Lecture.**

A. Study questions for Chapter 7. (See *PowerPoint Slide 2* for Chapter 7.)

1. How are motivation, job satisfaction, and performance related?

2. What are job-design approaches?

3. What are the keys to designing motivating jobs?

4. How are technology and job design related?

5. What alternative work arrangements are used today?

B. The lecture material for Chapter 7 is organized around the study questions.

1. Point out to the students that the text's "Chapter At A Glance" identifies the key topics contained in the chapter and links them to the appropriate study questions.

C. The chapter opens with a description of how automation and robotics are used in the design of work a Ford's Kansas City truck and SUV manufacturing facility.

II. **Study Question 1: How are motivation, job satisfaction, and performance related?**

A. Job satisfaction. (See *PowerPoint Slide 3* for Chapter 7.)

1. Job satisfaction is the degree to which individuals feel positively or negatively about their jobs.

2. Job satisfaction of other people may be inferred from careful observation of what they say and do while performing their jobs.

3. The Minnesota Satisfaction Questionnaire (MSQ) and the Job Descriptive Index (JDI) are two popular questionnaires that can be used for assessing job satisfaction. Both address important aspects of job satisfaction.

LECTURE ENHANCEMENT

Ask those students who have been gainfully employed to describe what they found to be satisfying about their jobs. Also ask them to discuss how those things affected their work behavior.

B. Job satisfaction and performance.

1. The importance of job satisfaction can be viewed in the context of two decisions people make about their work: a decision to belong and a decision to perform. (See *PowerPoint Slide 4* for Chapter 7.)

2. The decision to belong concerns an individual's attendance and longevity at work. Satisfied workers have more regular attendance and are less likely to quit their jobs. (See *PowerPoint Slide 4* for Chapter 7.)

3. The decision to perform is not as clear as the decision to belong. This is due to three possible alternative relationships between job satisfaction and performance. (See *PowerPoint Slide 4* for Chapter 7.)

    a. Satisfaction causes performance. (See *PowerPoint Slide 5* for Chapter 7.)

        (i) This alternative suggests that managers should focus on increasing employees' job satisfaction in order to increase their performance.

        (ii) Research indicates that no simple and direct link exists between individual job satisfaction at one point in time and work performance at a later point.

    b. Performance causes satisfaction. (See *PowerPoint Slide 6* for Chapter 7.)

        (i) This alternative suggests that managers should focus on increasing employees' job performance and as a result job satisfaction should increase.

        (ii) Research indicates an empirical relationship between individual performance measured at a certain time period and later job satisfaction.

        (iii) Rewards that equitably distributed serve to strengthen the linkage between performance and subsequent satisfaction.

    c. Rewards cause both satisfaction and performance. (See *PowerPoint Slide 7* for Chapter 7.)

        (i) The proper allocation of rewards can positively influence both performance and satisfaction.

        (ii) Research indicates that people who receive high rewards report high job satisfaction and that performance-contingent rewards influence a person's work performance.

        (iii) The size and value of the reward should vary in proportion to the level of one's performance accomplishment.

d. Managers should consider performance and satisfaction as two separate but interrelated work outcomes that are influenced by the allocation of rewards.

C. Integrating the motivation theories.

1. The linkage between satisfaction and performance helps to integrate the various motivation theories that were discussed in Chapter 6.

2. *Figure 7.1* from the textbook provides an integrated model of work motivation. (See *PowerPoint Slide 8* for Chapter 7.)

a. Note that *Figure 7.1* has much in common with Vroom's expectancy theory and the Porter-Lawler framework, both process theories of motivation.

b. According to the integrated model in *Figure 7.1*:

(i) Motivation leads to work effort that, when combined with appropriate individual abilities and organizational support, leads to job performance.

(ii) Job performance produces extrinsic and intrinsic rewards, and individuals consider the amount and value of these rewards in determining whether or not equity exists.

(iii) Appropriate intrinsic rewards will enhance motivation to work hard in the future.

(iv) Equitable extrinsic and intrinsic rewards will increase job satisfaction.

(v) Improved job satisfaction should lead to increased motivation to work hard in the future.

LECTURE ENHANCEMENT

Ask each student to identify a situation where he/she performed superbly and was highly satisfied as well as one where he/she performed not so well and was not very satisfied. Ask for volunteers to share their experiences and then analyze them in the context of the integrated model of individual work motivation in *Figure 7.1*. What insights does this analysis provide?

III. **Study Question 2: What are job-design approaches?**

A. Background on job design.

1. **Job design** is the process of planning and specifying job tasks and the work arrangements through which they are accomplished.

2. *Figure 7.2* in the textbook shows how alternative job-design approaches differ in the way required tasks are defined and in the amount of intrinsic motivation provided for the worker. (See *PowerPoint Slide 9* for Chapter 7.)

    a. Job simplification has a high degree of task specialization and a low level of intrinsic rewards.

    b. Job enlargement and rotation have moderate levels of both task specialization and intrinsic rewards.

    c. Job enrichment has high levels of both task specialization and intrinsic rewards.

LECTURE ENHANCEMENT

It might be instructive to point out to your students that the topic of job design is as old as work itself. The ancient Egyptians built their pyramids, the ancient Chinese built the Great Wall of China, and the Mesopotamians learned to irrigate their land and wall their cities. Undoubtedly, all of these tasks required jobs with well defined designs.

B. Scientific management. (See *PowerPoint Slide 10* for Chapter 7.)

1. Scholarly interest in job design can be traced in part to Frederick Taylor's work with scientific management in the early 1900s.

2. Scientific management took the approach of studying a job carefully, breaking it into its smallest components, establishing exact time and motion requirements for each task, and training workers to do these tasks in the same way over and over again.

3. **Job simplification**, which grows out of the scientific management tradition, is the approach of standardizing work procedures and employing people in clearly defined and highly specialized tasks.

    a. Job simplification has the potential advantages of increasing operating efficiency by reducing the skills required to do a job, being able to hire low-cost labor, and minimizing the need for training.

    b. Job simplification has the potential disadvantages of loss of efficiency due to lower quality, high rates of absenteeism and turnover, and demand for higher wages to compensate for unappealing jobs.

LECTURE ENHANCEMENT

To reinforce the job simplification strategy, ask students if they have ever had a job in which this strategy was employed. If any respond yes, ask them to describe their job. You can use one of these jobs to illustrate the characteristics of this strategy. Next, ask these students what they thought of their jobs and, if they no longer hold them, why they don't. Students will typically respond that they found the job to be boring so they quit. Responses such as these reflect the problems of boredom and turnover that are commonly associated with job simplification.

    C. Job enlargement and job rotation. (See *PowerPoint Slide 11* for Chapter 7.)

        1. **Job enlargement** increases task variety by combining into one job two or more tasks that were previously assigned to separate workers.

            a. Job enlargement is one form of horizontal loading.

            b. Horizontal loading increases job breadth by having the worker perform more and different tasks, but all at the same level of responsibility and challenge.

        2. **Job rotation** increases task variety by periodically shifting workers among jobs involving different tasks.

            a. Job rotation is another form of horizontal loading.

            b. Training is an important benefit of job rotation.

LECTURE ENHANCEMENT

Ask students what they think of the job rotation and job enlargement strategies. Usually, they respond that while these strategies may reduce some of the monotony of highly simplified jobs, their benefits are likely to be limited. In the words of Frederick Herzberg, "Why should a worker become motivated when one or more 'meaningless' tasks are added to previously existing ones or when work assignments are rotated among equally 'meaningless' tasks?" This point leads nicely into the material on job enrichment that follows.

    D. Job enrichment.

        1. Herzberg's two-factor theory of motivation (see Chapter 6) suggests that high levels of motivation should not be expected from jobs designed on the basis of simplification, enlargement, or rotation. To generate high levels of motivation, Herzberg advocates the use of job enrichment.

        2. **Job enrichment** is the practice of enhancing job content by building into it more motivating factors such as responsibility, achievement, recognition, and personal growth. (See *PowerPoint Slide 12* for Chapter 7.)

3. Job enrichment increases job content by giving workers more responsibility for planning and evaluating duties. (See *PowerPoint Slide 12* for Chapter 7.)

4. Job enrichment involves vertical loading to increase job depth. (See *PowerPoint Slide 12* for Chapter 7.)

5. Job depth can be increased by doing the following (see *PowerPoint Slide 13* for Chapter 7):

   a. Allow workers to plan.

   b. Allow workers to control.

   c. Maximize job freedom.

   d. Increase task difficulty.

   e. Help workers become task experts.

   f. Provide performance feedback.

   g. Increase performance accountability.

   h. Provide complete units of work.

LECTURE ENHANCEMENT

Point out to students that in recent years, technological changes have enriched secretarial jobs. You may want to ask students to identify these changes and explain their impact on secretarial work. The integration of personal computers into the modern office is the cause of many of these changes. For example, personal computers have reduced the number of simplified and repetitive tasks performed by secretaries. In addition, the scope and depth of many secretarial jobs have been expanded to include such responsibilities as word processing and the monitoring of budgets.

---

6. Concerns about job enrichment include the following (see *PowerPoint Slide 14* for Chapter 7):

   a. Job enrichment can be very costly, especially when it requires major changes in workflows, facilities, or technology.

   b. There is controversy concerning whether pay must be increased when jobs are enriched.

      (i) Herzberg argues that if employees are being paid a truly competitive wage or salary, the intrinsic motivation associated with enriched jobs will be enough and pay will not need to be increased.

IV.   **Study Question 3: What are the keys to designing motivating jobs?**

A. Job characteristics model.

1. *Figure 7.3* from the textbook presents the **job characteristics model** developed by Richard Hackman and Greg Oldham. According to this model, five different core job characteristics create three critical psychological states, which in turn produce four different work outcomes. In addition, the relationships between the core job characteristics and the critical psychological states and between the critical psychological states and individual work outcomes are influenced by three moderator variables. (See *PowerPoint Slide 15* for Chapter 7.)

2. Core job characteristics. (See *PowerPoint Slides 16* to *18* for Chapter 7.)

a. *Skill variety* — the degree to which a job requires a variety of different activities and involves the use of a number of different skills and talents of the individual.

b. *Task identity* — the degree to which the job requires the completion of a "whole" and identifiable piece of work; one that involves doing a job from beginning to end with a visible outcome.

c. *Task significance* — the degree to which the job is important and involves a meaningful contribution to the organization or society in general.

d. *Autonomy* — the degree to which the job gives the employee substantial freedom, independence, and discretion in scheduling the work and in determining the procedures used in carrying it out.

e. *Job feedback* — the degree to which carrying out the work activities provides direct and clear information to the employee regarding how well the job has been done.

LECTURE ENHANCEMENT

Ask a student who has worked in a fast-food restaurant, on an assembly line, or at some other type of simplified job to rate the job on a scale from 1 to 5 on each of the five core job characteristics (1 = low on the characteristic and 5 = high on the characteristic); then ask someone who has had a more enriched job to do the same. Discuss the insights that can be gained from this comparison.

---

3. The Job Diagnostic Survey (JDS) is used to measure the extent to which each core characteristic exists in a job. The higher a job scores on each characteristic, the more enriched it is considered to be.

4. JDS measures are used to develop a **motivating potential score**, which is shown below (see *PowerPoint Slide 19* for Chapter 7):

    a.   MPS = <u>Skill variety + task identity + task significance</u> x Autonomy x Feedback
                                         3

    b.   The MPS indicates the degree to which the job is capable of motivating people.

    c.   A job's MPS can be raised by:

        (i)   Combining tasks to create larger jobs.

        (ii) Opening feedback channels to enable workers to know how well they are doing.

        (iii) Establishing client relationships to experience feedback directly from customers.

        (iv) Employing vertical loading to create more planning and controlling responsibilities.

5.   *Critical psychological states* — the core job characteristics directly impact the following critical psychological states (see ***PowerPoint Slide 20*** for Chapter 7):

    a.   Experienced meaningfulness of work.

    b.   Experienced responsibility for the outcomes of the work.

    c.   Knowledge of actual results of work activities.

6.   *Individual work outcomes* — the critical psychological states, in turn, influence the following job outcomes (see ***PowerPoint Slide 20*** for Chapter 7):

    a.   High intrinsic work motivation.

    b.   High-quality work performance.

    c.   High job satisfaction with work.

    d.   Low absenteeism and turnover.

7.   The core job characteristics will not affect everyone in the same way. Employee growth-need strength, knowledge and skills, and context satisfaction will influence the extent to which people respond favorably to enriched jobs. (See ***PowerPoint Slide 21*** for Chapter 7.)

    a.   Growth-need strength is especially important in affecting whether or not people respond favorably to job enrichment.

      b. *Growth-need strength (GNS)* is the degree to which a person desires the opportunity for self-direction, learning, and personal accomplishment at work.

      c. People with "high GNS" will respond most positively to enriched jobs.

  8. Considerable research has been done on the job characteristics approach and the general conclusion is that the model and diagnostic approach are useful, but not yet perfect, guides to job design.

B. Social information processing. (See *PowerPoint Slide 22* for Chapter 7.)

  1. **Social information processing theory** argues that individual needs, task perceptions, and reactions are a result of socially constructed realities.

  2. Social information in organizations influences the way people perceive their jobs and respond to them.

  3. Research on social information processing indicates that both social information and core characteristics are important.

C. Managerial and global implications. (See *PowerPoint Slide 23* for Chapter 7.)

  1. Should everyone's job be enriched? The answer is clearly "No." The logic of individual differences suggests that not everyone will want an enriched job.

  2. Can job enrichment apply to groups? The answer is "Yes." The application of job-design strategies at the group level is growing in many types of settings.

  3. What is the impact of culture on job enrichment? The answer is: "Substantial." Research conducted in Belgium, Israel, Japan, the Netherlands, the United States, and Germany found unique aspects of what constitutes work in each country.

V.   Study Question 4: How are technology and job design related?

A. Background on technology and job design. (See *PowerPoint Slide 24* for Chapter 7.)

  1. **Sociotechnical systems** is an organizational behavior concept that reflects the importance of integrating people and technology to create high-performance work systems.

  2. As computers and information technologies continue to dominate the modern workplace, the sociotechnical systems concept is essential for job design.

B. Automation and robotics.

  1. **Automation** allows machines to do work previously accomplished by human beings.

  2. Automation increasingly involves the use of robots.

C. Flexible manufacturing systems. (See ***PowerPoint Slide 25*** for Chapter 7.)

    1. In **flexible manufacturing systems**, adaptive computer-based technologies and integrated job designs are used to shift work easily and quickly among alternative products.

    2. Workers in flexible manufacturing systems deal with changeover from one product configuration to another rather the performing routine assembly-line tasks.

    3. Workers in flexible manufacturing systems develop expertise across a wide range of functions, thereby enriching the core job characteristics.

D. Electronic offices.

    1. Continuing developments in electronic offices offer job enrichment possibilities for those workers equipped to handle the technology.

    2. Jobs in electronic offices can be stressful and difficult for those people who do not have the necessary education or skills.

    3. People who work continuously with computers may experience physical ailments associated with repetitive movements.

    4. Technology must be carefully integrated with the human factor.

E. Workflow and process reengineering. (See ***PowerPoint Slide 26*** for Chapter 7.)

    1. **Process reengineering** is the analysis, streamlining, and reconfiguration of actions and tasks required to reach a work goal.

    2. The process design approach systematically breaks processes down into their specific components and subtasks, analyzes each for relevance and simplicity, and then does everything possible to reconfigure the process to eliminate wasted time, effort, and resources.

    3. One simple question drives the process reengineering approach: "What is necessary and what else can be eliminated?"

LECTURE ENHANCEMENT

Have the students discuss how your college/university might apply process reengineering to the institution's course registration process.

VI.   **Study Question 5: What alternative work arrangements are used today?**

A. Background on alternative work arrangements.

1. Alternative ways of scheduling work are becoming increasing important because of demands for work-life balance and more family-friendly work environments.

2. Ethical and socially responsible management pays attention to the human factor in organizations — one way of accomplishing this is with alternative work arrangements.

B. Compressed workweeks.

   1. A **compressed workweek** is any scheduling of work that allows a full-time job to be completed in fewer than the standard five days. (See *PowerPoint Slide 27* for Chapter 7.)

   2. The most common form of compressed workweek is the "4/40" or 40 hours of work accomplished in four 10-hour days. (See *PowerPoint Slide 27* for Chapter 7.)

   3. The potential advantages of the compressed workweek include the following (see *PowerPoint Slide 28* for Chapter 7):

      a. Additional time off for workers.

      b. Lower employee absenteeism and improved recruiting of new employees for the organization.

   4. The potential disadvantages of the compressed workweek include the following (see *PowerPoint Slide 28* for Chapter 7):

      a. Individuals can experience increased fatigue from the extended workday and can have family adjustment problems.

      b. The organization can encounter work scheduling problems and customer complaints because of breaks in work coverage.

      c. Union opposition may occur in unionized companies.

C. Flexible working hours. (See *PowerPoint Slide 29* for Chapter 7.)

   1. **Flexible working hours**, or flextime, gives individuals a daily choice in the timing of their work commitments.

   2. *Flextime* increases individual autonomy in work scheduling and offers many opportunities and benefits such as shorter commuting time, more leisure time, more job satisfaction, and greater sense of responsibility.

   3. For the organization, flextime decreases absenteeism, tardiness, and turnover, and increases employee commitment and performance.

LECTURE ENHANCEMENT

Have any of your students' experienced compressed work weeks or flexible working hours? If so, have them discuss their experiences, and the impact of the alternative work arrangement on them and on the employing organization.

D. Job Sharing. (See *PowerPoint Slide 30* for Chapter 7.)

     1. **Job sharing** occurs when one full-time job is assigned to two or more persons who then divide the work according to agreed-upon hours.

     2. Organizations benefit from job sharing when they can attract talented people who would otherwise be unable to work.

     3. Some job sharers report less burnout and claim that they feel recharged each time they report to work.

     4. Job sharing should not be confused with a more controversial arrangement called work sharing, in which workers agree to cut back on the number of hours they work in order to protect against layoffs.

E. Work at home and the virtual office.

     1. **Telecommuting** refers to work at home or in a remote location via use of computers and advanced telecommunication linkages with a central office or other employment locations. (See *PowerPoint Slide 31* for Chapter 7.)

     2. *Flexiplace* is an arrangement wherein individuals work mostly from a home office and come into the corporate office only for special meetings. (See *PowerPoint Slide 31* for Chapter 7.)

     3. *Hoteling* involves workers using temporary office space that is reserved for them when they visit the main office. (See *PowerPoint Slide 31* for Chapter 7.)

     4. In the *virtual office*, the worker remains linked electronically with the home office while he/she works literally "from the road" and while traveling from place-to-place or customer-to-customer by car of airplane. (See *PowerPoint Slide 31* for Chapter 7.)

     5. The potential advantages of telecommuting include the following (see *PowerPoint Slide 32* for Chapter 7):

         a. For individuals, telecommuting offers flexibility, the comforts of home, and choice of location consistent with one's lifestyle.

         b. For organizations, telecommuting provides cost savings, efficiency, and employee satisfaction.

6. The potential disadvantages of telecommuting include the following (see *PowerPoint Slide 32* for Chapter 7):

    a. Telecommuters sometimes complain of isolation from co-workers, decreased identification with the work team, and technical difficulties with computer linkages essential to their work.

F. Part-time work.

1. **Temporary part-time work** occurs when an employee is classified as "temporary" and works less than the standard 40-hour work week. (See *PowerPoint Slide 33* for Chapter 7.)

2. **Permanent part-time work** occurs when an employee is considered to be a "permanent" member of the workforce and works less than the standard 40-hour work week. (See *PowerPoint Slide 33* for Chapter 7.)

3. The potential advantages of part-time work include the following (see *PowerPoint Slide 34* for Chapter 7.):

    a. Organizations use part-time work to control labor costs, help smooth out peaks and valleys in the business cycle, and retain highly skilled workers who only want to work part-time.

    b. Part-time work can help individuals who want something less than a full workweek for a variety of personal reasons.

4. The potential disadvantages of part-time work include the following (see *PowerPoint Slide 34* for Chapter 7):

    a. Increased stress for individuals who also hold a full-time job or one or more other part-time jobs.

    b. Part-timers often fail to qualify for fringe benefits and they may be paid less than their full-time counterparts.

LECTURE ENHANCEMENT

Have the students discuss which of the alternative work arrangement options that they find to be particularly appealing. Make sure they explain why they find them to be appealing? Ask them how, if at all, their preferences might change as they advance in their careers and grow in their personal lives.

VII.   **Study summary for Chapter 7.**

A. Point out to the students that the text's "Chapter 7 Study Guide" recaps the key theories, concepts, and ideas in the chapter in relation to the appropriate study questions.

CHAPTER STUDY GUIDE

Study Question 1: How are motivation, job satisfaction, and performance related?

- Job satisfaction is a work attitude that reflects the degree to which people feel positively or negatively about a job and its various factors.
- Common aspects of job satisfaction relate to pay, working conditions, quality of supervision, co-workers, and the task itself.
- Job satisfaction is empirically related to employee turnover and absenteeism.
- The relationship between job satisfaction and performance is more controversial; current thinking focuses on how rewards influence both satisfaction and performance.
- Reinforcement views emphasize contingent rewards as well as the speed of the rewards.
- The content theories help identify important needs and determine what a person values by way of rewards.
- Equity theory suggests that any rewards must be perceived as equitable in the social context of the workplace.
- Although motivation predicts work efforts, individual performance also depends on job-relevant abilities and organizational support.

Study Question 2: What are job-design approaches?

- Job design is the creation of tasks and work settings for specific jobs.
- Job design by scientific management or job simplification standardizes work and employs people in clearly defined and specialized tasks.
- Job enlargement increases task variety by combining two or more tasks previously assigned to separate workers.
- Job rotation increases task variety by periodically rotating workers among jobs involving different tasks.
- Job enrichment builds bigger and more responsible jobs by adding planning and evaluating duties.

Study Question 3: What are the keys to designing motivating jobs?

- Job characteristics theory offers a diagnostic approach to job enrichment based on the analysis of five core job characteristics: skill variety, task identity, task significance, autonomy, and feedback.
- Job characteristics theory does not assume that everyone wants an enriched job; it indicates that job enrichment will be more successful for persons with high growth needs, requisite job skills, and context satisfaction.
- The social information processing theory points out that information from co-workers and others in the workplace influences a worker's perceptions of and responses to a job.

- Not everyone's job should be enriched; job enrichment can be done for groups as well as individuals; cultural factors may influence job enrichment success.

Study Question 4: How are technology and job design related?

- Well-planned sociotechnical systems integrate people and technology for high performance.
- Robotics and complete automation are increasingly used to replace people to perform jobs that are highly simplified and repetitive.
- Workers in flexible manufacturing cells utilize the latest technology to produce high-quality products with short cycle times.
- The nature of office work is being changed by computer workstation technologies, networks, and various forms of electronic communication.
- Workflow and business process reengineering analyzes all steps in work sequences to streamline activities and tasks, save costs, and improve performance.

Study Question 5: What alternative work arrangements are used today?

- Today's complex society is giving rise to a number of alternative work arrangements designed to balance the personal demands on workers with job responsibilities and opportunities.
- The compressed workweek allows a full-time workweek to be completed in less than five days, typically offering four 10-hour days of work and three days free.
- Flexible working hours allow employees some daily choice in timing between work and nonwork activities.
- Job sharing occurs when two or more people divide one full-time job according to agreements among themselves and the employer.
- Telecommuting involves work at home or at a remote location while communicating with the home office as needed via computer and related technologies.
- Part-time work requires less than a 40-hour workweek and can be done on a schedule classifying the worker as temporary or permanent.

KEY TERMS

Automation: allows machines to do work previously accomplished by human beings.
Compressed workweek: any scheduling of work that allows a full-time job to be completed in fewer than the standard five days.
Flexible manufacturing systems: adaptive computer-based technologies and integrated job designs that are used to shift work easily and quickly among alternative products.
Flexible working hours: gives individuals a daily choice in the timing of their work commitments.
Job characteristics model: a model of job design specifying that five different core job characteristics create three critical psychological states, which in turn produce four different work outcomes.
Job design: the process of planning and specifying job tasks and the work arrangements through which they are accomplished.
Job enlargement: increases task variety by combining into one job two or more tasks that were previously assigned to separate workers.

Job enrichment: the practice of enhancing job content by building into it more motivating factors such as responsibility, achievement, recognition, and personal growth.

Job rotation: increases task variety by periodically shifting workers among jobs involving different tasks.

Job sharing: occurs when one full-time job is assigned to two or more persons who then divide the work according to agreed-upon hours.

Job simplification: the approach of standardizing work procedures and employing people in clearly defined and highly specialized tasks.

Motivating potential score: indicates the degree to which the job is capable of motivating people.

Permanent part-time work: occurs when an employee is considered to be a "permanent" member of the workforce and works less than the standard 40-hour work week.

Process reengineering: the analysis, streamlining, and reconfiguration of actions and tasks required to reach a work goal.

Social information processing theory: argues that individual needs, task perceptions, and reactions are a result of socially constructed realities.

Sociotechnical systems: an organizational behavior concept that reflects the importance of integrating people and technology to create high-performance work systems.

Telecommuting: refers to work at home or in a remote location via use of computers and advanced telecommunication linkages with a central office or other employment locations.

Temporary part-time work: occurs when an employee is classified as "temporary" and works less than the standard 40-hour work week.

Chapter 8
PERFORMANCE MANAGEMENT AND REWARDS

STUDY QUESTIONS

1.	What is goal setting?
2.	What is performance appraisal?
3.	What are compensation and rewards?
4.	What are human resource development and person-job fit?

LEARNING OBJECTIVES

After completing this chapter students should be able to:

1.	Explain the Locke and Latham goal-setting framework and describe its managerial implications.
2.	Explain management by objectives (MBO) as an application of goal setting.
3.	Explain the importance and purposes of performance appraisal.
4.	Discuss who should be involved in performance appraisals.
5.	Describe the comparative and absolute methods of performance appraisal, and the common measurement errors that are made in performance appraisal.
6.	Discuss how performance appraisals can be improved.
7.	Describe the importance of rewards in performance management and the methods that are commonly used in creatively rewarding people.
8.	Explain the concept of the person-job fit and how human resource development contributes to it.
9.	Explain how different human resource management policies, procedures, and practices contribute to achieving a good fit between people and jobs.

MATERIAL IN *THE OB SKILLS WORKBOOK* SUPPORTING THE CHAPTER

Cases for Critical Thinking	Case 8: I'm Not in Kansas Anymore
Experiential Exercise	Exercise 13: Annual Pay Raises
Self-Assessment	Assessment 8: Are You Cosmopolitan?

CHAPTER OVERVIEW

The chapter opens with a discussion of goal setting and goal-setting theory, with a focus on the Locke and Latham goal-setting framework. Based on this framework, five managerial implications of goal setting are described. The connection between goal setting and management by objectives (MBO) is also discussed, with emphasis being placed on how the MBO process works.

The second section of the chapter focuses on performance appraisal. The nature and purposes of performance appraisal are explained, and the issue of who conducts appraisals is examined from the perspective of multiple inputs. The use of output measures and activity measures to gauge performance is discussed next. Then three comparative methods of performance appraisal (*i.e.*, ranking, paired comparison, and forced distribution) and four absolute methods of appraisal (*i.e.*, graphic rating scales, critical incident diaries, behaviorally anchored rating sales, and management by objectives) are examined. Also considered are several different measurement errors that commonly occur in the performance appraisal process. This section concludes with a discussion with two sets of recommendations for improving performance appraisals.

The third section of the chapter focuses on compensation and rewards. The extrinsic reward of pay is examined, with particular emphasis on merit pay. In addition, several creative pay practices are discussed. These include skill-based pay, gain-sharing plans, profit-sharing plans, employee stock ownership plans (ESOPs), lump-sum increases, and flexible benefits plans.

The final section of the chapter focuses on human resource development and the person-job fit. This section describes how different human resource management policies, procedures, and practices contribute to achieving a good fit between people and jobs. The key HRM policies, procedures, and practices deal with the fundamental aspects of staffing, recruitment, selection, socialization, training, and career planning and development.

CHAPTER OUTLINE

I. **Study Question 1: What is goal setting?**
   A. Goal-setting theory
   B. Goal-setting guidelines
   C. Goal setting and MBO

II. **Study Question 2: What is performance appraisal?**
   A. Purposes of performance appraisal
   B. Who does the performance appraisal?
   C. Performance appraisal dimensions and standards
   D. Performance appraisal methods
   E. Measurement errors in performance appraisal
   F. Improving performance appraisal
   G. Group evaluation

III. **Study Question 3: What are compensation and rewards?**
   A. Pay as an extrinsic reward
   B. Creative pay practices

Study Question 4: What are human resource development and person-job fit?
    C. Staffing
    D. Recruitment
    E. Selection
    F. Socialization
    G. Training
    H. Career planning and development

CHAPTER LECTURE NOTES

I.   **Introduction to the Chapter 8 Lecture.**

    A. Study questions for Chapter 8. (See *PowerPoint Slide 2* for Chapter 8.)

        1. What is goal setting?

        2. What is performance appraisal?

        3. What are compensation and rewards?

        4. What are human resource development and person-job fit?

    B. The lecture material for Chapter 8 is organized around the study questions.

        1. Point out to the students that the text's "Chapter At A Glance" identifies the key topics contained in the chapter and links them to the appropriate study questions.

    C. The chapter opens with a description of boot camp training for the United States Marine Corps. The scenario illustrates how socialization and training contribute to the person-job fit of raw recruits becoming fighting Marines.

II.   **Study Question 1: What is goal setting?**

    A. Goal-setting theory.

        1. Goal setting is the process of developing, negotiating, and formalizing the targets or objectives that a person is responsible for accomplishing.

        2. *Figure 8.1* from the textbook depicts the Locke and Latham goal setting model. This model uses elements of expectancy theory (see Chapter 6) to help clarify the implications of goal setting for performance while taking into account certain moderating conditions, such as ability and task complexity. (See *PowerPoint Slide 3* for Chapter 8.)

    B. Goal-setting guidelines. (See *PowerPoint Slides 4* and *5* for Chapter 8.)

        1. Difficult goals are more likely to lead to higher performance than are less difficult ones. However, if the goals are seen as too difficult or impossible, the relationship with performance no longer holds.

2. Specific goals are more likely to lead to higher performance than are no goals or vague or very general ones.

3. Task feedback, or knowledge of results, is likely to motivate people toward high performance by encouraging the setting of higher performance goals.

4. Goals are most likely to lead to higher performance when people have the abilities and the feeling of self-efficacy required to accomplish them.

5. Goals are most likely to motivate people toward higher performance when they are accepted and there is commitment to them. Participating in the goal-setting process helps build such acceptance and commitment.

LECTURE ENHANCEMENT

If you state any goals in your syllabus, have the class analyze them and their implementation in light of the preceding goal-setting guidelines.

C. Goal setting and MBO.

1. Management by objectives is a practical goal setting approach for influencing individual performance at work. (See *PowerPoint Slide 6* for Chapter 8.)

2. **Management by objectives (MBO)** is a process of joint goal setting between a supervisor and a subordinate. (See *PowerPoint Slide 6* for Chapter 8.)

3. MBO involves managers working with their subordinates to establish performance goals and plans that are consistent with higher level work unit and organizational objectives. (See *PowerPoint Slide 6* for Chapter 8.)

4. *Figure 8.2* from the textbook shows how the MBO process works. This process is described below. (See *PowerPoint Slide 7* for Chapter 8.)

   a. The supervisor and subordinate jointly establish performance goals.

   b. The subordinate acts individually to perform the agreed upon tasks, and the superior acts individually to provide necessary support.

   c. The supervisor and subordinate jointly evaluate results and renew the MBO cycle.

5. Potential problems with MBO include the following (see *PowerPoint Slide 8* for Chapter 8):

   a. Too much paperwork in documenting goals and accomplishments.

    b. Too much emphasis on goal-oriented rewards and punishments, top-down goals, goals that are easily stated in objective terms, and individual goals instead of group goals.

    c. MBO may need to be implemented organization-wide if it is to work well.

III.   Study Question 2: What is performance appraisal?

    A. Background on performance appraisal. (See ***PowerPoint Slide 9*** for Chapter 8.)

        1. Performance appraisal helps both the manager and subordinate maintain the organization-job-employee characteristics match.

        2. **Performance appraisal** is a process of systematically evaluating performance and providing feedback on which performance adjustments can be made.

LECTURE ENHANCEMENT

Information on performance appraisal and a set of links to Web sites that focus on performance appraisal is available at http://www.zigonperf.com/Links.htm.

    B. Purposes of performance appraisal.

        1. The four functions of performance appraisals are (see ***PowerPoint Slide 10*** for Chapter 8):

            a. Define the specific job criteria against which performance will be measured.

            b. Measure past job performance accurately.

            c. Justify the rewards given to individuals and/or groups, thereby differentiating between high and low performance.

            d. Define the development experiences the ratee needs to have in order to enhance performance in the current job and to prepare for future responsibilities.

        2. The four functions of performance appraisal reflect two general purposes that are served by good performance appraisal systems: making evaluation decisions and making feedback and development decisions. (See ***PowerPoint Slide 11*** for Chapter 8.)

            a. *Evaluative decisions* are concerned with such issues as promotions, transfers, terminations, and salary increases.

      b. *Feedback and development decisions* let ratees know where they stand in terms of the organization's expectations and performance objectives, and include detailed consideration of the ratees' job-related strengths and weaknesses

---

LECTURE ENHANCEMENT

Many students are aware of the performance appraisal process. Students should be encouraged to share their experiences with performance appraisal. Many performance appraisals are ineffective, and, if poorly planned and carried out, actually undermine motivation.

C. Who does the performance appraisal? (See *PowerPoint Slide 12* for Chapter 8.)

    1. Traditionally, performance appraisals have been conducted by an individual's immediate superior, the presumption being that since the immediate superior is responsible for the subordinate's performance, the superior should do the appraisal.

    2. People other than the supervisor may be able to better appraise some aspects a person's job performance.

    3. To obtain as much appraisal information as possible, a 360-degree evaluation may be used. The **360-degree evaluation** uses evaluations of bosses, peers, and subordinates, as well as self-ratings, customer ratings, and ratings by others with whom the ratee deals outside the immediate work unit.

D. Performance appraisal dimensions and standards. (See *PowerPoint Slide 13* for Chapter 8.)

    1. Both performance outcomes and the behaviors or activities that result in these outcomes are important to performance appraisal.

    2. *Output measures* reflect the quantity or quality of a person's work performance, and usually they are obtained directly from written records or documents, such as production records.

    3. *Activity measures* reflect the behaviors that lead to outputs, and typically they are obtained from the evaluator's observations and rating.

E. Performance appraisal methods.

    1. Performance appraisal methods can be divided into two general categories: comparative methods and absolute methods.

    2. Comparative methods of performance appraisal.

a. Comparative methods of performance appraisal seek to identify a person's relative standing among those being rated.

b. Comparative methods can indicate that one person is better than another on a given dimension, but not how much better.

c. Comparative methods of performance appraisal include ranking, paired comparison, and forced distribution. (See *PowerPoint Slide 14* for Chapter 8.)

    (i) **Ranking** involves rank ordering each individual from best to worst on each performance dimension being considered.

    (ii) **Paired comparison** directly compares each person with every other person being rated.

    (iii) **Forced distribution** uses a small number of performance categories, such as "very good," "good," "adequate," "poor," and "very poor," and requires raters to place a specific proportion of employees into each of these categories.

3. Absolute methods of performance appraisal.

a. Absolute methods of performance appraisal specify precise measurement standards.

b. Absolute methods of performance appraisal include graphic rating scales, the critical incident diary, behaviorally anchored rating scales, and management by objectives. (See *PowerPoint Slides 15* and *16* for Chapter 8.)

    (i) **Graphic rating scales** list a variety of dimensions thought to be related to high performance outcomes in a given job and that the individual is expected to exhibit, and raters assign the ratees' scores on each dimension.

LECTURE ENHANCEMENT

The graphic rating scale system is a very common approach to performance appraisal. It is simple to implement and to use, but tends to be very subjective. For instance, on a scale from 1 to 5 for a certain characteristic, 4 means good. What does that mean really mean? Discuss this concept with the class. Have students provide examples from their own experiences.

    (ii) A **critical incident diary** records incidents of unusual success or failure in a given performance aspect.

(iii) A **behaviorally anchored rating scale (BARS)** describes observable job behaviors, each of which characterizes some degree of inferior versus superior job performance.

(iv) A *behavioral observation scale* (BOS) uses a five-point frequency scale (ranging from "almost always" to "almost never") to rate each of the observable job behaviors.

(v) *Management by objectives* is a process of joint goal setting between a supervisor and a subordinate, and the established goals are used as standards against which the subordinate's performance is evaluated.

F. Measurement errors in performance appraisal.

1. To be meaningful, an appraisal system must be both reliable and valid. (See *PowerPoint Slide 17* for Chapter 8.)

    a. *Reliability* means that the appraisal system provides consistent results each time it is used.

    b. *Validity* means that the appraisal system actually measures people on relevant job content.

2. Measurement errors that can threaten the reliability and validity of performance appraisals include the following:

    a. A **halo error** results when one person rates another person on several different dimensions and gives a similar rating for each dimension. (See *PowerPoint Slide 18* for Chapter 8.)

    b. A **leniency error** is the tendency to give relatively high ratings to virtually everyone. (See *PowerPoint Slide 18* for Chapter 8.)

    c. A **strictness error** occurs when a rater tends to give everyone a low rating. (See *PowerPoint Slide 18* for Chapter 8.)

    d. A **central tendency error** occurs when managers lump everyone together around the "average," or middle, category. (See *PowerPoint Slide 19* for Chapter 8.)

    e. A **low differentiation error** occurs when raters restrict themselves to a small part of the rating scale. (Leniency, strictness, and central tendency errors are specific types of the low differentiation error.) (See *PowerPoint Slide 19* for Chapter 8.)

    f. A **recency error** occurs when a rater allows recent events rather than earlier events to influence a performance rating. (See *PowerPoint Slide 20* for Chapter 8.)

      g. A **personal bias error** occurs when a rater allows specific biases, such as race, age, gender, or disability, to enter into performance appraisal. (See *PowerPoint Slide 20* for Chapter 8.)

      h. A *cultural bias error* occurs a rater allows cultural differences of employees to influence the performance appraisal. (See *PowerPoint Slide 20* for Chapter 8.)

G. Improving performance appraisal.

    1. Rating errors can be reduced and performance appraisals can be improved by doing the following (see *PowerPoint Slide 21* for Chapter 8):

      a. Train raters so that they understand the evaluation process rationale and can recognize the sources of measurement error.

      b. Make sure that raters observe ratees on an ongoing, regular basis and that they do not try to limit all their evaluations to the formally designated evaluation period.

      c. Do not have the rater rate too many ratees. The ability to identify performance differences drops, and fatigue sets in when the evaluation of large numbers of people is involved.

      d. Make sure that the performance dimensions and standards are stated clearly, and that the standards are as non-contaminating and non-deficient as possible.

      e. Avoid terms such as average because different evaluators tend to react differently to the terms.

    2. To have a legally defensible performance appraisal system that does not discriminate against employees, the following should be done (see *PowerPoint Slides 22* and *23* for Chapter 8):

      a. Appraisal must be based on an analysis of job requirements as reflected in performance standards.

      b. Appraisal is appropriate only where performance standards are clearly understood by employees.

      c. Clearly defined individual dimensions should be used rather than global measures.

      d. Dimensions should be behaviorally based and supported by observable evidence.

      e. If rating scales are used, abstract trait names, such as "loyalty," should be avoided unless they can be defined in terms of observable behavior.

      f.   Rating scale anchors should be brief and logically consistent.

      g.   The system must be validated and psychometrically sound, as must the ratings given by individual evaluators.

      h.   An appeal mechanism must be in place in the event the evaluator and the ratee disagree.

H. Group evaluation.

   1.   There is a growing trend toward group or team performance evaluations.

   2.   Group or team performance evaluations are consistent with self-managed teams and high-performance organizations.

IV.   **Study Question 3: What are compensation and rewards?**

A. Background on compensation and rewards.

   1.   The design and implementation of reward systems is an important complement to goal setting and performance appraisal.

   2.   *Extrinsic rewards* are positively valued work outcomes that are given to an individual or group by some other person or source in the work setting.

   3.   *Intrinsic rewards* are positively valued work outcomes that the individual receives directly as a result of task performance.

   4.   Managing intrinsic rewards presents a managerial challenge of designing work settings so that employees can reward themselves for a job well done.

B. Pay as an extrinsic reward. (See ***PowerPoint Slides 24*** and ***25*** for Chapter 8.)

   1.   Pay can help organizations attract and retain highly capable workers, and help satisfy and motivate these workers to work hard to achieve high performance.

   2.   For pay to serve as a source of work motivation, high levels of job performance must be viewed as the path through which high pay can be achieved.

   3.   **Merit pay** is a compensation system that bases an individual's salary or wage increase on a measure of the person's performance accomplishments during a specified time period.

   4.   To work well, a merit pay plan should be based on realistic and accurate measures of individual work performance and create a belief among employees that the way to achieve high pay is to perform at high levels.

   5.   Some people argue that merit pay plans are not consistent with the demands of modern organizations because they fail to recognize the high degree of task interdependence among employees.

C. Creative pay practices.

1. **Skill-based pay** rewards people for acquiring and developing job-relevant skills. (See *PowerPoint Slide 26* for Chapter 8.)

2. **Gain sharing** is a pay system that links pay and performance by giving the workers the opportunity to share in productivity gains through increased earnings. (See *PowerPoint Slide 26* for Chapter 8.)

   a. The Scanlon Plan and IMPROSHARE are well-known gain-sharing plans.

   b. The benefits of gain sharing include the following:

      (i) Increased worker motivation because of the pay-for-performance incentives.

      (ii) Greater personal responsibility for making performance contributions to the organization.

      (iii) Enhanced cooperation and teamwork.

3. **Profit-sharing plans** reward employees based on the entire organization's performance. (See *PowerPoint Slide 26* for Chapter 8.)

   a. Profit sharing does not reward employees for productivity gains.

   b. Profit sharing rewards employees on the basis of company profitability, which is often affected by factors that employees cannot control.

LECTURE ENHANCEMENT

Lincoln Electric pioneered profit sharing. In addition to paying its workers on a piece-rate basis, Lincoln Electric rewards employees with year-end profit-sharing payments that are contingent on their merit ratings and the firm's profits. The average profit sharing payment is approximately equal to the employee's annual salary. The motivating power of Lincoln's compensation policies is readily apparent from the fact that its workers produce about three times as much as other American workers in the same categories.

(Source: *Restoring Competitive Luster to American Industries: An Agenda for Success,* Cleveland: The Lincoln Electric Company.)

---

4. *Employee stock ownership plans* (**ESOPs**) either give company stock to employees, or allow them to purchase it at a price below market value. (See *PowerPoint Slide 27* for Chapter 8.)

5. **Lump-sum increases** reflect a pay system in which people elect to receive their wage or salary increase in one or more lump-sum payments. (See *PowerPoint Slide 27* for Chapter 8.)

    a. A related pan is the lump-sum payment wherein employers attempt to control labor costs while giving workers more money, if corporate earnings allow.

    6. **Flexible benefit plans** are systems that allow workers to select benefits according to their individual needs. (See *PowerPoint Slide 27* for Chapter 8.)

V.   **Study Question 4: What are human resource development and person-job fit?**

LECTURE ENHANCEMENT

An excellent online resource, named Workforce Management, deals with a broad range of human resource management issues. The Web site address is http://www.workforceonline.com/.

    A. Background on human resource development (HRD) and the person-job fit. (See *PowerPoint Slide 28* for Chapter 8.)

      1. Human resource development and the person-job fit are key contributing activities in performance management and rewards.

      2. **Human resource strategic planning** — the process of providing capable and motivated people to carry out the organization's mission and strategy — provides the foundation for human resource development and the person-job fit.

      3. Staffing, training, and career planning and development are important functions in human resource development and achieving a person-job fit.

LECTURE ENHANCEMENT

Ask the students to describe what they expect from a job and what they expect to bring to a job. Relate their stated expectations to the concept of person-job fit.

    B. Staffing.

      1. Job analysis. (See *PowerPoint Slide 29* for Chapter 8.)

        a. **Job analysis** refers to the process and procedures used to collect and classify information about tasks the organization needs to complete.

        b. Job analysis assists in the understanding of job activities required in a work process and helps define jobs, their interrelationships, and the demographic, aptitude and ability, and personality characteristics needed to do these jobs.

        c. The needed worker characteristics determined by job analysis are specified in the job description and are laid out in a job specification.

C. Recruitment. (See *PowerPoint Slide 30* for Chapter 8.)

    1. **Recruitment** is the process of attracting the best qualified individuals to apply for a job.

    2. Recruitment typically involves the following:

        a. Advertisement of a position vacancy.

        b. Preliminary contact with potential job candidates.

        c. Preliminary screening to obtain a pool of candidates.

    3. External versus internal recruitment.

        a. *External recruitment* involves such sources as general advertisements, often in newspapers, trade journals, or via external Internet; word-of-mouth suggestions from current employees; use of employment agencies; and applicant walk-ins.

        b. *Internal recruitment* is a process for attracting job applicants from those currently working for the firm.

        c. A **realistic job preview** provides applicants with an objective description of the prospective organization and job.

LECTURE ENHANCEMENT

A good way to reinforce the discussion of the recruitment process presented above is to see if any of your students are currently engaged in a job search. You can then ask students who respond affirmatively to describe their experiences with the recruiting process. This discussion typically helps students to see more clearly the relevance of recruiting from both a management perspective and their own personal perspectives as job candidates.

D. Selection. (See *PowerPoint Slide 31* for Chapter 8.)

    1. **Selection** involves the series of steps from initial applicant screening to final hiring of the new employee.

    2. Steps in selection process.

        a. *Completing application materials*: these materials may involve a traditional application form requesting various aspects of background and experience.

        b. *Conducting employment interviews*: interviews provide a rough idea regarding the applicant's fit with the job and organization.

c. *Completing any necessary tests*: tests may be administered either before or after the interview. They include aptitude or ability tests, personality tests, and tests for drug use.

    (i) Performance tests take many forms but often ask candidates to perform tasks that are identical to or at least closely related to what will be required on the job.

    (ii) *Assessment Centers* provide a firm with a comprehensive view of a candidate by evaluating the candidate's performance across many situations, typically involving various tests, simulations, role plays, and interviews, all based on dimensions the person occupying the job will need to demonstrate.

LECTURE ENHANCEMENT

Ask your students if they have ever been evaluated at an assessment center. Students with work experience, or students who are currently seeking employment, may have direct experience with this selection tool. If so, ask them to describe their experiences for the rest of the class.

---

d. *Doing a background investigation*: a background investigation can be used either early or late in the selection process, and it typically involves reference checks.

e. *Deciding to hire or not to hire*: based on the previous steps, the organization may choose to hire the applicant. At this point, a physical examination may be required if it is shown to be relevant for job performance.

E. Socialization. (See ***PowerPoint Slide 32*** for Chapter 8.)

1. **Socialization** is the process that adapts employees to the organization's culture.

2. Socialization occurs during and after completion of the staffing process.

3. Phases of socialization.

a. *Anticipatory socialization*: covers all of the learning that occurs before a new member joins an organization.

b. *Encounter*: the new recruit sees what the organization is truly like. Formal or informal orientation is part of this phase.

c. *Change and acquisition*: new hires master their on-the-job skills, perform their new roles successfully, adjust to their work group's values and norms, and become familiar with the organization's culture.

LECTURE ENHANCEMENT

Ask your students who are currently employed or have been employed in the past to describe the socialization process that they experienced. What was helpful about the socialization process? What was not helpful?

F. Training. (See *PowerPoint Slide 33* for Chapter 8.)

1. Training is a set of activities that provides the opportunity to acquire and improve job-related skills.

2. Training can be on-the-job, off-the-job, or both.

    a. *On-the-job training* (OJT) involves job instruction while performing the job in the actual workplace. Internships, apprenticeships, and job rotation are common forms of OJT.

        (i) Internships provide an opportunity for students to gain real-world experience.

        (ii) Apprenticeships involve learning a trade from an experienced worker.

        (iii) Job rotation provides a broad range of experience in different kinds of jobs in a firm.

    b. *Off-the-job training* commonly involves lectures, videos, and simulations, and increasingly is done through e-training.

G. Career planning and development.

1. **Career planning and development** involves individuals working with their managers and/or human resources (HR) experts on career issues.

2. *Figure 8.5* from the textbook offers a basic framework for formal career planning. The five steps in the framework begin with personal assessment and then progress through analysis of opportunities, selection of career objectives, selection and implementation of a career plan, and evaluation of results and revision of the career plan as necessary. (See *PowerPoint Slide 34* for Chapter 8.)

3. The manager's responsibility concerning career planning is twofold:

    a. Planning and managing a personal career.

    b. Assisting subordinates in assuming responsibility for their career planning and development.

4. The implications of constant change in the new workplace pressure people to continually review and reassess their career progress, take personal responsibility for their own career development, and be committed to lifelong learning.

   a. Outsourcing of jobs is becoming an increasingly common phenomenon in organizations, which in turn places an additional premium on each person continually developing his/her portfolio of skills.

5. Initial entry to a career.

   a. The full implications of the new workplace become apparent at the point of initial entry to a career.

   b. Whenever a job change is considered, the best advice is to know yourself and to learn as much as possible about the new job and the organization.

6. Adult life cycle and career stages. (See *PowerPoint Slide 35* for Chapter 8.)

   a. People mature they pass through the adult life cycle with many different problems and prospects, and it is especially important for managers to recognize the effects of this cycle on the people with whom they work.

   b. **Career stages** reflect the different work responsibilities and achievements through which people pass during the course of their work lives.

   c. *Entry and establishment* — or the provisional adulthood stage — involve on-the-job development of relevant skills and abilities.

   d. *Advancement* — or the first adulthood stage — involves growth and assumption of additional responsibility.

   e. *Maintenance, withdrawal, and retirement* — or the second adulthood stage — involve continued growth and accomplishments or career stability, and then ultimately retirement.

      (i) During this stage many people encounter a **career plateau** wherein they find themselves in a position from which they are unlikely to advance to a higher level of responsibility.

LECTURE ENHANCEMENT

A Web site referred to simply as "Monster" contains a vast amount of information about career planning and development, the current job market, starting your own business, information on how to investigate potential employers, mid-career strategies and more. The site is available at http://content.monster.com/.

VI. **Study summary for Chapter 8.**

A. Point out to the students that the text's "Chapter 8 Study Guide" recaps the key theories, concepts, and ideas in the chapter in relation to the appropriate study questions.

CHAPTER STUDY GUIDE

Study Question 1: What is goal setting?

- Goal setting is the process of developing, negotiating, and formalizing performance targets or objectives.
- Research supports predictions that the most motivational goals are challenging and specific, allow for feedback on results, and create commitment and acceptance.
- The motivational impact of goals may be affected by individual difference moderators such as ability and self-efficacy.
- Management by objectives is a process of joint goal setting between a supervisor and worker.
- The management by objectives process is a good action framework for applying goal-setting theory on an organizational basis.

Study Question 2: What is performance appraisal?

- Performance appraisal involves systematically evaluating performance and providing feedback on which performance adjustments can be made.
- Performance appraisals serve the two general purposes of evaluation and feedback and development.
- Performance appraisals traditionally are done by an individual's immediate superior but are moving toward 360-degree evaluations involving the full circle of contacts a person may have in job performance.
- Performance appraisals use either or both output measures and activity measures.
- Performance appraisal methods involve comparative methods and absolute methods.
- There are at least a half dozen rater errors important in performance appraisal.
- There are six steps that can be used to reduce errors and improve performance appraisals.

Study Question 3: What are compensation and rewards?

- Rewards involve the design and implementation of positively valued work outcomes.
- Reward systems emphasize a mix of extrinsic and intrinsic rewards.
- Pay as an extrinsic reward involves merit pay and creative pay practices.
- Creative pay practices include skill-based pay, gain-sharing plans, lump-sum pay increases, and flexible benefit plans.

Study Question 4: What are human resource development and person-job fit?

- HR strategic planning is the process of providing capable and motivated people to carry out the organization's mission and strategy.

- A key part of HR strategic planning, HR staffing involves job analysis, attracting individuals through recruitment, selecting those best qualified through screening and hiring, and socializing employees through initial orientation and follow-up over time. All these together help provide for person-job fit.
- Job analysis assists in understanding necessary job activities and helps define jobs, their interrelationships, and the demographic, aptitude and ability, and personality characteristics for these jobs. Information concerning the job itself appears in the job description. A job specification then merges requirements of the job analysis and job description. The above also help deal with legal requirements.
- Training is a set of activities that provide the opportunity to acquire and improve job-related skills.
- On-the-job training involves job instruction in the workplace and commonly utilizes internships, apprenticeships, and job rotation.
- Off-the-job training takes place off the job and commonly involves lectures, videos, and simulations.
- Career planning and development involves working with managers and HR experts on careers and involves the following: a five-stage planning framework, personal responsibility for developing a portfolio of skills to keep one marketable at any time, a balance sheet approach to evaluating each career opportunity, and recognition of the relationship between life and career stages and transitions.

KEY TERMS

Behaviorally anchored rating scale (BARS): an absolute method of performance appraisal that describes observable job behaviors, each of which characterizes some degree of inferior versus superior job performance.

Career planning and development: involves individuals working with their managers and/or human resources (HR) experts on career issues.

Career plateau: a position from which a person is unlikely to advance to a higher level of responsibility.

Career stages: the different work responsibilities and achievements through which people pass during the course of their work lives.

Central tendency error: occurs when managers lump everyone together around the "average," or middle, category.

Critical incident diary: an absolute method of performance appraisal that records incidents of unusual success or failure in a given performance aspect.

ESOPs: the acronym for employee stock ownership plans; these either give company stock to employees, or allow them to purchase it at a price below market value.

Flexible benefit plans: systems that allow workers to select benefits according to their individual needs.

Forced distribution: a comparative method of performance appraisal that uses a small number of performance categories, such as "very good," "good," "adequate," "poor," and "very poor," and requires raters to place a specific proportion of employees into each of these categories.

Gain sharing: a pay system that links pay and performance by giving the workers the opportunity to share in productivity gains through increased earnings.

Graphic rating scales: an absolute method of performance appraisal that lists a variety of dimensions thought to be related to high-performance outcomes in a given job and that the individual is expected to exhibit, and raters assign the ratees' scores on each dimension.

Halo error: results when one person rates another person on several different dimensions and gives a similar rating for each dimension.

Human resource strategic planning: the process of providing capable and motivated people to carry out the organization's mission and strategy.

Job analysis: the process and procedures used to collect and classify information about tasks the organization needs to complete.

Leniency error: the tendency to give relatively high ratings to virtually everyone.

Low differentiation error: occurs when raters restrict themselves to a small part of the rating scale. (Leniency, strictness, and central tendency errors are specific types of the low differentiation error.)

Lump-sum increases: a pay system in which people elect to receive their wage or salary increase in one or more lump-sum payments.

Management by objectives (MBO): a process of joint goal setting between a supervisor and a subordinate. Also used as an absolute method of performance appraisal.

Merit pay: a compensation system that bases an individual's salary or wage increase on a measure of the person's performance accomplishments during a specified time period.

Paired comparison: a comparative method of performance appraisal that directly compares each person with every other person being rated.

Performance appraisal: a process of systematically evaluating performance and providing feedback on which performance adjustments can be made.

Personal bias error: occurs when a rater allows specific biases, such as race, age, gender, or disability, to enter into performance appraisal.

Profit-sharing plans: reward employees based on the entire organization's performance.

Ranking: a comparative method of performance appraisal that involves rank ordering each individual from best to worst on each performance dimension being considered.

Realistic job preview: provides applicants with an objective description of the prospective organization and job.

Recency error: occurs when a rater allows recent events rather than earlier events to influence a performance rating.

Recruitment: the process of attracting the best qualified individuals to apply for a job.

Selection: the series of steps from initial applicant screening to final hiring of the new employee.

Skill-based pay: rewards people for acquiring and developing job-relevant skills.

Socialization: the process that adapts employees to the organization's culture.

Strictness error: occurs when a rater tends to give everyone a low rating.

Training: provides the opportunity to acquire and improve job-related skills.

360-degree evaluation: uses evaluations of bosses, peers, and subordinates, as well as self-ratings, customer ratings, and ratings by others with whom the ratee deals outside the immediate work unit.

Chapter 9
HOW GROUPS WORK

STUDY QUESTIONS

1.	What is the nature of groups in organizations?
2.	What are the stages of group development?
3.	What are the foundations of group performance?
4.	How do groups make decisions?

LEARNING OBJECTIVES

After completing this chapter students should be able to:

1.	Define "group" and describe the attributes of effective groups.
2.	Discuss the how synergy, social loafing, and social facilitation influence group accomplishments.
3.	Describe the differences between formal groups and informal groups.
4.	Discuss the stages of group development and their implications for group member behaviors and interactions.
5.	Describe the key group inputs.
6.	Describe the nature of required behaviors and emergent behaviors in group dynamics.
7.	Discuss the positive and negative aspects of intergroup dynamics.
8.	Explain the different communication networks that can be found in groups.
9.	Discuss how groups make decisions and the assets and liabilities of group decision-making.
10.	Explain what is meant by the term "groupthink" and describe how groupthink can be avoided.
11.	Discuss techniques for improving group decision making.

MATERIAL IN *THE OB SKILLS WORKBOOK* SUPPORTING THE CHAPTER

Cases for Critical Thinking	Case 9: The Forgotten Group Member
Experiential Exercises	Exercise 13: Annual Pay Raises
	Exercise 18: Serving on the Boundary
	Exercise 19: Eggsperiential Exercise
Self-Assessments	Assessment 9: Group Effectiveness
	Assessment 19: Decision-Making Biases

CHAPTER OVERVIEW

This chapter focuses on the nature of groups in organizations. The chapter begins by defining the term "group," discussing the attributes of an effective group, and examining the roles that synergy, social loafing, and social facilitation play in group accomplishments. Differences between formal and informal groups are explored as well. The second section of the chapter describes the five stages of group development — forming, storming, norming, performing, and adjourning — and their implications for the behavior and interaction of group members. The third section covers the foundations of group performance, focusing first on the group inputs of tasks; goals; rewards, and resources; technology; membership characteristics; and group size. The third section then examines group and intergroup dynamics as well as group communication networks. The final section of the chapter explores how groups make decisions, the assets and liabilities of group decision-making, groupthink and its implications, and methods for improving group decision making.

CHAPTER OUTLINE

I.   **Study Question 1: What is the nature of groups in organizations?**
A.   What is an effective group?
B.   Synergy and group accomplishments
C.   Formal and informal groups

II.   **Study Question 2: What are the stages of group development?**
A.   Forming stage
B.   Storming stage
C.   Norming stage
D.   Performing stage
E.   Adjourning stage

III.   **Study Question 3: What are the foundations of group performance?**
A.   Group inputs
B.   Group and intergroup dynamics
C.   Group communication networks

IV.   **Study Question 4: How do groups make decisions?**
A.   How groups make decisions
B.   Assets and liabilities of group decision making
C.   Groupthink
D.   Ways to improve group decisions

CHAPTER LECTURE NOTES

I.   **Introduction to the Chapter 9 Lecture.**

A.   Study questions for Chapter 9. (See *PowerPoint Slide 2* for Chapter 9.)

1.   What is the nature of groups in organizations?

2. What are the stages of group development?

3. What are the foundations of group performance?

4. How do groups make decisions?

B. The lecture material for Chapter 9 is organized around the study questions.

    1. Point out to the students that the text's "Chapter At A Glance" identifies the key topics contained in the chapter and links them to the appropriate study questions.

C. The chapter opens with a description of how the MacIntosh computer was developed by a team or workers at Apple Computer.

II.   **Study Question 1: What is the nature of groups in organizations?**

A. What is an effective group?

    1. A **group** is a collection of two or more people who work with one another regularly to achieve common goals. (See *PowerPoint Slide 3* for Chapter 9.)

    2. In a true group, members are mutually dependent on one another to achieve common goals, and they interact with one another regularly to pursue those goals over a sustained period of time. (See *PowerPoint Slide 3* for Chapter 9.)

    3. *Hot groups* thrive in conditions of crisis and competition; their creativity and innovativeness generate extraordinary returns. (See *PowerPoint Slide 3* for Chapter 9.)

    4. An **effective group** is one that achieves high levels of task performance, member satisfaction, and team viability. (See *PowerPoint Slide 4* for Chapter 9.)

        a. *Task performance* — an effective group achieves its performance goals in the standard sense of quantity, quality, and timeliness of work results.

        b. *Member satisfaction* — an effective group is one whose members believe that their participation and experiences are positive and meet important personal needs.

        c. *Team viability* — an effective group has members who are sufficiently satisfied to continue working well together on an ongoing basis and/or look forward to working together again at some future point in time.

LECTURE ENHANCEMENT

A good way to expose students to the nature of effective groups is to ask them how they feel about participating in groups. You will usually receive both highly positive and highly negative opinions. Students who have been members of successful athletic, social, extracurricular, class-based, and/or work groups will likely have quite positive attitudes. Those with less favorable experiences, such as students who have encountered nonproductive groups in their classes, will likely be more skeptical of the utility of groups and teams. For these students, the quip "A camel is a horse designed by a committee!" may ring true. Point out that despite their potential drawbacks, groups and teams are an essential organizational resource that all organizational members — but especially managers and leaders — must understand in order to tap their full potential.

B. Synergy and groups accomplishments.

    1. Effective groups offer the potential for **synergy** — the creation of a whole that is greater than the sum of the parts.

    2. Groups can help organizations in the following ways (see ***PowerPoint Slide 5*** for Chapter 9):

        a. Groups are good for people.

        b. Groups can improve creativity.

        c. Groups can make better decisions.

        d. Groups can increase commitments to action.

        e. Groups help control their members.

        f. Groups help offset large organization size.

    3. Groups often have performance advantages over individuals acting alone in following situations (see ***PowerPoint Slide 6*** for Chapter 9):

        a. When there is no clear expert in a particular task or problem.

        b. When problems are complex, requiring a division of labor and the sharing of information.

        c. Groups can be more creative and innovative because of their tendencies to make riskier decisions.

    4. Potential benefits for group members include the following (see ***PowerPoint Slide 7*** for Chapter 9):

    a. People learn from each other and share job skills and knowledge.

    b. Groups are important sources of need satisfaction for their members.

    c. Members can provide emotional support for each other in times of crisis or pressure.

    d. Members' contributions can help them experience self-esteem and personal involvement.

5. **Social loafing**, also known as the Ringelmann effect, is the tendency of people to work less hard in a group than they would individually. (See ***PowerPoint Slide 8*** for Chapter 9.)

    a. People may not work hard in groups for the following reasons:

        (i) Their individual contributions are less noticeable in the group context.

        (ii) They prefer to see others carry the workload.

6. Social loafing may be diminished or prevented by doing the following (see ***PowerPoint Slide 9*** for Chapter 9):

        (i) Define roles and tasks to maximize individual interests.

        (ii) Raise accountability by making individual performance expectations clear and identifiable.

        (iii) Tie individual rewards to their performance contribution to the group.

7. **Social facilitation** is the tendency for one's behavior to be influenced by the presence of others in a group or social setting. (See ***PowerPoint Slide 10*** for Chapter 9.)

    a. Social facilitation theory indicates that working in the presence of others creates an emotional arousal or excitement that stimulates behavior and therefore affects performance.

    b. Arousal tends to work positively when a person is proficient with the task.

    c. Arousal tends to work negatively when a the task is not well learned.

C. Formal and informal groups.

1. Formal groups.

    a. A **formal group** is officially designated to serve a specific organizational purpose. (See ***PowerPoint Slide 11*** for Chapter 9.)

LECTURE ENHANCEMENT

Discuss with students the various formal groups to which they belong, or have belonged.

---

    b. The head of a formal group is responsible for the group's performance accomplishments and serves a "linking-pin" role that ties the group horizontally and vertically with the rest of the organization. (See *PowerPoint Slide 11* for Chapter 9.)

    c. Formal groups may permanent or temporary. (See *PowerPoint Slide 11* for Chapter 9.)

    d. Permanent work groups, or command groups in the vertical structure, often appear on organization charts as departments, divisions, or teams. (See *PowerPoint Slide 11* for Chapter 9.)

    e. Temporary work groups are task groups specifically created to solve a problem or perform a defined task, and they often disband once the assigned purpose or tasks have been accomplished. (See *PowerPoint Slide 11* for Chapter 9.)

    f. Types of formal groups. (See *PowerPoint Slide 12* for Chapter 9.)

       (i) Cross-functional teams or task forces engage in special problem-solving efforts drawing on the perspectives and expertise of members representing each of the functional areas.

       (ii) Project teams, which often has cross-functional membership, are formed to complete a specific task with a well-defined end point.

       (iii) The **virtual group** is one whose members convene and work together electronically via computers.

  2. Informal groups.

    a. **Informal groups** emerge without being officially designated by the organization; they form spontaneously through personal relationships or special interests. (See *PowerPoint Slide 13* for Chapter 9.)

LECTURE ENHANCEMENT

Discuss with students the various informal groups to which they belong, or have belonged.

---

    b. Types of informal groups. (See *PowerPoint Slide 13* for Chapter 9.)

        (i) *Friendship groups* consist of persons with natural affinities for one another.

        (ii) *Interest groups* consist of persons who share common interests.

    c. Effect of informal groups. (See *PowerPoint Slide 14* for Chapter 9.)

        (i) Informal groups help people get their jobs done.

        (ii) Informal groups can speed up the workflow as people assist each other in ways that formal lines of authority fail to provide.

        (iii) Informal groups help individuals satisfy needs that are thwarted or unmet by a formal group.

        (iv) Informal groups provide their members with social satisfactions, security, and a sense of belonging.

III.   **Study Question 2: What are the stages of group development?**

    A. Stages of group development.

        1. All groups pass through a series of life cycle stages.

        2. Depending on the stage the group has reached, the leader and members face different challenges.

        3. *Figure 9.1* from the textbook describes five stages of group development: forming, storming, norming, performing, and adjourning. (See *PowerPoint Slide 15* for Chapter 9.)

    B. Forming stage. (See *PowerPoint Slide 16* for Chapter 9.)

        1. In the *forming stage* of group development, a primary concern is the initial entry of members to a group.

        2. Members are interested in getting to know each other and discovering what is considered acceptable behavior, in determining the real task of the group, and in defining group rules.

    C. Storming stage. (See *PowerPoint Slide 17* for Chapter 9.)

        1. The *storming stage* of group development is a period of high emotionality and tension among the group members.

        2. Hostility and infighting may occur, the group typically experiences many changes, and coalitions or cliques may form

3. Members' expectations tend to be clarified, and attention shifts toward obstacles standing in the way of group goals.

4. Individuals begin to understand one another's interpersonal styles.

5. Efforts are made to find ways to accomplish group goals while satisfying individual needs.

D. Norming stage. (See *PowerPoint Slide 18* for Chapter 9.)

1. The *norming stage* of group development, sometimes called initial integration, is the point at which the group begins to come together as a coordinated unit.

2. The turmoil of the storming stage gives way to a precarious balancing of forces.

3. Group members strive to maintain a positive balance and the desire for group harmony may obscure group problems.

4. Some members may mistake norming as the stage of ultimate maturity.

E. Performing stage. (See *PowerPoint Slide 19* for Chapter 9.)

1. The *performing stage*, sometimes called total integration, marks the emergence of a mature, organized, and well-functioning group.

2. Complex tasks and internal disagreements are handled in creative ways.

3. Members are motivated by group goals and are generally satisfied.

4. The primary challenges are continued efforts to improve relationships and performance.

5. Group members are able to adapt successfully to changing opportunities and demands.

6. A group that has achieved total integration will reflect the maturity end of the ten continua that are shown in *Figure 9.2* from the textbook. (See *PowerPoint Slide 20* for Chapter 9.)

F. Adjourning stage. (See *PowerPoint Slide 21* for Chapter 9.)

1. In the *adjourning stage*, a well-integrated group is able to disband, if required, with its work is accomplished.

2. The adjourning stage is especially important for temporary groups.

3. The willingness to disband when the job is done and to work well together in future responsibilities, group or otherwise, is an important long-run test of group success.

LECTURE ENHANCEMENT

Ask students to describe their experiences with different teams within the context of stages of group development. What happened for them at each stage? How do the students' experiences compare to the ideas presented above? Did anyone have an experience wherein the group seemed to get stuck at one particular stage — say, the storming stage? What happened, and what insights does it provide?

IV.   Study Question 3: What are the foundations of group performance?

A. *Figure 9.3* from the textbook portrays the work group as an open system that transforms resource input into product outputs. (See *PowerPoint Slide 22* for Chapter 9.)

LECTURE ENHANCEMENT

If you have assigned group projects to your students, be sure to relate the open systems model in *Figure 9.3* to their group experiences. Throughout your discussion, ask students to indicate how the various group inputs (*i.e.*, tasks; goals, rewards, and resources; technology; membership diversity; and group size) and group processes (*i.e.*, group and intergroup dynamics) affected their group performance, satisfaction, and future viability.

B. Group inputs.

1. Key group inputs include the nature of tasks; goals, rewards, resources; technology; membership diversity; and group size.

2. Tasks. (See *PowerPoint Slides 23* and *24* for Chapter 9.)

a. Tasks place different demands on groups, with varying implications for group effectiveness.

b. The *technical demands* of a group's task include its routineness, difficulty, and information requirements.

c. The *social demands* of a task involve relationships, ego involvement, controversies over ends and means, and the like.

d. Tasks that are complex in technical demands require unique solutions and more information processing.

e. Tasks that are complex in social demands involve difficulties reaching agreement on goals or methods for accomplishing them.

3. Goals, rewards, and resources. (See *PowerPoint Slide 25* for Chapter 9.)

a. Appropriate goals, well-designed reward systems, and adequate resources are essential to support long-term performance accomplishments.

b. A group's performance can suffer under each of the following conditions:

   (i) When goals are unclear, insufficiently challenging, or arbitrarily imposed.

   (ii) When goals are focused too much on individual-level instead of group-level accomplishments.

   (iii) When adequate budgets, the right facilities, good work methods and procedures, and the best technologies are not available.

4. Technology. (See *PowerPoint Slide 26* for Chapter 9.)

   a. *Technology* provides the means to get work accomplished.

   b. It is always necessary to have the right technology available for the task at hand.

   c. The nature of workflow technology can influence the way group members interact with one another while performing their tasks

5. Membership characteristics.

   a. To achieve success a group must have the right skills and competencies available for task performance and problem solving. (See *PowerPoint Slide 27* for Chapter 9.)

   b. In *homogeneous groups*, members may find it very easy to work together but they may also suffer performance limitations if their collective skills, experiences and perspectives are not a good match for complex skills. (See *PowerPoint Slide 27* for Chapter 9.)

   c. In *heterogeneous groups*, a wide pool of talent and viewpoints is available for problem solving but this diversity may also create difficulties as members try to define problems, share information, and handle interpersonal conflicts. (See *PowerPoint Slide 27* for Chapter 9.)

   d. The **diversity-consensus dilemma** is the tendency for increasing diversity among group members is to make it harder for group members to work together, even though the diversity expands the skills and perspectives available for problem solving. (See *PowerPoint Slide 28* for Chapter 9.)

   e. **FIRO-B theory** (with "FIRO" standing for fundamental interpersonal orientation) identifies differences in how people relate to one another in groups based on their needs to express and receive feelings of inclusion, control, and affection. (See *PowerPoint Slide 29* for Chapter 9.)

(i) Groups whose members have <u>compatible</u> characteristics are likely to be <u>more</u> effective.

(ii) Groups whose members have <u>incompatible</u> characteristics are likely to be <u>less</u> effective.

f. *Status* is a person's relative rank, prestige, or standing in a group. (See *PowerPoint Slide 30* for Chapter 9.)

g. **Status congruence** occurs when a person's position within the group is equivalent in status to positions held outside of the group. (See *PowerPoint Slide 30* for Chapter 9.)

6. Group size. (See *PowerPoint Slide 31* for Chapter 9.)

a. The size of a group, as measured by the number of its members, can make a difference in a group's effectiveness.

b. As a group becomes larger, more people are available to divide up the work and accomplish needed tasks, which can increase performance and member satisfaction, but only up to a point.

c. As a group size continues to grow, communication and coordination problems often set in, and in turn satisfaction may decline while turnover, absenteeism, social loafing, and group logistical problems may increase.

d. A good size for problem-solving groups is between five and seven members.

C. Group and intergroup dynamics.

1. **Group dynamics** refer to the forces operating in groups that affect the way members relate to and work with one another. (See *PowerPoint Slide 32* for Chapter 9.)

2. In the open systems model of groups, group dynamics are the processes through which inputs are transformed into outputs. (See *PowerPoint Slide 32* for Chapter 9.)

3. What goes on within groups.

a. George Homans's model of group dynamics specifies two sets of work group behaviors (*i.e.*, required and emergent) and three types of member relationships (*i.e.*, activities, interactions, and sentiments), all of which have their required and emergent forms.

b. Work group behaviors. (See *PowerPoint Slide 33* for Chapter 9.)

(i) *Required behaviors* are those formally defined and expected by the organization.

        (ii) *Emergent behaviors* are those that group members display in addition to what the organization asks of them.

   c. Member relationships. (See *PowerPoint Slide 34* for Chapter 9.)

        (i) *Activities* are the things people do or the actions they take in groups while working on tasks.

        (ii) *Interactions* are interpersonal communications and contacts.

        (iii)*Sentiments* are the feelings, attitudes, beliefs, or values held by group members.

4.   What goes on between groups.

   a. **Intergroup dynamics** refers to the dynamics that take place between two or more groups. (See *PowerPoint Slide 35* for Chapter 9.)

   b. Competition and intergroup problems often develop within an organization and have both positive and negative consequences.

   c. Organizations and their managers go to great lengths to avoid the negative aspects and achieve the positive aspects of intergroup dynamics.

   d. Common methods for achieving these results are the following (see *PowerPoint Slide 35* for Chapter 9):

        (i) Refocusing group members on a common enemy or a common goal.

        (ii) Direct negotiations.

        (iii)Training members to work more cooperatively.

        (iv)Refocusing rewards on contributions to the total organization and how much groups help each other.

D. Group communication networks.

1.   *Figure 9.4* from the textbook describes three interaction patterns and the associated communication networks that are found within groups. (See *PowerPoint Slide 36* for Chapter 9.)

2.   *Interacting groups* have members who work closely together on tasks and in which close coordination of activities takes place. Interacting groups use **decentralized communication networks** — also known as all-channel or star networks — in which all group members communicate directly and share information with one another.

3. *Coacting groups* have members who work on tasks independently while linked together through some form of central coordination. Coacting groups use **centralized communication networks** — also known as wheel or chain networks — in which group members are linked together through a central control point.

4. *Counteracting groups* exist when subgroups disagree on some aspect of workplace operations Counteracting groups use **restricted communications networks** in which polarized subgroups contest one another's positions and sometimes maintain antagonistic relations with one another.

LECTURE ENHANCEMENT

If you have assigned group projects to your students, have them describe the kind of communication network that developed in their groups. What were the advantages and disadvantages of the network they used?

V.   **Study Question 4: How do groups make decisions?**

A. How groups make decisions.

1. Edgar Schein has noted that groups may make decisions through any of the following six methods:

a. Decision by *lack of response* — one idea after another is suggested without any discussion-taking place; when the group finally accepts the idea, all others have been bypassed and discarded by simple lack of response rather than by critical evaluation. (See *PowerPoint Slide 37* for Chapter 9.)

b. Decision by *authority rule* — the chairperson, manager, or leader makes a decision for the group. (See *PowerPoint Slide 37* for Chapter 9.)

c. Decision by *minority rule* — two or three people are able to dominate or "railroad" the group into making a decision to which they agree. (See *PowerPoint Slide 37* for Chapter 9.)

d. Decision by *majority rule* — formal voting may take place, or members may be polled to find the majority viewpoint. (See *PowerPoint Slide 38* for Chapter 9.)

e. Decision by **consensus** — discussion leads to one alternative being favored by most members and the other members agree to support it. (See *PowerPoint Slide 38* for Chapter 9.)

f. Decision by *unanimity* — all group members agree totally on the course of action to be taken. (See *PowerPoint Slide 38* for Chapter 9.)

LECTURE ENHANCEMENT

Give a group "pop" quiz on the text material. Form groups of five or six members. Only one copy of the quiz should be given to each group. Students are permitted to talk to each other, but must arrive at one answer to each of the quiz questions. Grade the quizzes. Discuss how the different groups made their decisions regarding the correct answers. Consider how their different decision-making approaches affected the results.

B. Assets and liabilities of group decision making.

LECTURE ENHANCEMENT

Ask students to think about their various group experiences. Drawing on these experiences, have the students brainstorm on the advantage and disadvantages of groups. Use the students' examples as a lead-in to the following material.

---

1. The potential advantages of group decision making include the following (see *PowerPoint Slide 39* for Chapter 9):

    a. Information — more knowledge and expertise is applied to solve the problem.

    b. Alternatives — a greater number of alternatives are examined, avoiding tunnel vision.

    c. Understanding and acceptance — the final decision is better understood and accepted by all group members.

    d. Commitment — there is more commitment among all group members to make the final decision work.

2. The potential disadvantages of group decision making include the following (see *PowerPoint Slide 40* for Chapter 9):

    a. Social pressure to conform —individuals may feel compelled to go along with the apparent wishes of the group.

    b. Minority domination — the group's decision may be forced or "railroaded" by one individual or a small coalition.

    c. Time demands — with more people involved in the dialogue and discussion, group decisions usually take longer to make than individual decisions.

C. Groupthink

    1. **Groupthink** is the tendency of cohesive group members to lose their critical evaluative capabilities.

    2. Groupthink can result in poor decisions being made.

    3. Groupthink can be avoided by doing the following (see *PowerPoint Slides 41 and 42* for Chapter 9):

        a. Assign the role of critical evaluator to each group member.

        b. Have the leader avoid seeming partial to one course of action.

        c. Create subgroups that each work on the same problem.

        d. Have group members discuss issues with outsiders and report back.

        e. Invite outside experts to observe and react to group processes.

        f. Assign someone to be a "devil's advocate" at each meeting.

        g. Write alternative scenarios for the intentions of competing groups.

        h. Hold "second-chance" meetings after consensus is apparently achieved.

LECTURE ENHANCEMENT

Ask the students whether they have ever been in a group that succumbed to groupthink. If so, have them describe what happened and how they attempted to deal with groupthink.

D. How to improve group decisions.

    1. Brainstorming.

        a. In **brainstorming**, group members actively generate as many ideas and alternatives as possible, and they do so relatively quickly and without inhibitions. (See *PowerPoint Slide 43* for Chapter 9.)

        b. Brainstorming rules.

            (i) All criticism is ruled out.

            (ii) "Freewheeling" is welcomed.

            (iii) Quantity of ideas is emphasized.

(iv) "Piggy-backing" off of other ideas is encouraged.

2. Nominal group technique.

    a. The **nominal group technique** puts people in small groups of six to seven members and asks everyone to respond individually and in writing to a "nominal" question. (See *PowerPoint Slide 43* for Chapter 9.)

    b. Steps in nominal group technique.

        (i) Individuals list alternatives or ideas.

        (ii) In a round-robin fashion, participants read aloud their alternatives or ideas.

        (iii) In a round-robin fashion, participants ask questions that clarify but do not criticize the alternatives or ideas.

        (iv) A structured voting procedure is then used to prioritize the alternatives or ideas.

3. Delphi technique.

    a. The **Delphi technique** involves generating decision-making alternatives through a series of survey questionnaires. (See *PowerPoint Slide 44* for Chapter 9.)

4. Computer-mediated decision making.

    a. Information and computer technologies enable group decision making to take place across great distances with the aid of group decision support systems. (See *PowerPoint Slide 44* for Chapter 9.)

    b. Electronic brainstorming occurs through the use of special software that facilitates the entry of ideas at will through one's personal computer.

VI. **Study summary for Chapter 9.**

A. Point out to the students that the text's "Chapter 9 Study Guide" recaps the key theories, concepts, and ideas in the chapter in relation to the appropriate study questions.

CHAPTER STUDY GUIDE

Study Question 1: What is the nature of groups in organizations?

-   A group is a collection of people who interact with one another regularly to attain common goals.

- Groups can help organizations by helping their members to improve task performance and experience more satisfaction from their work.
- One way to view organizations is as interlocking networks of groups whose managers serve as leaders in one group and subordinates in another.
- Synergy occurs when groups are able to accomplish more than their members could by acting individually.
- Formal groups are designated by the organization to serve an official purpose; examples are work units, task forces, and committees; informal groups are unofficial and emerge spontaneously because of special interests.

Study Question 2: What are the stages of group development?

- Groups pass through various stages in their life cycles, and each stage poses somewhat distinct management problems.
- In the forming stage, groups have problems managing individual entry.
- In the storming stage, groups have problems managing expectations and status.
- In the norming or initial integration stage, groups have problems managing member relations and task efforts.
- In the performing or total integration stage, groups have problems managing continuous improvement and self-renewal.
- In the adjourning stage, groups have problems managing task completion and the process of disbanding.

Study Question 3: What are the foundations of group performance?

- An effective group is one that achieves high levels of task accomplishment and member satisfaction, and achieves viability to perform successfully over the long term.
- As open systems, groups must interact successfully with their environments to obtain resources that are transformed into outputs.
- Group input factors establish the core foundations for effectiveness, including goals, rewards, resources, technology, the task, membership characteristics, and group size.
- Group dynamics are the ways members work together to utilize inputs; they are another foundation of group effectiveness.
- Group dynamics are based on the interactions, activities, and sentiments of group members as well as on the required and emergent ways in which members work together.
- Intergroup dynamics are the forces that operate between two or more groups.
- The disadvantages of intergroup competition can be reduced through management strategies to direct, train, and reinforce groups to pursue cooperative instead of purely competitive actions.
- Groups in organizations work with different interaction patterns and use different communication networks.
- Interacting groups with decentralized networks tend to perform well on complex tasks; coacting groups with centralized networks may do well at simple tasks.
- Restricted communication networks are common in counteracting groups involving subgroup disagreements.

Study Question 4: How do groups make decisions?

- Groups can make decisions by lack of response, authority rule, minority rule, majority rule, consensus, and unanimity.
- The potential assets of group decision making include having more information available and generating more understanding and commitment.
- The potential liabilities of group decision making include social pressures to conform and greater time requirements.

- Groupthink is the tendency of some groups to lose critical evaluative capabilities.
- Techniques for improving creativity in group decision making include brainstorming, the nominal group technique, and the Delphi technique, including computer applications.

KEY TERMS

Brainstorming: group members actively generate as many ideas and alternatives as possible, and they do so relatively quickly and without inhibitions.

Centralized communication network: a network in which group members are linked together through a central control point.

Consensus: a group decision-making method in which discussion leads to one alternative being favored by most members and the other members agree to support it.

Decentralized communication network: a network in which all group members communicate directly and share information with one another.

Delphi technique: involves generating decision-making alternatives through a series of survey questionnaires.

Diversity-consensus dilemma: the tendency for increasing diversity among group members is to make it harder for group members to work together, even though the diversity expands the skills and perspectives available for problem solving.

Effective groups: ones that achieve high levels of task performance, member satisfaction, and team viability.

FIRO-B theory: identifies differences in how people relate to one another in groups based on their needs to express and receive feelings of inclusion, control, and affection.

Formal groups: groups that are officially designated to serve a specific organizational purpose.

Group dynamics: the forces operating in groups that affect the way members relate to and work with one another.

Groups: collections of two or more people who work with one another regularly to achieve common goals.

Groupthink: the tendency of cohesive group members to lose their critical evaluative capabilities.

Informal groups: groups that emerge without being officially designated by the organization; they form spontaneously through personal relationships or special interests.

Intergroup dynamics: the dynamics that take place between two or more groups.

Nominal group technique: puts people in small groups of six to seven members and asks everyone to respond individually and in writing to a "nominal" question.

Restricted communication network: a network in which polarized subgroups contest one another's positions and sometimes maintain antagonistic relations with one another.

Social facilitation: the tendency for one's behavior to be influenced by the presence of others in a group or social setting.

Social loafing: the tendency of people to work less hard in a group than they would individually.

Status congruence: occurs when a person's position within the group is equivalent in status to positions held outside of the group.

Synergy: the creation of a whole that is greater than the sum of the parts.

Virtual group: a group whose members convene and work together electronically via computers.

Chapter 10
TEAMWORK AND TEAM PERFORMANCE

STUDY QUESTIONS

1.	What is the nature of teams and teamwork?
2.	What is team building?
3.	How does team building improve performance?
4.	How do teams contribute to the high-performance workplace?

LEARNING OBJECTIVES

After completing this chapter students should be able to:

1.	Discuss the importance of teams in business organizations, and describe the types of teams that are typically found in businesses.
2.	Discuss the nature of teamwork, and describe the characteristics of high-performance teams.
3.	Explain how diversity influences team performance.
4.	Describe some of the common approaches to team building.
5.	Describe some of the challenges involved in teamwork, including the entry of new members and task and maintenance leadership.
6.	Explain the concepts of role ambiguity, role overload, role underload, and role conflict.
7.	Discuss the nature of group norms and group cohesiveness, and how the two are related in influencing group performance.
8.	Describe the typical types of teams that appear in business settings, include problem-solving teams, cross-functional teams, virtual teams, and self-managing teams.
9.	Describe the operational implications of self-managing teams.

MATERIAL IN *THE OB SKILLS WORKBOOK* SUPPORTING THE CHAPTER

Case for Critical Thinking	Case 10: NASCAR's Racing Teams
Experiential Exercises	Exercise 20: Scavenger Hunt Team Building
	Exercise 21: Work Team Dynamics
	Exercise 22: Identifying Groups Norms
	Exercise 23: Workgroup Culture
	Exercise 24: The Hot Seat
Self-Assessments	Assessment 9: Group Effectiveness
	Assessment 15: Empowering Others

CHAPTER OVERVIEW

This chapter focuses on teamwork and team performance. Most students have some experience working in teams. As a result, this should be a high-interest chapter that stimulates interesting classroom discussion.

The chapter begins by defining teams, discussing the types of teams found in organizations, the nature of teamwork, the characteristics of high-performance teams, and diversity and team performance. Next, the chapter focuses on team building. The nature and process of team building and different approaches to team building are examined. A model of the team-building process is presented and the formal retreat approach, the continuous improvement approach, and the outdoor experience approach to team building are described within this section.

The next section of the chapter focuses on improving team processes. Some of the challenges associated with the entry of new team members and the execution of task and maintenance leadership roles are examined. Role ambiguity, role overload, role underload, and different types of role conflict are discussed within the context of roles and role dynamics in a team setting. Different types of group norms with positive and negative implications are identified and examined in relation to group cohesiveness; the impact of norms and cohesiveness on group performance are identified as well.

The final section of the chapter describes the specific types of teams that exist in businesses, including problem-solving teams, cross-functional teams, virtual teams, and self-managing teams. Insight is provided into the operational implications of self-managing teams.

CHAPTER OUTLINE

I. **Study Question 1: What is the nature of teams and teamwork?**
    A. Types of teams
    B. The nature of teamwork
    C. Diversity and team performance

II. **Study Question 2: What is team building?**
    A. How team building works
    B. Approaches to team building

III. **Study Question 3: How does team building improve performance?**
    A. Entry of new members
    B. Task and maintenance leadership
    C. Roles and role dynamics
    D. Positive norms
    E. Team cohesiveness

IV. **Study Question 4: How do teams contribute to the high-performance workplace?**
    A. Problem-solving teams
    B. Cross-functional teams
    C. Virtual teams
    D. Self-managing teams

CHAPTER LECTURE NOTES

I.   Introduction to the Chapter 10 Lecture.

    A. Study questions for Chapter 10. (See ***PowerPoint Slide 2*** for Chapter 10.)

        1. What is the nature of teams and teamwork?

        2. What is team building?

        3. How does team building improve performance?

        4. How do teams contribute to the high-performance workplace?

    B. The lecture material for Chapter 10 is organized around the study questions.

        1. Point out to the students that the text's "Chapter At A Glance" identifies the key topics contained in the chapter and links them to the appropriate study questions.

    C. The chapter opens with a discussion of the importance of teams and teamwork in the contemporary business world. This argument is reinforced with an example that focuses on Donald Katz, founder of Audible.com.

II.   Study Question 1: What is the nature of teams and teamwork?

    A. Background on teams and teamwork. (See ***PowerPoint Slide 3*** for Chapter 10.)

        1. A **team** is a small group of people with complementary skills, who work actively together to achieve a common purpose for which they hold themselves collectively accountable.

        2. Teams are one of the major forces behind today's revolutionary changes in contemporary organizations.

LECTURE ENHANCEMENT

To get students involved with the topic, ask them to identify the different types of teams to which they have belonged while working for an organization or during their educational career or both. These examples can be related to the different types of teams that are discussed below. This exercise helps students relate to the material and recognize its relevance to their own experiences.

    B. Types of teams. (See ***PowerPoint Slide 4*** for Chapter 10.)

        1. *Teams that recommend things* are established to study specific problems and recommend solutions to them.

            a. These teams typically work with a target completion date and disband once their purpose has been fulfilled.

2. *Teams that run things* consist of people with the formal authority for leading other groups.

   a. These teams may exist at all levels of responsibility, from the individual work unit composed of a team leader and team members to the top management team composed of a CEO and other senior executives.

3. *Teams that make or do things* are functional groups and work units that perform ongoing tasks, such as marketing or manufacturing.

   a. Members of these teams must have good long-term working relationships with one another, solid operating systems, and the external support needed to achieve effectiveness over a sustained period of time.

C. The nature of teamwork.

1. **Teamwork** occurs when group members actively work together in such a way that all their respective skills are well utilized to achieve a common purpose. (See *PowerPoint Slide 5* for Chapter 10.)

2. A high-performing team can be created by doing the following:

   a. Communicating high-performance standards.

   b. Setting the tone in the first team meeting.

   c. Creating a sense of urgency.

   d. Making sure members have the right skills.

   e. Establishing clear rules for team behavior.

   f. As a leader, modeling expected behaviors.

   g. Finding ways to create early successes.

   h. Continually introducing new information.

   i. Having members spend time together.

   j. Giving positive feedback.

   k. Rewarding high performance.

3. High-performance teams have the following special characteristics that allow them to excel at teamwork and achieve special performance advantages (see *PowerPoint Slide 6* for Chapter 10):

    a.   High-performance teams have strong core values that help guide their attitudes and behaviors in directions consistent with the team's purpose.

    b.   High-performance teams turn a general sense of purpose into specific performance objectives.

    c.   High-performance teams have the right mix of skills, including technical skills, problem-solving and decision-making skills, and interpersonal skills.

    d.   High-performance teams possess creativity.

LECTURE ENHANCEMENT

Have each student analyze a team of which he/she has been a member in light of the above characteristics. Then in small groups, have the students share and compare their analyses. Which teams were more like high-performance teams?

D. Diversity and team performance.

    1. In order to create and maintain high performance teams, all of the various elements of group effectiveness discussed in Chapter 9 must be addressed and successfully managed.

    2. Membership diversity is an important group input.

        a.   Homogeneous teams. (See *PowerPoint Slide 7* for Chapter 10.)

           (i)   Homogeneous teams have members who are similar with respect to such variables as age, gender, race, experience, ethnicity, and culture.

           (ii) Members of homogeneous teams can quickly build social relations and engage in the interactions needed for teamwork.

           (iii) Homogeneity may limit the team in terms of ideas, viewpoints, and creativity.

        b.   Heterogeneous teams. (See *PowerPoint Slides 8* and *9* for Chapter 10.)

           (i)   Heterogeneous teams have members who are diverse in demography, experiences, life styles, and cultures, among other variables.

           (ii) Diversity offers a rich pool of information, talent, and varied perspectives that can help improve team problem solving and increase creativity.

           (iii) Research indicates that diversity among team members may create performance difficulties early in the team's life or stage of development.

(iv) Even though diverse teams may struggle in the short run to resolve issues, they are also likely to develop enhanced performance potential once things are worked out.

(v) Unlocking the full potential of teams and teamwork rich in diversity is one of the great advantages of high-performance organizations.

LECTURE ENHANCEMENT

Involve students in the generation of: (a) examples of the stresses and conflicts that occur through diversity, and (b) examples of enhanced performance that occur through diversity.

III.   **Study Question 2: What is team building?**

A.   Background on team building. (See *PowerPoint Slide 10* for Chapter 10.)

1.   When newly founded, work groups and teams must master challenges as members come together and begin the process of growing and working together as they pass through the various stages of group development.

2.   **Team building** is a sequence of planned activities designed to gather and analyze data on the functioning of a group and to initiate changes designed to improve teamwork and increase group effectiveness.

B.   How team building works.

1.   *Figure 10.1* from the textbook highlights the action steps and continuous improvement theme of the typical team-building process. The process begins when someone notices that a problem exists or may develop with team effectiveness. Members then work together to gather data relating to the problem, analyze these data, plan for improvements, implement the action plan, and evaluate the results. (See *PowerPoint Slide 11* for Chapter 10.)

2.   Team building is collaborative and data based.

3.   The goal of team building is to get good answers to such questions as:

a.   "How well are we doing in terms of task accomplishment."

b.   "How satisfied are we as individual members with the group and the way it operates?"

C.   Approaches to team building. (See *PowerPoint Slide 12* for Chapter 10.)

1.   *Formal retreat approach* — team building takes place during an off-site "retreat" that may last from one to several days with group members working intensively on a variety of assessment and planning tasks.

2. *Continuous improvement approach* — the manager, team leader, or group members take responsibility for regularly engaging in the team-building process.

3. *Outdoor experience approach* — this approach places group members in a variety of physically challenging situations that must be mastered through teamwork, not individual work.

IV. Study Question 3: How does team building improve performance?

A. Entry of new members.

1. Special difficulties are likely to occur when members first get together in a new group or work team, or when new members join an existing one.

2. New members may worry about the following factors (see *PowerPoint Slide 13* for Chapter 1.):

a. Participation — "Will I be allowed to participate?"

b. Goals — "Do I share the same goals as others?"

c. Control — "Will I be able to influence what takes place?"

d. Relationships — "How close do people get?"

e. Processes — "Are conflicts likely to be upsetting?"

LECTURE ENHANCEMENT

Identify individuals in the class who have started a new job recently. Have them discuss their experiences in terms of new member problems.

---

3. The following three behavior profiles describe how people may cope with individual entry problems in self-serving ways that might hinder group operations (see *PowerPoint Slide 14* for Chapter 10):

a. The *tough battler* is frustrated by a lack of identity in the new group and may act aggressively or reject authority.

b. The *friendly helper* is insecure, suffering uncertainties of intimacy and control.

c. The *objective thinker* is anxious about how personal needs will be met in the group.

B. Task and maintenance leadership.

1. The achievement of sustained high performance by groups requires that both "task needs" and "maintenance needs" be met. (See *PowerPoint Slide 15* for Chapter 10.)

2. Although anyone who is formally appointed as a group leader should help fulfill these needs, all members should also contribute. (See *PowerPoint Slide 15* for Chapter 10.)

3. **Distributive leadership** is the sharing among team members of the responsibilities for task and maintenance contributions that move a group forward. (See *PowerPoint Slide 15* for Chapter 10.)

4. *Figure 10.2* from the textbook describes the factors that are involved in leading by task contribution and leading by maintenance contributions. (See *PowerPoint Slide 16* for Chapter 10.)

   a. **Task activities** refer to the various things members do that directly contribute to the performance of important tasks.

   b. **Maintenance activities** refer to the various things members do to support the group's social and interpersonal relationships.

5. Group members also share the additional responsibility of avoiding the following disruptive behaviors (see *PowerPoint Slide 17* for Chapter 10):

   a. Being overly aggressive toward other members.

   b. Withdrawing and refusing to cooperate with others.

   c. Horsing around when there is work to be done.

   d. Using the group as a forum for self-confession.

   e. Talking too much about irrelevant matters.

   f. Trying to compete for attention and recognition.

LECTURE ENHANCEMENT

Ask students to describe examples of task activities, maintenance activities, and dysfunctional activities that they have encountered in their group experiences.

C. Roles and role dynamics.

   1. A **role** is a set of expectations associated with a job or position on a team. (See *PowerPoint Slide 18* for Chapter 10.)

2. When team members are unclear about their roles or experience conflicting role demands, performance problems can occur.

3. **Role ambiguity** occurs when someone is uncertain about what is expected in his/her role. (See *PowerPoint Slide 18* for Chapter 10.)

4. **Role overload** occurs when too much is expected and the individual feels overwhelmed with work. (See *PowerPoint Slide 18* for Chapter 10.)

5. **Role underload** occurs when too little is expected and the individual feels underutilized. (See *PowerPoint Slide 18* for Chapter 10.)

6. **Role conflict** occurs when someone is unable to respond to role expectations that conflict with one another. Four common types of role conflict are the following (see *PowerPoint Slide 19* for Chapter 10):

   a. *Intrasender role conflict* occurs when the same person sends conflicting expectations.

   b. *Intersender role conflict* occurs when different people send conflicting and mutually exclusive expectations.

   c. *Person-role conflict* occurs when one's personal values and needs come into conflict with role expectations.

   d. *Interrole conflict* occurs when the expectations of two or more roles held by the same individual become incompatible, such as the conflict between work and family demands.

LECTURE ENHANCEMENT

Divide the class into seven groups. Assign a different one of the following types of conflicting role demands to each group: role ambiguity, role overload, role underload, intrasender conflict, intersender conflict, person-role conflict, and interrole conflict. In a five-minute period, have each group come up with as many examples of its assigned type as possible. Have each group share some of its examples with the rest of the class.

---

7. One way of managing role dynamics is by *role negotiation,* which is a process through which individuals negotiate to clarify the role expectations each holds for the other. *Figure 10.3* from the textbook provides an example of a role negotiations agreement. (See *PowerPoint Slide 20* for Chapter 10.)

D. Positive norms.

1. **Norms** represent ideas or beliefs about how members of a group or team are expected to behave; they are rules or standards of conduct. (See *PowerPoint Slide 21* for Chapter 10.)

2. Managers, task force heads, committee chairs, and team leaders should help their groups adopt positive norms that support organizational goals. (See *PowerPoint Slide 21* for Chapter 10.)

   a. This can be accomplished by doing the following:

      (i) Acting as a positive role model.

      (ii) Holding meetings to agree on goals.

      (iii) Selecting members who can and will perform.

      (iv) Providing support and training for members.

      (v) Reinforcing and rewarding desired behaviors.

      (vi) Holding meetings for performance feedback.

      (vii) Holding meetings to plan for improvements.

3. A key norm in any setting is the performance norm, which conveys expectations about how hard group members should work. (See *PowerPoint Slide 22* for Chapter 10.)

4. Other norms that operate with positive and negative implications for groups and organizations include the following (see *PowerPoint Slide 22* for Chapter 10):

   a. Ethics norms.

   b. Organizational and personal pride norms.

   c. High-achievement norms.

   d. Support and helpfulness norms.

   e. Improvement and change norms.

LECTURE ENHANCEMENT

Ask students to provide examples of both positive and negative performance norms that they have encountered in the different groups of which they were members. Discuss how these norms influenced the members' behavior.

E. Team cohesiveness.

1. Group or team **cohesiveness** is the degree to which members are attracted to and motivated to remain part of it. (See *PowerPoint Slide 23* for Chapter 10.)

2. Cohesiveness tends to he higher when group members are similar in age, attitudes, needs, and backgrounds; when the group is of small size; where members respect one another's competencies, agree on common goals, and work on interdependent tasks; when they are physically isolated from others; and when they experience performance success or crisis. (See *PowerPoint Slide 23* for Chapter 10.)

3. *Figure 10.4* in the textbook shows how cohesiveness and conformity to performance norms affect group performance. (See *PowerPoint Slide 24* for Chapter 10.)

   a. The *basic rule of conformity* in group dynamics states that the more cohesive the group, the greater the conformity of members to group norms.

   b. When cohesiveness is high and performance norms are positive, performance will be high.

   c. When cohesiveness is low and performance norms are positive, performance will be moderate.

   d. When cohesiveness is low and performance norms are negative, performance will be low to moderate.

   e. When cohesiveness is high and performance norms are negative, performance will be low.

4. Team leaders and managers must be aware of the steps they can take to build cohesiveness. *Figure 10.5* in the textbook shows how group cohesiveness can be increased or decreased by making changes in group goals, membership composition, interactions, size, rewards, competition, location, and duration. (See *PowerPoint Slide 25* for Chapter 10.)

V.   **Study Question 4: How do teams contribute to the high-performance workplace?**

A. Background on teams in the high-performance workplace.

   1. The keys to new approaches to teamwork are empowerment, participation, and involvement.

   2. Teamwork settings in organizations are increasingly described as "lateral' or "horizontal" rather than "vertical."

B. Problem-solving teams. (See *PowerPoint Slide 26* for Chapter 10.)

   1. **Employee involvement teams** describe a wide variety of teams whose members meet regularly to examine workplace issues.

2. A special type of employee involvement group is the **quality circle** (QC), which is a small group of persons who meet periodically to discuss and develop solutions for problems relating to quality, productivity, or cost.

C. Cross-functional teams. (See *PowerPoint Slide 27* for Chapter 10.)

1. **Cross-functional teams** bring together persons from different functions to work on a common task.

2. Cross-functional teams help overcome the **functional silos problem** that occurs when members of functional units stay focused on matters internal to the function and minimize their interactions with members of other functions.

3. Cross-functional teams are used to solve problems with a positive combination of functional expertise and integrative systems thinking.

D. Virtual teams.

1. **Virtual teams** are ones whose members meet at least part of the time electronically and with computer support.

2. The potential advantages of virtual teams include the following (see *PowerPoint Slide 28* for Chapter 10):

   a. Cost-effectiveness and speed where members are unable to meet easily face-to-face.

   b. The power of the computer is brought to bear on typical team needs for information processing and decision making.

   c. Communication is possible among people separated by great distances.

   d. Interaction and decision making are focused on facts and objective information rather than emotional considerations.

3. The potential disadvantages of virtual teams include the following (see *PowerPoint Slide 29* for Chapter 10):

   a. The lack of personal contact between team members.

   b. Group decisions are made in a limited social context.

E. Self-managing teams.

1. A **self-managing team** is a small group whose members are empowered to make the decisions needed to manage themselves on a day-to-day basis.

2. *Figure 10.6* from the textbook compares the organizational structure and activities of a traditional organization with those of an organization with self-managing teams. (See *PowerPoint Slide 30* for Chapter 10.)

   a. Self-managing teams, also called *self-directed teams* or *empowered teams*, are permanent and formal elements in the organizational structure that replace the traditional work group headed by a supervisor.

   b. Members of self-managing teams assume duties — such as planning and work scheduling, assigning work tasks, training of workers, performance evaluation, and quality control — that otherwise would be performed by a manager or first-line supervisor.

3. **Multiskilling** — whereby team members are trained in performing more than one job on the team — enables members of self-managing teams to have substantial discretion in determining work pace and in distributing tasks.

4. The potential advantages of self-managing teams include the following (see *PowerPoint Slide 31* for Chapter 10):

   a. Productivity and quality improvements.

   b. Production flexibility and faster response to technological change.

   c. Reduced absenteeism and turnover.

   d. Improved work attitudes and quality of work life.

5. The potential disadvantages of self-managing teams include the following (see *PowerPoint Slide 32* for Chapter 10):

   a. Structural changes in job classifications and management levels eliminate the need for first-line supervisors.

   b. Managers must learn to deal with teams rather than individuals.

   c. Supervisors who are displaced by self-managing teams may feel threatened.

6. Self-managing teams are probably not right for all organizations, work situations, and people.

7. The essence of any self-managing team — high involvement, participation, and empowerment — must be consistent with the values and culture of the organization.

VI.   **Study summary for Chapter 10.**

A. Point out to the students that the text's "Chapter 10 Study Guide" recaps the key theories, concepts, and ideas in the chapter in relation to the appropriate study questions.

CHAPTER STUDY GUIDE

Study Question 1: What is the nature of teams and teamwork?

- A team is a small group of people working together to achieve a common purpose for which they hold themselves collectively accountable.
- High-performance teams have core values, clear performance objectives, and the right mix of skills, and creativity.
- Teamwork occurs when members of a team work together so that their skills are well utilized to accomplish common goals.

Study Question 2: What is team building?

- Team building is a data-based approach to analyzing group performance and taking steps to improve it in the future.
- Team building is participative and engages all group members in collaborative problem solving and action.

Study Question 3: How does team building improve group performance?

- Individual entry problems are common when new teams are formed and when new members join existing teams.
- Task leadership involves initiating and summarizing, making direct contributions to the group's task agenda; maintenance leadership involves gatekeeping and encouraging, helping to support the social fabric of the group over time.
- Role difficulties occur when expectations for group members are unclear, overwhelming, underwhelming, or conflicting.
- Norms, as rules or standards for what is considered appropriate behavior by group members, can have a significant impact on group processes and outcomes.
- Members of highly cohesive groups value their membership and are very loyal to the group; they also tend to conform to group norms.

Study Question 4: How do teams contribute to the high-performance workplace?

- An employee involvement team is one whose members meet regularly to address important work-related problems and opportunities.
- Members of a quality circle, a popular type of employee involvement group, meet regularly to deal with issues of quality improvement in work processes.
- Self-managing teams are small workgroups that operate with empowerment and essentially manage themselves on a day-to-day basis.
- Members of self-managing teams typically, plan, complete, and evaluate their own work; train and evaluate one another in job tasks; and share tasks and responsibilities.

- Self-managing teams have structural and management implications for organizations because they largely eliminate first-line supervision.

KEY TERMS

Cohesiveness: the degree to which members are attracted to and motivated to remain part of a group or team.

Cross-functional teams: teams that bring together persons from different functions to work on a common task.

Distributed leadership: the sharing among team members of the responsibilities for task and maintenance contributions that move a group forward.

Employee involvement team: a team whose members meet regularly to examine workplace issues.

Functional silos problem: occurs when members of functional units stay focused on matters internal to the function and minimize their interactions with members of other functions.

Maintenance activities: the various things members do to support the group's social and interpersonal relationships.

Multiskilling: occurs when team members are trained in performing more than one job on the team.

Norms: ideas or beliefs about how members of a group or team are expected to behave; rules or standards of conduct.

Quality circle: a small group of persons who meet periodically to discuss and develop solutions for problems relating to quality, productivity, or cost.

Role: a set of expectations associated with a job or position on a team.

Role ambiguity: occurs when someone is uncertain about what is expected in his/her role.

Role conflict: occurs when someone is unable to respond to role expectations that conflict with one another.

Role overload: occurs when too much is expected and the individual feels overwhelmed with work.

Role underload: occurs when too little is expected and the individual feels underutilized.

Self-managing team: a small group whose members are empowered to make the decisions needed to manage themselves on a day-to-day basis.

Task activities: the various things members do that directly contribute to the performance of important tasks.

Team building: a sequence of planned activities designed to gather and analyze data on the functioning of a group and to initiate changes designed to improve teamwork and increase group effectiveness.

Teams: small groups of people with complementary skills, who work actively together to achieve a common purpose for which they hold themselves collectively accountable.

Teamwork: occurs when group members actively work together in such a ways that all their respective skills are well utilized to achieve a common purpose.

Virtual team: a team whose members meet at least part of the time electronically and with computer support.

Chapter 11
LEADERSHIP

STUDY QUESTIONS

1.	What is leadership and how does it differ from management?
2.	What are situational contingency approaches to leadership?
3.	What are attributional approaches to leadership?
4.	What are some emerging leadership perspectives and why are they especially important in today's organizations?

LEARNING OBJECTIVES

After completing this chapter students should be able to:

1.	Explain how managers and leaders differ.
2.	Describe the orientation of the trait theories of leadership, and identify traits that have positive implications for successful leadership.
3.	Describe the basic emphasis of the Michigan Studies, the Ohio State studies, the leadership grid, and Leader-Member Exchange theory.
4.	Discuss the leader behaviors and situational contingencies that characterize Fiedler's leadership contingency theory, House's path-goal theory, and Hersey and Blanchard's situational leadership model.
5.	Explain the concept of substitutes for leadership.
6.	Discuss attribution theory and the application of attribution theory to leadership.
7.	Discuss the charismatic, transformational, and transactional approaches to leadership.
8.	Discuss the role of leadership in self-managing work teams.
9.	Identify and describe emerging issues regarding charismatic, transformational, and transactional leadership.

MATERIAL IN *THE OB SKILLS WORKBOOK* SUPPORTING THE CHAPTER

Case for Critical Thinking	Case 14: Perot Systems
Experiential Exercises	Exercise 28: Interview a Leader
	Exercise 29: Leadership Skills Inventories
	Exercise 30: Leadership and Participation in Decision Making
Self-Assessments	Assessment 12: Least Preferred Coworker Scale
	Assessment 13: Leadership Style
	Assessment 14: "IT"Leadership Style

CHAPTER OVERVIEW

This chapter discusses the vital role of leadership in business organizations. The chapter begins by discussing the differences between managers and leaders, and draws attention to the unique attributes of leaders. The chapter next discusses the trait and behavioral approaches to leadership. Traits that have positive implications for successful leadership are identified within the context of the trait approach. Under the umbrella of the behavioral approach, the Michigan Studies, the Ohio State Studies, the leadership grid, and Graen's Leader-Member Exchange Theory are discussed. Emphasis is placed on two key leader behaviors — task orientation and relationship orientation — that run through much of leader behavior theory. The situational contingency theories are also discussed, including Fiedler's leadership contingency theory, House's path-goal theory, and Hersey and Blanchard's situational leadership model. The situational contingency models build on leader behavior theory and research., by emphasizing the circumstances under which different leader behaviors seem to be most effective.

The chapter also explores characteristics of individuals, jobs, and organizations as substitutes for leadership; the nature and impact of leadership protypes or mental models of what leaders should be like; and the potential exaggeration of leadership's actual impact, particularly at the top levels of large organizations. The chapter concludes with a discussion of charismatic, transformational, and transactional leaders; leadership in self-managing work teams; and the emerging issues regarding charismatic, transformational, and transactional leadership.

CHAPTER OUTLINE

I.   **Study Question 1: What is leadership and how does it differ from management?**
      A. Trait theories
      B. Behavioral theories

II.   **Study Question 2: What are situational contingency approaches to leadership?**
      A. Fiedler's leadership contingency theory
      B. House's path-goal theory of leadership
      C. Hersey and Blanchard's situational leadership model
      D. Substitutes for leadership

III. **Study Question 3: What are attributional approaches to leadership?**
      A. Leadership prototypes
      B. Exaggeration of the leadership difference

IV.   **Study Question 4: What are some emerging leadership perspectives and why are they especially important in today's organizations?**
      A. Charismatic approaches
      B. Transformational versus transactional approaches
      C. Leadership in self-managing work teams
      D. Emerging leadership issues

CHAPTER LECTURE NOTES

I. Introduction to the Chapter 11 Lecture.

   A. Study questions for Chapter 11. (See ***PowerPoint Slide 2*** for Chapter 11.)

   1. What is leadership and how does it differ from management?

   2. What are situational contingency approaches to leadership?

   3. What are attributional approaches to leadership?

   4. What are some emerging leadership perspectives and why are they especially important in today's organizations?

   B. The lecture material for Chapter 11 is organized around the study questions.

   1. Point out to the students that the text's "Chapter At A Glance" identifies the key topics contained in the chapter and links them to the appropriate study questions.

   C. The chapter opens with poem by Robert Frost and a quotation from the Chinese classic *Tao Te Ching*. The purpose is get the reader to ponder the nature of leadership and the conditions under which it occurs.

II. Study Question 1: What is leadership and how does it differ from management?

   A. Background on leadership and management.

   1. The role of management is to promote stability or to enable the organization to run smoothly. (See ***PowerPoint Slide 3*** for Chapter 11.)

   2. The role of leadership is to promote adaptive or useful changes. (See ***PowerPoint Slide 3*** for Chapter 11.)

   3. Persons in managerial positions can be involved with both management and leadership activities. (See ***PowerPoint Slide 3*** for Chapter 11.)

   4. Both management and leadership are needed in an organization. (See ***PowerPoint Slide 3*** for Chapter 11.)

   5. **<u>Leadership</u>** is a special case of interpersonal influence that gets an individual or group to do what the leader or manager wants done. (See ***PowerPoint Slide 4*** for Chapter 11.)

   6. Leadership appears in two forms (see ***PowerPoint Slide 4*** for Chapter 11):

   a. Formal leadership, which is exerted by persons appointed to or elected to positions of formal authority in organizations.

   b. Informal leadership, which is exerted by persons who become influential because they have special skills that meet the resource needs of others.

     c. Although both types are important in organizations, this chapter will emphasize formal leadership.

    7. Approaches to leadership include (see ***PowerPoint Slide 5*** for Chapter 11):

     a. Trait and behavioral perspectives.

     b. Situational contingency perspectives.

     c. Attributional perspectives.

     d. New leadership perspectives (*i.e.*, charismatic approaches, transformational approaches, and leadership of self-directing work teams).

B. Trait theories.

    1. **Trait perspectives** assume that traits play a central role in differentiating between leaders and nonleaders or in predicting leader or organizational outcomes. (See ***PowerPoint Slide 6*** for Chapter 11.)

    2. The great person-trait approach reflects this leader and nonleader difference and is the earliest approach in studying leadership, having been introduced more than a century ago. (See ***PowerPoint Slide 6*** for Chapter 11.)

    3. According to ***Figure 11.1*** in the textbook, the following traits have positive implications for successful leadership (see ***PowerPoint Slide 7*** for Chapter 11):

     a. Energy and adjustment or stress tolerance.

     b. Prosocial power motivations.

     c. Achievement orientation.

     d. Emotional maturity.

     e. Self-confidence.

     f. Integrity.

     g. Perseverance or tenacity.

     h. Cognitive ability, intelligence, social intelligence.

     i. Task-relevant knowledge.

     j. Flexibility.

LECTURE ENHANCEMENT

One way to demonstrate to students the objectives as well as the shortcomings of the trait approach to leadership is to ask them to identify the traits of effective leaders. You can do this by asking a generic question such as "What are the traits of effective leaders?" and then recording their responses. Alternatively, you could provide more direction and distinguish between physical and personality traits by respectively asking, "What do leaders look like?" and "What personality characteristics do leaders typically possess?" If you use the former approach, you may want to record separately the physical and personality traits the students identify. Once a reasonable number of traits are listed, you can review them and cross out physical traits such as tall, strong, and good-looking, which have not been substantiated by research. You can also note that while the leadership traits of drive, desire to lead, motivation, honesty and integrity, self-confidence, intelligence, knowledge, and flexibility are seen as desirable, researchers have not found a definitive, universal profile of leadership traits.

    C. Behavioral theories.

        1. The **behavioral perspective** assumes that leaders' behaviors are central to performance and other outcomes. (See *PowerPoint Slide 8* for Chapter 11.)

        2. Instead of dealing with underlying traits, behaviors are considered. (See *PowerPoint Slide 8* for Chapter 11.)

        3. The major behavioral theories are the following (see *PowerPoint Slide 8* for Chapter 11):

            a. Michigan leadership studies.

            b. Ohio State leadership studies.

            c. Leadership Grid.

            d. Leader-Member Exchange (LMX) theory.

        5. Two classic research programs — at the University of Michigan and Ohio State University — provide useful insights into leadership behaviors.

        6. The Michigan studies identified two basic forms of leader behaviors: employee centered and production centered. (See *PowerPoint Slide 9* for Chapter 11.)

            a. *Employee-centered supervisors* are those who place strong emphasis on their subordinates' welfare.

            b. *Production-centered supervisors* are more concerned with getting the work done.

c. Employee-centered supervisors were found to have more productive work groups than did the production-centered supervisors.

d. Employee-centered behaviors and production-centered behaviors may be conceptualized as anchoring opposite ends of a continuum.

e. Employee-centered behaviors are also known as human relations oriented behaviors and production-centered behaviors are labeled task oriented behaviors.

7. The Ohio State Studies identified two leader behavior dimensions similar to those found in the Michigan studies: consideration and initiating structure. (See **PowerPoint Slide 10** for Chapter 11.)

a. <u>**Consideration**</u> refers to the extent to which a leader is sensitive to people's feelings and tries to make things pleasant for his or her followers. A leader high in consideration is similar to the employee-centered supervisor.

b. <u>**Initiating structure**</u> refers to the extent to which a leader is concerned with defining task requirements and other aspects of the work agenda. A leader high in initiating structure is similar to the production-centered supervisor,

c. To have highly satisfied and better performing subordinates, leaders should be high on both consideration and initiating structure behaviors, a dual emphasis that is reflected in the leadership grid approach.

8. Robert Blake and Jane Mouton have developed the *leadership grid* approach wherein leadership is plotted on a 9 x 9 grid that identifies the following key styles (see **PowerPoint Slides 11** and *12* for Chapter 11):

a. 1/1 reflecting a low concern for production and a low concern for people is called "impoverished management."

b. 1/9 reflecting a low concern for production and a high concern for people is called "country club management."

c. 9/1 reflecting a high concern for production and a low concern for people is called "task management."

d. 5/5 reflecting a moderate concern for production and a moderate concern for people is called "middle of the road management."

e. 9/9 reflecting a high concern for production and a high concern for people is called "team management."

LECTURE ENHANCEMENT

Divide the class into groups of five or six students. Assign each group one of the above five leadership styles from the Blake and Mouton grid. In a six to eight minute period, have each group come up with as many examples of its assigned style as possible, giving particular attention to describing the leaders' actual behaviors. Have each group report out two or three examples to the class.

---

    9. Graen's *Leader-Member Exchange (LMX) theory* focuses on the quality of the working relationships between leaders and followers with respect to the leader's behaviors influencing the followers. (See ***PowerPoint Slide 13*** for Chapter 11.)

        a. Followers (*i.e.*, employees, are designated as part of the "in-group" or "out-group." In group-followers tend to function as assistants or advisers and have higher quality exchanges with the leader than do out-group followers.

        b. Research suggests that high-quality LMX is associated with increased follower satisfaction and productivity, decreased turnover, increased salaries, and faster promotion rates.

   10. Leader behaviors may need to be carried out in different ways in different cultures.

III.   **Study Question 2: What are situational contingency approaches to leadership?**

   A. Background on situational contingency theories.

     1. The trait and behavioral perspectives assume that leadership, by itself, has a strong impact on outcomes.

     2. Leader traits and behaviors can act in conjunction with situational contingencies to predict outcomes. (See ***PowerPoint Slide 14*** for Chapter 11.)

     3. The effects of traits are enhanced by their relevance to the leader's situational contingencies. (See ***PowerPoint Slide 14*** for Chapter 11.)

     4. The major situational contingency theories include the following (see ***PowerPoint Slide 14*** for Chapter 11):

        a. Fiedler's leadership contingency theory.

        b. Fiedler's cognitive resource theory.

        c. House's path-goal theory of leadership.

        d. Hersey and Blanchard's situational leadership model.

B. Fiedler's leadership contingency theory.

1. Fred *Fiedler's situational contingency theory* holds that group effectiveness depends on an appropriate match between a leader's style (essentially a trait measure) and the demands of the situation.

2. Fiedler considers **situational control** — the extent to which a leader can determine what his or her group is going to do — to be the primary contingency factor in determining the effectiveness of leader behavior. (See *PowerPoint Slide 15* for Chapter 11.)

3. Situational control reflects a combination of the following three variables (see *PowerPoint Slide 15* for Chapter 11):

   a. *Leader-member relations* (good versus poor), which captures membership support for the leader.

   b. *Task structure* (high versus low), which spells out the leader's task goals, procedures, and guidelines for the group.

   c. *Position power* (strong versus weak), which describes the leader's task expertise and reward or punishment authority.

4. The **least preferred co-worker (LPC) scale** measures a person's leadership style based on a description of the individual with whom he/she has been able to work least well. (See *PowerPoint Slide 16* for Chapter 11.)

5. High-LPC leaders (those describing their LPC very positively) have a relationship-motivated style, whereas low-LPC leaders (those describing their LPC negatively) have a task-motivated style. (See *PowerPoint Slide 15* for Chapter 11.)

6. *Figure 11.2* from the text shows the task-motivated leader achieves greater group effectiveness under conditions of high and low situational control, whereas the relationship-motivated leader has a more effective group under a moderate-control situation. (See *PowerPoint Slide 17* for Chapter 11.)

7. Fielder's cognitive resource theory. (See *PowerPoint Slide 18* for Chapter 11.)

   a. *Cognitive resource theory* specifies that a leader's use of directive or nondirective behavior depends on the following situational contingencies:

      (i) The leader's or subordinate group members' ability or competency.

      (ii) Stress.

      (iii) Experience.

      (iv) Group support of the leader.

       b. Leader directiveness is most helpful for performance when the leader is competent, relaxed, and supported.

  8. The biggest controversy regarding Fiedler's contingency approach concerns exactly what the LPC instrument measures. Additional controversy concerns the interpretation of the relationship between situational control and leader motivations.

  9. **Leader match training** applies Fiedler's contingency theory by training leaders to diagnose the situation to match their high or low LPC scores with situational control.

C. House's path-goal theory of leadership.

  1. Path-goal theory is rooted in the expectancy model of motivation (see Chapter 6). (See *PowerPoint Slide 19* for Chapter 11.)

  2. **House's path-goal theory of leadership** focuses on how a leader influences subordinates' perceptions of both work goals and personal goals and the links, or paths, found between these two sets of goals. (See *PowerPoint Slide 19* for Chapter 11.)

       a. Performance should improve when the leader clarifies the effort-performance (or expectancy) paths and the performance-reward (or instrumentality) paths.

  3. *Figure 11.3* in the textbook summarizes the major path-goal relationships in House's leadership approach. (See *PowerPoint Slide 20* for Chapter 11.)

       a. The figure identifies four types of leader behaviors — directive, supportive, achievement-oriented, and participative — and two categories of situational contingency variables — subordinate attributes and work-setting attributes.

          (i) **Directive leadership** spells out the what and how of subordinates' tasks. It is similar to initiating structure.

          (ii) **Supportive leadership** focuses on subordinate needs and well-being and promoting a friendly work climate. It is similar to consideration.

          (iii) **Achievement-oriented leadership** emphasizes setting challenging goals, stressing excellence in performance, and showing confidence in the group members' abilities to achieve high standards of performance.

          (iv) **Participative leadership** focuses on consulting with subordinates and seeking and taking their suggestions into account before making decisions.

       b. Leader behaviors are adjusted to complement the contingency variables in order to influence subordinate satisfaction, acceptance of the leader, and motivation for task performance.

4. Predictions of path-goal theory.

    a. Directive leadership will have a positive impact on subordinates when tasks are ambiguous and the opposite effect when tasks are clear. (See *PowerPoint Slide 21* for Chapter 11.)

    b. Supportive leadership will increase the satisfaction of subordinates who work on tasks that are highly repetitive, unpleasant, stressful, or frustrating. (See *PowerPoint Slide 21* for Chapter 11.)

    c. Achievement-oriented leadership will encourage subordinates to strive for higher performance standards and to have more confidence in their ability to meet challenging goals when subordinates are working at ambiguous, nonrepetitive tasks. (See *PowerPoint Slide 22* for Chapter 11.)

    d. Participative leadership will promote satisfaction on nonrepetitive tasks that allow for the ego involvement of subordinates. (See *PowerPoint Slide 22* for Chapter 11.)

5. While path-goal theory has been in existence for about 30 years, many aspects of it have not been tested adequately.

6. Possible applications of path-goal theory include the following:

    a. Training could be used to change leadership behavior to fit the situational contingencies.

    b. The leader could be taught to diagnose the situation and to learn how to change the contingencies.

D. Hersey and Blanchard's situational leadership model.

1. This model focuses on the situational contingency of maturity, or "readiness," of followers.

2. Readiness refers to the extent to which people have the ability and willingness to accomplish a specific task.

3. A leader should adjust his/her leadership style based on the degree of readiness of the followers.

4. *Figure 11.4* from the textbook depicts the Hersey and Blanchard model and shows how four different leadership styles are related to follower readiness. (See *PowerPoint Slide 23* for Chapter 11.)

    a. A *telling style* (*i.e.*, high emphasis on task behavior and low emphasis on relationship behavior) is best for low follower readiness (*i.e.*, unable and unwilling or insecure).

b. A *selling style* (*i.e.*, high emphasis on task behavior and high emphasis on relationship behavior) is best for moderately low follower readiness (*i.e.*, unable but willing or confident).

c. A *participating style* (*i.e.*, low emphasis on task behavior and high emphasis on relationship behavior) is best for moderately high follower readiness (*i.e.*, able but unwilling or insecure).

d. A *delegating style* (*i.e.*, low emphasis on task behavior and low emphasis on relationship behavior) is best for high follower readiness (*i.e.*, able and willing or confident).

LECTURE ENHANCEMENT

Hersey and Blanchard's four levels of follower readiness can be compared to student classifications on a high school or college sports team. Freshmen are essentially low readiness subordinates who require a telling style of leadership. Sophomores are willing to assume more responsibility, but lack some of the skills; they respond well to a selling style. Juniors are able to handle more responsibility, but may lack confidence; they respond well to a participating style. Finally, since seniors are able, willing, and confident, they respond best to the delegating style.

---

e. The Hersey-Blanchard situational leadership model requires the leader to develop the capability to diagnose situational demands and then chose and implement the appropriate leadership response.

LECTURE ENHANCEMENT

Compare and contrast the three major situational contingency theories discussed above using the following table. Point out that while Fiedler argues that its hard for leaders to change their style, the other theorists recommend that leaders should be flexible in adjusting their styles to match the situation. Therefore, the theory that works best for a particular individual may depend upon the extent to which he or she is capable of changing styles.

CONTINGENCY THEORIES

Comparison Points	Fiedler's Approach	House's Approach	Hersey and Blanchard's Approach
Concern	Situational Control	Situational Attributes	Situational Attributes
Diagnostic Focus	Task Structure, Position Power, Leader-member Relations	Subordinate Characteristics, Task Demands	Follower Readiness
Leadership Styles	Task-motivated, Relationship-motivated	Directive, Supportive, Participative, Achievement-Oriented	Telling, Selling, Participating, Delegating
Managerial Implications	Effective leader matches style with situation	Effective leader chooses style to complement situational attributes	Effective leader chooses style to complement situational attributes

---

E. Substitutes for leadership.

1. The substitutes for leadership theory argues that sometimes hierarchical leadership makes essentially no difference.

2. This approach contends that certain individual, job, and organizational variables can either serve as **substitutes for leadership** or neutralize a leader's impact on subordinates. Some examples of these variables are shown in *Figure 11.5* of the textbook. (See *PowerPoint Slide 24* for Chapter 11.)

IV. **Study Question 3: What are attributional approaches to leadership?**

A. Background on attributional approaches to leadership. (See *PowerPoint Slide 25* for Chapter 11.)

1. The traditional leadership theories discussed so far have all assumed that leadership and its substantive effects can be identified and measured objectively.

2. Attribution theory provides a competing perspective to that of traditional leadership theory.

3. *Attribution theory* suggests that leadership is influenced by attempts to understand causes of behavior and to assess responsibilities for behavior.

B. Leadership prototypes. (See *PowerPoint Slide 26* for Chapter 11.)

1. A **leadership prototype** refers to the view that people have an image in their minds of what a model leader should look like.

2. These implicit theories or prototypes usually consist of a mix of specific and more general characteristics. For example, a prototype of a bank president would differ in many ways from that of a high-ranking military officer.

3. Leadership prototypes differ across countries and national cultures.

4. The closer the behavior of a leader is to the implicit theories of his or her followers, the more favorable the leader's relations and key outcomes tend to be.

C. Exaggeration of the leadership difference. (See *PowerPoint Slide 27* for Chapter 11.)

1. Top leaders of organizations have little impact on profits and effectiveness compared to environmental and industry forces.

2. Much of the impact of top leaders is symbolic. This occurs especially when performance is either extremely high or extremely low or when the situation is such that many people could have been responsible for the performance

3. The **romance of leadership** refers to people attributing romantic, almost magical, qualities to leadership.

V. **Study Question 4: What are some emerging leadership perspectives and why are they especially important in today's organizations?**

A. Background on emerging leadership perspectives.

1. The **new leadership** emphasizes charismatic and transformational approaches and various aspects of vision related to them, and the leadership of self-directing work teams.

2. The new leadership is considered especially important in changing and transforming individuals and organizations with a commitment to high performance.

B. Charismatic approaches.

1. <u>**Charismatic leaders**</u> are those who, by force of their personal abilities, are capable of having a profound and extraordinary effect on followers. (See *PowerPoint Slide 28* for Chapter 11.)

2. Charismatic leaders are high in the need for power and have high feelings of self-efficacy and conviction in the moral rightness of their beliefs. (See *PowerPoint Slide 28* for Chapter 11.)

3. The negative (or dark) side of charismatic leadership emphasizes personalized power that serves the leader's personal interests, whereas the positive (or bright) side emphasizes socialized power that tends to empower the followers. (See *PowerPoint Slide 29* for Chapter 11.)

4. Conger and Kanungo's three-stage charismatic leadership model.

    a. The three stages are as follows (see *PowerPoint Slide 30* for Chapter 11):

        (i)   Stage 1: the leader critically evaluates the status quo.

        (ii) Stage 2: the leader formulates and articulates the goals along with an idealized future vision.

        (iii) Stage 3: the leader shows how these goals and vision can be achieved.

    b. If leaders use behaviors such as vision articulation, environmental sensitivity, and unconventional behavior, rather than maintaining the status quo, followers will attribute charismatic leadership to them.

5. *Figure 11.6* from the textbook describes the traits and behaviors of "distant charismatics" (*i.e.*, where leaders seldom, if ever, have close contact with followers) and "close charismatics" (*i.e.*, where leaders have direct contact with followers). (See *PowerPoint Slide 31* for Chapter 11.)

C. Transformational versus transactional approaches.

1. <u>**Transactional leadership**</u> involves leader-follower exchanges necessary for achieving routine performance agreed upon between leaders and followers. (See *PowerPoint Slide 32* for Chapter 11.)

2. Dimensions of transactional leadership include contingent rewards, active management by exception, passive management by exception, and laissez-faire management. (See *PowerPoint Slide 32* for Chapter 11.)

    a. *Contingent rewards* provide various kinds of rewards in exchange for mutually agreed upon goal accomplishment.

    b. *Active management by exception* involves watching for deviation from rules and standards and taking corrective action.

      c. *Passive management by exception* involves intervening only if standards are not met.

      d. *Laissez-faire management* involves abdicating responsibilities and avoiding decisions.

  3. **Transformational leadership** occurs when leaders broaden and elevate their followers' interests, when they generate awareness and acceptance of the group's purposes and mission, and when they stir followers to look beyond their own interests for the good of others. (See ***PowerPoint Slide 33*** for Chapter 11.)

  4. Dimensions of transformational leadership include charisma, inspiration, intellectual stimulation, and individualized consideration. (See ***PowerPoint Slide 33*** for Chapter 11.)

      a. *Charisma* provides vision and a sense of mission, and it instills pride, along with follower respect and trust.

      b. *Inspiration* communicates high expectations, uses symbols to focus efforts, and expresses important purposes in simple ways.

      c. *Intellectual stimulation* promotes intelligence, rationality, and careful problem solving.

      d. *Individualized consideration* provides personal attention, treats each employee individually, and coaches and advises.

  5. Transformational leadership is likely to be strongest at the top management level, where there is the greatest opportunity for proposing and communicating a vision., but it can be found throughout an organization.

D. Leadership in self-managing work teams.

  1. The duties of an outside leader of a self-managing team are quite different from the duties of outside leaders that are traditional, formally designated first-line supervisors. A key aspect of their jobs is to provide resources or liaisons with other units but without the trappings of authority associated with traditional first-line supervisors. (See ***PowerPoint Slide 34*** for Chapter 11.)

  2. Internal leadership is a process that facilitates team performance.

  3. Conditions for creating and maintaining team performance include the following (see ***PowerPoint Slide 34*** for Chapter 11):

      a. Efficient, goal-directed effort.

      b. Adequate resources.

      c. Competent, motivated performance.

        d. A productive, supportive climate.

        e. Commitment to continuous improvement and adaptation.

    4. The conditions for creating and maintaining team performance often encourage member self-leadership activities, where key leadership aspects are carried out with little or no aspects from an outside leader or sometimes even an inside leader.

E. Emerging leadership issues.

    1. Can people be trained in the new leadership? (See *PowerPoint Slide 35* for Chapter 11.)

        a. People can be trained to adopt new leadership approaches.

        b. Leaders can devise improvement programs to address their weaknesses and work with trainers to develop their leadership skills.

        c. Leaders can be trained in charismatic skills.

    2. Is new leadership always good? (See *PowerPoint Slide 36* for Chapter 11.)

        a. New leadership is not always good.

        b. Dark-side charismatics can have negative effects on the population of followers.

        c. New leadership is not always needed; sometimes emphasis on a vision diverts energy from more important day-to-day activities.

        d. New leadership by itself is not sufficient; new leadership needs to be used in conjunction with traditional leadership.

        e. New leadership is not important only at the top; it applies at all levels of organizational leadership.

LECTURE ENHANCEMENT

Consider asking your students the following set of questions: Would you rather work for a boss or a leader? Would you rather be a boss or a leader? Do you think that there is a difference? Consider the following list of contrasts between bosses and leaders from the preface to *The Quality School* by William Glasser, M.D. (The book is about putting Deming's quality principles into public schools.)

Bosses	**Leaders**
A boss drives.	A leader leads.
A boss relies on authority.	A leader relies on cooperation.
A boss says, "I."	A leader says, "We."
A boss creates fear.	A leader creates confidence.
A boss knows how.	A leader shows how.
A boss creates resentment.	A leader creates enthusiasm.
A boss fixes blame.	A leader fixes mistakes.
A boss makes work drudgery.	A leader makes work interesting

VI.   **Study summary for Chapter 11.**

A. Point out to the students that the text's "Chapter 11 Study Guide" recaps the key theories, concepts, and ideas in the chapter in relation to the appropriate study questions.

CHAPTER STUDY GUIDE

Study Question 1: What is leadership and how does it differ from management?

- Leadership is a special case of interpersonal influence that gets an individual or group to do what the leader wants done.
- Leadership and management differ in that management is designed to promote stability or to make the organization run smoothly, whereas the role of leadership is to promote adaptive change.
- Trait, or great person, approaches argue that leader traits have a major impact on differentiating between leaders and nonleaders and predicting leadership outcomes.
- Traits are considered relatively innate and hard to change.
- Similar to trait approaches, behavior theories argue that leader behaviors have a major impact on outcomes.
- The Michigan, Ohio State, and Graen's leader-member exchange (LMX) approaches are particularly important leader behavior theories.
- Leader behavior theories are especially suitable for leadership training.

Study Question 2: What are situational contingency approaches to leadership?

- Leader situational contingency approaches argue that leadership, in combination with various situational contingency variables, can have a major impact on outcomes.
- The effects of traits are enhanced to the extent of their relevance to the situational contingencies faced by the leader.
- Strong or weak situational contingencies influence the impact of leadership traits.
- Fiedler's contingency theory, House's path-goal theory, Hersey and Blanchard's situational leadership theory, and Kerr and Jerimer's substitutes for leadership theory are particularly important, specific situational contingency approaches.
- Sometimes, as in the case of the substitutes for leadership approach, the role of situational contingencies replaces that of leadership, so that leadership has little or no impact in itself.

Study Question 3: What are attributional approaches to leadership?

- Attribution theory extends traditional leadership approaches by recognizing that substantive effects cannot always be objectively identified and measured.
- Leaders form attributions about why their employees perform well or poorly and respond accordingly.
- Leaders and followers often infer that there is good leadership when their group performs well.
- Leaders and followers often have in mind a good leader prototype; compare the leader against such a prototype; and conclude that the closer the fit, the better the leadership.
- Some contend that leadership makes no real difference and is largely symbolic; others, following the "romance of leadership" notion, embrace the symbolic emphasis and attribute almost magical qualities to leadership.

Study Question 4: What are emerging leadership perspectives and why are they especially important in today's organizations?

- Some emerging leadership perspectives consist of charismatic, transformational, and visionary leadership as well as leadership of self-directing work teams.
- Charismatic, transformational, and visionary attributions help move followers to achieve goals that transcend their own self-interests and help transform the organization.
- Particularly important emerging leadership approaches are Bass's transformational theory and House's and Conger and Kanungo's charismatic theories.
- Transformational approaches are broader than charismatic ones and often include charisma as one of their dimensions.
- Leadership in high-performance work teams, particularly involved in today's organizations, often changes the external leadership role by making it a facilitative one so as to encourage team members to lead themselves.
- Behaviors of team coordinators are assumed to work best when reinforced by leaders who provide empowerment and stress various aspects of the new leadership.
- The new leadership, in general, is important because it goes beyond traditional leadership in facilitating change in the increasingly fast-moving workplace.

KEY TERMS

Achievement-oriented leadership: in House's leadership model, this refers to leader behavior that emphasizes setting challenging goals, stressing excellence in performance, and showing confidence in the group members' ability to achieve high standards of performance.

Behavioral perspective: assumes that leaders behaviors are central to performance and other outcomes.

Charismatic leaders: leaders who, by force of their personal abilities, are capable of having a profound and extraordinary effect on followers.

Consideration: the extent to which a leader is sensitive to people's feelings and tries to make things pleasant for his or her followers.

Directive leadership: in House's leadership model, this refers to leader behavior that spells out the what and how of subordinates' tasks.

House's path-goal theory of leadership: focuses on how a leader influences subordinates' perceptions of both work goals and personal goals and the links, or paths, found between these two sets of goals.

Initiating structure: the extent to which a leader is concerned with defining task requirements and other aspects of the work agenda.

Leader match training: applies Fiedler's contingency theory by training leaders to diagnose the situation to match their high or low LPC scores with situational control.

Leadership: a special case of interpersonal influence that gets an individual or group to do what the leader or manager wants done.

Leadership prototype: the view that people have an image in their minds of what a model leader should look like.

Least preferred co-worker (LPC) scale: in Fiedler's contingency theory, the LPC measures a person's leadership style based on a description of the individual with whom he/she has been able to work least well.

New leadership: emphasizes charismatic and transformational approaches and various aspects of vision related to them, and the leadership of self-directing work teams.

Participative leadership: in House's leadership model, this refers to leader behavior that focuses on consulting with subordinates and seeking and taking their suggestions into account before making decisions.

Romance of leadership: refers to people attributing romantic, almost magical, qualities to leadership.

Situational control: the extent to which a leader can determine what his or her group is going to do.

Substitutes for leadership: an approach contending that certain individual, job, and organizational variables can either substitute for or neutralize a leader's impact on subordinates.

Supportive leadership: in House's leadership model, this refers to leader behavior that focuses on subordinate needs and well-being and promoting a friendly work climate.

Trait perspectives: assume that traits play a central role in differentiating between leaders and nonleaders or in predicting leader or organizational outcomes.

Transactional leadership: involves leader-follower exchanges necessary for achieving routine performance agreed upon between leaders and followers.

Transformational leadership: occurs when leaders broaden and elevate their followers' interests, when they generate awareness and acceptance of the group's purposes and mission, and when they stir followers to look beyond their own interests for the good of others.

Chapter 12
POWER AND POLITICS

STUDY QUESTIONS

1.	What are power and influence in an organization?
2.	How are power, obedience, and formal authority intertwined in an organization?
3.	What is empowerment?
4.	What is organizational politics?

LEARNING OBJECTIVES

After completing this chapter students should be able to:

1.	Define "power" in an organizational context, and describe the different types of position power and personal power.
2.	Explain how people build position power and personal power in organizations.
3.	Describe how power is developed through the use of information and influence techniques.
4.	Discuss the basic nature and implications of Milgram's obedience experiments.
5.	Describe the acceptance theory of authority and its relationship to the zone of indifference.
6.	Explain the concept of empowerment and describe how power can be changed or expanded.
7.	Describe the two different traditions in organizational politics.
8.	Discuss the nature and implications of political interpretation, political forecasting, subunit power, and politics and corporate strategy.
9.	Describe the mechanisms that individuals can employ to protect themselves from organizational politics.
10.	Describe the relationship between politics and organizational governance from the perspectives of agency theory, resource dependency theory, and ethics.

MATERIAL IN *THE OB SKILLS WORKBOOK* SUPPORTING THE CHAPTER

Case for Critical Thinking	Case 12: Power or Empowerment at GM?
Experiential Exercises	Exercise 26: Interview a Leader
	Exercise 29: My Best Manager: Revisited
	Exercise 32: Power Circle Exercise
Self-Assessments	Assessment 15: Empowering Others
	Assessment 16: Machiavellianism
	Assessment 20: Conflict Management Styles

CHAPTER OVERVIEW

This chapter focuses on the topics of power and politics in organizations. Most of the chapter focuses on power and it implications. The chapter begins by defining power, and describing the difference between position power (*i.e.*, reward, coercive, legitimate, process, information, and representative) and personal power (*i.e.*, expert, rational persuasion, and referent). Ways to build position power and personal power as well as using information and influence techniques are explained. The next section of the chapter covers power, formal authority, and obedience. The Milgram experiments on obedience are summarized and their implications for human behavior are outlined. Barnard's acceptance theory of authority and the concept of zone of indifference in people's reactions to authoritative directives complete this section of the chapter. This next part of the chapter focuses on empowerment, identifying ways of changing position power and expanding the zone of indifference. Empowerment conceives of power as an expanding resource rather than as a limited resource.

In the final section of the chapter, the related topic of organizational politics is discussed. Two traditions of organizational politics —the Machiavellian tradition and the creative compromise tradition — are introduced and discussed. Issues of political interpretation, political forecasting, subunit power, and politics and corporate strategy are examined. Organizational politics is depicted as a double-edged sword, and as being neither inherently good nor bad. The self-protection mechanisms that people use to shield themselves from politics are discussed; these mechanisms include avoidance, redirecting responsibility, and defending turf. This section of the chapter concludes with a discussion of politics and organizational governance that draws heavily on agency theory and resource dependency theory and emphasizes the role of ethics in organizational governance.

CHAPTER OUTLINE

I.   **Study Question 1: What are power and influence in an organization?**
   A. Position power
   B. Personal power
   C. Building influence

II. **Study Question 2: How are power, obedience, and formal authority intertwined in an organization?**
   A. Obedience
   B. Acceptance of authority
   C. Zone of indifference

III. **Study Question 3: What is empowerment?**
   A. Keys to empowerment
   B. Power as an expanding pie

IV. **Study Question 4: What is organizational politics?**
   A. The traditions of organizational politics
   B. The politics of self-protection
   C. Politics and governance

CHAPTER LECTURE NOTES

I. **Introduction to the Chapter 12 Lecture.**

A. Study questions for Chapter 12. (See *PowerPoint Slide 2* for Chapter 12.)

1. What are power and influence in an organization?

2. How are power, obedience, and formal authority intertwined in an organization?

3. What is empowerment?

4. What is organizational politics?

B. The lecture material for Chapter 12 is organized around the study questions.

1. Point out to the students that the text's "Chapter At A Glance" identifies the key topics contained in the chapter and links them to the appropriate study questions.

C. The chapter opens with a brief description of the how Edward J. Zore, 16th president of Northwestern Mutual, views the company's operations in the context of fairness and the avoidance of conflict.

II. **Study Question 1: What are power and influence in an organization?**

A. Background on power and influence. (See *PowerPoint Slide 3* for Chapter 12.)

1. **Power** is the ability to get someone to do something you want done or the ability to make things happen or get things done the way you want.

2. **Influence** is expressed by others' behavioral response to the exercise of power.

B. Position power.

1. Position power derives from an individual's position in the organizational hierarchy.

2. Six bases of power are associated with a manager's position in the organization. These are reward, coercive, legitimate, process, information, and representative power. (See *PowerPoint Slide 4* for Chapter 12.)

3. **Reward power** is the extent to which a manager can use extrinsic and intrinsic rewards to control other people. (See *PowerPoint Slide 5* for Chapter 12.)

4. **Coercive power** is the extent to which a manager can deny desired rewards and administer punishment to control other people. (See *PowerPoint Slide 5* for Chapter 12.)

5. <u>**Legitimate power**</u>, or formal hierarchical authority, is the extent to which a manager can use subordinates' internalized values or beliefs that the boss has the "right of command" to control other people. (See *PowerPoint Slide 6* for Chapter 12.)

6. <u>**Process power**</u> is the control over methods of production and analysis that a manager has due to being in a position to influence how inputs are transformed into outputs. (See *PowerPoint Slide 6* for Chapter 12.)

7. <u>**Information power**</u> is the access to and/or control of information. (See *PowerPoint Slide 7* for Chapter 12.)

8. <u>**Representative power**</u> is the formal right conferred by the firm to speak for a potentially important group composed of individuals across departments or outside the firm. (See *PowerPoint Slide 7* for Chapter 12.)

9. Legitimacy in most organizations reflects an implicit moral and technical order.

C. Personal power.

1. Personal power resides in the individual and is independent of that individual's position. (See *PowerPoint Slide 8* for Chapter 12.)

2. Three bases of personal power are expertise, rational persuasion, and reference. (See *PowerPoint Slide 8* for Chapter 12.)

3. <u>**Expert power**</u> is the ability to control another's behavior through the possession of knowledge, experience, or judgment that the other person does not have but needs. (See *PowerPoint Slide 9* for Chapter 12.)

4. <u>**Rational persuasion**</u> is the ability to control another's behavior because through an individual's efforts the other person accepts the desirability of an offered goal and a reasonable way of achieving it. (See *PowerPoint Slide 9* for Chapter 12.)

   a. Rational persuasion rests on trust.

   b. To develop trust, a manager should, at a minimum, do the following:

      (i) Always honor implied and explicit social contracts.

      (ii) Seek to prevent, avoid, and rectify harm to others.

      (iii) Respect the unique needs of others.

5. <u>**Referent power**</u> is the ability to control another's behavior because the person wants to identify with the power source. (See *PowerPoint Slide 10* for Chapter 12.)

LECTURE ENHANCEMENT

Ask the students if they have encountered any leaders who have had a truly significant impact on their lives. Have the students describe the types of power these leaders used and the impacts that were achieved.

D. Building influence.

1. A considerable portion of any manager's time is directed toward power-oriented behavior (*i.e.*, action that is directed primarily at developing or using relationships in which other people are to some degree willing to defer to one's wishes).

2. *Figure 12.1* from the textbook shows three basic dimensions of managerial power and influence — downward, upward, and lateral — and how each is achieved. (See *PowerPoint Slide 11* for Chapter 12.)

    a. Personal power is used to achieve upward influence.

    b. Personal power is used to achieve lateral influence.

    c. Position power and personal power are used to achieve downward influence.

3. The effective manager is one who succeeds in building and maintaining high levels of both position and personal power.

4. Building position power. (See *PowerPoint Slide 12* for Chapter 12.)

    a. Position power can be enhanced when:

        (i)   Managers are able to demonstrate to others that their work units are highly relevant to organizational goals and are able to respond to urgent organizational needs.

        (ii) When managers attempt to increase the relevance of their tasks and those of their unit to the organization.

    b. Managers may attempt to build position power by defining tasks so that they are difficult to evaluate; in turn this will have a negative effect on the organization:

5. Building personal power.

    a. Three personal characteristics — expertise, political savvy, and likeability — have special potential for enhancing personal power in an organization. (See *PowerPoint Slide 13* for Chapter 12.)

          (i) *Building expertise* — gaining additional expertise by advanced training and education, participation in professional associations, and involvement in the early stages of projects.

          (ii) *Political savvy* — learning better ways to negotiate, persuade individuals, and understand the goals and means people are most willing to accept.

          (iii)*Likability* — having or developing personal characteristics that create personal attraction in relationships with other people.

    b. From a purely analytical standpoint, most sources of power can be traced to position power or personal power.

6. Most managers attempt to increase the visibility of their job performance by doing the following (see ***PowerPoint Slide 14*** for Chapter 12):

    a. Expanding the number of contacts they have with senior people.

    b. Making oral presentations of written work.

    c. Participating in problem-solving task forces.

    d. Sending out notices of accomplishment.

    e. Generally seeking additional opportunities to increase personal name recognition.

7. Expert power is often relational and embedded within the organizational context.

8. Controlling decision premises. (See ***PowerPoint Slide 15*** for Chapter 12.)

    a. Executives also attempt to control, or at least influence, decision premises.

    b. A decision premise is a basis for defining the problem and for selecting among alternatives.

    c. Executives who want to increase their power often make their goals and needs clear, and bargain effectively to show that their preferred goals and needs are best.

9. The most common techniques for exercising relational influence include the following (see ***PowerPoint Slide 16*** for Chapter 12):

    a. *Reason* — using facts and data to support a logical argument.

    b. *Friendliness* — using flattery, goodwill, and favorable impressions.

    c. *Coalition* — using relationships with other people for support.

      d. *Bargaining* — using the exchange of benefits as a basis for negotiation.

      e. *Assertiveness* — using a direct and forceful personal approach.

      f. *Higher authority* — gaining higher-level support for one's requests.

      g. *Sanctions* — using organizationally derived rewards and punishments.

10. Truly effective managers are able to influence their bosses as well as their subordinates, but little empirical research is available to document how to best exercise upward influence.

III.   **Study Question 2: How are power, obedience, and formal authority intertwined in an organization?**

A. Two important practical issues in the exercise of power and formal authority. (See **PowerPoint Slide 17** for Chapter 12.)

   1. Why should subordinates respond to a manager's authority (or "right to command")?

   2. Given that subordinates are willing to obey, what determines the limits of obedience?

B. Obedience.

   1. The Milgram experiments.

      a. Milgram designed a series of experiments to determine the extent to which people obey the commands of an authority figure, even if they believe they are endangering the life of another person. (See **PowerPoint Slide 18** for Chapter 12.)

      b. Subjects were falsely told that the purpose of the experiment was to determine the effects of punishment on learning of word pairs.

      c. Subjects were instructed to give successively higher levels of electric shocks to people who missed the word pairs. Of course, the shocks were fictitious since the "learner" was an experimental confederate.

      d. The experimental results revealed that 65 percent of the subjects subjected the "learner" to the maximum level of shock and the remaining 35 percent refused to obey the experimenter at various intermediate points. (See **PowerPoint Slide 18** for Chapter 12.)

      e. Subsequent experimentation showed that the subject's tendencies toward compliance were somewhat reduced when:

(i) Experimentation took place in a rundown office rather than a university lab.

(ii) The victim was closer.

(iii) The experimenter was farther away.

(iv) The experimental subject could observe other subjects.

f. The basic conclusion of Milgram's studies is there is a tendency for individuals to comply with and be obedient to authority. (See ***PowerPoint Slide 18*** for Chapter 12.)

LECTURE ENHANCEMENT

A discussion of the Milgram experiments, along with a classroom exercise that assesses some of the same human traits (*i.e.*, obedience to authority) studied by Milgram, is available at http://www.unc.edu/~emgallag/teachconf/milgramexp.html.

C. Acceptance of authority.

1. Chester Barnard's acceptance theory of authority provides insight into why so many organizations appear to drift into apparent chaos even though the tendency to follow instructions is great and defiance is rare.

2. Barnard argued that subordinates accepted or followed a directive from the boss only under special circumstances, all four of which must be met.

3. The four circumstances are the following (see ***PowerPoint Slide 19*** for Chapter 12):

    a. The subordinate can and must understand the directive.

    b. The subordinate must feel mentally and physically capable of carrying out the directive.

    c. The subordinate must believe that the directive is not inconsistent with the purpose of the organization.

    d. The subordinate must believe that the directive is not inconsistent with his or her personal interests.

D. Zone of indifference.

1. In exchange for certain inducements, subordinates recognize the authority of the organization and its managers to direct their behavior in certain ways (*i.e.*, there is a "zone of indifference" in which directives are obeyed). (See ***PowerPoint Slide 20*** for Chapter 12.)

2. A **zone of indifference** is the range of authoritative requests to which a subordinate is willing to respond without subjecting the directives to critical evaluation or judgment. (See ***PowerPoint Slide 20*** for Chapter 12.)

3. *Figure 12.2* from the textbook provides examples of directives that would likely fall inside and outside of a typical employee's zone of indifference. (See ***PowerPoint Slide 21*** for Chapter 12.)

4. Research on ethical managerial behavior shows that supervisors can become sources of pressure for subordinates to do such things as support incorrect viewpoints, sign false documents, overlook the supervisor's wrongdoing, and do business with the supervisor's friends.

IV. **Study Question 3: What is empowerment?**

A. Background on empowerment.

1. **Empowerment** is the process by which managers help others to acquire and use the power needed to make decisions affecting themselves and their work. (See ***PowerPoint Slide 22*** for Chapter 12.)

2. The concept of empowerment is part of the sweeping change being witnessed in today's corporations.

3. Empowerment provides the foundation for self-managing work teams and other employee involvement groups. (See ***PowerPoint Slide 22*** for Chapter 12.)

B. Keys to empowerment.

1. *Empowerment* emphasizes the ability to make things happen. Power is still relational, but in terms of problems and opportunities, not individuals. (See ***PowerPoint Slide 22*** for Chapter 12.)

2. Changing position power. (See ***PowerPoint Slide 23*** for Chapter 12.)

   a. When an organization attempts to move power down the hierarchy, it must also alter the existing pattern of position power.

   b. Changing this pattern raises the following important questions:

      (i) Can "empowered" individuals give rewards and sanctions based on task accomplishment?

      (ii) Has their new right to act been legitimized with formal authority?

3. Expanding the zone of indifference. (See *PowerPoint Slide 24* for Chapter 12.)

   a. When embarking on an empowerment program, management needs to recognize the current zone of indifference and systematically move to expand it.

   b. Management should show precisely how empowerment will benefit the individuals involved and provide the inducement needed to expand the zone of indifference.

LECTURE ENHANCEMENT

Max DePree, the chairperson of Herman Miller, Inc., a Michigan-based office furniture maker provides an excellent example of empowering workers through the practice of leadership. In his book, *Leadership is an Art*, DePree, who is the son of the firm's founder, outlines a leadership style based on respect for others and diversity. Respect of this nature ensures that the organization can benefit from everyone's contributions. DePree also emphasizes the difference between "hierarchical" and "roving" leadership. His point? Often it is the roving, or informal leader, who really counts. What does the hierarchical leader do? If he/she is smart, this person — or manager — "supports" the roving leader and helps him or her lead. DePree says: "Roving leadership is the expression of the ability of hierarchical leaders to permit others to share ownership of problems — to take possession of the situation."

An example of how "roving," "lateral," and "bottom-up" leadership works at Herman Miller is provided by research manager Bill Foley's decision to forbid the use of rosewood and Honduran mahogany in one of the firm's hallmark products — the $2,000 plus Eames chair, because use of these woods contributed to the destruction of the rainforests. While his decision lead to considerable debate, it ultimately was supported. Foley claims the company's strong ethics and commitment to participatory management helped him feel empowered to make the decision. Herman Miller's success at capitalizing on these strengths is apparent from its ranking as one of *Fortune* magazine's "most admired" American corporations.

C. Power as an expanding pie. (See *PowerPoint Slides 25* and *26* for Chapter 12.)

   1. Along with empowerment, employees need to be trained to expand their power and their new influence potential.

   2. The key is to change the concept of power within the organization from a view that stresses power over others to one that emphasizes the use of power to get things done.

   3. A clearer definition of roles and responsibilities may help managers empower others.

   4. Empowerment means that all mangers need to emphasize different ways of exercising influence.

5. Special support may be needed for individuals so that they become comfortable in developing their own power over events and activities.

V.   Study Question 4: What is organizational politics?

A. The traditions of organizational politics.

1. There are two quite different traditions in the analysis of organizational politics: one that focuses on politics in terms of self-interest and the use of nonsanctioned means, and the other that treats politics as a necessary function resulting from differences in the self-interests of individuals.

2. The tradition of self-interest and the use of nonsanctioned means. (See *PowerPoint Slide 27* for Chapter 12.)

   a. This tradition builds on the philosophy outlined in Machiavelli's *The Prince*.

   b. In this tradition, **organizational politics** is the management of influence to obtain ends not sanctioned by the organization or to obtain sanctioned ends through nonsanctioned influence means.

3. The tradition that treats politics as a necessary function resulting from differences in the self-interests of individuals. (See *PowerPoint Slide 28* for Chapter 12.)

   a. In this tradition, **organizational politics** is viewed as the art of creative compromise among competing interests.

   b. Politics arise because individuals and organizations need to develop compromises, avoid confrontation, and live together.

   c. Organizational politics involves the use of power to develop socially acceptable means and ends that balance individual and collective interests.

4. Political interpretation.

   a. The two different traditions of organizational politics are reflected in the ways executives describe their effects on managers and their organizations.

   b. In one survey, 53 percent of those interviewed indicated that organizational politics enhanced the achievement of organizational goals and survival, while 44 percent suggested that it distracted individuals from organizational goals.

   c. In this same survey, 60 percent of respondents suggested that organizational politics was good for career advancement, whereas 39 percent reported that it led to a loss of power, position, and credibility.

   d. Organizational politics serve important functions, including overcoming personnel inadequacies, coping with change, and substituting for formal authority.

    e.   Use of the following political skills can lower executive stress:

        (i)   The ability to use practical intelligence (as opposed to analytical and creative intelligence).

        (ii) The ability to be calculating and shrewd about social connections.

        (iii) The ability to inspire trust and confidence.

        (iv) The ability to deal with individuals having a wide variety of backgrounds, styles, and personalities.

5.   Political forecasting.

    a.   Managers may gain a better understanding of political behavior to forecast future actions by placing themselves in the position of other persons involved in critical decisions or events.

    b.   *Figure 12.3* from the textbook provides an example of using a payoff matrix for political forecasting. (See *PowerPoint Slide 29* for Chapter 12.)

6.   Subunit power.

    a.   Line units are typically more powerful than are staff groups. (See *PowerPoint Slide 30* for Chapter 12.)

    b.   Units toward the top of the organizational hierarchy are often more powerful than those toward the bottom. (See *PowerPoint Slide 30* for Chapter 12.)

    c.   Power differentials are not as pronounced among units at or near the same level in an organization. (See *PowerPoint Slide 30* for Chapter 12.)

    d.   Political actions for influencing lateral, intergroup relationships include the following (see *PowerPoint Slide 31* for Chapter 12):

        (i)   *Workflow linkages* — involve contacts with units that precede or follow in a sequential production chain.

        (ii) *Service linkages* — involve contacts with units established to help with problems.

        (iii) *Advisory linkages* — involve formal staff units having special expertise.

        (iv) *Auditing linkages* — involve units that have the right to evaluate the actions of others after action has been taken.

        (v) *Approval linkages* — involve units whose approval must be obtained before action may be taken.

7. Politics and corporate strategy.

   a. In corporations there is a growing awareness of the importance of political strategy.

   b. Important aspects of corporate political strategy include the following (see *PowerPoint Slide 32* for Chapter 12):

      (i) The absence of a political strategy can be damaging to a corporation.

      (ii) Corporate political strategy should be targeted toward turning the government from a regulator against industry to a protector of it.

      (iii) Decisions need to be made about when and how to get involved in the public policy processes.

B. The politics of self-protection.

LECTURE ENHANCEMENT

Ask the students to provide examples of how they have protected themselves in interpersonal, group, and organizational settings. Relate these examples to the following lecture material on the politics of self-protection.

---

1. While organizational politics may be helpful to the organization as a whole, it is probably more commonly known and better understood in terms of self-protection.

2. Individuals can utilize three common strategies to protect themselves: avoiding action and risk taking, redirecting accountability and responsibility, or defending their turf.

3. Avoidance. (See *PowerPoint Slide 33* for Chapter 12.)

   a. Avoidance is quite common in controversial areas where the employee must risk being wrong or where actions may yield a sanction.

   b. Common avoidance approaches are working to the rules, playing dumb, depersonalization, and routine stalling.

4. Redirecting responsibility.

   a. Politically sensitive individuals will also protect themselves from accepting blame for the negative consequences of their actions.

   b. Common approaches for redirecting responsibility include the following (see *PowerPoint Slide 34* for Chapter 12):

(i) Passing the buck — defining the task in such a way that it becomes someone else's formal responsibility.

(ii) Buffing (or rigorous documentation) — taking action only when all the paperwork is in place and it is clear that they are merely following procedure.

(iii) Preparing a blind memo — taking action but drafting a memo that explains an objection to the implemented action.

(iv) Rewriting history — claiming to be an early supporter of something that turns out to be successful, or one who had initial reservations if a programs fails.

(v) Redirecting techniques for those who are really devious.

    1. Scapegoating — blaming the problem on someone or some group that has difficulty engaging in self-defense.

    2. Blaming the problem on uncontrollable events.

    3. Escalating commitment to a losing course of action.

5. Defending turf. (See *PowerPoint Slide 35* for Chapter 12.)

    a. Defending turf is a time-honored tradition in most large organizations.

    b. Defending turf results when:

        (i) Managers seek to increase their power by expanding the jobs their groups perform.

        (ii) Competing interests exist among various departments and groups.

C. Politics and governance.

1. Agency theory.

    a. An important power problem in today's modern corporation arises from the separation of owners and managers. (See *PowerPoint Slide 36* for Chapter 12.)

    b. **Agency theory** reflects the notion that managers are "agents" of the owners and suggests that public corporation can function effectively even though its managers are self-interested and do not automatically bear the full consequences of their managerial actions. (See *PowerPoint Slide 36* for Chapter 12.)

    c. The key arguments of agency theory are the following (see ***PowerPoint Slide 37*** for Chapter 12):

        (i) By protecting stockholder interests, all the interests of society are served.

        (ii) Stockholders have a clear interest in greater returns.

        (iii) Managers are self-interested and unwilling to sacrifice these self-interests for others (particularly stockholders) and must be controlled.

    d. Types of controls that are instituted for agents include the following (see ***PowerPoint Slide 38*** for Chapter 12):

        (i) Pay plan incentives that align the interests of management and stockholders.

        (ii) The establishment of a strong, independent board of directors.

        (iii) Stockholders with a large stake in the firm taking an active role on the board.

2. Resource dependencies.

    a. Executive behavior can sometimes be explained in terms of *resource dependencies* — the firm's need for resources that are controlled by others. (See ***PowerPoint Slide 39*** for Chapter 12.)

    b. The resource dependence of an organization increases as (see ***PowerPoint Slide 39*** for Chapter 12):

        (i) Needed resources become more scarce.

        (ii) Outsiders have more control over needed resources.

        (iii) There are fewer substitutes for a particular type of resource controlled by a limited number of outsiders.

    c. One political role of the chief executive is to develop workable compromises among the competing resource dependencies facing the organization.

    d. Strategies that alter the firm's degree of resource dependence include the following:

        (i) Mergers and acquisitions to exercise control over key resources.

        (ii) Changing the "rules of the game" to secure protection from powerful outsiders.

      e.   International competition has narrowed the range of options for chief executives.

   3.   Organizational governance.

      a.   **<u>Organizational governance</u>** refers to the pattern of authority, influence, and acceptable managerial behavior established at the top of an organization. (See ***PowerPoint Slide 40*** for Chapter 12.)

      b.   Organizational governance establishes what is important, how issues will be defined, who should and should not be involved in key choices, and the boundaries for acceptable implementation. (See ***PowerPoint Slide 40*** for Chapter 12.)

      c.   Analysis of organizational governance builds on resource dependence and suggests that a dominant coalition comprised of powerful organizational actors is a key to understanding a firm's governance.

         (i)   Through the governance system, the dominant coalition attempts to define organizational reality.

      d.   While organizational governance was an internal and rather private matter in the past, it is now becoming more public and openly controversial.

LECTURE ENHANCEMENT

An excellent site on corporate governance is available online at http://www.corpgov.net/. The site explains compelling issues pertaining to corporate governance in the United States in a crisp and fairly short narrative.

---

   4.   Politics, organizational governance, and ethics.

      a.   Negative views of organizational governance. (See ***PowerPoint Slide 41*** for Chapter 12.)

         (i)   Unbalanced organizational governance by some United States corporations may limit their ability to manage global operations effectively.

        (ii) Organizational governance is too closely tied to the short-term interests of stockholders and the pay of the CEO.

      b.   Positive views of organizational governance. (See ***PowerPoint Slide 42*** for Chapter 12.)

         (i)   The governance of United States firms is extending well beyond the limited interests of the owners to include employees and communities.

(ii) Organization governance should be based on the following ethical criteria:

1. The behavior must result in optimizing the satisfaction of people both inside and outside the organization to produce the greatest good for the greatest number of people.

2. The behavior must respect the rights of all affected parties.

3. The behavior must respect the rules of justice by treating people equitably and fairly, as opposed to arbitrarily.

(iii) When the above criteria cannot be fulfilled in a given situation, the criterion of overwhelming factors should be invoked.

(iv) Choosing to be ethical often involves considerable personal sacrifice, and at all corporate levels it involves avoiding common rationalizations.

LECTURE ENHANCEMENT

Consider the following two positions:

Position 1: The primary, if not sole, purpose of the leaders of a business is to produce a profit for its owners.
Position 2: The purpose of the leaders of a business is to serve the needs of society by producing useful goods and services.

Take a quick poll of the class to determine who is more supportive of position 1 and who is more supportive of position 2. Everyone must choose one or the other, even though they may not totally agree with the position. Divide each of groups into two subgroups: groups **A** and **B** are those students who support position **1**. Groups **C** and **D** are those students who support position **2**. The students should prepare for and conduct an in-class debate on these two positions, according to the following scheme: Group **A**, which believes in position **1** argues for position **1**. Group **B**, which believes in position **1** argues for position **2**. Group **C**, which believes in position **2** argues for position **2**. Group **D**, which believes in position **2** argues for position **1**. Thus, each position will be more thoroughly examined and will help the students to gain greater insight about opposing viewpoints regarding the moral role of business leaders.

VI.   **Study summary for Chapter 12.**

A. Point out to the students that the text's "Chapter 12 Study Guide" recaps the key theories, concepts, and ideas in the chapter in relation to the appropriate study questions.

CHAPTER STUDY GUIDE

Study Question 1: What are power and influence in an organization?

- Power is the ability to get someone else to do what you want him or her to do.
- Power vested in managerial positions derives from three sources: rewards, punishments, and legitimacy (formal authority).
- Influence is what you have when you exercise power.
- Position power is formal authority that is based on the manager's position in the hierarchy.
- Personal power is based on one's expertise and referent capabilities.
- Managers can pursue various ways of acquiring high position and personal power.
- They can also become skilled at using various techniques — such as reason, friendliness, ingratiation, and bargaining — to influence superiors, peers, and subordinates.

Study Question 2: How are power, obedience, and formal authority intertwined in an organization?

- Individuals are socialized to accept power (the potential to control the behavior of others) and formal authority (the potential to exert such control through the legitimacy of a managerial position).
- The Milgram experiments illustrate that people have a tendency to obey directives coming from others who appear powerful and authoritative.
- Power and authority work only if the individual "accepts" them as legitimate.
- The zone of indifference defines the boundaries within which people in organizations let others influence their behavior.

Study Question 3: What is empowerment?

- Empowerment is the process through which managers help others acquire and use the power needed to make decisions that affect themselves and their work.
- Clear delegation of authority, integrated planning, and the involvement of senior management are all important to implementing empowerment.
- Empowerment emphasizes power as the ability to get things done rather than the ability to get others to do what you want.

Study Question 4: What is organizational politics?

- Politics involves the use of power to obtain ends not officially sanctioned and the use of power to find ways of balancing individual and collective interests in otherwise difficult circumstances.
- For the manager, politics often occurs in decision situations where the interests of another manager or individual must be reconciled with one's own.
- For managers, politics also involves subunits that jockey for power and advantageous positions vis-à-vis one another.
- Politics can also be used strategically.
- The politics of self-protection involve efforts to avoid accountability, redirect responsibility, and defend one's turf.

- While some suggest that executives are agents of the owners, politics also come into play as resource dependencies with external environmental elements that must be strategically managed.
- Organizational governance is the pattern of authority, influence, and acceptable managerial behavior established at the top of the organization.
- CEOs and managers can develop an ethical organizational governance system that is free from rationalizations.

KEY TERMS

Agency theory: reflects the notion that managers are "agents" of the owners and suggests that public corporations can function effectively even though its managers are self-interested and do not automatically bear the full consequences of their managerial actions.

Coercive power: the extent to which a manager can deny desired rewards and administer punishment to control other people.

Empowerment: the process by which managers help others to acquire and use the power needed to make decisions affecting themselves and their work.

Expert power: the ability to control another's behavior through the possession of knowledge, experience, or judgment that the other person does not have but needs.

Influence: is expressed by others' behavioral responses to the exercise of power.

Information power: the access to and/or control of information.

Legitimate power: the extent to which a manager can use subordinates' internalized values or beliefs that the boss has the "right of command" to control other people.

Organizational governance: the pattern of authority, influence, and acceptable managerial behavior established at the top of an organization.

Organizational politics: one view of organizational politics is the management of influence to obtain ends not sanctioned by the organization or to obtain sanctioned ends through nonsanctioned influence means; an alternate view of organizational politics is that it is the art of creative compromise among competing interests.

Power: the ability to get someone to do something you want done or the ability to make things happen or get things done the way you want.

Process power: the control over methods of production and analysis that a manager has due to being in a position to influence how inputs are transformed into outputs.

Rational persuasion: the ability to control another's behavior because through an individual's efforts the other person accepts the desirability of an offered goal and a reasonable way of achieving it.

Referent power: the ability to control another's behavior because the person wants to identify with the power source.

Representative power: the formal right conferred by the firm to speak for a potentially important group composed of individuals across departments or outside the firm.

Reward power: the extent to which a manager can use extrinsic and intrinsic rewards to control other people.

Zone of indifference: the range of authoritative requests to which a subordinate is willing to respond without subjecting the directives to critical evaluation or judgment.

Chapter 13
INFORMATION AND COMMUNICATION

STUDY QUESTIONS

1.	What is the nature of communication in organizations?
2.	What are the essentials of interpersonal communication?
3.	What are the barriers to effective communication?
4.	What are current issues in organizational communication?

LEARNING OBJECTIVES

After completing this chapter students should be able to:

1.	Describe the key elements of the communication process.
2.	Discuss the importance of feedback in the communication process.
3.	Explain the difference between formal and informal channels of communication.
4.	Describe the key communication directions and flows that occur within organizations.
5.	Differentiate between effective and efficient communication, and explain how nonverbal communication, active listening, and cross-cultural communication influence the effectiveness of interpersonal communication.
6.	Identify and describe the barriers to effective communication.
7.	Explain the implications of the organizational communication issues of electronic communication, virtual workspaces, workplace privacy, and the social context of communication.

MATERIAL IN *THE OB SKILLS WORKBOOK* SUPPORTING THE CHAPTER

Case for Critical Thinking	Case 13: The Poorly Informed Walrus
Experiential Exercises	Exercise 23: Active Listening
	Exercise 24: Upward Appraisal
Self-Assessments	Exercise 12: "TT" Leadership Style
	Exercise 13: Empowering Others

CHAPTER OVERVIEW

This chapter focuses on the important topics of information and communication. The material in this chapter should be of high interest to students, because everyone deals with the challenges

Associated with communicating effectively, and we are all affected by the vast amount of information that crosses our paths daily.

The chapter begins by describing the communication process and examining each of its components in some detail. Particular emphasis is given to the role of feedback in communication, communication channels, and downward, upward, and lateral communication. Next, the essential components of interpersonal communications are explored, including effective and efficient communication, nonverbal communication, active listening, and cross-cultural communication. Particular attention is given to the implications of each of these phenomena for effective interpersonal communications, and suggestions are offered for improving interpersonal communications in each area.

The next section of the chapter focuses on the barriers to effective communication, including physical distractions, semantic problems, mixed messages, absence of feedback, and status effects. The chapter concludes with a section on issues in organizational communication. Included among these issues are electronic communication, virtual workspaces, workplace privacy, and the social context of communication.

CHAPTER OUTLINE

I.   **Study Question 1: What is the nature of communication in organizations?**
      A. The communication process
      B. Feedback and communication
      C. Communication channels
      D. Communication directions and flows

II.   **Study Question 2: What are the essentials of interpersonal communication?**
      A. Effective and efficient communication
      B. Nonverbal communication
      C. Active listening
      D. Cross-cultural communication

III. **Study Question 3: What are the barriers to effective communication?**
      A. Physical distractions
      B. Semantic problems
      C. Mixed messages
      D. Absence of feedback
      E. Status effects

IV.   **Study Question 4: What are current issues in organizational communication?**
      A. Electronic communication
      B. Virtual workspaces
      C. Workplace privacy
      D. Communication and social context

CHAPTER LECTURE NOTES

I.   **Introduction to the Chapter 13 Lecture.**

A.   Study questions for Chapter 13. (See ***PowerPoint Slide 2*** for Chapter 13.)

1.   What is the nature of communication in organizations?

2.   What are the essentials of interpersonal communication?

3.   What are the barriers to effective communication?

4.   What are current issues in organizational communication?

B.   The lecture material for Chapter 13 is organized around the study questions.

1.   Point out to the students that the text's "Chapter At A Glance" identifies the key topics contained in the chapter and links them to the appropriate study questions.

C.   The chapter opens with a brief description of Sun Microsystems' organizational communications programs. Building on this example, the point is made that communication is one essential component of operating a great organization that has a sustainable competitive advantage in the marketplace.

II.   **Study Question 1: What is the nature of communication in organizations?**

A.   The communication process.

1.   **Communication** is the process of sending and receiving messages with attached meanings.

2.   *Figure 13.1* from the textbook describes the keys elements of the communication process, which are a source, a communication channel, a receiver, feedback, and noise. (See ***PowerPoint Slide 3*** for Chapter 13.)

a.   A *source* who encodes an intended meaning into a message.

(i)   Encoding is the process of translating an idea or thought into a message consisting of verbal, written, or nonverbal symbols.

b.   A *communication channel* by which the source transmits the message to a receiver.

(i)   **Communication channels** are the pathways through which messages are sent, including face-to-face meetings, electronic mail and online discussions, written letters or memorandums, and telephone or voice-mail, among others.

(ii) Some people are better at using certain channels over others, and specific channels are better for some messages.

c. A *receiver* who decodes the message into a perceived meaning.

(i) Decoding is the process of assigning meaning to the received message.

d. Feedback that the receiver may or may not give to the source.

e. **Noise,** which is any disturbance that disrupts the communication process and interferes with the transference of messages.

LECTURE ENHANCEMENT

One way to enhance the discussion of the communication process is to focus on the lecture mode of teaching. As the teacher/lecturer, you are occupying the role of sender, whereas the students are receivers. To communicate with them, you use a variety of symbols including spoken and written words, gestures, transparencies, PowerPoint slides, etc. to send them messages. As receivers, the students decode these messages into perceived meanings, which may or may not be the same as the intended meanings.

B. Feedback and communication.

1. **Feedback** is the process through which the receiver communicates with the sender by returning another message. (See *PowerPoint Slide 4* for Chapter 13.)

2. Giving feedback is often associated with one or more persons communicating an evaluation of what another person has said or done. (See *PowerPoint Slide 4* for Chapter 13.)

3. **360-degree feedback** occurs when a person's supervisor, peers, co-workers, and direct reports provide feedback on performance. (See *PowerPoint Slide 4* for Chapter 13.)

4. To be effective at giving constructive feedback, a person should do the following (see *PowerPoint Slide 5* for Chapter 13):

a. Give feedback directly and in a spirit of mutual trust.

b. Be specific, not general; use clear examples.

c. Give feedback when the receiver is most ready to accept it.

d. Be accurate; check validity with others.

e. Focus on things that the receiver can control.

f. Limit how much feedback the receiver gets at one time.

LECTURE ENHANCEMENT

Divide the class into groups of four or five students. Using the guidelines for providing constructive feedback, have each group devise a plan for how they would go about providing feedback to a fellow group member who is not carrying his/her fair share of the group's work load. Select two or three of the groups to share their feedback plans with the entire class.

C. Communication channels.

    1. Information flows in organizations through both formal and informal channels of communication.

    2. **Formal channels** follow the chain of command established by an organization's hierarchy of authority. (See ***PowerPoint Slide 6*** for Chapter 13.)

    3. **Informal channels** do not follow an organization's hierarchy of authority. (See ***PowerPoint Slide 6*** for Chapter 13.)

        a. The **grapevine** is a network of friendships and acquaintances through which rumors and other unofficial information are passed from person to person. (See ***PowerPoint Slide 6*** for Chapter 13.)

        b. The potential advantages of grapevines include the following:

            (i) Enabling the quick and efficient transmission of information.

            (ii) Helping to fulfill people's needs, such as providing a sense of security or providing social satisfaction.

        c. The primary disadvantage of grapevines in the transmission of incorrect or untimely information.

    4. *Channel richness* refers to the capacity of a channel to convey information effectively. (See ***PowerPoint Slide 7*** for Chapter 13.)

        a. The richest channels are face-to-face.

        b. Telephone, e-mail, written memos, and letters have moderate channel richness.

        c. Posted notices and bulletins are the leanest channels.

        d. Richer channels should be used to achieve effective communication with more complex and open-ended messages.

     e.   Leaner channels work well for more routine and straightforward messages.

  D. Communication directions and flows.

      1. **Organizational communication** is the specific process through which information moves and is exchanged throughout an organization. (See *PowerPoint Slide 8* for Chapter 13.)

      2. Information flows through the formal and informal structures described above in sections "II, C, 2" and "II, C, 3" as well as downward, upward, and laterally. (See *PowerPoint Slide 8* for Chapter 13.)

      3. *Figure 13.2* from the textbook illustrates downward, upward, and lateral information flows in organizations. (See *PowerPoint Slide 9* for Chapter 13.)

         a. *Downward communication* follows the chain of command from top to bottom.

           (i) One of its major functions is to achieve influence through information.

           (ii) Lower-level personnel need to know what higher levels are doing and to be regularly reminded of key policies, strategies, objectives, and technical developments.

           (iii) A lack of adequate downward communication is often cited as a management failure.

      4. *Upward communication* is the flow of messages from lower to higher levels in the organization.

         a. Upward communication keeps higher levels informed about what lower-level workers are doing, what their problems are, what suggestions they have for improvements, and how they feel about the organization and their jobs.

      5. *Lateral communication* provides for timely and accurate feedback and product information to be shared between customers and workers, and for internal communication across department or functional boundaries.

         a. New organizational designs are emphasizing lateral communication in the form of cross-departmental committees, teams, or task forces, and the matrix organization.

         b. Organizational ecology is the study of how building design may influence communication and productivity by improving lateral communication.

III.   **Study Question 2: What are the essentials of interpersonal communication?**

  A. Effective and efficient communication. (See *PowerPoint Slide 10* for Chapter 13.)

1. **Effective communication** occurs when the intended meaning of the source and the perceived meaning of the receiver are virtually the same.

2. **Efficient communication** occurs at minimum cost in terms of resources expended.

3. An effective communication may not be efficient or vice versa.

LECTURE ENHANCEMENT

Using the example of the lecture mode of teaching, you can reinforce the concepts of effective and efficient communication by noting that while you can communicate quite "efficiently" with students through straight lectures, their involvement and feedback is needed to insure "effective" communication.

B. Nonverbal communication. (See *PowerPoint Slide 11* for Chapter 13.)

1. **Nonverbal communication** takes place through facial expressions, body motions, eye contact, and other physical gestures.

2. *Kinesics* is the study of gestures and body postures.

3. The nonverbal side to communication can often hold the key to what someone is really thinking or meaning, and can affect the impressions we make on others.

4. *Proxemics* — the study of how space is utilized — is also important to nonverbal communication.

LECTURE ENHANCEMENT

A fun way to illustrate the power of nonverbal communication is to call on volunteers to "act out" various emotions without speaking verbally. Specifically, you may whisper to one volunteer to "act angry," another to "be sad," another to "be happy," etc. Alternatively, you may ask one student to portray all of these emotions, plus any others that you choose. Then you can ask the students' classmates to guess which emotion is being portrayed.

C. Active listening.

1. The ability to listen well is a distinct asset to anyone whose job involves a large proportion of time spent communicating with other people. (See *PowerPoint Slide 12* for Chapter 13.)

2. Everyone in the new workplace should develop good skills in **active listening** — the ability to help the source of a message say what he or she really means. (See *PowerPoint Slide 12* for Chapter 13.)

3. Guidelines for active listening include the following (see *PowerPoint Slide 13* for Chapter 13):

    a. Listen for content — try to hear exactly what is being said.

    b. Listen for feelings — try to identify how the source feels about things.

    c. Respond to feelings — let the source know that his or her feelings are recognized.

    d. Note all cues — be sensitive to both verbal and nonverbal expressions.

    e. Reflect back — repeat in your own words what you think you are hearing.

LECTURE ENHANCEMENT

Active listening and effective listening are closely related topics Simple rules for effective listening include the following: (1) Stop talking. (2) Help the speaker feel at ease. (3) Have an attitude that shows you want to listen. (4) Avoid distractions. (5) Have empathy for the speaker. (6) Be patient.

D. Cross-cultural communication. (See *PowerPoint Slide 14* for Chapter 13.)

1. A common problem in cross-cultural communication is *ethnocentrism* — the tendency to believe one's culture and its values are superior to those of others.

2. The difficulties with cross-cultural communication are perhaps most obvious with respect to language differences.

3. Gestures may also be used quite differently in different cultures.

4. One of the best ways to understand cultural differences is to learn at least some of the language of the country with which dealings take place.

LECTURE ENHANCEMENT

A very entertaining website that provides a collection of cultural misunderstanding (or communications "goofs" in translating phrases from one language to another) is available at http://www.css.edu/users/dswenson/web/335ARTIC/CULTCOMM.HTM. Consider reading some of these "goofs" to your students to illustrate the difficulties inherent in cross-cultural communication.

IV. **Study Question 3: What are the barriers to effective communication?**

LECTURE ENHANCEMENT

Using the example of the lecture mode of teaching, you can preview the discussion of communication barriers by asking students to identify sources of "noise" which sometimes interfere with the effectiveness of lectures. An added benefit of this discussion is that instructors may obtain some useful feedback on their lecturing styles.

A. The six sources of noise that can cause communication problems are: physical distractions, semantic problems, mixed messages, cultural differences, absence of feedback, and status effects.

B. Physical distractions. (See *PowerPoint Slide 15* for Chapter 13.)

1. Any number of physical distractions — such as interruptions from telephone calls or drop-in visitors — can interfere with the effectiveness of a communication attempt.

C. Semantic problems. (See *PowerPoint Slide 16* for Chapter 13.)

1. Semantic barriers to communication involve a poor choice or use of words and mixed messages.

2. The **KISS principle** of communication means "keep it short and simple."

D. Mixed messages. (See *PowerPoint Slide 17* for Chapter 13.)

1. **Mixed messages** occur when a person's words communicate one thing while actions or "body language" communicates another.

2. Mixed messages are important to spot since nonverbals can add important insight into what is really being said in face-to-face communication.

E. Absence of feedback. (See *PowerPoint Slide 18* for Chapter 13.)

1. One-way communication flows from sender to receiver only, with no direct and immediate feedback from the recipient.

2. Two-way communication goes from sender to receiver and back again, and it is characterized by the normal interactive conversations in our daily experiences.

3. Research indicates that two-way communication is more accurate and effective than one-way communication, even though it is also more costly and time consuming.

F.   Status effects. (See *PowerPoint Slide 19* for Chapter 13.)

1.   Status differences in organizations create potential communication barriers between persons of higher and lower ranks.

2.   The **mum effect** occurs when people are reluctant to communicate bad news or desire to be polite.

3.   Management by wandering around (**MBWA**) involves getting out of the office to directly communicate with others as they do their jobs.

V.   **Study Question 4: What are current issues in organizational communication?**

A.   Electronic communication.

1.   Advances in information technology are allowing organizations to do the following (See *PowerPoint Slide 20* for Chapter 13):

a.   Distribute information much faster than before.

b.   Make more information available than ever before.

c.   Allow broader and more immediate access to this information.

d.   Encourage participation in the sharing and use of information.

e.   Integrate systems and functions, and use information to link with environments in unprecedented ways.

2.   The potential disadvantages of electronic communications include the following (see *PowerPoint Slide 21* for Chapter 13):

a.   People interact with machines, not one another

b.   Nonverbal communications are removed from the situation.

c.   The electronic medium can alter the emotional aspects of communication.

(i)   *Flaming* describes rudeness in electronic communication.

d.   Information overload may occur.

B.   Virtual workspaces.

1.   New communication technologies will continue to keep changing the nature of work and of office work in particular.

a.   **Virtual workspaces** are online sites that allow users to share information, documents, calendars, and discussion continuously and on demand.

    C. Workplace privacy.

        1. Workplace privacy is an important controversy in organizational communication.

            a. Progressive organizations are developing internal policies regarding the privacy of employee communications, and the issue is gaining attention from legislators.

    D. Communication and social context. (See ***PowerPoint Slide 22*** for Chapter 13.)

        1. Women are socialized into relationship building in communication; men are socialized to seek status through communication.

        2. Either women or men may dominate communications in situations where they are in the majority.

        3. Early socialization and training better prepare women for the skills involved in communication and may make them more sensitive in interpersonal relations.

        4. Men may be more socialized in ways that cause communication problems — such as aggression, competitiveness, and individualism.

        5. Contemporary society values the political correctness of communication in the workplace.

LECTURE ENHANCEMENT

Mindtools, which is a British site dedicated towards self-improvement, provides an excellent set of tips and recommendations that can help people improve their overall communication skills. The Internet address is: http://www.mindtools.com/page8.html.

VI.   **Study summary for Chapter 13.**

    A. Point out to the students that the text's "Chapter 13 Study Guide" recaps the key theories, concepts, and ideas in the chapter in relation to the appropriate study questions.

CHAPTER STUDY GUIDE

Study Question 1: What is the nature of communication in organizations?

- Communication is the process of sending and receiving messages with attached meanings.
- The communication process involves encoding an intended meaning into a message, sending the message through a channel, and receiving and decoding the message into perceived meaning.

- Noise is anything that interferes with the communication process.
- Feedback is a return message from the original recipient back to the sender.
- To be constructive, feedback must be direct, specific, and given at an appropriate time.
- Organizational communication is the specific process through which information moves and is exchanged within an organization.
- Organizations depend on complex flows of information — upward, downward, and laterally — to operate effectively.

Study Question 2: What are the essentials of interpersonal communication?

- Communication is effective when both sender and receiver interpret a message in the same way.
- Communication is efficient when messages are transferred at a low cost.
- Nonverbal communication occurs through facial expressions, body position, eye contact, and other physical gestures.
- Active listening encourages a free and complete flow of information from the sender to the receiver; it is nonjudgmental and encouraging.
- Communication in organizations uses a variety of formal and informal channels; the richness of the channel, or its capacity to convey information, must be adequate for the message.

Study Question 3: What are the barriers to effective communication?

- The possible barriers to communication include physical distractions, semantic problems, and cultural differences.
- Mixed messages that give confused or conflicting verbal and nonverbal cues may interfere with communications.
- The absence of feedback can make it difficult to know whether or not an intended message has been accurately received.
- Status effects in organizations may result in restricted and filtered information exchanges between subordinates and their superiors.

Study Question 4: What are current issues in organizational communication?

- As new electronic communication technologies change the workplace, the emphasis on electronic communications and virtual workspaces brings many performance advantages.
- Potential disadvantages in a world of information technology include the loss of emotion and personality in the communication process.
- Researchers are interested in possible differences in communication styles between men and women and in the relative effectiveness of these styles for conditions in the new workplace.
- Current issues in organizational communication also include those of privacy and political correctness in workplace communication.

KEY TERMS

Active listening: the ability to help the source of a message say what he or she really means.
Communication: the process of sending and receiving messages with attached meanings.
Communication channels: the pathways through which messages are sent, including face-to-face meetings, electronic mail and online discussions, written letters or memorandums, and telephone or voice-mail, among others.

Effective communication: communication that occurs when the intended meaning of the source and the perceived meaning of the receiver are virtually the same.

Efficient communication: communication that occurs at minimum cost in terms of resources expended.

Feedback: the process through which the receiver communicates with the sender by returning another message.

Formal channels: channels that follow the chain of command established by an organization's hierarchy of authority.

Grapevine: a network of friendships and acquaintances through which rumors and other unofficial information are passed from person to person.

Informal channels: channels that do not follow an organization's hierarchy of authority

KISS principle: a communication principle that means "keep it short and simple."

MBWA: involves getting out of the office to directly communicate with others with others as they do their jobs.

Mixed messages: messages that occur when a person's words communicate one thing while actions or "body language" communicate another.

Mum effect: occurs when people are reluctant to communicate bad news or desire to be polite.

Noise: any disturbance that disrupts the communication process and interferes with the transference of messages.

Nonverbal communication: the type of communication that takes place through facial expressions, body motions, eye contact, and other physical gestures.

Organizational communication: the specific process through which information moves and is exchanged throughout an organization.

360-degree feedback: occurs when a person's supervisor, peers, co-workers, and direct reports provide feedback on performance.

Virtual workspaces: online sites that allow users to share information, documents, calendars, and discussion continuously and on demand.

Chapter 14
DECISION MAKING

STUDY QUESTIONS

1.	What is the decision-making process in organizations?
2.	What are the useful decision making models?
3.	How do intuition, judgment, and creativity affect decision making?
4.	How do you manage the decision-making process?
5.	What are some of the current issues in decision making?

LEARNING OBJECTIVES

After completing this chapter students should be able to:

1.	Describe the five basic steps involved in systematic decision making.
2.	Describe the differences among certain environments, risk environments, uncertain environments, and organized anarchy.
3.	Explain the differences among programmed decisions, nonprogrammed decisions, and associative choices.
4.	Describe the classical, behavioral decision, and garbage can models of decision making.
5.	Describe the different judgmental heuristics and general biases that occur in decision making.
6.	Explain the stages of creative thinking and describe methods for fostering creativity in decision making.
7.	Explain how to manage the decision-making process with respect to choosing problems to address, deciding who should participate, and knowing when to quit.
8.	Discuss the impact of information technology, culture, and ethics on decision making.

MATERIAL IN *THE OB SKILLS WORKBOOK* SUPPORTING THE CHAPTER

Case for Critical Thinking	Case 14: Johnson & Johnson
Experiential Exercises	Exercise 32: Role Analysis Negotiation
	Exercise 33: Lost at Sea
	Exercise 34: Entering the Unknown
	Exercise 36; The Ugli Orange
	Exercise 38: Force-Field Analysis
Self-Assessments	Assessment 16: Your Intuitive Ability
	Assessment 17: Decision Making Biases

CHAPTER OVERVIEW

This chapter focuses on decision making, a process that takes place on a continuous basis in business organizations. The chapter begins by reviewing the basic steps involved in systematic decision making. Decision environments are discussed, including certain environments, risk environments, uncertain environments, and organized anarchy. The differences between programmed and nonprogrammed decisions are also discussed, along with associative choices.

The chapter progresses to discuss the principle decision-making models, which include classical decision theory, behavioral decision theory, and the garbage can model. These different models are placed in the context of the realities facing decision makers in the business world. The next section of the chapter reviews the concepts of intuition, judgment, and creativity. Judgmental heuristics are introduced and discussed, including the availability heuristic, the representativeness heuristic, and the anchoring and adjustment heuristic. General biases in decision making, including the confirmation trap and the hindsight trap, are also discussed. Stages of creative thinking and methods for fostering creativity in decision making are examined as well.

The next portion of the chapter focuses on managing the decision-making process, with attention being given to choosing problems to address, deciding who should participate, and knowing when to quit. In the discussion of who should participate, emphasis is placed on the Vroom, Yetton, and Jago model for selecting the decision-making method that is most appropriate for the situation at hand. The chapter concludes with a discussion of current issues in decision making, including the impact of information technology, culture, and ethics on decision making.

CHAPTER OUTLINE

I.   **Study Question 1: What is the decision-making process in organizations?**
     A. Decision environments
     B. Types of decisions

II. **Study Question 2: What are the useful decision-making models?**
     A. Classical and behavioral decision theory
     B. The garbage can model
     C. Decision-making realities

III. **Study Question 3: How do intuition, judgment, and creativity affect decision making?**
     A. Judgmental heuristics
     B. Creativity

IV. **Study Question 4: How do you manage the decision-making process?**
     A. Choosing to address problems
     B. Deciding who should participate
     C. Knowing when to quit

V.   **Study Question 5: What are some of the current issues in decision making?**
     A. Information technology and decision making

B. Culture factors and decision making

C. Ethical issues and decision making

CHAPTER LECTURE NOTES

I.   **Introduction to the Chapter 14 Lecture.**

A. Study questions for Chapter 14. (See *PowerPoint Slides 2* and *3* for Chapter 14.)

1. What is the decision-making process in organizations?

2. What are the useful decision-making models?

3. How do intuition, judgment, and creativity affect decision making?

4. How do you manage the decision-making process?

5. What are some of the current issues in decision making?

B. The lecture material for Chapter 14 is organized around the study questions.

1. Point out to the students that the text's "Chapter At A Glance" identifies the key topics contained in the chapter and links them to the appropriate study questions.

C. The chapter opens with a discussion of Plante Moran's Principle of Decision Making, which states that: "It is our intent to maintain timely yet thorough decision-making processes, with decisions made at the most appropriate level. We will strive to be effective by keeping a balance between participation and efficiency."

II.   **Study question 1: What is the decision-making process in organizations?**

A. Background on the decision-making process.

1. **Decision making** is the process of choosing a course of action for dealing with a problem or opportunity. (See *PowerPoint Slide 4* for Chapter 14.)

LECTURE ENHANCEMENT

Prior to introducing the steps of the decision-making process, ask students to describe how they have gone about making a major decision, such as which college or university to attend. Make sure they describe the sequence of steps they went through, and then relate their discussion to the five basic steps involved in systematic decision making.

---

2. The five basic steps involved in systematic decision making are (see *PowerPoint Slide 4* for Chapter 14):

a. Recognize and define the problem or opportunity.

    b. Identify and analyze alternative courses of action, and estimate their effects on the problem or opportunity.

    c. Choose a preferred course of action.

    d. Implement the preferred course of action.

    e. Evaluate the results and follow up as necessary.

B. Decision environments.

   1. Problem solving and opportunity seeking decisions in organizations are typically made under three different conditions or environments: certainty, risk, and uncertainty.

     a. **Certain environments** exist when information is sufficient to predict the results of each alternative in advance of implementation. (See *PowerPoint Slide 5* for Chapter 14.)

     b. **Risk environments** exist when decision makers lack complete certainty regarding the outcomes of various courses of action, but they are aware of the probabilities associated with their occurrence. (See *PowerPoint Slide 5* for Chapter 14.)

     c. **Uncertain environments** exist when managers have so little information on hand that they cannot even assign probabilities to various alternatives and their possible outcomes. (See *PowerPoint Slide 6* for Chapter 14.)

      (i) Uncertain decision environments can be characterized as a rapidly changing setting in terms of the following (see *PowerPoint Slide 6* for Chapter 14):

        1. External conditions.

        2. The information technology requirements needed for analyzing and making decisions.

        3. The people who influence problem and choice definitions.

      (ii) **Organized anarchy** refers to a firm or division in a firm that is in a transition characterized by very rapid change and lack of a legitimate hierarchy and collegiality.

      (iii) Uncertain decision environments can also be assessed in terms of the types of risks encountered by the organization. (See *PowerPoint Slide 7* for Chapter 14.)

        1. Strategic risks are threats to overall business success.

2. Operational risks are threats inherent in the technologies used to reach business success.

3. Reputation risks are threats to a brand or to the firm's reputation.

LECTURE ENHANCEMENT

As an out-of-class assignment to enhance understanding of different types of decision environments, have each student or small groups of students select a company from the *Fortune 500* list. Have them do some background research on the company's business environment, using the company's Web site or periodicals such as *Fortune* magazine or *The Wall Street Journal*. Have the students describe the company's business environment and characterize it as being one certainty, risk, or uncertainty.

C. Types of decisions. (See *PowerPoint Slide 8* for Chapter 14.)

1. **Programmed decisions** implement solutions that have already been determined by past experience as appropriate for addressing routine problems that arise on a regular basis.

2. **Nonprogrammed decisions** implement solutions that are specifically crafted or tailored for addressing a nonroutine problem.

LECTURE ENHANCEMENT

To stimulate discussion of the programmed decisions versus nonprogrammed decisions, ask students to provide examples of each type. You can either solicit student examples as a prelude to your own illustrations, or present your examples first to get them started.

---

3. Higher-level managers generally spend more of their time dealing within nonroutine problems.

4. **Associative choices** are decisions that can be loosely linked to nagging continual problems but that were not specifically developed to solve the problem.

III. **Study Question 2: What are useful decision-making models?**

A. Background on decision-making models.

1. *Figure 14.1* from the textbook provides a comparison of the classical and behavioral models of decision making. (See *PowerPoint Slide 9* for Chapter 14.)

2. **Classical decision theory** views the manager as acting in a world of complete certainty.

3. <u>**Behavioral decision theory**</u> accepts the notion of bounded rationality and suggests that people act only in terms of what they perceive about a given situation.

B. Classical and behavioral decision theory.

1. Classical decision theory assumes that the manager faces a clearly defined problem, knows all possible action alternatives and their consequences, and then chooses the alternative that offers the best, or "optimum," solution to the problem. (See *PowerPoint Slide 10* for Chapter 14.)

2. Behavioral scientists are cautious about applying classical decision theory to many decision situations because human beings have cognitive limitations that restrict their information-processing capabilities. This is known as bounded rationality. (See *PowerPoint Slide 10* for Chapter 14.)

3. Classical decision theory does not appear to fit today's chaotic world of globalizing high-tech operations, yet it can be used toward the bottom of many firms. (See *PowerPoint Slide 11* for Chapter 14.)

4. As indicated earlier, behavioral decision theory accepts the notion of bounded rationality and suggests that people act only in terms of what they perceive about a given situation. This ultimately leads to <u>**satisficing**</u> wherein decision makers choose the first alternative that appears to give an acceptable or a satisfactory solution to the problem. (See *PowerPoint Slide 11* for Chapter 14.)

C. The garbage can model.

1. The <u>**garbage can model**</u> views the main components of the choice process — problems, solutions, participants, and choice situations — as all mixed up together in the "garbage can" of the organization. (See *PowerPoint Slide 12* for Chapter 14.)

2. When the organizational setting is stable and the technology is well known and fixed, traditions, strategy, and the administrative structure help order the contents of the "garbage can."

3. When the organizational setting is dynamic, the technology is changing, demands are conflicting, or the goals are unclear, the components of the "garbage can" get mixed up.

4. The garbage can model highlights two important organizational facts of life. (See *PowerPoint Slide 12* for Chapter 14.)

a. Different individuals may do choice making and implementation.

b. Many problems go unsolved.

D. Decision-making realities. (See *PowerPoint Slides 13* and *14* for Chapter 14.)

1. A key difference between a manager's ability to make an optimum decision in the classical style and the manager's tendency to make a satisficing decision in the behavior style is the availability of information.

2. The organizational realities of bounded rationality and cognitive limitations affect the way people define problems, identify action alternatives, and choose preferred courses of action.

3. Most decision making in organizations involves more than linear and step-by-step rational choice but it is not necessarily as chaotic as the garbage can model suggests.

4. Decisions must be made under risk and uncertainty, in response to nonroutine problems, and under the pressure of information and time limitations.

5. Decisions should be made on an ethical foundation.

LECTURE ENHANCEMENT

Ask students to provide examples of when they have used optimizing decision making and examples of when they have used satisficing decision making. These examples should help students to understand the conditions under which these two approaches usually occur.

IV. **Study Question 3: How do intuition, judgment, and creativity affect decision making?**

A. Intuition. (See *PowerPoint Slide 15* for Chapter 14.)

1. A key element in decision making under risk and uncertainty is **intuition** — the ability to know or recognize quickly and readily the possibilities of a given situation.

2. Managers are more likely to gather data and to make decisions in a relational or interactive way that in a systematic step-by-step fashion.

3. Since managers work in chaotic settings, they should be confident in using their intuitive skills and combine analytical and intuitive approaches to create new and novel solutions to complex problems.

LECTURE ENHANCEMENT

Ask students to raise their hands if they think that they rely predominantly on a *systematic step-by-step approach to decision making*. Make a note of these students. Do the same for those who believe that they use an *intuitive approach to decision making* most often. From here, several avenues to generating discussion of these alternative ways of making decision are available. For example, you may ask students who believe that they rely more on the systematic (or intuitive) approach to elaborate on the ways in which they typically make decisions. What do they consider to be the advantages of their approach? The disadvantages? Another option is to create panels of users of the intuitive and systematic approaches to engage each other in a debate on the relative merits of their decision-making styles. Or you could create panels of intuitive and systematic decision makers, but instead of having them debate one another, you could instruct them to ask the students with alternative styles questions about the ways in which they typically approach various problems. Any of these options can be used to generate a lively discussion of the relative strengths and weaknesses of the systematic and intuitive decision-making approaches.

        B.   Judgmental heuristics.

            1.   Judgment, or the use of one's intellect, is important in all aspects of decision making.

            2.   **Heuristics** are simplifying strategies or "rules of thumb" used to make decisions. (See *PowerPoint Slide 16* for Chapter 14.)

            3.   Hueristics make it easier to deal with uncertainty and limited information in problem situations. (See *PowerPoint Slide 16* for Chapter 14.)

            4.   The **availability heuristic** involves assessing a current event based on past occurrences that are easily available in one's memory. (See *PowerPoint Slide 17* for Chapter 14.)

            5.   The **representative heuristic** involves assessing the likelihood that an event will occur based on its similarity to one's stereotypes of similar occurrences. (See *PowerPoint Slide 17* for Chapter 14.)

            6.   The **anchoring and adjustment heuristic** involves assessing an event by taking an initial value determined by historical precedent or an outside source, and then incrementally adjusting this value to make a current assessment. (See *PowerPoint Slide 17* for Chapter 14.)

            7.   The **confirmation trap** is the tendency for the decision maker to seek confirmation for what is already thought to be true and to not search for disconfirming information. (See *PowerPoint Slide 18* for Chapter 14.)

            8.   The **hindsight trap** is the tendency for the decision maker to overestimate the degree to which an event that has already taken place could have been predicted. (See *PowerPoint Slide 18* for Chapter 14.)

C. Creativity.

1. **Creativity** in decision making involves the development of unique and novel responses to problems and opportunities.

2. Creative thinking may unfold in a series of five stages. (See *PowerPoint Slide 19* for Chapter 14.)

   a. Stage 1 — *preparation*: people engage in the active learning and day-to-day sensing required to deal successfully with complex environments.

   b. Stage 2 — *concentration*: actual problems are defined and framed so that alternatives can be considered for dealing with the problems.

   c. Stage 3 — *incubation*: people look at the problems in diverse ways that permit the consideration of unusual alternatives, avoiding tendencies toward purely linear and systematic problem solving.

   d. Stage 4 — *illumination*: people respond to flashes of insight and recognize when all pieces to the puzzle suddenly fit into place.

   e. Stage 5 — *certification*: proceeds with logical analysis to confirm that good problem-solving decisions have really been made.

3. All of these stages of creativity need support and encouragement in the organizational environment.

4. Decision makers may foster creativity in the following ways (see *PowerPoint Slide 20* for Chapter 14):

   a. Diversifying teams to include members with different backgrounds, training, and perspectives.

   b. Encouraging analogical reasoning.

   c. Stressing periods of silent reflection.

   d. Recording all ideas so that the same ones are not rediscovered.

   e. Establishing high expectations for creativity.

   f. Developing a physical space that encourages fun, divergent ideas.

5. Research demonstrates that creativity is higher when (see *PowerPoint Slides 21* and *22* for Chapter 14):

    a.   Linguistic ability, willingness to engage in divergent thinking, and intelligence are present.

    b.   Individuals are motivated by and derive satisfaction from task accomplishment.

    c.   The decision maker provides opportunities for creativity, eliminates as many constraints as possible, and provides rewards for creative efforts.

    d.   The decision maker emphasizes engagement in the creative process and counsels individuals to share their ideas with others.

    e.   The decision maker encourages subordinates to recognize ambiguity, contact others with different views, and be prepared to make considerable changes.

V.   Study Question 4: How do you manage the decision-making process?

A. Choosing to address problems.

    1.   The effective manager and team leader knows when to delegate decisions to others, how to set priorities, and when to abstain from acting altogether.

    2.   When faced with the dilemma of whether or not to deal with a specific problem, asking and answering the following questions can sometimes help. (See *PowerPoint Slide 23* for Chapter 14.)

        a.   Is the problem easy to deal with?

        b.   Might the problem resolve itself?

        c.   Is this my decision to make?

        d.   Is this a solvable problem within the context of the organization?

    3.   Half of the decisions in organizations fail for the following reasons (see *PowerPoint Slide 24* for Chapter 14):

        a.   Managers may merely copy the choices of others and try to sell them to subordinates.

        b.   Subordinates may believe the manager is just imposing his or her will rather than working for the best interests of everyone.

        c.   Managers may tend to focus on the problems they see rather than the outcomes they want.

        d.   Managers may underutilize participation.

B. Deciding who should participate.

1. Good organizational decisions are made by individuals acting alone, by individuals consulting with others, and by groups of people working together.

2. Who participates and how decisions are made should reflect the issues at hand. *Figure 14.2* from the textbook shows a model developed by Victor Vroom, Philip Yetton, and Arthur Jago that helps managers choose the decision-making method that is most appropriate for various problem situations. (See *PowerPoint Slide 25* for Chapter 14.)

    a. The model seeks to sequentially array the key factors that should guide participation choices.

    b. The key problem attributes are the following (see *PowerPoint Slide 26* for Chapter 14):

        (i) The required quality of the decision.

        (ii) The commitment needed from subordinates.

        (iii) The amount of information the leader has.

        (iv) The problem structure.

        (v) Commitment probability (*i.e.*, the chances subordinates would be committed if the leader made the choice).

        (vi) Goal congruence (*i.e.*, the degree to which subordinates share the goals to be obtained by the choice).

        (vii) Subordinate conflict.

        (vii) Subordinate information.

    c. The key to effectively managing participation in decision making is first knowing when to use each decision method and then knowing how to implement each of them well.

    d. Types of decision methods in the model.

        (i) **Authority decisions** are made when the manager or team leader uses information that he or she possesses and decides what to do without involving others. (See *PowerPoint Slide 27* for Chapter 14.)

            1. Variant 1 — the manager solves the problem or makes the decision alone, using information available at the time.

2. Variant 2 — the manager obtains the necessary information from subordinate(s) or other group members and then decides on the problem solution.

(ii) **Consultative decisions** are made when the manager or team leader solicits input from other people and then, based on this information and its interpretation, makes a final choice. (See *PowerPoint Slide 28* for Chapter 14.)

1. Variant 1 — the manager shares the problem with relevant subordinates or other group members individually, getting their ideas and suggestions without bringing them together as a group. The manager then makes a decision that may or may not reflect the subordinates' input.

2. Variant 2 — the manager shares the problem with subordinates or other group members, collectively obtaining their ideas and suggestions. The manager then makes a decision that may or may not reflect the subordinates' input.

(iii) **Group decisions** are made by both consulting with others and allowing them to help make the final choice. (See *PowerPoint Slide 29* for Chapter 14.)

C. Knowing when to quit. (See *PowerPoint Slide 30* for Chapter 14.)

1. The organization's natural desire to continue on a selected course of action reinforces some natural tendencies among decision makers.

2. **Escalating commitment** is the tendency to continue and renew effort on a previously chosen course of action, even though it is not working.

3. The tendency to escalate commitments often outweighs the willingness to disengage from them.

4. Good decision makers are willing to reverse previous decisions and stop investing time and other resources in unsuccessful courses of action.

LECTURE ENHANCEMENT

Explain to students that escalating commitment is encouraged by the popular saying, "If at first you don't succeed, try, try again." Current wisdom supports an alternative view, illustrated in this quote by the late W.C. Fields: "If at first you don't succeed, try, try again. Then quit. No use being a damn fool about it."

VI. **Study Question 5: What are some of the current issues in decision making?**

A. Workplace trends that are affecting organizational decision makers include the following (see ***PowerPoint Slide 31*** for Chapter 14):

1. Business units are becoming smaller in size as they do more outsourcing and employ fewer full-time workers.

2. New, more flexible, and adaptable organizational forms are replacing the traditional pyramid structures.

3. Multifunctional understanding is increasingly important as organizations emphasize lateral coordination.

4. Workers with both technical knowledge and team skills are increasingly desirable.

5. The nature of "work" is in a state of flux as jobs change fast, require continuous learning, and are less bound by the "9-to-5" tradition.

B. Information technology and decision making. (See ***PowerPoint Slides 32*** and ***33*** for Chapter 14.)

1. **Artificial intelligence** (AI) is the study of how computers can be programmed to think like the human brain.

2. The applications of AI to organizational decision making include the following:

a. Decision-making support from expert systems that reason like human experts and follow "either-or" rules to make deductions.

b. In the very near future, fuzzy logic that reasons beyond "either-or" choices and neural networks that reason inductively by simulating the brain's parallel processing capabilities will become operational realities.

c. Computer support for group decision making.

3. New information technology will not be able to deal with the issues raised by the garbage can model of decision making.

C. Culture factors and decision making. (See ***PowerPoint Slide 34*** for Chapter 14.)

1. Since culture can be described as "the way in which a group of people solves problems," it is only reasonable to expect decision-making approaches will vary across cultures.

2. The North American view of decision making stresses decisiveness, speed, and individual selection of alternatives, with more emphasis on choice than on implementation.

3. Other cultures place less emphasis on individual choice than on developing implementations that work.

4. The more important role of culture in decision making concerns not how problems are solved but which concerns are elevated to the status of problems solvable within the firm.

D. Ethical issues and decision making.

1. An *ethical dilemma* is a situation in which a person must decide whether or not to do something that, although personally or organizationally beneficial, may be considered unethical and perhaps illegal.

2. Often, ethical dilemmas are associated with risk and uncertainty, and with nonroutine problem situations.

3. Ethics can be infused into decision making by doing the following (see *PowerPoint Slide 35* for Chapter 14):

   a. Develop a code of ethics and follow it.

   b. Establish procedures for reporting violations.

   c. Involve employees in identifying ethical issues.

   d. Monitor ethical performance.

   e. Reward ethical behavior.

   f. Publicize efforts.

4. Moral conduct is involved in choosing problems, deciding who should be involved, estimating the impacts of alternatives, and selecting an alternative for implementation. (See *PowerPoint Slide 36* for Chapter 14.)

5. Effective implemented decisions need to solve a problem or capitalize on choices as well as match the decision maker's moral values and help others. (See *PowerPoint Slide 36* for Chapter 14.)

25

LECTURE ENHANCEMENT

There are organizations that follow the decisions made by businesses that affect the environment and other sensitive issues. While these organizations may have a point of view that is not mainstream, it still behooves managers to be sensitive to the fact that many of their decisions are being "watched" by some stakeholder group or other constituency. An example of one of these "watchdog" organizations is Corporate Watch at http://www.corpwatch.org/.

VII.   Study summary for Chapter 14.

A. Point out to the students that the text's "Chapter 14 Study Guide" recaps the key theories, concepts, and ideas in the chapter in relation to the appropriate study questions.

CHAPTER STUDY GUIDE

Study Question 1: What is the decision-making process in organizations?

- Decision making is a process of identifying problems and opportunities and choosing among alternative courses of action for dealing successfully with them.
- Organizational decisions are often made in risky and uncertain environments, where situations are ambiguous and information is limited.
- Routine and repetitive problems can be dealt with through programmed decisions; nonroutine or novel problems require nonprogrammed decisions that are crafted to fit the situation at hand.

Study Question 2: What are the useful decision-making models?

- Classical, behavioral, and garbage can models are often useful views of decision making.
- According to classical decision theory, optimum decisions are made after carefully analyzing all possible alternatives and their known consequences.
- According to behavioral decision theory, most organizational decisions are made with limited information and by satisficing — choosing the first acceptable or satisfactory solution to problems.
- According to the garbage can model, the main components of the choice process — problems, solutions, participants, and choice situations — are all mixed up together in the garbage can of the organization.
- The pressures of time and the lack of information are two important decision-making realities.

Study Question 3: How do intuition, judgment, and creativity affect decision making?

- Both systematic decision making and intuitive decision making are important in today's complex work environments.

- Intuition is the ability to quickly recognize the action possibilities for resolving a problem situation.
- The use of judgmental heuristics, or simplifying rules of thumb, is common in decision making but can lead to biased results.
- Common heuristics include availability decisions based on recent events, representativeness decisions based on similar events, and anchoring and adjustment decisions based on historical precedents.
- Creativity in finding unique and novel solutions to problems can be enhanced through both individual and group problem-solving strategies.

Study Question 4: How do you manage the decision-making process?

- Good managers know that not every problem requires an immediate decision; they also know how and when to delegate decision-making responsibilities.
- A common mistake is for a manager or team leader to make all decisions alone; instead, a full range of individual, consultative, and group decision-making methods should be utilized.
- The Vroom-Yetton-Jago model offers a way of matching problems with appropriate decision methods, based on quality requirements, information availability, and time constraints.
- Tendencies toward escalating commitment, continuing previously chosen courses of action even when they are not working, should be recognized in work settings.

Study Question 5: What are some of the current issues in decision making?

- Technology, culture, and ethics are key issues in decision making.
- Technological developments are continuing to change the nature of organizational decision making.
- Culture counts; differences in culture alter by whom, how, when, and why decisions are made.
- Ethics is involved in each stage of the decision-making process, and effective decision making includes individual moral criteria and values.

KEY TERMS

Anchoring and adjustment heuristic: involves assessing an event by taking an initial value determined by historical precedent or an outside source, and then incrementally adjusting this value to make a current assessment.

Artificial intelligence: the study of how computers can be programmed to think like the human brain.

Associative choices: decisions that can be loosely linked to nagging continual problems but that were not specifically developed to solve the problem.

Authority decisions: decisions that are made when the manager or team leader uses information that he or she possesses and decides what to do without involving others.

Availability heuristic: involves assessing a current event based on past occurrences that are easily available in one's memory.

Behavioral decision theory: accepts the notion of bounded rationality and suggests that people act only in terms of what they perceive about a given situation.

Certain environments: exist when information is sufficient to predict the results of each alternative in advance of implementation.

Classical decision theory: views the manager as acting in a world of complete certainty.

Confirmation trap: the tendency for the decision maker to seek confirmation for what is already thought to be true and to not search for disconfirming information.

Consultative decisions: decisions that are made when the manager or team leader solicits input from other people and then, based on this information and its interpretation, makes a final choice.

Creativity: the development of unique and novel responses to problems and opportunities.

Decision making: the process of choosing a course of action for dealing with a problem or opportunity.

Escalating commitment: the tendency to continue and renew effort on a previously chosen course of action, even though it is not working.

Garbage can model: views the main components of the choice process — problems, solutions, participants, and choice situations — as all mixed up together in the "garbage can" of the organization.

Group decisions: decisions that are made by both consulting with others and allowing them to help make the final choice.

Heuristics: simplifying strategies or "rules of thumb" used to make decisions.

Hindsight trap: the tendency for the decision maker to overestimate the degree to which an event that has already taken place could have been predicted.

Intuition: the ability to know or recognize quickly and readily the possibilities of a given situation.

Nonprogrammed decisions: implement solutions that are specifically crafted or tailored for addressing a nonroutine problem.

Organized anarchy: refers to a firm or division in a firm that is in a transition characterized by very rapid change and lack of a legitimate hierarchy and collegiality.

Programmed decisions: implement solutions that have already been determined by past experience as appropriate for addressing routine problems that arise on a regular basis.

Representativeness heuristic: involves assessing the likelihood that an event will occur based on its similarity to one's stereotypes of similar occurrences.

Risk environments: exist when decision makers lack complete certainty regarding the outcomes of various courses of action, but they are aware of the probabilities associated with their occurrence.

Satisficing: decision makers choose the first alternative that appears to give an acceptable or a satisfactory solution to the problem.

Uncertain environments: exist when managers have so little information on hand that they cannot even assign probabilities to various alternatives and their possible outcomes.

Chapter 15
CONFLICT AND NEGOTIATION

STUDY QUESTIONS

1.	What is conflict?
2.	How can conflict be managed successfully?
3.	What is negotiation?
4.	What are the different strategies involved in negotiation?

LEARNING OBJECTIVES

After completing this chapter students should be able to:

1.	Describe the nature of conflict and the different types and levels of conflict..
2.	Explain the difference between functional and dysfunctional conflict, and how conflict may be affected by culture.
3.	Describe the different stages of conflict and the various causes of conflict.
4.	Explain the different indirect conflict management approaches.
5.	Explain the different direct conflict management approaches.
6.	Describe the basic nature of negotiation and how negotiation is affected by goals and outcomes, ethics, organizational settings, and cultural differences.
7.	Discuss the nature and implications of distributive negotiation and integrative negotiation.
8.	Describe how to make negotiations effective, including gaining integrative agreements, avoiding common negotiation pitfalls, and using third-party roles.

MATERIAL IN *THE OB SKILLS WORKBOOK* SUPPORTING THE CHAPTER

Case for Critical Thinking	Case 15: Faculty Empowerment and the Changing University Environment
Experiential Exercises	Exercise 35: The Vacation Puzzle Exercise 36: The Ugli Orange Exercise 37: Conflict Dialogues
Self-Assessments	Assessment 18: Conflict Management Styles

CHAPTER OVERVIEW

This chapter focuses on conflict and negotiation, which are important topics in organizational behavior. The first half of the chapter focuses on conflict, which is inevitable anytime a group of people work together. As a result, it is important for managers to understand the dynamics of conflict and how conflict can be effectively resolved. The chapter begins by defining conflict, identifying different types and levels of conflict, differentiating between functional and dysfunctional conflict, and exploring cultural differences in conflict and conflict management. The second section of the chapter focuses on various aspects of managing conflict. Included among the topics in this section are stages of conflict; causes of conflict; the indirect conflict management approaches of reduced interdependence, appeals to common goals, hierarchical referral, and altering scripts and myths; and the direct conflict management approaches that include lose-lose conflict, win-lose conflict, and win-win conflict.

The second half of the chapter, with two sections, focuses on negotiation. All managers engage in negotiations on some level. This third section of the chapter defines negotiation and then discusses negotiation goals and outcomes, ethical aspects of negotiation, organizational settings for negotiation, and cultural differences in negotiations. The final section of the chapter focuses on negotiation strategies, contrasting distributive negotiation with integrative negotiation. Emphasis is placed on how to gain integrative agreements and how to avoid common negotiation pitfalls. The section concludes with a description of alternative dispute resolution, arbitration, and mediation as third-party roles in negotiations.

CHAPTER OUTLINE

I.   **Study Question 1: What is conflict?**
    A. Types of conflict
    B. Levels of conflict
    C. Functional and dysfunctional conflicts
    D. Culture and conflict

II. **Study Question 2: How can conflict be managed successfully?**
    A. Stages of conflict
    B. Causes of conflict
    C. Indirect conflict management approaches
    D. Direct conflict management approaches

III. **Study Question 3: What is negotiation?**
    A. What is negotiation?
    B. Negotiation goals and outcomes
    C. Ethical aspects of negotiation
    D. Organizational settings for negotiation
    E. Culture and negotiation

IV. **Study Question 4: What are the different strategies involved in negotiation?**
    A. Distributive negotiation
    B. Integrative negotiation
    C. How to gain integrative agreements

    D. Common negotiation pitfalls

    E. Third-party roles in negotiation

CHAPTER LECTURE NOTES

I.   **Introduction to the Chapter 15 Lecture.**

    A. Study questions for Chapter 15 (see ***PowerPoint Slide 2*** for Chapter 15).

        1. What is conflict?

        2. How can conflict be managed successfully?

        3. What is negotiation?

        4. What are the different strategies involved in negotiation?

    B. The lecture material for Chapter 15 is organized around the study questions.

        1. Point out to the students that the text's "Chapter At A Glance" identifies the key topics contained in the chapter and links them to the appropriate study questions.

    C. The chapter opens with an example that contrasts the negotiating styles of women and men.

II.   **Study Question 1: What is conflict?**

    A. Background on conflict.

        1. **Conflict** occurs whenever disagreements exist in a social situation over issues of substance or whenever emotional antagonisms create frictions between individuals or groups. (See ***PowerPoint Slide 3*** for Chapter 15.)

        2. The manager or leader may be directly involved in conflict or be a mediator of it.

        3. Managers and team leaders must be comfortable with interpersonal conflict, be able to recognize situations that have the potential for conflict, and effectively deal with conflict situations.

LECTURE ENHANCEMENT

One way to get students involved in your discussion of conflict is to ask them to note on a piece of paper a situation where they were involved in a conflict at work or at school. You can either (a) collect and sort through these papers to find good conflict examples [in which case you may suggest that students write their names on their papers], or (b) simply ask students to share their experiences with the class. Regardless of the option you choose, you can count on this approach to supply you with numerous examples that you can then refer back to in discussing substantive and emotional conflicts or functional and dysfunctional conflicts.

B. Types of conflict. (See *PowerPoint Slide 4* for Chapter 15.)

    1. **Substantive conflict** is a fundamental disagreement over ends or goals to be pursued and the means for their accomplishment.

    2. **Emotional conflict** involves interpersonal difficulties that arise over feelings of anger, mistrust, dislike, fear, resentment, and the like. This type of conflict is commonly known as a "clash of personalities."

C. Levels of conflict.

    1. Conflict within an individual. (See *PowerPoint Slide 5* for Chapter 15.)

        a. **Intrapersonal conflicts** often involve actual or perceived pressures from incompatible goals or expectations of the following types: approach-approach, avoidance-avoidance, and approach-avoidance.

        b. Approach-approach conflict occurs when a person must choose between two positive and equally attractive alternatives.

        c. Avoidance-avoidance conflict occurs when a person must choose between two negative and equally unattractive alternatives.

        d. Approach-avoidance conflict occurs when a person must decide to do something that has both positive and negative consequences.

    2. Conflict between two or more individuals.

        a. **Interpersonal conflict** occurs between two or more individuals who are in opposition to one another. (See *PowerPoint Slide 6* for Chapter 15.)

        b. Interpersonal conflict often arises in the performance evaluation process. It may be substantive or emotional or both.

    3. Conflict between groups.

a. **Intergroup conflict** occurs among members of different teams or groups. (See *PowerPoint Slide 6* for Chapter 15.)

b. Intergroup conflict can make the coordination and integration of task activities very difficult.

c. Cross-functional teams and task forces can help to minimize intergroup conflict.

4. Conflict between organizations. (See *PowerPoint Slide 7* for Chapter 15.)

a. **Interorganizational conflict** commonly refers to the competition and rivalry that characterizes firms operating in the same markets, but it actually encompasses disagreements that exist between any two or more organizations.

D. Functional and dysfunctional conflicts.

1. *Figure 15.1* from the textbook identifies two faces of conflict — functional and dysfunctional — in relation o the intensity of conflict and the impact of conflict on performance. (See *PowerPoint Slide 8* for Chapter 15.)

2. **Functional conflict**, alternatively called constructive conflict, results in positive benefits to individuals, the group, or the organization.

LECTURE ENHANCEMENT

Ask the students to provide examples of functional conflict that they have personally experienced.

---

3. The potential benefits of functional conflict the following (see *PowerPoint Slide 9* for Chapter 15):

a. Conflict can bring important problems to the surface so that they can be addressed.

b. Conflict can cause decisions to be considered carefully and perhaps reconsidered to ensure that the right path of action is being followed.

c. Conflict can increase the amount of information used for decision making.

d. Conflict can offer opportunities for creativity that can improve individual, team, or organizational performance.

4. **Dysfunctional conflict**, or destructive conflict, works to the disadvantage of an individual or group.

LECTURE ENHANCEMENT

Ask the students to provide examples of dysfunctional conflict that they have personally experienced.

---

5. The potential disadvantages of dysfunctional conflict include the following (see *PowerPoint Slide 10* for Chapter 15):

   a. Dysfunctional conflict diverts energies.

   b. Dysfunctional conflict hurts group cohesion.

   c. Dysfunctional conflict promotes interpersonal hostilities.

   d. Dysfunctional conflict creates a negative environment for workers.

   e. Dysfunctional conflict can decrease work productivity and job satisfaction.

   f. Dysfunctional conflict can contribute to absenteeism and job turnover.

E. Culture and conflict. (See *PowerPoint Slide 11* for Chapter 15.)

   1. Culture and cultural differences must be considered for their conflict potential.

   2. Individuals who are not able to recognize and respect the impact of culture on behavior may contribute to the emergence of dysfunctional situations

   3. By approaching a cross-cultural work situation with sensitivity and respect, ways can be found to work together without great difficulty and even with the advantages that constructive conflict may offer.

III. **Study Question 2: How can conflict be managed successfully?**

A. True **conflict resolution** occurs when the underlying reasons for a given destructive conflict are eliminated.

B. Stages of conflict.

   1. *Figure 15.2* from the textbook identifies four stages of conflict: conflict antecedents, perceived conflict, felt conflict, and manifest conflict. (See *PowerPoint Slide 12* for Chapter 15.)

      a. *Conflict antecedents* establish the conditions for which conflicts are likely to develop.

    b. *Perceived conflict* occurs when the antecedent conditions become the basis for substantive or emotional differences between people or groups.

    c. *Felt conflict* occurs when conflict is experienced as tension that motivates the person to take action to reduce feelings of discomfort.

    d. For conflict to be resolved, all parties should both perceive it and feel the need to do something about it.

    e. *Manifest conflict* occurs when it is expressed openly in behavior.

    f. A state of manifest conflict may be resolved by removing or correcting its antecedents.

2. *Suppression* is a superficial and often temporary form of conflict resolution.

3. Unresolved substantive conflicts can result in sustained emotional discomfort and escalate into dysfunctional emotional conflict between individuals.

4. Truly resolved conflicts may establish conditions that reduce the potential for future conflicts to make it easier to deal with them

C. Causes of conflict.

1. *Vertical conflict* occurs between hierarchical levels, and commonly involves supervisor-subordinate disagreements over resources, goals, deadlines, or performance results. (See *PowerPoint Slide 13* for Chapter 15.)

2. *Horizontal conflict* occurs between persons or groups at the same hierarchical level, and commonly involve goal incompatibilities, resource scarcities, or purely interpersonal factors. (See *PowerPoint Slide 13* for Chapter 15.)

3. A common variation of horizontal conflict is *line-staff conflict* that involves disagreements over who has authority and control over specific matters. (See *PowerPoint Slide 13* for Chapter 15.)

4. *Role conflicts* occur when communication of task expectations proves inadequate or upsetting. (See *PowerPoint Slide 14* for Chapter 15.)

5. *Workflow interdependencies* refer to the disputes and open disagreements that may erupt among people and units who are required to cooperate to meet challenging goals. (See *PowerPoint Slide 14* for Chapter 15.)

6. *Domain ambiguities* involve misunderstandings over such things as customer jurisdiction or scope of authority. (See *PowerPoint Slide 14* for Chapter 15.)

7. *Resource scarcity* refers to destructive competition that can result when resources are scarce or being redistributed. (See ***PowerPoint Slide 15*** for Chapter 15.)

8. *Power or value asymmetries* exist when interdependent people or groups differ substantially from one another in status and influence or in values. (See ***PowerPoint Slide 15*** for Chapter 15.)

D. Indirect conflict management approaches.

1. Indirect conflict management approaches share the common ground of avoiding direct dealings with personalities.

2. *Reduced interdependence* refers to managers adjusting the level of interdependency among units or individuals when workflow conflicts exist. (See ***PowerPoint Slide 16*** for Chapter 15.)

   a. *Decoupling* is taking action to eliminate or reduce the required contact between conflicting parties.

   b. *Buffering* refers to building an inventory to remove direct performance pressures when the outputs of one group are the inputs of another group.

   c. Persons in *linking pin roles*, such as project liaison, are expected to understand the operations, members, needs, and norms of their host group. They are supposed to use this knowledge to help their group work better with other groups in order to accomplish mutual tasks.

3. An *appeal to common goals* can focus the attention of potentially conflicting parties on one mutually desirable conclusion. (See ***PowerPoint Slide 16*** for Chapter 15.)

4. *Hierarchical referral* makes use of the chain of command for conflict resolution. Problems are simply referred up the hierarchy for more senior managers to reconcile. (See ***PowerPoint Slide 17*** for Chapter 15.)

5. *Altering scripts and myths* refers to the superficial management of conflict by using behavioral routines that become part of the organization's culture. (See ***PowerPoint Slide 17*** for Chapter 15.)

E. Direct conflict management approaches.

LECTURE ENHANCEMENT

To introduce the material on direct conflict management approaches, ask the students the following questions: (1) To what extent do you attempt to satisfy your own concerns when you're trying to resolve a conflict? (2)) To what extent do you attempt to satisfy the other party' concerns when you're trying to resolve a conflict? Select several students to share their self-assessments with respect to these two questions, and ask them to describe how they typically go about trying to resolve a conflict. Relate this discussion to the different conflict resolution strategies identified in *Figure 15.3*.

---

1. *Figure 15.3* from the textbook describes five different approaches for managing conflict. These approaches reflect differing combinations of assertiveness (*i.e.*, attempting to satisfy one's own concerns) and cooperativeness (*i.e.*, attempting to satisfy the other party's concerns). (See *PowerPoint Slide 18* for Chapter 15.)

2. Each conflict management style can be effective in different circumstances.

   a. Collaboration and problem solving is preferred to gain true conflict resolution when time and cost permit.

   b. Avoidance may be used when an issue is trivial, when more important issues are pressing, or when people need to cool down temporarily and regain perspective.

   c. Authoritative command may be used when quick and decisive action is vital or when unpopular actions must be taken.

   d. Accommodation may be used when issues are more important to others than to yourself or when you want to build "credits" for use in later disagreements.

   e. Compromise may be used to arrive at temporary settlements of complex issues or to arrive at expedient solutions when time is limited.

3. Lose-lose conflict. (See *PowerPoint Slide 19* for Chapter 15.)

   a. *Lose-lose conflict* occurs when nobody really gets what he or she wants.

   b. **Avoidance** is an extreme form of inattention; everyone simply pretends that the conflict does not really exist and hopes that it will go away. This is a low-assertiveness and low-cooperativeness situation.

      (i) Avoidance may be used when an issue is trivial or more important issues are pressing, or when people need to cool down temporarily and regain perspective.

    c. **Accommodation**, or **smoothing** as it is sometimes called, involves playing down differences among the conflicting parties and highlighting similarities and areas of agreement. This is a low-assertiveness and high-cooperativeness situation.

        (i) Accommodation may be used when issues are more important to others than to yourself or when you want to build "credits" for use in later issues.

    d. **Compromise** occurs when each party gives up something of value to the other; but with no one's desires being fully satisfied, the antecedent conditions for future conflicts are established. This is a moderate-assertiveness and moderate-cooperativeness situation.

        (i) Compromise may be used for temporary settlements to complex issues or to arrive at expedient solutions when time is limited.

4. Win-lose conflict. (See *PowerPoint Slide 20* for Chapter 15.)

    a. In *win-lose conflict*, one party achieves its desires at the expense and to the exclusion of the other party's desires. This is a high-assertiveness and low-cooperativeness situation.

    b. **Competition** occurs when one party achieves a victory through the use of force, superior skills, or domination. This is a high-assertiveness and low-cooperativeness situation.

    c. **Authoritative command** refers to the use of formal authority to dictate a solution and specify who gains what and who loses what. This is a high-assertiveness and low-cooperativeness situation.

        (i) Authoritative command may be used when quick and decisive action is vital or when unpopular actions must be taken.

5. Win-win conflict.

    a. *Win-win conflict* is achieved by a blend of both high cooperativeness and high assertiveness. (See *PowerPoint Slide 21* for Chapter 15.)

    b. **Collaboration** or **problem solving** involves recognition by all conflicting parties that something is wrong and needs attention, and it stresses gathering and evaluating information in solving disputes and making choices. (See *PowerPoint Slide 21* for Chapter 15.)

    c. Collaboration and problem solving are preferred to gain true conflict resolution when time and cost permit. (See *PowerPoint Slide 21* for Chapter 15.)

d. The ultimate test for a win-win solution is whether or not the conflicting parties see that the solution accomplishes the following (see ***PowerPoint Slide 22*** for Chapter 15):

(i) Achieves each other's goals.

(ii) Is acceptable to both parties.

(iii) Establishes a process whereby all parties involved see a responsibility to be open and honest about facts and feelings.

e. Potential disadvantages of collaboration include the following (see ***PowerPoint Slide 23*** for Chapter 15):

(i) Collaboration requires time and energy.

(ii) Both parties to the conflict need to be assertive and cooperative.

(iii) Collaboration may not be feasible if the organization's culture does not value cooperation.

LECTURE ENHANCEMENT

Note that each of the conflict management styles has some value; each is appropriately utilized in different situations. For example, <u>avoidance</u> is appropriate when an issue is trivial or there is no chance of resolution. <u>Accommodation</u> or has merit when issues are more important to others than yourself or when you realize you are wrong. <u>Competition</u> or is useful in situations where quick, decisive action is vital. <u>Compromise</u> is helpful in achieving a temporary solution to a complex issue or when conflicting parties have equal power but are committed to mutually exclusive goals. <u>Collaboration</u> or is appropriate when an integrative solution needs to be found without sacrificing either party's concerns, both of which are very important.

(Additional information can be found in D. Tjosvold, *The Conflict Positive Organization*, Boston: Addison-Wesley Publishing Company, Inc. 1991.)

IV. **Study Question 3: What is negotiation?**

A. What is negotiation?

1. **Negotiation** is the process of making joint decisions when the parties involved have different preferences.

B. Negotiation goals and outcomes.

1. *Substance goals* deal with outcomes that relate to the "content" issues under negotiation. (See ***PowerPoint Slide 24*** for Chapter 15.)

2. *Relationship goals* deal with outcomes that relate to how well people involved in the negotiation and any constituencies they may represent are able to work with one another once the process is concluded. (See **PowerPoint Slide 24** for Chapter 15.)

LECTURE ENHANCEMENT

An excellent article on negotiation, entitled "Consider Both Relationships and Substance When Negotiating Strategically," by G.T. Savage, J.D. Blair, and R.L. Sorenson is available in the *Academy of Management Executive*, 1989, 3(1): 37-48.

---

3. *Effective negotiation* occurs when substance issues are resolved and working relationships are maintained or even improved. (See **PowerPoint Slide 25** for Chapter 15.)

4. Negotiations are effective when the following conditions are met (see **PowerPoint Slide 25** for Chapter 15):

   a. *Quality* — the negotiation results offer a "quality" agreement that is wise and satisfactory to all sides.

   b. *Harmony* — the negotiation is "harmonious" and fosters rather than inhibits good interpersonal relations.

   c. *Efficiency* — the negotiation is "efficient" and no more time consuming or costly than absolutely necessary.

LECTURE ENHANCEMENT

Consider the following scenario: Suppose that you have given the class a complex project assignment which has a due date four weeks in the future, will count for 40 percent of their course grade, and must be done in groups. Some students complain that project, with its short time line, will overload their schedules. Other students are concerned about their grades, wanting to receive as much guidance and feedback as possible.

Divide the class into groups of four or five students. Have each group devise a plan for negotiating among themselves and with you regarding the above scenario. Select two or three of the teams to share their negotiation plans with the entire class.

After the plans are presented, discuss how the plan reflects negotiation goals and the three criteria for effective negotiations. Also discuss how well the plan follows the negotiation rules for integrative agreements. To what extent is each plan likely to result in a win-win situation for the students and the instructor?

C. Ethical aspects of negotiation. (See *PowerPoint Slide 26* for Chapter 15.)

   1. To maintain good working relationships in negotiations, managers and other involved parties should strive for high ethical standards.

   2. Negotiating parties often try to rationalize questionable ethics as unavoidable, harmless, or justified, but these rationalizations are offset by long-run negative consequences.

   3. The unethical negotiating party may become a target of revenge.

   4. Unethical negotiating actions may become habitual.

D. Organizational settings for negotiation. (See *PowerPoint Slides 27* and *28* for Chapter 15.)

   1. *Two-party negotiation* occurs when the manager negotiates directly with one other person.

   2. *Group negotiation* occurs when the manager is part of a team or group whose members are negotiating to arrive at a common decision.

   3. *Intergroup negotiation* occurs when the manager is part of a group that is negotiating with another group to arrive at a decision regarding a problem or situation affecting both.

   4. *Constituency negotiation* occurs when the manager is involved in negotiation with other persons, with each party representing a broader constituency.

E. Culture and negotiation.

   1. The existence of cultural differences in time orientation, individualism-collectivism, and power distance can have a substantial impact on negotiation.

V. **Study Question 4: What are the different strategies involved in negotiation?**

A. Background on negotiation strategies. (See *PowerPoint Slide 29* for Chapter 15.)

   1. **Distributive negotiation** focuses on positions staked out or declared by the parties involved, and each party is trying to claim certain portions of the available pie.

   2. **Integrative negotiation** — also called *principled negotiation* — focuses on the merits of the issues, and everyone involved tries to enlarge the available pie rather than stake claims to certain portions of it.

LECTURE ENHANCEMENT

There are many books, videos, and web-based resources available on how to negotiate effectively. The Web site entitled at http://top7business.com/archives/negotiation/ provides access to a sample of this material.

B. Distributive negotiation. (See *PowerPoint Slide 30* for Chapter 15.)

    a. Participants in distributive negotiation focus on the question: "Who is going to get this resource?"

    b. *"Hard" distributive negotiation* takes place when each party holds out to get its own.

    c. *"Soft" distributive negotiation* takes place when one party is willing to make concessions to the other to resolve things.

    d. The **bargaining zone** is the range between one party's minimum reservation point and the other party's maximum reservation point.

        (i) *Figure 15.4* from the textbook illustrates the bargaining zone in a classic two-party negotiation.

C. Integrative negotiation. (See *PowerPoint Slide 31* for Chapter 15.)

    1. Participants in integrative negotiation focus on the question: "How can the resource best be utilized?" Being much less confrontational, addressing this question permits a broad range of alternatives to be considered and there is much more of a "win-win" orientation.

    2. Integrative negotiation may occur in any of the following forms:

        a. Integrative negotiation may involve selective guidance in which both parties realize that there are more important things on which to focus their time and attention.

        b. Compromise can play a role in integrative negotiation, but it must have an enduring basis.

        c. Integrative negotiation may involve true collaboration.

D. How to gain integrative agreements.

    1. The foundations for gaining truly integrative agreements include supportive attitudes, constructive behaviors, and good information.

2. The attitudinal foundations of integrative agreements include the following (see ***PowerPoint Slide 32*** for Chapter 15):

   a. Willingness to trust the other party.

   b. Willingness to share information with the other party.

   c. Willingness to ask concrete questions of the other party.

3. The behavioral foundations of integrative agreements include the following (see ***PowerPoint Slide 33*** for Chapter 15):

   a. The ability to separate the people from the problem to avoid allowing emotional considerations to affect the negotiation.

   b. The ability to focus on interests rather than positions.

   c. The ability to avoid making premature judgments.

   d. The ability to keep alternative creation separate from evaluation.

   e. The ability to judge possible agreements on an objective set of criteria or standards.

4. The information foundations of integrative agreements include the following (see ***PowerPoint Slide 34*** for Chapter 15):

   a. Each party must know what he or she will do if an agreement can't be reached. In other words, each party must become familiar with his/her BATNA, or "best alternative to a negotiated agreement."

   b. Each party must determine what is personally important in the situation.

   c. Each party must achieve an understanding of what the other party values, even to the point of determining the other party's BANTA.

E. Common negotiation pitfalls. (See ***PowerPoint Slide 35*** for Chapter 15.)

1. *Myth of the fixed pie* — the tendency in negotiation to stake out your position based on the assumption that in order to gain your way, something must be subtracted from that of the other party.

2. *Escalating commitment* — once demands have been stated, people become committed to them and are reluctant to back down.

3. *Overconfidence* — negotiators often develop overconfidence that their positions are the only correct ones, consequently leading them to ignore the other party's needs.

4. Telling and hearing problems.

   a. "Negotiation is the process of communicating back and forth for the purpose of reaching a joint decision."

   b. *Telling problem* — the parties don't really talk to one another, at least not in the sense of making themselves truly understood.

   c. *Hearing problem* — the parties are unable or unwilling to listen well enough to understand what each other is saying.

F. Third-party roles in negotiation. (See *PowerPoint Slides 36* and *37* for Chapter 15.)

   1. Negotiation may sometimes be accomplished through the intervention of third parties, such as when stalemates occur and matters appear irresolvable under current circumstance.

   2. **Alternative dispute resolution** occurs when a neutral third party works with persons involved in a negotiation to help them resolve impasses and settle disputes.

   3. **Arbitration** occurs when a neutral third party acts as a "judge" with the power to issue a decision that is binding on all parties.

   4. **Mediation** occurs when a neutral third party tries to engage the conflicting parties in a negotiated solution through persuasion and rational argument.

LECTURE ENHANCEMENT

The Negotiation Institute Web site at http://www.negotiation.com/ provides materials that may be used to support and amplify on your discussion of negotiation.

VI. **Study summary for Chapter 15.**

   A. Point out to the students that the text's "Chapter 15 Study Guide" recaps the key theories, concepts, and ideas in the chapter in relation to the appropriate study questions.

CHAPTER STUDY GUIDE

Study Question 1: What is conflict?

- Conflict appears in a social situation as any disagreement over issues of substance or emotional antagonisms that create friction between individuals or groups.

- Conflict can either be emotional — based on personal feelings — or substantive — based on work goals.
- When kept within tolerable limits, conflict can be a source of creativity and performance enhancement; it becomes destructive when these limits are exceeded.
- Conflict situations in organizations occur in vertical and lateral working relations and in line-staff relations.
- Most typically, conflict develops through a series of stages, beginning with antecedent conditions and progressing into manifest conflict.
- Unresolved prior conflicts set the stage for future conflicts of a similar nature.

Study Question 2: How can conflict be managed successfully?

- Indirect forms of conflict management include appeals to common goals, hierarchical referral, organizational redesign, and the use of mythology and scripts.
- Direct conflict management proceeds with different contributions of assertiveness and cooperativeness by conflicting parties.
- Win-win conflict resolution is preferred; it is achieved through collaboration and problem solving.
- Win-lose conflict resolution should be avoided; it is associated with competition and authoritative command.

Study Question 3: What is negotiation?

- Negotiation occurs whenever two or more people with different preferences must make joint decisions.
- Managers may find themselves involved in various types of negotiation situations, including two-party, group, intergroup, and constituency negotiation.
- Effective negotiation occurs when issues of substance are resolved and human relationships are maintained, or even improved, in the process.
- Ethical conduct is important to successful negotiations.

Study Question 4: What are the different strategies involved in negotiation?

- In distributive negotiation, the focus of each party is on staking out positions in the attempt to claim desired portions of a "fixed pie."
- In integrative negotiation, sometimes called principled negotiation, the focus is on determining the merits of the issues and finding ways to satisfy one another's needs.
- The success of the strategies depends on avoiding common negotiating pitfalls and building good communications.

KEY TERMS

Accommodation or smoothing: involves playing down differences among the conflicting parties and highlighting similarities and areas of agreement.

Alternative dispute resolution: occurs when a neutral third party works with persons involved in a negotiation to help them resolve impasses and settle disputes.

Arbitration: occurs when a neutral third party acts as a judge with the power to issue a decision that is binding on all parties.

Authoritative command: the use of formal authority to dictate a solution and specify who gains what and who loses what.

Avoidance: an extreme form of inattention; everyone simply pretends that the conflict does not really exist and hopes that it will go away.

Bargaining zone: the range between one party's minimum reservation point and the other party's maximum reservation point.

Collaboration: involves recognition by all conflicting parties that something is wrong and needs attention, and it stresses gathering and evaluating information in solving disputes and making choices. Also known as problem solving.

Competition: occurs when one party achieves a victory through the use of force, superior skills, or domination.

Compromise: occurs when each party gives up something of value to the other; but with no one's desires being fully satisfied, the antecedent conditions for future conflicts are established.

Conflict: occurs whenever disagreements exist in a social situation over issues of substance or whenever emotional antagonisms create frictions between individuals or groups.

Conflict resolution: occurs when the underlying reasons for a given destructive conflict are eliminated.

Distributive negotiation: focuses on positions staked out or declared by the parties involved, and each party is trying to claim certain portions of the available pie.

Dysfunctional conflict: conflict that works to the disadvantage of an individual or group.

Emotional conflict: involves interpersonal difficulties that arise over feelings of anger, mistrust, dislike, fear, resentment, and the like.

Functional conflict: conflict that results in positive benefits to individuals, the group, or the organization.

Integrative negotiation: focuses on the merits of the issues, and everyone involved tries to enlarge the available pie rather than stake claims to certain portions of it.

Intergroup conflict: occurs among members of different teams or groups.

Interorganizational conflict: commonly refers to the competition and rivalry that characterizes firms operating in the same markets, but it actually encompasses disagreements that exist between any two or more organizations.

Interpersonal conflict: occurs between two or more individuals who are in opposition to one another.

Intrapersonal conflict: often involve actual or perceived pressures from incompatible goals or expectations of the following types: approach-approach, avoidance-avoidance, and approach-avoidance.

Mediation: occurs when a neutral third party tries to engage the conflicting parties in a negotiated solution through persuasion and rational argument.

Negotiation: the process of making joint decisions when the parties involved have different preferences.

Problem solving: involves recognition by all conflicting parties that something is wrong and needs attention, and it stresses gathering and evaluating information in solving disputes and making choices. Also known as collaboration.

Substantive conflict: involves a fundamental disagreement over ends or goals to be pursued and the means for their accomplishment.

Chapter 16
CHANGE, INNOVATION, AND STRESS

STUDY QUESTIONS

1.	What is organizational change?
2.	What change strategies are used in organizations?
3.	How is resistance to change best managed?
4.	How do organizations innovate?
5.	How does stress affect people in change environments?

LEARNING OBJECTIVES

After completing this chapter students should be able to:

1.	Identify different types of change, key forces for changes, and key targets of change.
2.	Describe Kurt Lewin's three-phase model of planned change.
3.	Describe the differences among the force-coercion, rational persuasion, and shared power change strategies.
4.	Explain why people resist change and how to deal with resistance
5.	Describe the innovation process and the distinctive features of innovative organizations.
6.	Discuss the nature and implications of stress and stressors.
7.	Explain the difference between constructive stress and destructive stress, and relate both to performance and personal health
8.	Discuss the concepts of stress prevention and stress management.

MATERIAL IN *THE OB SKILLS WORKBOOK* SUPPORTING THE CHAPTER

Case for Critical Thinking	Case 16: The New Vice President
Experiential Exercises	Exercise 31: Role Analysis Negotiation
	Exercise 37: Force-Field Analysis
Self-Assessments	Assessment 19: Your Personality Type
	Assessment 20: Time Management Profile

CHAPTER OVERVIEW

This chapter focuses on change, innovation, and stress. These three issues are extremely important in the daily lives of most managers. Change and innovation are becoming commonplace occurrences in many industries. To illustrate this point, ask your students to think about the changes and innovations that have taken place during their school years. When your students entered grade school, most managers sat at a desk with no computer, had a phone with a single line, had no idea what a pager or cell-phone was, used an overhead projector to make presentations, asked a secretary to "type a letter" when correspondence was necessary, and wouldn't know what you were talking about if you mentioned the words Internet, World Wide Web, Yahoo, Amazon.com, or virtual reality — all phenomena which have developed within the last decade or so. Today, things are much different — and the differences have been caused by innovation, change, and in many cases, both positive and negative forms of stress.

The initial focus of the chapter is on organizational change. Different types of changes are described, and the various forces for and targets of change are identified. Kurt Lewin's three phase model of change is examined; emphasis is placed on the dynamics associated with the unfreezing, change, and refreezing phases. Next, three strategies for facilitating change — force-coercion, rational persuasion, and shared power — are discussed. The third section of the chapter identifies different reasons underlying people's resistance to change and explains how to deal effectively with resistance to change.

The second major issue of this chapter is innovation within organizations. This section is brief, but substantive. Product and process innovations are defined. The innovation process — idea creation, initial experimentation, feasibility determination, and final application — and features of innovative organizations are described.

The chapter concludes with a third major issue — stress. Stress is defined, then work stressors and life stressors are identified. Constructive stress and destructive stress are examined within the context of stress and performance. The impact of stress on health is discussed briefly, before stress prevention and stress management are explored.

CHAPTER OUTLINE

I.   **Study Question 1: What is organizational change?**
    A. Planned and unplanned change
    B. Forces and targets for change
    C. Phases of planned change

II.   **Study Question 2: What change strategies are used in organizations?**
    A. Force-coercion
    B. Rational persuasion
    C. Shared power

III.   **Study Question 3: How is resistance to change best managed?**
    A. Why people resist change
    B. Ways of dealing with resistance

IV.   **Study Question 4: How do organizations innovate?**
    A. The innovation process
    B. Features of innovative organizations

V.   **Study Question 5: How does stress affect people in change environments?**
    A. Sources of stress
    B. Stress and performance

    C. Stress and health

    D. Stress management

CHAPTER LECTURE NOTES

I. **Introduction to the Chapter 16 Lecture.**

    A. Study questions for Chapter 16. (See *PowerPoint Slide 2* for Chapter 16.)

        1. What is organizational change?

        2. What change strategies are used in organizations?

        3. How is resistance to change best managed?

        4. How do organizations innovate?

        5. How does stress affect people in change environments?

    B. The lecture material for Chapter 16 is organized around the study questions.

        1. Point out to the students that the text's "Chapter At A Glance" identifies the key topics contained in the chapter and links them to the appropriate study questions.

    C. The chapter opens by describing how change, innovation, and stress are expected and normal adjuncts of a modern business environment that can be characterized with the words "turmoil" and "turbulence."

II. **Study Question 1: What is organizational change?**

LECTURE ENHANCEMENT

The following quote from Kurt Lewin provides a nice introduction to the topic of change: "If you want to truly understand something, try to change it."

    A. Background on change.

        1. **Transformational change** results in a major overhaul of the organization or its component systems. (See *PowerPoint Slide 3* for Chapter 16.)

            a. Transformational change may be described as *radical change* or *frame-breaking change*.

            b. Organizations experiencing transformational change undergo a significant shift in basic characteristic features.

2. *Incremental change*, or *frame-bending change*, is part of the organization's natural evolution in that it builds on the existing ways of operating to enhance or extend them in new directions. (See *PowerPoint Slide 4* for Chapter 16.)

   a. Incremental change includes the introduction of new products, new technologies, and new systems and processes.

   b. The capability of improving continuously through incremental change is an important asset in today's demanding environments.

3. **Change agents** are individuals and groups who lead and support the change process by taking responsibility for changing the existing behavior patterns of other people or the social system. (See *PowerPoint Slide 5* for Chapter 16.)

   a. The success of both transformational change and incremental change depends in part on change agents.

   b. Being an effective change agent means being a great *change leader*.

B. Planned and unplanned change.

   1. **Unplanned change** occurs spontaneously and without a change agent's direction, and such change may be disruptive. (See *PowerPoint Slide 6* for Chapter 16.)

   2. When unplanned change occurs, the appropriate goal is to act quickly to minimize the negative consequences and maximize any possible benefits. (See *PowerPoint Slide 6* for Chapter 16.)

   3. **Planned change** is the result of specific efforts by a change agent and is a direct response to someone's perception of a performance gap. (See *PowerPoint Slide 7* for Chapter 16.)

   4. A **performance gap** is the discrepancy between the desired and actual state of affairs. (See *PowerPoint Slide 7* for Chapter 16.)

   5. Performance gaps may represent problems to be resolved or opportunities to be explored. (See *PowerPoint Slide 7* for Chapter 16.)

C. Forces and targets for change.

   1. Forces for change include the following (see *PowerPoint Slide 8* for Chapter 16):

      a. Organization-environment relationships.

      b. Organizational life cycle.

      c. Political nature of organizations.

2. Planned change based on any of these forces can be internally directed toward a wide variety of organizational components.

3. *Figure 16.1* from the textbook identifies various organizational targets for planned change. (See *PowerPoint Slide 9* for Chapter 16.)

   a. The targets for change include organizational purpose, objectives, strategy, culture, people, task, structure, and technology.

   b. These targets are highly interconnected in the workplace.

D. Phases of planned change.

1. Transformational change efforts can fail for the following reasons (see *PowerPoint Slide 10* for Chapter 16):

   a. No sense of urgency.

   b. No powerful guiding coalition.

   c. No compelling vision.

   d. Failure to communicate the vision.

   e. Failure to empower others to act.

   f. Failure to celebrate short-term wins.

   g. Failure to build on accomplishments.

   h. Failure to institutionalize results.

2. Psychologist Kurt Lewin recommends that any change effort be viewed as a process with three distinct phases — unfreezing, changing, and refreezing — that must be well handled for a change to be successful.

   a. **<u>Unfreezing</u>** is the managerial responsibility of preparing a situation for change, and it involves disconfirming existing attitudes and behaviors to create a felt need for something new. (See *PowerPoint Slide 11* for Chapter 16.)

      (i) Large systems seem particularly susceptible to what is sometimes called the *boiled frog phenomenon*, which refers to the notion that a live frog will immediately jump when placed in a pan of hot water, but when placed in cold water that is then heated very slowly, however, the frog will stay in the water until the water boils the frog to death.

(ii) When managers fail to monitor their environments, recognize the important trends, or sense the need to change, their organizations may slowly suffer and lose their competitive edge.

(iii) The best organizations are led by people who are always on the alert and understand the importance of unfreezing in the change process.

b. **Changing** involves taking action to modify a situation by changing things, such as the people, tasks, structure, or technology of the organization. (See *PowerPoint Slide 11* for Chapter 16.)

(i) Lewin believes that many change agents are prone to an activity trap — they bypass the unfreezing stage and start changing things prematurely to too quickly.

c. **Refreezing** is designed to maintain the momentum of a change and eventually institutionalize it as part of the normal routine. (See *PowerPoint Slide 11* for Chapter 16.)

(i) Refreezing secures the full benefits of long-lasting change.

(ii) Refreezing involves the following activities:

1. Positively reinforcing desired outcomes.

2. Providing extra support when difficulties are encountered.

3. Evaluating progress and results.

4. Assessing the costs and benefits of change.

5. Allowing for modifications to be made in the change to increase its success over time.

LECTURE ENHANCEMENT

Have the students identify something they believe should be changed about the way your college or university operates. Then have them analyze how this change could be managed using the three phase model of planned change for guidance.

III.   Study Question 2: What change strategies are used in organizations?

A. *Figure 16.2* from the textbook identifies three different change strategies — force-coercion, rational persuasion, and shared power — and the power bases, change agent behaviors, and predicted outcomes associated with each strategy. (See *PowerPoint Slide 12* for Chapter 16.)

B. Force-coercion.

1. The **force-coercion strategy** uses legitimacy, rewards, or punishments as primary inducements to change.

2. The change agent acts unilaterally to "command" change through the formal authority of his or her position, to induce change via an offer of special rewards, or to bring about change via threats of punishment.

3. People respond to this strategy mainly out of the fear of being punished if they do not comply with a change directive or out of the desire to gain a reward if they do.

4. Compliance is usually temporary.

C. Rational persuasion.

1. The **rational persuasion strategy** attempts to bring about change through the use of special knowledge, empirical support, or rational arguments.

2. This strategy assumes that rational people will be guided by reason and self-interest in deciding whether or not to support a change.

3. The strategy is sometimes referred to as an *empirical-rational strategy of planned change*.

4. When successful, this strategy results in a longer lasting, more naturalized change than does force-coercion.

D. Shared-power.

1. The **shared-power strategy** actively and sincerely involves the people who will be affected by a change in planning and making key decisions relating to this change.

2. This strategy is sometimes called a *normative-reeducative approach*.

3. This strategy tries to develop directions and support for change through involvement and empowerment.

4. Given the high level of involvement, this strategy is likely to result in longer lasting and internalized change.

LECTURE ENHANCEMENT

If you used the previous *Enhancement*, discuss with the students the viability of using force-coercion, rational persuasion, or shared power to achieve the planned change in your college or university.

IV.   **Study Question 3: How is resistance to change best managed?**

    A. Background on resistance to change. (See *PowerPoint Slide 13* for Chapter 16.)

         1. **Resistance to change** is any attitude or behavior that indicates unwillingness to make or support a desired change.

         2. Change agents often view resistance as something that must be overcome for change to be successful.

         3. It is helpful to view resistance to change as feedback that the change agent can use to facilitate achieving the change objectives.

    B. Why people resist change.

         1. People resist change for the following reasons (see *PowerPoint Slide 14* for Chapter 16):

             a. Fear of the unknown.

             b. Lack of good information.

             c. Fear of loss of security.

             d. No reasons to change.

             e. Fear of loss of power.

             f. Lack of resources.

             g. Bad timing.

             h. Habit.

         2. Forms of resistance to change include resistance to the change itself, resistance to the change strategy, and resistance to the change agent.

         3. Resistance to the change itself. (See *PowerPoint Slide 15* for Chapter 16.)

             a. People may reject a change because they believe it is not worth their time, effort, or attention.

    b.   To deal with this form of resistance, the change agent should inform all those affected by the change as to how it satisfies the following criteria:

        (i)   *Benefit* — the change should have a clear relative advantage for the people being asked to change, it should be perceived as "a better way."

        (ii)   *Compatibility* — the change should be as compatible as possible with existing values and experiences of the people being asked to change.

        (iii) *Complexity* — the change should be no more complex than necessary; it must be as easy as possible for people to understand and use.

        (iv) *Triability* — the change should be something that people can try on a step-by-step basis and make adjustments as things progress.

4.   Resistance to the change strategy. (See ***PowerPoint Slide 16*** for Chapter 16.)

    a.   Using the force-coercion strategy may create resistance among individuals who resent management by "command" or the use of threatened punishment.

    b.   Using the rational persuasion strategy may create resistance when the data are suspect or the expertise of advocates is unclear.

    c.   Using the shared-power strategy may create resistance if it appears manipulative and insincere.

5.   Resistance to the change agent. (See ***PowerPoint Slide 17*** for Chapter 16.)

    a.   Resistance to the change agent is directed at the person implementing the change and often involves personality and other differences.

LECTURE ENHANCEMENT

Assuming that you used the preceding two enhancements, ask the students to identify potential sources of resistance for the planned change in your college or university.

C. How to deal with resistance. (See ***PowerPoint Slide 18*** for Chapter 16.)

1.   *Education and communication* — the objective is to educate people about a change before it is implemented and to help them understand the logic of the change.

2.   *Participation and support* — with the goal of allowing others to help design and implement the changes, this approach asks people to contribute ideas and advice or to work on task forces or committees that may be leading the change.

3. *Facilitation and support* — involves providing assistance, both emotional and material, for people experiencing the hardships of change.

4. *Negotiation and agreement* — offers incentives to actual or potential change resistors; tradeoffs are arranged to provide special benefits in exchange for assurances that the change will not be blocked.

5. *Manipulation and cooptation* — makes use of covert attempts to influence others, selectively providing information and consciously structuring events so that the desired change occurs.

6. *Explicit or implicit coercion* — employs the force of authority to get people to accept change.

7. *Figure 16.3* from the textbook provides additional information regarding each of the above methods for dealing with resistance to change. The additional information describes when to use each method as well as the advantages and disadvantages of each method. (See *PowerPoint Slide 19* for Chapter 16.)

LECTURE ENHANCEMENT

Assuming that you used the preceding three enhancements, have the students discuss ways of overcoming resistance to planned change in your college or university.

V. **Study Question 4: How do organizations innovate?**

A. Background on innovation. (See *PowerPoint Slide 20* for Chapter 16.)

1. **Innovation** is the process of creating new ideas and putting them into practice.

2. **Product innovations** result in the introduction of new or improved goods or services to better meet customer needs.

3. **Process innovations** result in the introduction of new and better work methods and operations.

B. The innovation process.

1. *Figure 16.4* from the textbook describes the basic steps in a typical process of organizational innovation. (See *PowerPoint Slide 21* for Chapter 16.)

2. The steps include the following:

a. *Idea creation* — to create an idea through spontaneous creativity, ingenuity, and information processing.

b. *Initial experimentation* — to establish the idea's potential value and application.

c. *Feasibility determination* — to identify anticipated costs and benefits.

d. *Final application* — to produce and market a new product or service, or to implement a new approach to operations.

C. Features of innovative organizations. (See ***PowerPoint Slide 22*** for Chapter 16.)

1. *Strategies and cultures* — highly innovative organizations have strategies and cultures that are built around a commitment to innovation, including having a tolerance for mistakes and respect for well-intentioned ideas that turn out to not work..

2. *Structures* — highly innovative organizations have structures that support innovation by emphasizing creativity through teamwork and cross-functional integration and the use of decentralization and empowerment.

3. *Staffing* — in highly innovative organizations, staffing is done with a clear commitment to innovation by giving proper attention to the innovation roles of idea generators, information gatekeepers, product champions, and project leaders.

4. *Top-management support* — innovative organizations have senior managers who provide good examples for others, eliminate obstacles to innovation, and try to get things done that make innovation easier.

LECTURE ENHANCEMENT

To illustrate the value of innovation to organizations, share with students the classic story on the origins of "post-it" notes in the 3M Corporation. To embellish the information provided, explain how Art Fry, a 3M employee got the idea for "post-it" notes while attempting to mark pages in his Sunday hymnal. He found that a light adhesive developed by a colleague, Spencer Silver, was perfect for the task. To this point, Spencer's adhesive had been considered a failure because it wasn't sticky enough. Even after the "post-it" application of the adhesive was identified, Fry had trouble getting the full support of management. To win them over, he distributed "post-it" notes throughout the company. Within a short time, top executives were hooked on them. When market tests proved successful, the product received the green light. Ultimately, "post-it" notes became one of the five best selling office products in history. Innovations such as this are encouraged at 3M through formal practices such as "bootlegging" in which small groups of researchers and marketers work together to bring new products to market.

(Source: *A Passion for Excellence,* New York: Random House, 1985; *Breakthroughs!,* New York: Rawson Associates, 1986; C. Knowlton, "What Makes America Best, *Fortune,* March 28, 1988, pp. 40-54; B. Dumaine, "Ability to Innovate," *Fortune,* January 29, 1990; pp. 43, 46; S. Weiner, "A Hard Way to Make a Buck," *Forbes,* April 29, 1991, pp. 134-137; *The Economist,* November 30, 1991, pp. 70-72.)

VI.   Study Question 5: How does stress affect people in change environments?

A. Background on stress.

1. Change and innovation often create new and increased pressures on the people involved.

2. **Stress** is a state of tension experienced by individuals facing extraordinary demands, constraints, or opportunities. (See *PowerPoint Slide 23* for Chapter 16.)

LECTURE ENHANCEMENT

An interesting on-line stress quiz (or assessment) is available at http://www.stress-less.com/WebStressScale.cfm. The quiz helps you determine: situations at work and in your personal life that you perceive as stressful; your signs and symptoms of stress; and the effectiveness of your current coping skills and resources. The answers are processed on-line.

B. Sources of stress.

1. **Stressors** are the wide variety of things that cause stress for individuals. (See *PowerPoint Slide 24* for Chapter 16.)

2. **Work stressors** can arise from many sources, including excessively high or low task demands, role conflicts or ambiguities, poor interpersonal relations, or career progress that is either to slow or too fast.

3. Common work stressors include the following (see *PowerPoint Slide 25* for Chapter 16):

(i)   Task demands.

(ii) Role ambiguities.

(iii) Role conflicts.

(iv) Ethical dilemmas.

(v)   Interpersonal problems.

(vi) Career developments.

(vii) Physical setting.

4. Life stressors. (See *PowerPoint Slide 26* for Chapter 16.)

a. The *spillover effect* results when forces in people's personal lives "spillover" to affect them at work.

b. **Life stressors** occur as family events (*e.g.*, the birth of a new child), economic difficulties (*e.g.*, the sudden loss of a big investment), and personal affairs (*e.g.*, a separation or divorce).

c. Stressors also include personal factors such as individual needs, capabilities, and personality.

LECTURE ENHANCEMENT

Ask the students to identify the things that cause stress for them. Treating their role as a student as their work, have them identify the work, nonwork, and personal stressors in their lives.

C. Stress and performance.

1. **Constructive stress**, or *eustress*, occurs at moderate levels and prompts increased work effort, stimulates creativity, and encourage greater diligence, thereby having a positive impact on performance. (See *PowerPoint Slide 27* for Chapter 16.)

2. **Destructive stress**, or *distress*, is dysfunctional for both the individual and the organization. It occurs as low or high levels of stress. (See *PowerPoint Slide 27* for Chapter 16.)

3. **Job burnout** occurs as a loss of interest in and satisfaction with a job due to stressful working conditions. (See *PowerPoint Slide 27* for Chapter 16.)

4. Extreme reactions to stress include desk rage and workplace rage.

5. *Toxic workplaces* exist when too much stress overloads and breaks down a person's physical and mental systems resulting in absenteeism, turnover, errors, accidents, dissatisfaction, reduced performance, unethical behavior, and illness.

D. Stress and health. (See *PowerPoint Slide 28* for Chapter 16.)

1. Stress can impact a person's health.

2. Health problems associated with stress include heart attack, stroke, hypertension, migraine headache, ulcers, substance abuse, overeating, depression, and muscle aches.

3. Managers and team leaders should be alert to signs of excessive stress in themselves and their co-workers.

LECTURE ENHANCEMENT

There are some startling statistics about workplace stress that have been published by the American Institute of Stress, available on the organization's Web site at http://www.stress.org/. The statistics are based on surveys of American employees and other American Institute of Stress research. These statistics may stimulate interesting classroom discussion.

E. Stress management. (See *PowerPoint Slides 29* and *30* for Chapter 16.)

1. **Stress prevention** involves taking action to keep stress from reaching destructive levels in the first place.

2. Once stress has reached a destructive point, special techniques of stress management can be implemented.

3. **Stress management** begins with the recognition of stress symptoms and continues with actions to maintain a positive performance edge.

4. **Personal wellness** involves the pursuit of one's job and career goals with the support of a personal health promotion program.

5. **Employee assistance programs** are designed to provide help for employees who are experiencing personal problems and the stress associated with them.

LECTURE ENHANCEMENT

Ask the students to identify the techniques that they use for managing stress. Common examples are likely to include both effective and ineffective coping mechanisms. Effective coping mechanisms could include exercise, listening to music, resting, visiting with friends, etc. Ineffective coping mechanisms could include such actions as engaging in angry outbursts, becoming sullen, mistreating family or friends, excessive consumption of alcohol, etc.

VII. **Study summary for Chapter 16.**

A. Point out to the students that the text's "Chapter 16 Study Guide" recaps the key theories, concepts, and ideas in the chapter in relation to the appropriate study questions.

CHAPTER STUDY GUIDE

Study Question 1: What is organizational change?

- Planned change takes place because change agents — individuals and groups — make it happen to resolve performance problems or realize performance opportunities.

- Transformational change naturally shifts fundamental aspects of organizations such as purpose and mission, beliefs and values, strategies, and structures.
- Organizational targets for planned change include purpose, strategy, culture, structure, people, tasks, and technology.
- The planned change process requires attention to the three phases — unfreezing, changing, and refreezing.

Study Question 2: What change strategies are used in organizations?

- Change strategies are the means change agents use to bring about desired change in people and systems.
- Force-coercion change strategies use position power to bring about change through direct command or through rewards and punishments.
- Rational persuasion change strategies use logical arguments and appeals to knowledge and facts to convince people to change.
- Shared-power change strategies involve other persons in planning and implementing change.

Study Question 3: How is resistance to change best managed?

- Resistance to change should be expected and not feared; it is a source of feedback that can be used to improve a change effort.
- People usually resist change because they are defending something of value; they may focus their resistance on the change itself, the change strategy, or the change agent as a person.
- Strategies for dealing with resistance to change include education and communication, participation and involvement, facilitation and support, negotiation and agreement, manipulation and cooptation, and explicit or implicit coercion.

Study Question 4: How do organizations innovate?

- Innovation is the process of creating new ideas and then implementing them in practical applications.
- Product innovations result in improved goods or services; process innovations result in improved work methods and operations.
- Steps in the innovation process normally include idea generation, initial experimentation, feasibility determination, and final application.
- Common features of highly innovative organizations include supportive strategies, cultures, structures, staffing, and senior leadership.

Study Question 5: How does stress affect people in change environments?

- Stress emerges when people experience tensions caused by extraordinary demands, constraints, or opportunities in their jobs.
- Work-related stressors arise from such things as excessive task demands, interpersonal problems, unclear roles, ethical dilemmas, and career disappointments.
- Nonwork stress can spill over to affect people at work; nonwork stressors may be traced to family situations, economic difficulties, and personal problems.

- Personal stressors derive from personality type, needs, and values; they can influence how stressful different situations become for different people.
- Stress can be managed by prevention — such as making adjustments in work and nonwork factors; it can also be dealt with through personal wellness — taking steps to maintain a healthy body and mind capable of better withstanding stressful situations.

KEY TERMS

Change agents: individuals and groups who lead and support the change process by taking responsibility for changing the existing behavior patterns of other people or the social system.

Changing: the second stage in Lewin's change model that involves taking action to modify a situation by changing things, such as the people, tasks, structure, or technology of the organization.

Constructive stress: stress that occurs at moderate levels and prompts increased work effort, stimulates creativity, and encourage greater diligence, thereby having a positive impact on performance.

Destructive stress: stress that is dysfunctional for both the individual and the organization.

Employee assistance programs: programs that are designed to provide help for employees who are experiencing personal problems and the stress associated with them.

Force-coercion strategy: a change strategy that uses legitimacy, rewards, or punishments as primary inducements to change.

Innovation: the process of creating new ideas and putting them into practice.

Job burnout: occurs as a loss of interest in and satisfaction with a job due to stressful working conditions.

Life stressors: occur as family events (*e.g.*, the birth of a new child), economic difficulties (*e.g.*, the sudden loss of a big investment), and personal affairs (*e.g.*, a separation or divorce).

Performance gap: the discrepancy between the desired and actual state of affairs.

Personal wellness: involves the pursuit of one's job and career goals with the support of a personal health promotion program.

Planned change: change that is the result of specific efforts by a change agent and is a direct response to someone's perception of a performance gap.

Process innovations: innovations that result in the introduction of new and better work methods and operations.

Product innovations: innovations that result in the introduction of new or improved goods or services to better meet customer needs.

Rational persuasion strategy: a change strategy that attempts to bring about change through the use of special knowledge, empirical support, or rational arguments.

Refreezing: the third stage in Lewin's change model that is designed to maintain the momentum of a change and eventually institutionalize it as part of the normal routine.

Resistance to change: any attitude or behavior that indicates unwillingness to make or support a desired change.

Shared-power strategy: a change strategy actively and sincerely involves the people who will be affected by a change in planning and making key decisions relating to this change.

Stress: a state of tension experienced by individuals facing extraordinary demands, constraints, or opportunities.

Stress management: begins with the recognition of stress symptoms and continues with actions to maintain a positive performance edge.

Stressors: the wide variety of things that cause stress for individuals.

Stress prevention: involves taking action to keep stress from reaching destructive levels in the first place.

Transformational change: results in a major overhaul of the organization or its component systems.

Unfreezing: the first stage in Lewin's change model that involves the managerial responsibility of preparing a situation for change, and it involves disconfirming existing attitudes and behaviors to create a felt need for something new.

Unplanned change: change that occurs spontaneously and without a change agent's direction, and such change may be disruptive.

Work stressors: stressors that arise from many sources, including excessively high or low task demands, role conflicts or ambiguities, poor interpersonal relations, or career progress that is either to slow or too fast.

Chapter 17
ORGANIZING FOR PERFORMANCE

STUDY QUESTIONS

1.	What is strategy and how is it linked to different types of organizational goals?
2.	What are the basic attributes of organizations?
3.	How is work organized and coordinated?
4.	What are bureaucracies and what are the common structures?

LEARNING OBJECTIVES

After completing this chapter students should be able to:

1.	Define mission, strategy, societal goals, output goals, and systems goals, and explain how the various types of goals influence the formulation and implementation of mission and strategy.
2.	Explain how principles regarding organization charts, the chain of command, unity of command, span of control, and line and staff units are used to create hierarchy or vertical specialization.
3.	Describe the nature and effects of output controls, process controls, formalization, standardization, and total quality management.
4.	Describe the differences between centralization and decentralization.
5.	Discuss the different ways that businesses organize horizontally.
6.	Discuss the differences between personal methods of coordination and impersonal methods of coordination.
7.	Describe the nature and implications of mechanistic structures, organic structures, and hybrid structures.

MATERIAL IN *THE OB SKILLS WORKBOOK* SUPPORTING THE CHAPTER

Case for Critical Thinking	Case 17: First Community Financial
Experiential Exercises	Exercise 13: Tinkertoys
	Exercise 39: Organizations Alive!
	Exercise 40: Fast-Food Technology
	Exercise 41: Alien Invasion
Self-Assessments	Assessment 2: A 21st Century Manager
	Assessment 21: Organizational Design Preference

CHAPTER OVERVIEW

This chapter focuses on the basic attributes of organizations. The chapter begins by discussing the nature of mission and strategy in business organizations and how societal goals, output goals, and systems goals influence the formulation and implementation of mission and strategy. Successful organizations develop structures that are consistent with their strategies — often expressed as "strategy drives structure." The chapter examines the structural attributes of organizations, focusing first on hierarchy or vertical specialization, control, and centralization versus decentralization. The discussion of hierarchy includes concepts regarding organization charts, chain of command, unity of command, span of control, and line and staff units. The examination of control covers output controls, process controls, formalization, standardization, and total quality management. The discussion of centralization and decentralization stresses the impact of each approach on people's behavior at work. The chapter then turns to an examination of horizontal specialization and the coordination of work across horizontally differentiated organizational units. Horizontal differentiation is explored within the context of traditional departmental structures — functional, divisional, and matrix. Next, the chapter examines personal and impersonal methods of coordinating departmental structures. The chapter concludes with a discussion of mechanistic structures (or machine bureaucracies), organic structures (or professional bureaucracies) and hybrid structures, which combine features of the mechanistic and organic types.

CHAPTER OUTLINE

I. **Study Question 1: What is strategy and how is it linked to different types of organizational goals?**
   A. What is strategy?
   B. Organizations and society
   C. Output goals of organizations
   D. Systems goals of organizations

II. **Study Question 2: What are the basic attributes of organizations?**
   A. Hierarchy
   B. Controls
   C. Centralization and decentralization

III. **Study Question 3: How is work organized and coordinated?**
   A. Traditional departmental structures
   B. Coordination

IV. **Study Question 4: What are bureaucracies and what are the common structures?**
   A. Mechanistic structures
   B. Organic structures
   C. Hybrid structures

CHAPTER LECTURE NOTES

I.   **Introduction to the Chapter 17 Lecture.**

    A. Study questions for Chapter 17. (See ***PowerPoint Slide 2*** for Chapter 17.)

        1. What is strategy and how is it linked to different types of organizational goals?

        2. What are the basic attributes of organizations?

        3. How is work organized and coordinated?

        4. What are bureaucracies and what are the common structures?

    B. The lecture material for Chapter 17 is organized around the study questions.

        1. Point out to the students that the text's "Chapter At A Glance" identifies the key topics contained in the chapter and links them to the appropriate study questions.

    C. The chapter opens with description of how George Schaefer, president and CEO of Fifth Third Bank, approaches issues of how to organize the bank's extensive operations.

II.   **Study Question 1: What is strategy and how is it linked to different types of organizational goals?**

    A. What is strategy?

        1. <u>**Strategy**</u> is the process of positioning the organization in the competitive environment and implementing actions to compete successfully. (See ***PowerPoint Slide 3*** for Chapter 17.)

        2. Strategy is a pattern in the stream of decisions that reflect goal choices and the way the firm organizes to achieve them. (See ***PowerPoint Slide 3*** for Chapter 17.)

        3. Conventional strategy decisions begin with the following elements (see ***PowerPoint Slide 4*** for Chapter 17):

            a. Choosing the types of contributions the firm intends to make to society.

            b. Precisely whom the firm will serve.

            c. Exactly what the firm will provide to others.

        4. By selecting goals, firms also define who they are and what they will try to become.

        5. The goals of the firm should be consistent and consistent with the way in which it is organized.

B. Organizations and society.

1. **Societal goals** reflect an organization's intended contributions to the broader society. (See *PowerPoint Slide 5* for Chapter 17.)

2. By contributing to the larger society, organizations gain legitimacy, a social right to operate, and more discretion for their non-societal goals and operating practices. (See *PowerPoint Slide 5* for Chapter 17.)

3. By claiming to provide specific types of societal contributions, an organization can make legitimate claims over resources, individuals, markets, and products. (See *PowerPoint Slide 5* for Chapter 17.)

4. A firm's societal contribution is often part of its **mission statement**, which is a written statement of organizational purpose. (See *PowerPoint Slide 6* for Chapter 17.)

5. A good mission statement identifies whom the firm will serve and how it will go about accomplishing its societal purpose. (See *PowerPoint Slide 6* for Chapter 17.)

6. Organizations that can more effectively translate the positive character of their societal contribution into a favorable image have an advantage over firms that neglect this sense of purpose.

LECTURE ENHANCEMENT

Bring a copy of the mission statement for your college or university to class. Discuss the institution's strategic objectives in light of the mission statement.

C. Output goals of organizations. (See *PowerPoint Slide 7* for Chapter 17.)

1. Although an organization may have a primary beneficiary, its mission statement may also recognize the interests of many other parties.

2. **Output goals** define the type of business an organization is in and which provide some substance to the more general aspects of mission statements.

D. Systems goals of organizations.

1. **Systems goals** are concerned with conditions within the organization that are expected to increase its survival potential. (See *PowerPoint Slide 8* for Chapter 17.)

2. For many organizations, systems goals include growth, productivity, stability, harmony, flexibility, prestige, and human resource maintenance. (See *PowerPoint Slide 8* for Chapter 17.)

3. Systems goals must often be balanced against one another. (See ***PowerPoint Slide 8*** for Chapter 17.)

4. Different parts of the organization are often asked to pursue different types of systems goals.

5. The relative importance of different systems goals can vary substantially across various types of organizations.

6. Well-defined systems goals can accomplish the following (see ***PowerPoint Slide 9*** for Chapter 17):

   a. They can focus managers' attention on what needs to be done.

   b. They can provide flexibility in devising ways to meet important targets.

   c. They can be used to balance the demands, constraints, and opportunities facing the firm.

   d. They can form a basis for dividing the work of the firm (*i.e.*, developing a formal structure).

III. **Study Question 2: What are the basic attributes of organizations?**

   A. Background on basic attributes of organizations. (See ***PowerPoint Slide 10*** for Chapter 17.)

   1. Successful organizations develop a structure that is consistent with the pattern of goals and strategy established by senior management.

   2. The formal structure that shows the planned configuration of positions, job duties, and the lines of authority among different parts of the enterprise.

   3. Traditionally, the formal structure of the firm has also been called the division of labor.

LECTURE ENHANCEMENT

To introduce material regarding basic attributes of organizations, describe for the students the organization structure that exists at your college/university. Focus on why the college/university is organized as it is and what is accomplished through this organization form. Also give attention to how this structure reflects the institution's strategy.

B. Hierarchy.

1. <u>**Vertical specialization**</u> is the hierarchical division of labor that distributes formal authority and establishes where and how critical decisions are to be made. (See *PowerPoint Slide 11* for Chapter 17.)

2. This division of labor creates a *hierarchy of authority* — an arrangement of work positions in order of increasing authority. (See *PowerPoint Slide 11* for Chapter 17.)

3. <u>**Organization charts**</u> are diagrams that depict the formal structures of organizations. (See *PowerPoint Slide 11* for Chapter 17.)

4. *Figure 17.1* from the textbook provides an example of a partial organization chart for a state university. As such, it shows the various positions, the position holders, and the lines of authority that link them to one another. (See *PowerPoint Slide 12* for Chapter 17.)

5. The *chain of command* is a listing of who reports to whom up and down the organizational hierarchy. (See *PowerPoint Slide 13* for Chapter 17.)

6. *Unity of command.* — the notion that each individual should have one boss and each unit one leader — is considered necessary to avoid confusion, to assign accountability to specific individuals, and to provide clear channels of communication up and down the organization. (See *PowerPoint Slide 13* for Chapter 17.)

7. <u>**Span of control**</u> refers to the number of individuals reporting to a supervisor. (See *PowerPoint Slide 13* for Chapter 17.)

    a. Narrower spans of control are expected when tasks are complex, when subordinates are inexperienced or poorly trained, or when tasks call for team effort.

    b. Narrow spans of control yield many organizational levels that are not only expensive but also make the organization unresponsive to necessary change.

8. <u>**Line units**</u> are work groups that conduct the major business of the organization. (See *PowerPoint Slide 14* for Chapter 17.)

9. <u>**Staff units**</u> are work groups that assist the line units by performing specialized services to the organization. (See *PowerPoint Slide 14* for Chapter 17.)

10. Some subordinate staff units are charged with conducting the major business of a higher-level staff unit; thus, the lower-level staff units have a line relationship with the higher-level staff unit.

11. Internal versus external units. (See *PowerPoint Slide 15* for Chapter 17.)

     a. *Internal line units* focus on transforming raw materials and information into products and services.

     b. *External line units* focus on maintaining linkages to suppliers, distributors, and customers.

     c. *Internal staff units* assist the line units in performing their functions.

     d. *External staff units* assist the line units, but the focus is on linking the firm to the environment and buffering internal operations.

12. ***Figure 17.2*** from the textbook illustrates how the placement of staff alters the structure of the firm. (See ***PowerPoint Slide 16*** for Chapter 17.)

13. Some firms are outsourcing many of their staff functions. (See ***PowerPoint Slide 17*** for Chapter 17.)

14. One of the foremost trends in management involves using information technology to streamline operations and reduce staff in order to lower costs and raise productivity. (See ***PowerPoint Slide 17*** for Chapter 17.)

15. Most organizations use a combination of line and staff units, alliances with specialized providers, and managerial techniques to specialize the vertical division of labor. (See ***PowerPoint Slide 17*** for Chapter 17.)

16. The most appropriate pattern of vertical specialization depends on the environment of the organization and the organization's size, technology, and goals. (See ***PowerPoint Slide 17*** for Chapter 17.)

LECTURE ENHANCEMENT

For small businesses that are unsure of how to organize, an excellent resource from which to obtain management advice is SCORE, or the Service Corps of Retired Executives. SCORE maintains a Web site at http://www.score.org/.

    C. Controls.

LECTURE ENHANCEMENT

Before you discuss controls, you may want to solicit student input by asking them to identify some examples of controls that are used in organizations. You can simply record these controls on the chalkboard, whiteboard, or overhead projector as they are offered. Students typically provide many examples ranging from a minimum GPA requirement to liquor laws to shoplifting guards. You can then use some of the examples to illustrate the different types of controls presented below.

1. **Control** is the set of mechanisms used to keep action or outputs within predetermined limits. (See *PowerPoint Slide 18* for Chapter 17.)

2. Control deals with setting standards, measuring results versus standards, and instituting corrective action. (See *PowerPoint Slide 18* for Chapter 17.)

3. Output controls. (See *PowerPoint Slide 19* for Chapter 17.)

   a. **Output controls** focus on desired targets and allow mangers to use their own methods for reaching defined targets.

   b. Most modern organizations use output controls as part of an overall method of managing by exception.

   c. Output controls promote flexibility and creativity as well as facilitate dialogue concerning corrective action.

4. Process controls.

5. **Process controls** attempt to specify the manner in which tasks are accomplished. (See *PowerPoint Slide 20* for Chapter 17.)

6. Types of process controls include the following (see *PowerPoint Slide 20* for Chapter 17):

   (i) Policies, procedures, and rules.

   (ii) Formalization and standardization

   (iii) Total quality management controls.

   b. Policies, procedures, and rules. (See *PowerPoint Slides 21* and *22* for Chapter 17.)

      (i) A *policy* is a guideline for action that outlines important objectives and broadly indicates how an activity is to be performed.

      (ii) *Procedures* indicate the best method for performing a task, show the aspects of a task that are most important, or outline how an individual is to be rewarded.

      (iii) *Rules* typically describe in detail how a task or a series of tasks is to be performed, or they indicate what cannot be done.

      (iv) Rules, procedures, and policies are often employed as substitutes for direct managerial supervision.

   c. Formalization and standardization. (See *PowerPoint Slide 23* for Chapter 17.)

(i) **Formalization** is the written documentation of work rules, policies, and procedures.

(ii) **Standardization** is the degree to which the range of actions in a job or series of jobs is limited so that actions are performed in a uniform manner.

d. Total quality management controls.

(i) Establishing a total quality management process within the firm is based on the ideas of the late W. Edwards Deming regarding continual improvement resting upon statistical analyses of the firm's operations

(ii) Deming's 14 points for achieving total quality management include the following (See *PowerPoint Slides 24* to *26* for Chapter 17.):

1. Create a consistency of purpose in the company to innovate, put resources into research and education, and put resources into maintaining equipment and new production aids.

2. Learn a new philosophy of quality to improve every system.

3. Require statistical evidence of process control and eliminate financial controls on production.

4. Require statistical evidence of control in purchasing parts; this will mean dealing with fewer suppliers.

5. Use statistical methods to isolate the sources of trouble.

6. Institute modern on-the-job training.

7. Improve supervision to develop inspired leaders.

8. Drive out fear and instill learning.

9. Break down barriers between departments.

10. Eliminate numerical goals and slogans.

11. Constantly revamp work methods.

12. Institute massive training programs for employees in statistical methods.

13. Retrain people in new skills.

14. Create a structure that will push, every day, on the above 13 points.

D. Centralization and decentralization.

1. **Centralization** is the degree to which the authority to make decisions is restricted to higher levels of management. (See *PowerPoint Slide 27* for Chapter 17.)

2. **Decentralization** is the degree to which the authority to make decisions is given to lower levels in an organization's hierarchy. (See *PowerPoint Slide 27* for Chapter 17.)

3. Greater centralization is often adopted when the firm faces a single major threat to its survival.

4. Decentralization has the following effects (see *PowerPoint Slide 28* for Chapter 17):

   a. It provides higher subordinate satisfaction.

   b. It provides a quicker response to a diverse series of unrelated problems.

   c. It assists in on-the-job training of subordinates for higher-level positions.

   d. Decentralization encourages participation in decision making.

IV. **Study Question 3: How is work organized and coordinated?**

A. Background on organizing and coordinating work. (See *PowerPoint Slide 29* for Chapter 17.)

1. **Horizontal specialization** is a division of labor that establishes specific work units or groups within an organization; it is often referred to as the process of departmentation.

2. Whenever managers divide tasks and group similar types of skills and resources together, they must also be concerned with how each group's individual efforts will be integrated with others — this is *coordination*.

B. Traditional departmental structures.

1. Functional departments.

   a. **Functional departmentation** groups individuals by skill, knowledge, and action.

   b. *Figure 17.3* from the textbook identifies the major advantages and disadvantages of functional departmentation or *functional specialization*. (See *PowerPoint Slide 30* for Chapter 17.)

   c. Advantages of departmentation by function include the following:

(i) Yields very clear task assignments, consistent with an individual's training.

(ii) Individuals within a department can easily build on one another's knowledge, training, and experience.

(iii) Provides an excellent training ground for new managers.

(iv) It is easy to explain.

(v) Takes advantage of employee technical quality.

d. Disadvantages of departmentation by function include the following:

(i) May reinforce the narrow training of individuals.

(ii) May yield narrow, boring, and routine jobs.

(iii) Communication across technical area is complex and difficult.

(iv) "Top management overload" with too much attention to cross-functional problems.

(v) Individuals may look up the organizational hierarchy for direction and reinforcement rather than focus attention on products, services, or clients.

LECTURE ENHANCEMENT

Ask students to think about how the curriculum at their college/university addresses the different functions of business. Are marketing, finance, production, and human resource management, for instance, taught as stand-alone courses, or are they taught in some integrated fashion? As stand-alone courses, what does this convey to students about the functional chimneys of business? What does any integrated format convey about tearing down these functional chimneys?

---

2. Divisional departments.

a. **Divisional departmentation** groups individuals and resources by products, territories, services, clients, or legal entities.

b. *Figure 17.4* from the textbook shows a divisional pattern of organization grouped around products, regions, and customers for three divisions of a conglomerate. (See *PowerPoint Slide 31* for Chapter 17.)

(i) This pattern is often used to meet diverse external threats and opportunities.

(ii) *Figure 17.4* also identifies the major advantages and disadvantages of *divisional specialization.*

c. Advantages of divisional departmentation include the following:

(i) Promotes adaptability and flexibility in meeting the demands of important external groups.

(ii) Allows for spotting external changes as they emerge.

(iii) Provides for the integration of specialized personnel.

(iv) Focuses on the success or failure of particular products, services, clients, or territories.

d. Disadvantages of divisional departmentation include the following:

(i) Does not provide a pool or highly trained individuals with similar expertise to solve problems and train others

(ii) Allows duplication of effort, as each division attempts to solve similar problems.

(iii) May give priority to divisional goals over the health and welfare of the overall organization.

(iv) Creates conflict between divisions over shared resources.

3. Matrix structures.

a. <u>**Matrix departmentation**</u> is the simultaneous use of both the functional and divisional forms of departmentation.

b. *Figure 17.5* provides an example of the matrix pattern of departmentation and identifies its major advantages and disadvantages. (See *PowerPoint Slide 32* for Chapter 17.)

c. Advantages of matrix departmentation include the following:

(i) Combines strengths of both functional and divisional departmentation.

(ii) Blends technical and market emphasis.

(iii) Provides a series of managers able to converse with both technical and marketing personnel.

d. Disadvantages of matrix departmentation include the following:

(i) Very expensive.

(ii) Unity of command is loose (individuals have more than one supervisor).

(iii) Authority and responsibilities of managers may overlap, causing conflicts and gaps in effort across units and inconsistencies in priorities.

(iv) It is difficult to explain to employees.

LECTURE ENHANCEMENT

Ask students to consider the project teams on which they most likely have worked in one or more of their courses. Have them describe the challenges they have encountered in responding to the expectations of both the project team leader and the course instructor. Relate their descriptions to the preceding discussion of the advantages and disadvantages of matrix departmentation.

---

4. Mixed forms of departmentation.

   a. Organizations often use a mixture of departmentation forms.

   b. It is often desirable to divide the effort (*i.e.*, group people and resources) by two methods at the same time in order to balance the advantages and disadvantages of each.

C. Coordination.

   1. **Coordination** is the set of mechanisms that an organization uses to link the actions of its units into a consistent pattern. (See *PowerPoint Slide 33* for Chapter 17.)

   2. Much of the coordination within a unit is handled by its manager.

   3. Smaller organizations may rely on their management hierarchy to provide the necessary consistency and integration. (See *PowerPoint Slide 33* for Chapter 17.)

   4. As the organization grows, managers become overloaded and the organization needs to develop more efficient and effective ways of linking work units to one another. (See *PowerPoint Slide 33* for Chapter 17.)

   5. Personal methods of coordination. (See *PowerPoint Slide 34* for Chapter 17.)

      a. *Personal methods of coordination* produce synergy by promoting dialogue, discussion, innovation, creativity, and learning, both within and across organizational units.

      b. The most common personal methods of coordination are direct contact between and among organizational members and committee memberships.

    c.   The appropriate mix of personal coordination methods should be tailored to the individual skills, abilities, and experiences of subordinates.

    6.   Impersonal methods of coordination. (See ***PowerPoint Slide 35*** for Chapter 17.)

        a.   *Impersonal methods of coordination* produce synergy by stressing consistency and standardization so that individual pieces fit together.

        b.   Impersonal coordination methods are often refinements and extensions of process controls with an emphasis on formalization and standardization.

        c.   Historically, firms used specialized departments to coordinate across units.

        d.   Two powerful impersonal methods of coordination are the matrix form of departmentation and management information systems.

    7.   While control involves the vertical exercise of formal authority involving targets, measures, and corrective action, coordination stresses cooperative problem solving.

V.   **Study Question 4: What are bureaucracies and what are the common structures?**

    A. Background on bureaucracies.

       1.   Bureaucracy is an ideal form of organization, the characteristics of which were defined by the German sociologist Max Weber. (See ***PowerPoint Slide 36*** for Chapter 17.)

       2.   **Bureaucracies** rely on a division of labor, hierarchical control, promotion by merit with career opportunities for employees, and administration by rule. (See ***PowerPoint Slide 36*** for Chapter 17.)

       3.   *Figure 17.6* from the textbook illustrates three basic types of bureaucracies: the mechanistic, the organic, and the divisionalized approaches. (See ***PowerPoint Slide 37*** for Chapter 17.)

    B. Mechanistic structures.

       1.   The **mechanistic type** (or *machine bureaucracy*) emphasizes vertical specialization and control. (See ***PowerPoint Slide 38*** for Chapter 17.)

       2.   Mechanistic organizations stress rules, policies, and procedures; specify techniques for decision making; and emphasize developing well-documented control systems backed by a strong middle management and supported by a centralized staff. (See ***PowerPoint Slide 38*** for Chapter 17.)

       3.   Firms often use the mechanistic design in pursuing a strategy of becoming a low cost leader. (See ***PowerPoint Slide 38*** for Chapter 17.)

4. The prime advantage of the mechanistic type is efficiency through extensive vertical and horizontal specialization. Tied together with elaborate controls and impersonal coordination mechanisms. (See *PowerPoint Slide 39* for Chapter 17.)

5. Disadvantages of the mechanistic type include the following (see *PowerPoint Slide 39* for Chapter 17):

   a. Employees may not like rigid designs, which may result in motivational problems.

   b. Unions further solidify narrow job description by demanding fixed work rules to protect employees from extensive vertical controls.

   c. Key employees may leave.

   d. The organization is less able to adjust to subtle external changes or new technologies.

C. Organic structures.

1. The **organic type** (or *professional bureaucracy*) is much less vertically oriented than its mechanistic counterpart and it emphasizes horizontal specialization. (See *PowerPoint Slide 40* for Chapter 17.)

2. Organic organizations have minimal procedures and rely on the judgments of experts and personal means of coordination. (See *PowerPoint Slide 40* for Chapter 17.)

3. Firms using the organic design find it easier to pursue strategies that emphasize product quality, quick response to customers, or innovation. (See *PowerPoint Slide 40* for Chapter 17.)

4. Advantages of the organic type include the following (see *PowerPoint Slide 41* for Chapter 17):

   a. It is better than the mechanistic type for problem solving and serving customer needs.

   b. Centralized direction by senior management is less intense.

   c. The organization is good at detecting external changes and adjusting to new technologies.

5. Disadvantages of the organic type include the following (see *PowerPoint Slide 41* for Chapter 17):

   a. It is not as efficient as the mechanistic type.

   b. It has restricted capacity to respond to central management direction.

LECTURE ENHANCEMENT

Xerox is an example of an organization that has moved back and forth between a mechanistic structure and an organic structure. Under Xerox's founder, Joseph Wilson, the company was positioned on the organic end of the continuum as evidenced by its "loose organizational structure." Wilson's successor as CEO, Peter McClough moved Xerox toward the mechanistic end through the implementation of much-needed controls. When David Kearnes took over as CEO, however, he found that slow decision making, unnecessary layers of management, and an inability to respond to face-paced market changes characterized the mechanistic structure McClough had implemented. Kearnes responded to these problems by moving Xerox back toward an organic design that included small product teams and encouraged diversification.

(Source: "Culture Shock at Xerox," *Business Week,* June 22, 1987; "Remaking the American CEO," *New York Times,* January 25, 1987, p. C-8.)

D. Hybrid structures.

1. Many very large firms have found that neither the mechanistic nor the organic approach was suitable for all their operations.

2. Common types of hybrid structures include the following:

    a. The *divisional firm,* an extension of the divisional pattern of departmentation, is composed of quasi-independent divisions so that different divisions can be more or less organic or mechanistic. (See ***PowerPoint Slide 42*** for Chapter 17.)

    b. A **conglomerate** is a single corporation that contains a number of unrelated businesses. (See ***PowerPoint Slide 42*** for Chapter 17.)

    c. The conglomerate simultaneously illustrates three key points that will be the focus of Chapter 18. These key points are (see ***PowerPoint Slide 43*** for Chapter 17):

        (i) All structures are combinations of the basic elements.

        (ii) There is no one best structure — the appropriate structure depends on factors such as the size of the firm and its environment, technology, and strategy.

        (iii) The firm does not stand alone but is part of a larger network of firms that compete against other networks.

LECTURE ENHANCEMENT

Have the students analyze the structure of the college/university they are attending. Is it a mechanistic structure, an organic structure, or a hybrid structure? What particular characteristics of the organization did they consider in arriving at their analytical conclusions?

VI. Study summary for Chapter 17.

    A. Point out to the students that the text's "Chapter 17 Study Guide" recaps the key theories, concepts, and ideas in the chapter in relation to the appropriate study questions.

CHAPTER STUDY GUIDE

Study Question 1: What is strategy and how is it linked to different types of organizational goals?

- Strategy and goals are closely intertwined.
- Strategy is a process.
- Strategy is positioning the organization in the competitive environment.
- Strategy is a pattern in a stream of actions.
- Organizations make specific contributions to society and gain legitimacy from these contributions.
- A societal contribution focused on a primary beneficiary may be represented in the firm's mission statement.
- As managers consider how they will accomplish their firm's mission, many begin with a very clear statement of which businesses they are in.
- Firms often specify output goals by detailing the specific products and services they offer.
- Corporations have systems goals to show the conditions managers believe will yield survival and success.
- Growth, productivity, stability, harmony, flexibility, prestige, and human resource maintenance are examples of systems goals.

Study Question 2: What are the basic attributes of organizations?

- The formal structure defines the intended configuration of positions, job duties, and lines of authority among different parts of the enterprise.
- The formal structure is also known as the firm's division of labor.
- Vertical specialization is used to allocate formal authority within the organization and may be seen on an organization chart.
- Vertical specialization is the hierarchical division of labor that specifies where formal authority is located.
- Typically, a chain of command exists to link lower-level workers with senior managers.

- The distinction between line and staff units also indicates how authority is distributed, with the line units conducting the major business of the firm and staff providing support.
- Managerial techniques, such as decision support and expert computer systems, are used to expand the analytical reach and decision-making capacity of managers to minimize staff.
- Control is the set of mechanisms the organizations uses to keep action or outputs within predetermined levels.
- Output controls focus on desired targets and allow managers to use their own methods for reaching these targets.
- Process controls specify the manner in which tasks are to be accomplished through (1) policies, rules, and procedures; (2) formalization and standardization; and (3) total quality management processes.
- Firms are learning that decentralization often provides substantial benefits.
- With centralization, discretion to decide is moved farther up the hierarchy.
- With decentralization, discretion to decide is moved farther down the hierarchy.

Study Question 3: How is work organized and coordinated?

- Horizontal specialization is the division of labor that results in various work units and departments in the organization.
- Three main types or patterns of departments are observed: functional, divisional, and matrix. Each pattern has a mix of advantages and disadvantages.
- Organizations may successfully use any type, or mixture, as long as the strengths of the structure match the needs of the organization.
- Coordination is the set of mechanisms the organization uses to link the actions of separate units into a consistent pattern.
- Personal methods of coordination produce synergy by promoting dialogue, discussion, innovation, creativity, and learning.
- Impersonal methods of control produce synergy by stressing consistency and standardization so that individual pieces fit together.

Study Question 4: What are bureaucracies and what are the common structures?

- The bureaucracy is an ideal form based on legal authority, logic, and order that provides superior efficiency and effectiveness.
- The mechanistic type emphasizes vertical specialization and control.
- The organic type emphasizes horizontal specialization and coordination.
- Hybrid types are combinations of mechanistic and organic elements and include the divisionalized form and the conglomerate.

KEY TERMS

Bureaucracy: a structural form that relies on a division of labor, hierarchical control, promotion by merit with career opportunities for employees, and administration by rule.
Centralization: the degree to which the authority to make decisions is restricted to higher levels of management.
Conglomerate: a single corporation that contains a number of unrelated businesses.
Control: the set of mechanisms used to keep action or outputs within predetermined limits.

Coordination: the set of mechanisms that an organization uses to link the actions of its units into a consistent pattern.

Decentralization: the degree to which the authority to make decisions is given to lower levels in an organization's hierarchy.

Divisional departmentation: groups individuals and resources by products, territories, services, clients, or legal entities.

Formalization: the written documentation of work rules, policies, and procedures.

Functional departmentation: groups individuals by skill, knowledge, and action.

Horizontal specialization: a division of labor that establishes specific work units or groups within an organization; it is often referred to as the process of departmentation.

Line units: work groups that conduct the major business of the organization.

Matrix departmentation: the simultaneous use of both the functional and divisional forms of departmentation.

Mechanistic type: a structural type that emphasizes vertical specialization and control.

Mission statements: written statements of organizational purpose.

Organic type: a structural type that is much less vertically oriented than its mechanistic counterpart and which emphasizes horizontal specialization.

Organization charts: diagrams that depict the formal structures of organizations.

Output controls: controls that focus on desired targets and allow mangers to use their own methods for reaching defined targets.

Output goals: goals that define the type of business an organization is in and which provide some substance to the more general aspects of mission statements.

Process controls: controls that attempt to specify the manner in which tasks are accomplished.

Societal goals: goals that reflect an organization's intended contributions to the broader society.

Span of control: the number of individuals reporting to a supervisor.

Staff units: work groups that assist the line units by performing specialized services to the organization.

Standardization: the degree to which the range of actions in a job or series of jobs is limited so that actions are performed in a uniform manner.

Strategy: the process of positioning the organization in the competitive environment and implementing actions to compete successfully.

Systems goals: goals that are concerned with conditions within the organization that are expected to increase its survival potential.

Vertical specialization: the hierarchical division of labor that distributes formal authority and establishes where and how critical decisions are to be made.

Chapter 18
ORGANIZATION DESIGN FOR STRATEGIC COMPETENCY

STUDY QUESTIONS

1.	What is organizational design and how is it linked to strategy?
2.	What is information technology and how is it used?
3.	Can the design of the firm co-evolve with the environment?
4.	How does a firm and continue to learn over time?

LEARNING OBJECTIVES

After completing this chapter students should be able to:

1.	Describe the basic nature of organizational design.
2.	Explain how strategy influences organizational design.
3.	Explain why it is easier for smaller organizations to maintain a simple design.
4.	Discuss James D. Thompson's and Joan Woodward's views of technology, and explain how operations technology influences organizational design.
5.	Describe an adhocracy and explain when it becomes an organizational design option.
6.	Explain how information technology can influence organizational design, particularly as it enables strategic capabilities, learning, and e-business.
7.	Discuss the impact of environmental richness, environmental interdependence, and environmental uncertainty and volatility on organizational design.
8.	Describe how network organizations and alliances enable organizational designs to co-evolve with the environment.
9.	Describe how virtual organizations contribute to organizational learning.
10.	Describe the challenges of distributing, interpreting, and retrieving information.
11.	Explain deficit cycles and benefit cycles in the context of organizational learning.

MATERIAL IN *THE OB SKILLS WORKBOOK* SUPPORTING THE CHAPTER

Case for Critical Thinking	Case 18: Mission Management and Trust
Experiential Exercises	Exercise 13: Tinkertoys
	Exercise 39: Organizations Alive!
	Exercise 41: Alien Invasion
Self-Assessment Inventories	Assessment 2: A 21st Century Manager
	Assessment 9: Group Effectiveness
	Assessment 21: Organizational Design Preference

CHAPTER OVERVIEW

This chapter focuses on organizational design and key factors that influence it. The chapter begins by explaining the concept of organizational design and discussing how strategic decisions, organizational size, and operations technology affect organizational design. Two aspects of strategy — positioning the organization in its environment and a pattern in the stream of decisions — are examined in relation to organizational design. The discussion of size and organizational design emphasizes the point that small organizations tend operate with a simple structural design whereas large organizations require more complex designs. The organizational design impact of operations technology is examined from the perspectives of Thompson's and Woodward's technology classification systems. This section of the chapter concludes with a discussion of adhocracy as a design option with intensive technology and some small-batch processes.

The second section of the chapter addresses information technology and organizational design. Particular emphasis is placed on why information technology makes a difference in organizational design, using information technology as a strategic capability, how information technology promotes learning, and how information technology fosters the development of e-business.

The third section of the chapter explores how the environment influences organizational design. Emphasis is placed on the very important concept of environmental complexity and its component parts — environmental richness, environmental interdependence, and environmental uncertainty and volatility. This section also examines the roles of network organizations and alliances in enabling organizational designs to co-evolve with the environment.

The final section of the chapter focuses on organizational learning. The key topics in this section include virtual organizations; methods by which organizations acquire knowledge: how information is distributed, interpreted, and retrieved in organizations; and the existence of deficit cycles and benefit cycles in organizational learning.

CHAPTER OUTLINE

I.   **Study Question 1: What is organizational design and how is it linked to strategy?**
   A. Organizational design defined
   B. Organizational design and strategic decisions
   C. Size and organizational design
   D. Operations technology and organizational design
   E. Adhocracy as a design option

II.   **Study Question 2: What is information technology and how is it used?**
   A. Why IT makes a difference
   B. IT as a strategic capability
   C. IT and learning
   D. IT and e-business

III.   **Study Question 3: Can the design of the firm co-evolve with the environment?**
   A. Environmental complexity
   B. Network organizations and alliances

    C. Virtual organizations

IV.   **Study Question 4: How does a firm learn and continue to learn over time?**
    A. How organizations acquire knowledge
    B. Information distribution, interpretation, and retention
    C. Dynamics of organizational learning

CHAPTER LECTURE NOTES

I.   **Introduction to the Chapter 18 Lecture.**

    A. Study questions for Chapter 18. (See *PowerPoint Slide 2* for Chapter 18.)

        1. What is organizational design and how is it linked to strategy?

        2. What is information technology and how it is used?

        3. Can the design of the firm co-evolve with the environment?

        4. How does a firm learn and continue to learn over time?

    B. The lecture material for Chapter 18 is organized around the study questions.

        1. Point out to the students that the text's "Chapter At A Glance" identifies the key topics contained in the chapter and links them to the appropriate study questions.

    C. The chapter opens with a description of IBM's initiatives at stimulating the development of e-businesses.

II.   **Study Question 1: What is organizational design and how is it linked to strategy?**

    A. Organizational design defined. (See *PowerPoint Slide 3* for Chapter 18.)

        1. **<u>Organizational design</u>** is the process of choosing and implementing a structural configuration.

        2. The choice of an appropriate organizational design is contingent upon several factors, including the size of the firm, its operations and information technology, its environment, and the strategy it selects for growth and survival.

    B. Organizational design and strategic decisions.

        1. Strategy is both a positioning of the firm in its environment to provide it with the capability to succeed and a pattern in the stream of decisions.

        2. The structural configuration of organizations (or organizational design) should accomplish the following (see *PowerPoint Slide 4* for Chapter 18):

a. It should enable senior executives to emphasize the skills and abilities that their firms need to compete as well as to remain agile and dynamic in a rapidly changing world.

b. It should allow for individuals to experiment, grow, and develop competencies so that the strategy of the firm can evolve.

3. Co-evolution is a process by which the firm can adjust to external changes even as it shapes some of the challenges facing it. (See *PowerPoint Slide 5* for Chapter 18.)

a. Shaping capabilities via the organization's design is a dynamic aspect of co-evolution.

b. Even with co-evolution, managers must maintain a recognizable pattern of choices in the design that leads to accomplishing a broadly shared view of where the firm is going.

C. Size and organizational design.

1. Large organizations cannot be just bigger versions of their smaller counterparts. (See *PowerPoint Slide 6* for Chapter 18.)

a. As the number of individuals in a firm increases arithmetically, the number of possible interconnections among them increases geometrically.

b. The design of small firms is directly influenced by core operations technology.

c. Larger firms have many core operations technologies in a variety of much more specialized units, thereby resulting in greater organizational complexity than in smaller firms.

2. The **simple design** is a configuration involving one or two ways of specializing individuals and units. (See *PowerPoint Slide 7* for Chapter 18.)

a. Vertical specialization and control typically emphasize levels of supervision without elaborate formal mechanisms (*e.g.*, rule books and policy manuals), and the majority of the control resides in the manager.

b. The simple design is appropriate for many small firms, such as family businesses, retail stores, and small manufacturing firms.

c. The strengths of the simple design are simplicity, flexibility, and responsiveness to the desires of a central manager.

D. Operations technology and organizational design.

1. Organizational design must be adjusted to fit technological opportunities and requirements. (See *PowerPoint Slide 8* for Chapter 18.)

2. **Operations technology** is the combination of resources, knowledge, and techniques that creates a product or service output for an organization. (See *PowerPoint Slide 8* for Chapter 18.)

3. **Information technology** is the combination of machines, artifacts, procedures, and systems used to gather, store, analyze, and disseminate information for translating it into knowledge. (See *PowerPoint Slide 8* for Chapter 18.)

4. Two common classifications of operations technology are Thompson's classification and Woodward's classification.

5. Thompson's view of technology.

   a. Thompson classified technologies based on the degree to which the technology could be specified and the degree of interdependence among the work activities. (See *PowerPoint Slide 9* for Chapter 18.)

   b. Under *intensive technology*, there is uncertainty as to how to produce desired outcomes. (See *PowerPoint Slide 9* for Chapter 18.)

      (i) Coordination and knowledge exchange are of critical importance with this kind of technology.

   c. *Mediating technologies* link parties that want to become interdependent. (See *PowerPoint Slide 10* for Chapter 18.)

      (i) The degree of coordination among the individual tasks with pooled technology is substantially reduced.

      (ii) Information management becomes more important than coordinated knowledge application

   d. Under *long-linked technology* — also called mass production or industrial technology — the way to produce the desired outcome is known. (See *PowerPoint Slide 10* for Chapter 18.)

      (i) The task is broken down into a number of sequential steps.

      (ii) Control is critical, and coordination is restricted to making the sequential linkages work in harmony.

6. Woodward's view of technology.

   a. In *small-batch production*, a variety of custom products are tailor-made to fit customer specifications. (See *PowerPoint Slide 11* for Chapter 18.)

    b. In *mass production*, the organization produces one or a few products through an assembly-line system. (See ***PowerPoint Slide 11*** for Chapter 18.)

    c. Organizations using *continuous-process technology* produce a few products using considerable automation. (See ***PowerPoint Slide 11*** for Chapter 18.)

    d. The combination of structure and technology is critical to organizational success. (See ***PowerPoint Slide 12*** for Chapter 18.)

        (i) Successful small-batch and continuous-process plants have flexible structures with small work groups at the bottom; more rigidly structured plants are less successful.

        (ii) Successful mass production operations are rigidly structured and have large work groups at the bottom.

E. Adhocracy as a design option.

    1. In those instances where managers and employees simply do not know the appropriate way to service a client or to produce a particular product, an adhocracy may be an appropriate structural design. (See ***PowerPoint Slide 13*** for Chapter 18.)

    2. **Adhocracy** is an organizational structure that is characterized by few rules, policies, and procedures; substantial decentralization; shared decision-making among members; extreme horizontal specialization; few levels of management; and virtually no formal controls. (See ***PowerPoint Slide 14*** for Chapter 18.)

    3. The adhocracy is particularly useful when an aspect of the firm's operations technology presents two sticky problems (see ***PowerPoint Slide 15*** for Chapter 18):

        a. The tasks facing the firm vary considerably and provide many exceptions.

        b. Problems are difficult to define and resolve.

III.   Study Question 2: What is information technology and how is it used?

A. Why IT makes a difference.

    1. From an organizational standpoint IT can be used in the following ways (see ***PowerPoint Slide 16*** for Chapter 18):

        a. As a partial substitute for some operations as well as some process controls and impersonal methods of coordination.

        b. As a strategic capability.

        c. As a capability for transforming information to knowledge for learning.

2. Old bureaucracies prospered and dominated other organizational forms, in part, because they provided more efficient production through specialization and their approach to dealing with information.

3. In many organizations, the initial implementation of IT displaced the most routine, highly specified, and repetitious jobs but it did not alter the fundamental character or design of the organization. (See *PowerPoint Slide 17* for Chapter 18.)

4. A second wave of substitution replaced process controls and informal coordination mechanisms with decision support systems (DSS), and a second wave of implementation brought some marginal changes in organizational design. Firms often needed fewer levels of management and fewer internal staff, and in some instances some internal staff operations could be outsourced. (See *PowerPoint Slide 17* for Chapter 18.)

5. The emphasis on direct substitution was still the norm in many organizations well into the 1990s, and in smaller firms it continues today.

LECTURE ENHANCEMENT

CIO.com is a Web site that contains a vast array of information pertaining to the role of information technology in the workplace. Access the Web site at http://www.cio.com/CIO/.

B. IT as a strategic capability. (See *PowerPoint Slide 18* for Chapter 18.)

1. Traditionally, IT has been used to improve the efficiency, speed of responsiveness, and effectiveness of operations.

2. Instead of just substituting for process controls, IT now provides individuals deep within the organization the information they need to plan, make choices, coordinate with others, and control their own operations.

3. This new strategic IT capability resulted from IT being broadly available to everyone in an organization.

C. IT and learning.

1. With the adoption of WINTEL, which refers to Microsoft Windows in combination with an Intel microprocessing chip, three important IT changes occurred.

   a. IT applications for tasks found across many organizations were quickly developed and received broad acceptance.

   b. WINTEL expanded to incorporate existing telecommunications systems such as the Internet.

     c. IT was transformed from a substitute to a mechanism for learning.

  2. The impact of IT includes the following (see *PowerPoint Slide 19* for Chapter 18):

     a. New IT systems empower individuals, expanding their jobs and making the jobs both interesting and challenging.

     b. IT encourages the development of a "virtual" network of task forces and temporary teams to both define and solve problems.

     c. IT transforms how people manage — instead of telling others what to do, managers will need to treat colleagues as unpaid volunteers who expect to participate in decisions.

  3. For the production segment of firms using long-linked technology, IT can be linked to total quality management (TQM) programs and embedded in the machinery.

     a. To make TQM work with IT, all employees must plan, do, and control.

D. IT and e-business.

  1. IT has spawned a whole new series of corporations called e-businesses, and is transforming bricks-and-mortar firms.

  2. E-businesses include business-to-business (B2B) and business-to-consumers (B2C) firms.

  3. Many dot-com firms adopted a variation of the adhocracy as their design pattern because e-business was conceived as being fundamentally different from the old bricks-and-mortar operations. (See *PowerPoint Slide 20* for Chapter 18.)

  4. Many dot-coms quickly failed because the managers of these firms forgot about the following key liabilities of the adhocracy (see *PowerPoint Slide 20* for Chapter 18):

     a. There are limits on the size of an effective adhocracy.

     b. The actual delivery of products and services did not require continual innovation but rested more on responsiveness to clients and maintaining efficiency.

IV.   **Study Question 3: Can the design of the firm co-evolve with the environment?**

A. Background on the environment and organizational design. (See *PowerPoint Slide 21* for Chapter 18.)

1. Understanding organizational environments is important because organizations are open systems that receive inputs from the environment and in turn sell outputs to the environment.

2. The *general environment* is the set of cultural, economic, legal-political, and educational conditions found in the areas in which the organization operates.

3. The *specific environment* consists of the owners, suppliers, distributors, government agencies, and competitors with which an organization must interact to grow and survive.

4. A firm typically has much more choice in the composition of its specific environment than its general; environment

---

LECTURE ENHANCEMENT

As an out-of class assignment for student groups, have each group select a well-known company to examine with regard to its organizational environment. Have the students identify the general environmental conditions that are affecting many organizations at the present point in time. Also have them try to identify some stakeholders in the specific environment that are relevant to resource inputs, transformation process, and product outputs.

B. Environmental complexity.

1. **Environmental complexity** is the magnitude of the problems and opportunities in the organization's environment as evidenced by three main factors: the degree of richness, the degree of interdependence, and the degree of uncertainty stemming from both the general and the specific environment. (See *PowerPoint Slide 22* for Chapter 18.)

2. Environmental richness. (See *PowerPoint Slide 23* for Chapter 18.)

   a. The environment is richer when the economy is growing, when individuals are improving their education, and when those on whom the organization relies are prospering.

   b. For businesses, a richer environment means that economic conditions are improving, customers are spending more money, and suppliers (especially banks) are willing to invest in the organization's future.

   c. A rich environment has more opportunities and dynamism (*i.e.*, the potential for change), and the organizational design must enable the firm to recognize these opportunities and capitalize on them

   d. The opposite of richness is decline, such as a general recession.

3. Environmental interdependence. (See *PowerPoint Slide 24* for Chapter 18.)

a. The link between external interdependence and organizational design is often subtle and indirect in that the organization may co-opt powerful outsiders by including them, or adjust its overall design strategy to absorb or buffer the demands of a more powerful external element.

4. Uncertainty and volatility. (See *PowerPoint Slide 25* for Chapter 18.)

a. Environmental uncertainty and volatility can be particularly damaging to large bureaucracies since investments quickly become outmoded and internal operations no longer work as expected.

b. The more organic form of organization design is the appropriate response to uncertainty and volatility.

c. With extreme uncertainty and volatility, movement toward an adhocracy may be needed.

C. Network organizations and alliances.

1. In a complex global economy, firms must learn to co-evolve by altering their environment. Two important ways of accomplishing this is through the management of networks and the development of alliances. (See *PowerPoint Slide 26* for Chapter 18.)

2. How networks and alliances are operationalized in different areas of the world.

a. In Europe, *informal combines* or *cartels* exist wherein competitors work cooperatively to share the market in order to decrease uncertainty and improve favorability for all. (See *PowerPoint Slide 27* for Chapter 18.)

b. In the United States, informal combines and cartels are illegal except in rare cases. (See *PowerPoint Slide 27* for Chapter 18.)

c. In Japan, the network of relationships among well-established firms in many industries is called *keiretsu*. (See *PowerPoint Slide 27* for Chapter 18.)

(i) In a *bank-centered keiretsu*, firms are linked directly to one another through cross ownership and historical ties to one bank.

(ii) In a *vertical keiretsu*, a key manufacturer is at the hub of a network of supplier firms or distributor firms.

d. In the United States, *outsourcing* is developing as a specialized form of network organization. (See *PowerPoint Slide 27* for Chapter 18.)

(i) With outsourcing, the central firm specializes in core activities and works with a comparatively small number of suppliers on a long-term basis for both component development and manufacturing efficiency.

         (ii) With too much outsourcing, firms become too highly dependent upon others and lose the capacity to be flexible in response to new opportunities.

    e. **Interfirm alliances**, which are announced cooperative agreements or joint ventures between two independent firms, often involve corporations that are headquartered in different nations. (See *PowerPoint Slide 28* for Chapter 18.)

         (i) Alliances are quite common in high technology industries, because they seek not only to develop technology but also to ensure that their solutions become standardized across regions of the world.

         (ii) In alliances, firms cooperate rather than compete; consequently, both the alliance managers and the sponsoring executives must be patient, flexible, and creative in pursuing the goals of the alliance and each sponsor.

D. Virtual organizations.

  1. A **virtual organization** — an ever-shifting constellation of firms, with a lead corporation, that pool skills, resources, and experiences to thrive jointly — is a design option when internal and external contingencies are changing quickly. (See *PowerPoint Slide 29* for Chapter 18.)

  2. The virtual organization works if it operates by some unique rules and is led in a most untypical way. (See *PowerPoint Slide 30* for Chapter 18.)

    a. The production system yielding the products and services customers desire needs to be in a partner network among independent firms where they are bound together by mutual trust and collective survival.

    b. The partner network needs to develop and maintain an advanced information technology, trust and cross-owning of problems and solutions, and a common shared culture.

    c. The lead firm must take responsibility for the whole constellation and coordinate the actions and evolution of autonomous member firms.

    d. The lead corporation and the members of the partner network need to rethink how they are internally organized and managed.

  3. The *boundaryless organization* is a design option that seeks to eliminate vertical, horizontal, external, and geographic barriers that block desired action. (See *PowerPoint Slide 31* for Chapter 18.)

    a. Boundaryless organizations do not seek to eliminate all boundaries; rather they seek to make boundaries more permeable.

b. To create a boundaryless organization, the following actions need to be undertaken (see *PowerPoint Slide 31* for Chapter 18):

(i) Executives should systematically examine the culture of the firm, catalog its competencies, chart how accountability is actually determined, study the organizational design, assess the actual work processes, and evaluate leadership.

(ii) Employees, managers, and executives initiate a process of improving how they can cooperate rather than compete with others inside and outside the firm.

LECTURE ENHANCEMENT

Ask the students if any of them have taken an on-line course that utilized a discussion board and perhaps required students to work together in some fashion over the Internet. Have them provide some details about these experiences and then relate the discussion to the concepts of boundaryless organizations and virtual organizations.

V. **Study Question 4: How does a firm learn and continue to learn over time?**

A. Background on organizational learning. (See *PowerPoint Slide 32* for Chapter 18.)

1. **Organizational learning** is the process of knowledge acquisition, information distribution, information interpretation, and organizational retention in adapting successfully to changing circumstances.

2. Organizational learning involves the adjustment of the organization's and individual's actions based on its experience and that of others.

3. Organizational learning is the key to successful co-evolution.

B. How organizations acquire knowledge.

1. Firms obtain information and knowledge in a variety of ways and at different rates during their histories.

2. Mimicry. (See *PowerPoint Slide 33* for Chapter 18.)

a. **Mimicry** occurs when managers copy what they believe are the successful practices of others.

b. Mimicry is important to the new firm for the following reasons:

(i) It provides workable, if not ideal, solutions to many problems.

(ii) It reduces the number of decisions that need to be analyzed separately, allowing managers to concentrate on more critical issues

(iii) It establishes legitimacy or acceptance by employees, suppliers, and customers and narrows the choices calling for detailed explanations.

c. Failure often results from simply copying others without attempting to understand the issues involved or the cause-effect relationships

3. Experience. (See *PowerPoint Slide 34* for Chapter 18.)

a. A primary way to acquire knowledge is through experience.

b. Besides learning by doing, managers can also systematically embark on structured programs to capture the lessons to be learned from failure and success.

c. The major problem with emphasizing learning by doing is the inability to forecast precisely what will change and how it will change.

4. Vicarious learning.

a. *Vicarious learning* involves capturing the lessons of others' experiences.

b. At the individual level, managers are building on individualized "social learning" and using it to help transform their potential for organizational improvement.

(i) *Social learning* is learning that is achieved through the reciprocal interactions among people, behavior, and environment.

(ii) *Figure 18.1* from the textbook illustrates and elaborates on this individualized view of learning. (See *PowerPoint Slide 35* for Chapter 18.)

1. The individual uses modeling or vicarious learning to acquire behavior by observing and imitating others.

2. Symbolic processes are used to help communicate values, beliefs, and goals that serve as guides to the individual's behavior.

3. *Self-control* is important in influencing an individual's behavior.

4. *Self-efficacy* — the person's belief that he or she can perform adequately in a situation — is an important part of self-control.

c. **Scanning** involves looking outside the firm and bringing back useful solutions to problems. (See *PowerPoint Slide 36* for Chapter 18.)

    (i) Astute managers can contribute to organizational learning by scanning external sources, such as competitors, suppliers, industry consultants, customers, and leading firms.

    (ii) The critical problem in scanning is translating obtained knowledge in action.

  d. **Grafting** is the process of acquiring individuals, units, and/or firms to bring in useful knowledge to the organization. (See *PowerPoint Slide 36* for Chapter 18.)

    (i) The critical problem in grafting is translating obtained knowledge in action.

C. Information distribution, interpretation, and retention.

  1. Once information is obtained, managers must establish mechanisms to distribute relevant information to the individuals who may need it.

  2. Although data collection is helpful, it is not enough. Data are not information; the information must be interpreted.

  3. Information interpretation.

    a. Information within organizations is a collective understanding of the firm's goals and of how the data relate to one of the firm's stated or unstated objectives within the current setting.

    b. Common problems in information interpretation include the following (see *PowerPoint Slide 37* for Chapter 18):

      (i) *Self-serving interpretations* occur when people see what they have seen in the past or see what they want to see.

      (ii) A **managerial script** is a series of well-known routines for problem identification and alternative generation and analysis common to managers within a firm.

    c. An **organizational myth** is a commonly held cause-effect relationship or assertion that cannot be supported. (See *PowerPoint Slide 38* for Chapter 18.)

      (i) Three common myths often block the development of multiple interpretations. (See *PowerPoint Slide 38* for Chapter 18.)

        1. *Single organizational truth* — this myth is often expressed as: "Although others may be biased, I am able to define problems and develop solutions objectively." The more complex the issue, the stronger the likelihood of many different supportable interpretations.

    2. *Presumption of competence* — managers at all levels are subject to believing that their part of the firm is okay and just needs minor improvements in implementation.

    3. *Denial of tradeoffs* — most managers believe that their group, unit, or firm can avoid making undesirable tradeoffs and simultaneously please nearly every constituency.

4. Information retention.

    a. Organizations contain a variety of mechanisms that can be used to retain useful information. Seven important mechanisms are: individuals, culture, transformation mechanisms, formal structures, ecology, external archives, and internal information technologies. (See *PowerPoint Slide 39* for Chapter 18.)

    b. Individuals are the most important storehouses of information for organizations. Organizations that retain a large and comparatively stable group of experienced individuals are expected to have a higher capacity to acquire, retain, and retrieve information.

    c. Culture is an important repository of the shared experiences of corporate members. The culture often maintains the organizational memory via rich, vivid, and meaningful stories that outlive those who experienced the event.

    d. Transformational mechanisms refer to the documents, rule books, written procedures, and even standard but unwritten methods of operation that are used to store accumulated information.

    e. The organization's formal structure and the positions in an organization are less obvious but equally important mechanisms for sorting information.

    f. Physical structures (or *ecology*) are potentially important but often-neglected mechanisms used to store information.

    g. External archives can be tapped to provide valuable information on most larger organizations, and they provide a view of events that is quite different from that held by the organization.

    h. Internal informational technology can provide a powerful and individually tailored mechanism for storing information. All too often, however, managers are not using their IT systems strategically and are not tapping into them as mechanisms for retention.

D. Dynamics of organizational learning.

1. Learning cycles help explain why many organizations apparently fail to learn, while others appear to improve rapidly.

2. Deficit cycles. (See *PowerPoint Slide 40*for Chapter 18.)

    a. A **deficit cycle** is a pattern of deteriorating performance that is followed by even further deterioration.

    b. Major factors associated with deficit cycles include the following:

        (i) *Organizational inertia* — it is very difficult to change organizations, and the larger the organization, the more inertia it often has.

        (ii) *Hubris* — too few senior executives are willing to challenge their own actions or those of their firms because they see a history of success.

        (iii) *Detachment* — executives often believe they can manage far-flung, diverse operations through analysis of reports and financial records.

3. Benefit cycles. (See *PowerPoint Slide 41* for Chapter 18.)

    a. Firms can successfully co-evolve by initiating a **benefit cycle**, which is a pattern of successful adjustment followed by further improvements.

    b. The same problems do not keep reoccurring because the firm develops adequate mechanisms for learning.

VI.   **Study summary for Chapter 18.**

    A. Point out to the students that the text's "Chapter 18 Study Guide" recaps the key theories, concepts, and ideas in the chapter in relation to the appropriate study questions.

CHAPTER STUDY GUIDE

Study Question 1: What is organizational design and how is it linked to strategy?

- Organizational design is the process of choosing and implementing a structural configuration for an organization.
- Organization design is a way to implement the positioning of the firm in its environment.
- Organizational design provides a basis for a consistent stream of decisions.
- Strategy and organizational design are interrelated. The organization's design must support the strategy if the firm is to be successful.
- Smaller firms often adopt a simple structure because it works, is cheap, and stresses the influence of the leader.
- Operations technology and organizational design should be interrelated to ensure that the firm produces the desired goods and/or services.
- In highly intensive and small-batch technologies, organizational designs may tend toward adhocracy, a very decentralized form of operation.

Study Question 2: What is information technology and how is it used?

- Information technology is the combination of machines, artifacts, procedures, and systems used to gather, store, analyze, and disseminate information for translating it into knowledge.
- Information technology and organizational design can be interrelated. IT provides an opportunity to change the design by substitution, for learning, and to capture strategic advantages.
- IT has now progressed to the point where it can be a fundamental part of the pattern of decisions and the adaptations firms make to the environment.
- Changes can occur from the bottom up so that firms can learn quickly.
- IT and e-business are inseparable, and e-business has become a part of the mix for many firms.

Study Question 3: Can the design of the firm co-evolve with the environment?

- In more effective firms, environmental conditions and organizational design are interrelated as the firm is influenced by and influences its setting.
- In analyzing environments, both the general (background conditions) and specific (key actors and organizations) environments are important.
- The more complex the environment, the greater the demands on the organization; and firms should respond with more complex designs, such as the use of interfirm alliances.
- No firm stands alone; it needs to connect with others and develop partners to thrive.
- A virtual organization is an ever-shifting constellation of firms, with a lead corporation, that pool skills, resources, and experiences to thrive jointly.
- A virtual organization is used with extremes in environmental complexity and technological change.

Study Question 4: How does a firm learn and continue to learn over time?

- Organizational learning is the process of knowledge acquisition, information distribution, information interpretation, and organizational memory used to adapt successfully to changing circumstances.
- Firms use mimicry, experience, vicarious learning, scanning, and grafting to acquire information.
- Firms establish mechanisms to convert information into technology.
- These mechanisms need to avoid self-serving interpretation and an overreliance on scripts and common myths.
- Firms retain information via individuals, transformation mechanisms, formal structure, physical structure, external archives, and their IT system.
- Organizational learning cycles are helpful in understanding organizational behavior because learning is not automatic.
- Noting the presence of a deficit cycle or a benefit cycle helps us understand how some organizations continually decline while others appear to be rising stars.

KEY TERMS

Adhocracy: an organizational structure that is characterized by few rules, policies, and procedures; substantial decentralization; shared decision-making among members; extreme horizontal specialization; few levels of management; and virtually no formal controls.

Benefit cycle: a pattern of successful adjustment followed by further improvements.

Deficit cycle: a pattern of deteriorating performance that is followed by even further deterioration.

Environmental complexity: the magnitude of the problems and opportunities in the organization's environment as evidenced by three main factors: the degree of richness, the degree of interdependence, and the degree of uncertainty stemming from both the general and the specific environment.

Grafting: the process of acquiring individuals, units, and/or firms to bring in useful knowledge to the organization.

Information technology: the combination of machines, artifacts, procedures, and systems used to gather, store, analyze, and disseminate information for translating it into knowledge.

Interfirm alliances: announced cooperative agreements or joint ventures between two independent firms, often involve corporations that are headquartered in different nations.

Managerial script: a series of well-known routines for problem identification and alternative generation and analysis common to managers within a firm.

Mimicry: occurs when managers copy what they believe are the successful practices of others.

Operations technology: the combination of resources, knowledge, and techniques that creates a product or service output for an organization.

Organizational design: the process of choosing and implementing a structural configuration.

Organizational learning: the process of knowledge acquisition, information distribution, information interpretation, and organizational retention in adapting successfully to changing circumstances.

Organizational myth: a commonly held cause-effect relationship or assertion that cannot be supported.

Scanning: involves looking outside the firm and bringing back useful solutions to problems.

Simple design: a configuration involving one or two ways of specializing individuals and units.

Virtual organization: an ever-shifting constellation of firms, with a lead corporation, that pool skills, resources, and experiences to thrive jointly.

Chapter 19
ORGANIZATIONAL CULTURE AND DEVELOPMENT

STUDY QUESTIONS

1.	What is organizational culture?
2.	How do you understand an organizational culture?
3.	How can the organizational culture be managed?
4.	How can you use organization development to improve the firm?

LEARNING OBJECTIVES

After completing this chapter students should be able to:

1.	Describe the basic nature of organizational culture as well as the external adaptation and internal integration functions of organizational culture.
2.	Discuss the importance of dominant cultures, subcultures, and countercultures in organizations, and relate them to multicultural organizations.
3.	Describe the three levels of cultural analysis.
4.	Discuss the importance of stories, rites, rituals, and symbols in organizations.
5.	Explain how cultural rules and roles; shared values, meanings, and organizational myths; and national culture help people understand an organization's culture.
6.	Explain how management philosophy and strategy influence the development of organizational culture.
7.	Describe different approaches to building, reinforcing, and changing cultures.
8.	Discuss the assumptions, values, and principles of organizational development (OD).
9.	Discuss the importance of action research in organizational development.
10.	Describe the organizationwide, group and intergroup, and individual OD interventions.

MATERIAL IN *THE OB SKILLS WORKBOOK* SUPPORTING THE CHAPTER

Case for Critical Thinking	Case 19: Motorola
Experiential Exercises	Exercise 9: How We View Differences
	Exercise 23: Workgroup Culture
	Exercise 40: Fast-Food Technology
	Exercise 41: Alien Invasion
Self-Assessments	Assessment 8: Are You Cosmopolitan?
	Assessment 9: Group Effectiveness
	Assessment 22: Which Culture Fits You?

CHAPTER OVERVIEW

This chapter focuses the steps necessary to build a high-performance organizational culture. Most students are familiar with the concept of organizational culture, but may not know the components of culture or the underlying assumptions. The chapter lays out these ideas in an organized fashion, and provides rich detail to build an understanding of the importance of organizational culture in business organizations.

The chapter begins by defining organizational culture or corporate culture, and then describes external adaptation and internal integration as the keys functions of organizational culture. The roles of dominant cultures, subcultures, and countercultures in organizations are discussed and related to the development of multicultural organizations. The chapter then examines different levels of cultural analysis, and considers how stories, rites, rituals, and symbols help people to understand an organization's culture. Cultural rules and roles as well as shared values, meanings, and organizational myths enable people to gain a fuller and richer understanding of an organization's culture. An appreciation for national culture also contributes to an understanding of organizational culture.

Next, the chapter turns to a discussion of how management philosophy and strategy influence the development of organizational culture. Different approaches to and methods of building, reinforcing, and changing cultures are described. Finally, the chapter explores the potential of organizational development (OD) for fostering planned change of organizational culture. This section of the chapter begins with an explanation of the assumptions, values and principles, and action research foundations of OD. The section concludes with a description of useful organizationwide, group and intergroup, and individual OD interventions.

CHAPTER OUTLINE

I.   **Study Question 1: What is organizational culture?**
        A. Functions of organizational culture
        B. Dominant culture, subcultures, and countercultures
        C. Valuing cultural diversity

II.   **Study Question 2: How do you understand an organizational culture?**
        A. Levels of cultural analysis
        B. Stories, rites, rituals, and symbols
        C. Cultural rules and roles
        D. Shared values, meanings, and organizational myths
        E. National cultural influences

III.   **Study Question 3: How can the organizational culture be managed?**
        A. Management philosophy and strategy
        B. Building, reinforcing, and changing culture

IV.   **Study Question 4: How can you use organization development to improve the firm?**
        A. Underlying assumptions of OD
        B. OD values and principles
        C. Action-research foundations of OD
        D. OD interventions

CHAPTER LECTURE NOTES

I. **Introduction to the Chapter 19 Lecture.**

    A. Study questions for Chapter 19. (See ***PowerPoint Slide 2*** for Chapter 19.)

        1. What is organizational culture?

        2. How do you understand an organizational culture?

        3. How can the organizational culture be managed?

        4. How can you use organizational development to improve the firm?

    B. The lecture material for Chapter 19 is organized around the study questions.

        1. Point out to the students that the text's "Chapter At A Glance" identifies the key topics contained in the chapter and links them to the appropriate study questions.

    C. The chapter opens with a discussion of the organizational culture at R&R Partners, a Las Vegas-based advertising agency and lobbying firm, and how that culture affects organizational members quality of work life.

II. **Study Question 1: What is organizational culture?**

    A. Background on organizational culture. (See ***PowerPoint Slide 3*** for Chapter 19.)

        1. **Organizational or corporate culture** is the system of shared actions, values, and beliefs that develops within an organization and guides the behavior of its members.

        2. No two organizational cultures are identical.

        3. Cultural differences can have a major impact on the performance of organizations and the quality of work life experienced by their members.

    B. Functions of organizational culture.

        1. **External adaptation** involves reaching goals and dealing with outsiders regarding tasks to be accomplished, methods used to achieve the goals, and methods of coping with success and failure. (See ***PowerPoint Slide 4*** for Chapter 19.)

        2. Three important aspects of external adaptation are (see ***PowerPoint Slide 4*** for Chapter 19):

            a. Separating more important from less important eternal forces.

            b. Developing ways to measure accomplishments.

            c. Creating explanations for why goals are not always met.

3. External adaptation involves answering the following important instrumental or goal-related questions concerning coping with reality (see **PowerPoint Slide 5** for Chapter 19):

   a. What is the real mission?

   b. How do we contribute?

   c. What are our goals?

   d. How do we reach our goals?

   e. What external forces are important?

   f. How do we measure results?

   g. What do we do if specific targets are not met?

   h. How do we tell others how good we are?

   i. When do we quit?

LECTURE ENHANCEMENT

Discuss how the college/university addresses some or all of the above questions regarding external adaptation.

---

4. **Internal integration** deals with the creation of a collective identity and with finding ways of matching methods of working and living together. (See **PowerPoint Slide 6** for Chapter 19.)

5. Three important aspects of working together are (see **PowerPoint Slide 6** for Chapter 19):

   a. Deciding who is a member and who is not.

   b. Developing an informal understanding of acceptable and unacceptable behavior.

   c. Separating friends from enemies.

6. Internal integration involves answering the following important questions associated with living together (see **PowerPoint Slide 7** for Chapter 19):

   a. What is our unique identity?

      b.   How do we view the world?

      c.   Who is a member?

      d.   How do we allocate power, status, and authority?

      e.   How do we communicate?

      f.   What is the basis for friendship?

LECTURE ENHANCEMENT

Discuss how the college/university addresses some or all of the above questions regarding internal integration.

C. Dominant cultures, subcultures, and countercultures.

    1. A **subculture** is a group of individuals with a unique pattern of values and philosophy that are not inconsistent with the organization's dominant values and philosophy. (See *PowerPoint Slide 8* for Chapter 19.)

    2. A **counterculture** is a group of individuals with a pattern of values and philosophy that outwardly reject the surrounding culture. (See *PowerPoint Slide 8* for Chapter 19.)

    3. Every large organization imports potentially important subcultural groupings when it hires employees from the larger society.

    4. The difficulty in importing groupings from the larger society lies in the relevance of these subgroups to the organization as a whole.

    5. The following three problems are associated with accepting subcultural divisions and working within the confines of the larger culture (see *PowerPoint Slide 9* for Chapter 19):

        a. Subordinate groups are likely to form into a counterculture and to work more diligently to change their status than to better the firm.

        b. The firm may encounter extreme difficulty in coping with broader cultural changes.

        c. Firms that accept and build on natural divisions from the larger culture may encounter extreme difficulty in developing sound international operations.

D. Valuing cultural diversity.

1. The *multicultural organization* is a firm that values diversity but systematically works to block the transfer of societally based subcultures into the fabric of the organization.

2. Taylor Cox suggests a five-step program for developing a multicultural organization. (See *PowerPoint Slide 10* for Chapter 19.)

a. Step 1 — the organization should develop pluralism with the objective of multibased socialization.

b. Step 2 — the organization should fully integrate its structure so that there is no direct relationship between a naturally occurring group and any particular job.

c. Step 3 — the organization must integrate the informal networks by eliminating barriers and increasing participation.

d. Step 4 — the organization should break the linkage between naturally occurring group identity and the identity of the firm.

e. Step 5 — the organization must actively work to eliminate interpersonal conflict based on either the group identity or the natural backlash of the largest societally based grouping.

3. The key problems with fully implementing Cox's five-step program are the following:

a. Separating the firm from the larger culture in which it must operate.

b. Eliminating some societally based groupings that are relevant for achieving the firm's goals.

III. **Study Question 2: How do you understand an organizational culture?**

A. Levels of cultural analysis.

1. As shown in *Figure 19.1* from the textbook, the three important levels of cultural analysis in organizations are observable culture, shared values, and common assumptions. (See *PowerPoint Slide 11* for Chapter 19.)

2. The first level of cultural analysis is *observable culture*, which refers to "the way we do things around here."

a. The observable culture includes unique stories, ceremonies, and corporate rituals that make up the history of the firm or a group within the firm.

3. The second level of cultural analysis involves the *shared values* that link people together and provide a powerful motivational mechanism for members of the culture.

    a. Every member may not agree with the shared values, but they have all been exposed to them and have often been told they are important.

4. The deepest level of cultural analysis involves *common cultural assumptions*, which are the taken-for-granted truths that collections of corporate members share as a result of their joint experience. It is often extremely difficult to isolate these patterns, but doing so helps explain why culture invades every aspect of organizational life.

LECTURE ENHANCEMENT

Divide the class into groups of five or six students. Have each group focus on a different campus organization — fraternities and sororities are excellent choices — and analyze the organization's observable culture, shared values, and common cultural assumptions.

B. Stories, rites, rituals, and symbols.

1. To begin understanding a corporate culture, it is often easiest to start with stories of the company's founding, its successes and failures, and its winners and losers.

2. **Sagas** are embellished heroic accounts of accomplishments. (See *PowerPoint Slide 12* for Chapter 19.)

3. **Rites** are standardized and recurring activities used at special times to influence the behaviors and understanding of organizational members. (See *PowerPoint Slide 12* for Chapter 19.)

4. **Rituals** are systems of rites. (See *PowerPoint Slide 12* for Chapter 19.)

5. Rites and rituals may be unique to subcultures within an organization.

6. A **cultural symbol** is any object, act, or event that serves to transmit cultural meaning. (See *PowerPoint Slide 12* for Chapter 19.)

C. Cultural rules and roles.

1. Organizational culture often specifies when various types of actions are appropriate and where individual members stand in the social system. These cultural rules and roles are part of the normative controls of the organization and emerge from its daily routines. (See *PowerPoint Slide 13* for Chapter 19.)

D. Shared values, meanings, and organizational myths.

1. *Shared values* help turn routine activities into valuable and important actions, tie the organization to the important values of society, and may provide a very distinctive source of competitive advantage. (See *PowerPoint Slide 14* for Chapter 19.)

2. An organization with a *strong culture* possesses a broadly and deeply shared value system, but this can reinforce a singular view of the organizational and its environment, thereby rendering change difficult.

3. Strong corporate cultures share the following characteristics (see *PowerPoint Slides 15* and *16* for Chapter 19):

    a. A widely shared real understanding of what the firm stands for, often embodied in slogans.

    b. A concern for individuals over rules, policies, procedures, and adherence to job duties.

    c. A recognition of heroes whose actions illustrate the company's shared philosophy and concerns.

    d. A belief in ritual and ceremony as important to members and to building a common identity.

    e. A well-understood sense of the informal rules and expectations so that employees and managers know what is expected of them.

    f. A belief that what employees and managers do is important and that it is essential to share information and ideas.

4. What you see as an outside observer may or may not be what organizational members see.

    a. Through interaction with one another, and as reinforced by the rest of the organization, workers may infuse a larger shared meaning — or sense of broader purpose — into their tasks.

    b. Organizational culture is a "shared" set of meanings and perceptions.

5. **Organizational myths** are unproven and often unstated beliefs that are accepted uncritically. (See *PowerPoint Slide 17* for Chapter 19.)

    a. Myths allow executives to redefine impossible problems into more manageable components.

    b. Myths can facilitate experimentation and creativity, and they allow managers to govern.

E. National cultural influences. (See *PowerPoint Slide 18* for Chapter 19.)

    1. Widely held common assumptions may often be traced to the larger culture of the corporation's host society.

    2. National cultural values may become embedded in the expectations of important organizational constituencies and in generally accepted solutions to problems.

IV.   Study Question 3: How can the organizational culture be managed?

A. Background on managing organizational culture.

    1. Good managers are able to reinforce and support an existing strong culture; good managers are also able to help build resilient cultures in situations where the features of strong cultures are absent.

    2. Two broad strategies for managing corporate culture have received considerable attention in the OB literature. (See *PowerPoint Slide 19* for Chapter 19.)

        a. One strategy calls for managers to help modify observable culture, shared values, and common assumptions directly.

        b. A second strategy involves the use of organizational development techniques to modify specific elements of the culture.

B. Management philosophy and strategy.

    1. **<u>Management philosophy</u>** links key goal-related issues with key collaboration issues to come up with general ways by which the firm will manage its affairs.

    2. A well developed management philosophy is important for the following reasons (see *PowerPoint Slide 20* for Chapter 19):

        a. It establishes generally understood boundaries on all members of the firm.

        b. It provides a consistent way of approaching new and novel situations.

        c. It helps hold individuals together by assuring them of a known path toward success.

C. Building, reinforcing, and changing culture.

    1. How managers can build, reinforce, and change culture. (See *PowerPoint Slide 21* for Chapter 19.)

        a. Managers can modify the visible aspects of culture, such as the language, stories, rites, rituals, and sagas.

      b. Managers can change the lessons to be drawn from common stories and even encourage individuals to see the reality they see.

      c. Top managers, in particular, can set the tone for a culture and for cultural change.

      d. Managers can help foster a culture that provides answers to important questions concerning external adaptation and internal integration.

  2. Mistakes that managers can make in building, reinforcing, and changing culture. (See *PowerPoint Slide 22* for Chapter 19.)

      a. Trying to change people's values from the top down while keeping the ways in which the organization operates the same.

      b. Trying to change people's values from the top down without recognizing the importance of individuals.

      c. Attempting to revitalize an organization by dictating major changes and ignoring shared values.

V.   Study Question 4: How can you use organization development to improve the firm?

  A. Background on organization development.

    1. To keep the culture fresh and competitive, the challenge today is to engage in a process of continuous self-assessment and planned change in order to stay abreast of problems and opportunities in a complex and demanding environment.

    2. **Organizational development (OD)** is the application of behavioral science knowledge in a long-range effort to improve an organization's ability to cope with change in its external environment and increase its internal problem-solving capabilities. (See *PowerPoint Slide 23* for Chapter 19.)

    3. OD is designed to work on both issues of external adaptation and internal integration. (See *PowerPoint Slide 24* for Chapter 19.)

    4. OD is used to improve organizational performance. (See *PowerPoint Slide 24* for Chapter 19.)

    5. OD seeks to achieve change in such a way that the organization's members become more active and confident in taking similar steps to maintain the culture and longer-run organizational effectiveness. (See *PowerPoint Slide 24* for Chapter 19.)

  B. Underlying assumptions of OD.

    1. The organizational development foundations for achieving change are rooted in underlying assumptions about individuals, groups, and organizations.

2. At the individual level, OD is guided by principles that reflect an underlying respect for people and their capabilities. (See *PowerPoint Slide 25* for Chapter 19.)

3. At the group level, OD is guided by principles that reflect a belief that groups can be good for both people and organizations. (See *PowerPoint Slide 25* for Chapter 19.)

4. At the organizational level, OD is guided by principles that show a respect for the complexity of an organization as a system of interdependent parts. (See *PowerPoint Slide 25* for Chapter 19.)

C. OD values and principles.

1. OD offers a systematic approach to planned change in organizations, which addresses two main goals: outcome goals (mainly issues of external adaptation) and process goals (mainly issues of internal integration). (See *PowerPoint Slide 26* for Chapter 19.)

2. OD is intended to help organizations and their members by (See *PowerPoint Slide 27* for Chapter 19.):

   a. Creating an open problem-solving climate throughout an organization.

   b. Supplementing formal authority with that of knowledge and competence.

   c. Moving decision making to points where relevant information is available.

   d. Building trust and maximizing collaboration among individuals and groups.

   e. Increasing the sense of organizational "ownership" among members.

   f. Allowing people to exercise self-direction and self-control at work.

D. Action-research foundations of OD.

1. **Action research** is the process of systematically collecting data on an organization, feeding it back for action planning, and evaluating results by collecting and reflecting on more data after the planned actions have been taken. (See *PowerPoint Slide 28* for Chapter 19.)

2. *Figure 19.2* from the textbook depicts the typical sequence of activities in the action research model. (See *PowerPoint Slide 29* for Chapter 19.)

3. *Figure 19.3* from the textbook portrays an open systems framework that can be used for conducting individual level, group level, and organization level diagnoses in the action research model. (See *PowerPoint Slide 30* for Chapter 19.)

a. At the organization level, effectiveness must be diagnosed in the context of the external environment and major organizational variables including strategy technology, structure, culture, and management systems.

b. At the group level, effectiveness must be diagnosed in the context of the organization environment and major group variables including tasks, membership, norms, cohesiveness, and group processes.

c. At the individual level, effectiveness must be diagnosed in the context of the workgroup environment and major individual variables including tasks, goals, needs, abilities, and interpersonal relationships.

LECTURE ENHANCEMENT

To clarify the action research process, give the example of a small firm that was experiencing a performance gap. Management perceived the problem and hired a consultant, who interviewed key people and planned a problem-solving workshop. Participants in the workshop were coached on how to analyze data and determine appropriate action directions; they also received information on group process techniques. The consultant continued to meet periodically with the group to review progress and additional help was given when needed. The problem-solving workshops became an annual event for the firm.

E. OD interventions.

1. **Organizational development interventions** are activities initiated to facilitate planned change and help the organizational system to develop its own problem-solving capabilities.

2. Organizationwide interventions. (See *PowerPoint Slides 31* and *32* for Chapter 19.)

    a. **Survey feedback** begins with the collection of data via questionnaires from organizational members or a representative sample of them, moves to the feedback of data to the members, and then engages the members in a collaborative process of interpreting the data and developing action plans.

    b. **Confrontation meetings** are designed to help determine quickly how an organization may be improved and to take initial actions to improve the situation.

    c. **Structural redesign** involves realigning the structure of the organization or major subsystems in order to improve performance.

    d. **Collateral organization** makes creative problem solving possible by pulling a representative set of members out of the formal organization structure to engage in periodic small-group, problem-solving sessions.

3. Group and intergroup interventions. (See ***PowerPoint Slide 33*** for Chapter 19.)

      a. <u>**Team building**</u> involves a consultant or manager engaging the members of a group in a series of activities designed to help them examine how the group functions and how it may function better.

      b. <u>**Process consultation**</u> helps a group improve on such things as norms, cohesiveness, decision-making methods, communication, conflict, and task and maintenance activities.

      c. <u>**Intergroup team building**</u> is designed to help two or more groups improve their working relationships with one another and to experience improved group effectiveness as a result.

4. Individual interventions. (See ***PowerPoint Slide 34*** for Chapter 19.)

      a. <u>**Role negotiation**</u> is a process through which individuals clarify expectations about what each should give and receive in their working relationship.

      b. <u>**Job redesign**</u> is the process of creating long-term congruence between individual goals and organizational career opportunities.

      c. <u>**Career planning**</u> provides structured opportunities for individuals to work with their managers or staff experts from the personnel or human resources department on career issues.

5. Successful high-tech firms use organization development interventions to facilitate external adaptation and internal integration as part of the ongoing evolution of the organization's culture.

VI.   **Study summary for Chapter 19.**

A. Point out to the students that the text's "Chapter 19 Study Guide" recaps the key theories, concepts, and ideas in the chapter in relation to the appropriate study questions.

CHAPTER STUDY GUIDE

Study Question 1: What is organizational culture?

- Organizational or corporate culture is the system of shared actions, values, and beliefs that develops within an organization and guides the behavior of its members.
- The functions of the corporate culture include responding to both external adaptation and internal integration issues.
- Most organizations contain a variety of subcultures, and a few have countercultures that can become the source of potentially harmful conflicts.

Study Question 2: How do you understand an organizational culture?

- A detailed understanding of the functions and manifestations of culture is needed.
- Organizational cultures may be analyzed in terms of observable actions, shared values, and common assumptions (the taken-for-granted truths).
- Observable aspects of culture include the stories, rites, rituals, and symbols that are shared by organization members.
- Cultural rules and roles specify when various types of actions are appropriate and where individual members stand in the social system.
- Shard meanings and understandings help everyone know how to act and expect others to act in various circumstances.
- Common assumptions are the taken-for-granted truths that are shared by collections of corporate members.
- The corporate culture also reflects the values and implicit assumptions of the larger national culture.

Study Question 3: How can the organizational culture be managed?

- Executives may manage many aspects of the observable culture directly.
- Nurturing shared values among the membership is a major challenge for executives.
- Adjusting actions to common understandings limits the decision scope of even the CEO.

Study Question 4: How can you use organizational development to improve the firm?

- All managers may use organizational development (OD) techniques in their attempts to manage, nurture, and guide cultural change.
- OD is a special application of knowledge gained from behavioral science to create a comprehensive effort to improve organizational effectiveness.
- With a strong commitment to collaborative efforts and human values, OD utilizes basic behavioral science principles with respect to individuals, groups, and organizations.
- OD has two main goals: outcome goals (mainly issues of external adaptation) and process goals (mainly issues of internal integration).
- Organizational development practitioners refer to action research as the process of systematically collecting data on an organization, groups, and individuals.
- Organizationwide interventions include survey feedback, confrontation meetings, structural redesign, and collateral organization.
- Group and intergroup interventions include team building, process consultation, and intergroup team building.
- Individual interventions include role negotiation, job redesign, and career planning.

KEY TERMS

Action research: the process of systematically collecting data on an organization, feeding it back for action planning, and evaluating results by collecting and reflecting on more data after the planned actions have been taken.

Career planning: a process that provides structured opportunities for individuals to work with their managers or staff experts from the personnel or human resources department on career issues.

Collateral organization: makes creative problem solving possible by pulling a representative set of members out of the formal organization structure to engage in periodic small-group, problem-solving sessions.

Confrontation meeting: a meeting that is designed to help determine quickly how an organization may be improved and to take initial actions to improve the situation.

Countercultures: groups of individuals with a pattern of values and philosophy that outwardly reject the surrounding culture.

Cultural symbol: any object, act, or event that serves to transmit cultural meaning.

External adaptation: involves reaching goals and dealing with outsiders regarding tasks to be accomplished, methods used to achieve the goals, and methods of coping with success and failure.

Intergroup team building: a process that is designed to help two or more groups improve their working relationships with one another and to experience improved group effectiveness as a result.

Internal integration: deals with the creation of a collective identity and with finding ways of matching methods of working and living together.

Job redesign: the process of creating long-term congruence between individual goals and organizational career opportunities.

Management philosophy: links key goal-related issues with key collaboration issues to come up with general ways by which the firm will manage its affairs.

Organizational or corporate culture: the system of shared actions, values, and beliefs that develops within an organization and guides the behavior of its members.

Organizational development (OD): the application of behavioral science knowledge in a long-range effort to improve an organization's ability to cope with change in its external environment and increase its internal problem-solving capabilities.

Organizational development interventions: activities initiated to facilitate planned change and help the organizational system to develop its own problem-solving capabilities.

Organizational myth: unproven and often unstated beliefs that are accepted uncritically.

Process consultation: helps a group improve on such things as norms, cohesiveness, decision-making methods, communication, conflict, and task and maintenance activities.

Rites: standardized and recurring activities used at special times to influence the behaviors and understanding of organizational members.

Rituals: systems of rites.

Role negotiation: a process through which individuals clarify expectations about what each should give and receive in their working relationship.

Sagas: embellished heroic accounts of accomplishments.

Structural redesign: involves realigning the structure of the organization or major subsystems in order to improve performance.

Subcultures: groups of individuals with a unique pattern of values and philosophy that are not inconsistent with the organization's dominant values and philosophy.

Survey feedback: begins with the collection of data via questionnaires from organizational members or a representative sample of them, moves to the feedback of data to the members, and then engages the members in a collaborative process of interpreting the data and developing action plans.

Team building: a process that involves a consultant or manager engaging the members of a group in a series of activities designed to help them examine how the group functions and how it may function better.

The OB Skills Workbook
THE JOSSEY-BASS/PFEIFFER CLASSROOM COLLECTION

STUDENT LEADERSHIP PRACTICES INVENTORY BY KOUZES AND POSNER

	ACTIVITY	SUGGESTED PART	OVERVIEW
1	Student Leadership Practices Inventory — Student Workbook	All	This workbook includes a worksheet to help interpret feedback and plan improvement in each leadership practice assessed, sections on how to compare scores with the normative sample and how to share feedback with constituents, and more than 140 actual steps yours students can take to get results.
2	Student Leadership Practices Inventory — Self	All	This 30-item inventory will help students evaluate their performance and effectiveness as a leader. Results from the simple scoring process helps students prepare plans for personal leadership development.
3	Student Leadership Practices Inventory — Observer	All	This version of the LPI is used by others to assess the individual's leadership tendencies, thus allowing for comparison with self-perceptions.

INSTRUCTOR'S NOTES

The *Student Leadership Practices Inventory — Student Workbook* begins on page W-9 of ***The OB Skills Workbook*** and concludes on page W-22. Five topics are covered — "Leadership: What People Do When They're Leading," "Questions Frequently Asked About the Student LPI," "Recording Your Scores," "Interpreting Your Scores," and "Summary and Action-Planning Worksheets." Collectively, this material provides the user with a solid conceptual foundation for understanding the LPI as well as detailed instructions for completing, scoring, and interpreting it.

The *Student Leadership Practices Inventory — Self* is located on pages W-23 through W-25 of the workbook, and the *Student Leadership Practices Inventory — Observer* is on pages W-26 through W-28.

EXPERIENTIAL EXERCISES FROM THE PFEIFFER ANNUAL: TRAINING

Assessments and Exercises: Guidelines for Use

The materials for this workbook were selected with several considerations in mind. Careful attention was given to make sure each selection satisfied the following criteria:

- Relevance — materials were chosen to represent contemporary and emerging topics of interest.
- Content — materials were chosen to match a variety of topics from the companion text; a primary topic is identified and, in some cases, secondary topics are also provided.
- Time — materials, with a couple of exceptions, were chosen to fit a traditional "one-hour" class meeting; alternatively, these can be used to break up a two- or three-hour meeting.
- Audience — materials were chosen to work in a variety of groups, particularly those that may be populated with young undergraduates that have little or no work experience.
- Simplicity — materials were chosen to be quickly engaging; in most cases, there is not a lot of time spent "setting up" the assessment/exercise and there are not too many details that require students' attention.

Assessments

Assessments are good tools to help students grasp and begin to understand the relevance of specific concepts in their lives. An effective approach for using assessments is to assign them one meeting in advance. Have students complete the instrument out of class and then score it during discussion of the corresponding topic. Alternately, the whole process can take place in class within 15 minutes.

General discussion should focus on what the assessment measures, what students discover when completing the assessment (particularly, any surprises), and what the scores mean. Be prepared for typical reactions (*e.g.*, "I already knew this," "I do not think this is true about me"). When students claim they already possessed certain knowledge (*i.e.*, insights about their personality, behavior) about themselves, press them to elaborate. Ask how they have been using this knowledge and how effective their strategies have been. For skeptical students, it may be helpful to talk about self-perception and whether the way we see ourselves is necessarily the way others see us. If enough skepticism about the results exists, you may want to consider having friends use the instrument to assess the student.

Experiential Exercises

Experiential exercises can be introduced in a number of ways. Labeling them "experientials" or "simulations" provides an opportunity to talk about why they are valuable learning tools. These exercises fulfill two main purposes: (1) they allow students to move from abstract to concrete by practicing what they read; and (2) the practice takes place in a safe learning environment (*i.e.*, one where the penalties for mistakes are minimal).

Two general rules are advisable. First, students should always follow directions. Experiential exercises are, by design, vague. Specific instructions, when they exist, may be critical for producing responses that create intended learning. Second, students must treat each exercise seriously. Because students will learn about behavior through the exercises, cavalier attitudes may lead to the wrong lessons.

A "warm-up" experiential during the first or second class meeting can be effective for helping students overcome the awkward feeling that often accompanies these exercises. Remind students that it is okay not to have all the answers and to feel as though they are not doing it the "right" way. Experiential exercises are often designed to produce "wrong" results in order to fully explore them (*e.g.*, why they occurred, how they can be avoided).

ACTIVITY 1 — SWEET TOOTH: BONDING STRANGERS INTO A TEAM

SUGGESTED PART	OVERVIEW
Parts 1, 3, 4	perception; teamwork; decision making; communication

INSTRUCTOR'S NOTES

Primary Topic(s): Introduction, Groups/Teams

Icebreakers can be effective tools for getting individuals to interact in a non-threatening way. As such, *Sweet Tooth* can be utilized at multiple points depending on the topic you want to explore. While the exercise is designed to be a small group activity, it can also be implemented in a large group (*i.e.*, full class) setting. In the latter case, you may want to consider displaying items on a transparency rather than individual handouts.

The first opportunity to use the exercise occurs during the first class meeting. Students are naturally apprehensive when arriving for new classes, particularly if they are experiential.

The exercise can also be used to explore various issues related to groups/teams. These include member diversity, group size, communication, and decision making.

If students are going to be assigned to project teams, a third opportunity for using the exercise exists. Effectiveness depends on the point you want to stress. If you want to promote interaction and stimulate communication between new group members, *Sweet Tooth* is appropriate. If you want to explore developmental issues (*e.g.*, developing effective norms), consider using *Interrogatories*.

Final Note: Be mindful that the examples and some clues are culturally bound. If you have international students without significant exposure to American culture, they may be confused by the exercise and withdraw. The end result is that you accomplish exactly the opposite of what you wanted. Adding a few international items (tailored to your audience) can encourage these individuals to get involved. Alternately, you could use this as an opportunity to explore the feelings of international students and to discuss the reasons for keeping everyone engaged (*e.g.*, their contributions will be needed later).

ACTIVITY 2 — INTERROGATORIES: IDENTIFYING ISSUES AND NEEDS

SUGGESTED PART	OVERVIEW
Parts 1, 3, 4	current issues; group dynamics; communication

INSTRUCTOR'S NOTES

Primary Topic(s): Groups/Teams, Conflict

In its simplest form, this exercise can be used as an icebreaker after assigning students to project teams. Having students generate questions related to specific topics can satisfy the "need to know" that accompanies new group experiences. Generating questions within the group beforehand can stimulate communication and allow group members to recognize shared experiences.

The recommended variation is a good way to help groups begin the process of developing productive norms and defining role expectations. Be prepared to spend a full class meeting (one hour) to fully explore all the issues. Rather than introduce topics one at a time, distribute lists with all the issues to each individual. Instruct groups to begin by identifying which issues are likely to be the key to successfully completing the project. In phase two, ask members to share personal group experiences (*i.e.*, actual problems encountered from one or more issues). In the final phase, have groups determine how they will deal with the issues to prevent them from impeding progress.

You may find it helpful to conclude the exercise by having groups develop and sign a team contract covering the procedures for dealing with potential problems.

ACTIVITY 3 — DECODE: WORKING WITH DIFFERENT INSTRUCTIONS

SUGGESTED PART	OVERVIEW
Parts 3, 4	decision making; leadership; conflict; teamwork

INSTRUCTOR'S NOTES

Primary Topic(s): Groups/Teams, Leadership

This exercise and *Get Smart* are similar. Both involve a group-based, problem-solving activity where groups only have a part of the final solution. Both require full cooperation to produce a successful outcome for everyone. It is possible for a subset of the class to solve the problem so that everyone does not experience success. You will not want to use both exercises unless your explicit goal is to see if they learned from the first experience. If this is the case, use *Decode* first because the instructions to cooperate are built into the exercise.

Two modifications to the original instructions may be in order. First, consider awarding actual bonus points to those individuals involved in solving the cryptogram. Also, you may want to adjust the time limits to allow a reasonable chance of success. Two- and three-minute limits may not be enough time, particularly if there are several groups that must approach you for clues and then interact with one another. At the same time, the time limits should provide a bit of challenge.

There are several points of discussion depending on your focus. If groups/teams are stressed, the conversation should concentrate on intragroup and intergroup dynamics. Begin by exploring behaviors that helped or hindered the group. Do not include the secret instructions at this point. Follow this discussion by talking about how well groups/teams worked together. Focus on the natural tendency to compete rather than cooperate. If groups/teams tended to be competitive, ask them why they failed to recognize that cooperation would make the task easier.

If leadership is the focal point, begin the debriefing by making everyone aware that one individual received a special set of instructions. Draw this individual into the discussion. Seek to understand what conditions made this individual more or less assertive during the exercise. Follow up by asking other members of the class why they accepted or rejected attempts by the "leader" to implement the special instructions.

Final Note: As with many experiential exercises, advance knowledge of the purpose(s) can limit the learning experience. While it is likely that some students may come into this exercise knowing that cooperation leads to a better outcome for all, it is unlikely that this information will be possessed by a sufficient number to create the critical mass needed for easy cooperation. In other words, there will always be enough skeptics in the audience to make it difficult for those with advance knowledge to "foil" the exercise.

However, it is possible that knowledge of the decoded cryptogram can put one group at a decided advantage over the others. It is recommended that you generate additional cryptograms and regularly change them out (you may even want to announce this at the start of the exercise), so that students are not tempted to take shortcuts.

ACTIVITY 4 — CHOICES: LEARNING EFFECTIVE CONFLICT MANAGEMENT STRATEGIES

SUGGESTED PART	OVERVIEW
Parts 1, 2, 3, 4, 5	conflict; negotiation; communication; decision making;

INSTRUCTOR'S NOTES

Primary Topic(s): Conflict, Groups/Teams

This exercise is designed to help groups develop the skills for handling conflict that is inevitable when individuals work together. The conflict-handling strategies used do not perfectly coincide with those identified in the text. However, the exercise is a good supplement to text discussion because it outlines conditions for using different strategies. Use this exercise carefully, with full explanations and comparison/contrasts of the strategies, to avoid confusing students:

Schermerhorn *et al.* Strategy	Exercise Strategy
Avoidance	Withdrawal
Authority	Authority
Accommodation	No Equivalent
Compromise	Compromise
Collaboration	Integration
No Equivalent	Suppression

Ten scenarios are provided. These can be useful for fully exploring the nature of conflict and the conditions for choosing a conflict-handling strategy. However, it is equally likely that students will become bored after analyzing a few scenarios. In order to make this exercise fit a traditional one-hour class meeting, selecting a limited subset is advisable. A complete discussion can be accomplished using Scenarios 1, 4, 7, 9, and 10. These scenarios cover each strategy as a primary solution with adequate opportunity for viewing all the strategies as secondary solutions.

While strategies such as withdrawal, authority, and suppression are less than optimal, conditions exist when they may be useful. A key advantage of this exercise is the ability to illustrate some of these conditions (*e.g.*, when laws/policies are being violated, when no direct benefit to getting involved exists).

A useful variation that may create additional opportunities to explore conflict handling is to have students complete the scenarios individually before class and then put them into groups for determining primary and secondary strategies. If this variation is used, end the session with discussion about the dynamics that took place as student groups chose their strategies. Focus on disagreements that may have been present and whether groups took advantage of the opportunity to apply what they were learning.

ACTIVITY 5 — INTERNAL/EXTERNAL MOTIVATORS: ENCOURAGING CREATIVITY

SUGGESTED PART	OVERVIEW
Parts 2, 4, 5	creativity; motivation; job design; decision making

INSTRUCTOR'S NOTES

Primary Topic(s): Motivation

This exercise has been modified to focus on academic work. All students should recognize the value of creativity in completing assignments. Likewise, they should be familiar with the role of motivation. De-emphasize the group aspects of this exercise and focus on the individual level. The handout on motivation and creativity is quite informative. You may want to consider assigning it before students begin working on the exercise.

Subgroup discussion can be eliminated to reduce the total time to complete this exercise. However, a full class discussion is likely to center on a few individuals are normal contributors. Be prepared to draw others, who normally do not voice opinions, into the discussion.

The main purpose of the exercise is to help students realize that both forms motivation are important. However, intrinsic motivation is more likely to encourage creativity. A clear understanding of the relationship between motivation, creativity, and performance will enable a richer discussion of the various job design approaches (Chapter 7 of the textbook).

ACTIVITY 6 — QUICK HITTER: FOSTERING THE CREATIVE SPIRIT

SUGGESTED PART	OVERVIEW
Parts 4, 5	creativity; decision making; communication

INSTRUCTOR'S NOTES

Primary Topic(s): Perception, Decision Making

This exercise focuses on enhancing individual creativity by identifying barriers that limit it. It also illustrates how perceptions and traditional thinking can hinder creativity and influence decision making. John Maxwell's *Thinking for a Change* (2003, Warner Business Books) is a useful resource to provide additional material for this exercise.

The movie is quite long (115 minutes), but a full showing is recommended for courses that emphasize decision making, creativity, and/or entrepreneurship. Patch's experience with his roommate at the psychiatric hospital illustrates the importance of framing (reframing) for solving problems. The notion of "thinking outside the box" is reinforced throughout the movie. This theme (non-conventional thinking) could be supplemented with scenes and discussion of the movie *K-Pax*. While *Patch Adams* is based on a true story, some students may have trouble seeing the relevance to business situations. Consider incorporating discussions using Fred Smith and Federal Express (initial idea written in a college term paper was rejected by his professor) or Sam Walton and Wal-Mart (traditional wisdom held that discount stores could not be successful in locations with a population less than 50,000).

If the aim of this exercise is to emphasize perceptions, you may wish to use selected scenes from *Finding Forrester* to illustrate how perceptions influence not only individual behavior but affect interpersonal interactions as well. The movie is loaded with examples of inaccurate race-based perceptions. Three scenes are particularly illustrative: the "BMW discussion" as Jamal Wallace encounters William Forrester's aide for the first the time; Forrester's remark as he and Jamal watch Jeopardy; and Robert Crawford's comments to colleagues about the authenticity of Jamal's submission to the annual essay competition.

The OB Skills Workbook
CASES FOR CRITICAL THINKING

CASE 1: DREXLER'S BAR-B-QUE

SUGGESTED CHAPTER		CROSS-REFERENCE AND INTEGRATION
1	Introducing Organizational Behavior	organizational structure; design and culture; organizational change and innovation; decision making; leadership

CASE SUMMARY

Drexler's Bar-B-Que is a family-owned restaurant. The restaurant is located in an economically disadvantaged neighborhood in Houston, Texas. Drexler's has been in the same family for many years and is currently operated by James Drexler and his mother, Mrs. Scott. Mrs. Scott has strong moral and religious beliefs, which she has projected onto the atmosphere of the restaurant. Consistent with Mrs. Scott's beliefs, Drexler's is actively involved in charity work in Houston. For many years the business operated in a consistent manner and was successful. In 1994, it closed for six months. During that time, the building was leveled and completely rebuilt. Shortly after the restaurant reopened, business doubled. A key event that affected the business was the arrival on the scene of James's brother Clyde, a NBA basketball player. On February 14, 1995, Clyde was traded from the Portland Trailblazers to the Houston Rockets. Clyde had played his collegiate ball at the local university and was popular in the city of Houston. The result was a significant amount of publicity for the Drexler's Bar-B-Que. The restaurant has since become the hub of several businesses located side-by-side. Clyde has since become a coach in Colorado, but when the basketball season is over, he comes back to Houston and the Drexler restaurant where he is a major draw.

RELATED WEB SITES

Description of Site	Web Site Address
Sidewalk Houston — includes a description and picture of Drexler's Bar-B-Que	http://houston.citysearch.com/detail/4975?brand=sidewalk

QUESTIONS AND SUGGESTED ANSWERS

1. Use the open systems model described in this chapter to show how Drexler's Bar-B-Que should operate as a learning organization.

    Answer:

    Like any business, Drexler's depends on receipt of resources and other inputs, including its employees and customers, from the external environment. These inputs must be well

341

used in restaurant operations — the throughputs that create the meals actually served — in order to satisfy the needs of the customers. With satisfied customers, the company can continue to prosper and grow as is the current situation. At any point where the customers become dissatisfied and the restaurant clientele decreases substantially in number, the company will have difficulty surviving financially. To avoid this situation, management and leadership at Drexler's must be continually communicating with customers to determine their satisfaction and needs, and develop the organizational responses appropriate to them. This means that the restaurant should operate in a manner of continuous learning while simultaneously always adapting to meet emerging needs while staying consistent with the core values.

2.   How do the "values" of Drexler's Bar-B-Que relate to the ethics and social responsibility issues raised in this chapter?

Answer:

One of the key ingredients of any successful organization, Drexler's Bar-B-Que included, is a clear sense of purpose that is supported by a core set of appropriate values. In this case, the purpose of the original restaurant seems clear — to make a reasonable profit while providing high quality and distinctive bar-b-que food to a local restaurant clientele. This purpose has served the organization well and it seems to have succeeded in continually meeting this purpose. In addition, however, Mrs. Scott has pursued this purpose with a strong and even growing commitment to the local community in which the restaurant is located. These values are reflected in the ways she personally treats everyone and the way the restaurant operates — right up to the present initiatives to provide free holiday meals to the poor. The challenge now will be to maintain these values in an expansion and diversification of the business, and under the glare of increased publicity brought about by Clyde Drexler's media appeal as a basketball star.

3.   What challenges of organization and managerial leadership face Drexler's in its current movement toward expansion?

Answer:

The "superstar" status of Clyde Drexler has brought a great deal of attention to this restaurant, and has increased its customer appeal substantially. This means that the financial resources are in place for the restaurant to expand and for the "family" to diversify its businesses beyond the traditional restaurant. The challenges in this respect will be to maintain the clear sense of purpose and core values as the size of the operations increases and as more non-family members join the ranks of employees. Eventually, the issue of management and leadership succession will have to be addressed when Mrs. Scott decides to reduce her direct role in the business or even retire. The opportunity to "institutionalize" her personality and presence, however, exists. Indeed, she is the cornerstone of the organizational culture and may be viewed relative to her family's business much like Walt Disney and Sam Walton were to theirs. Overall, the company looks to be in a very good position, assuming that management can maintain the integrity of its values and purpose even while pursuing expansion.

4.   By 2002 the restaurant was appealing to the local interest in Clyde Drexler. Discuss the pros and cons of that approach.

Answer:

Celebrity appeal can be an extremely valuable asset as long as the celebrity continues to be viewed as a hero and as long as the person continues to be available. The appeal of the restaurant had shifted to a person who ultimately moved out of the state and was in Houston only part of the year. While Clyde's presence might bring in additional customers when he is in town, the restaurant is in operation throughout the year. A team of employees and a group of local customers had been built around Mrs. Scott's leadership and food skills and the changed focus could detract from what had given the operation its success.

CASE 2: THE PANERA BREAD CASE — NOT BY BREAD ALONE

SUGGESTED CHAPTER		CROSS-REFERENCE AND INTEGRATION
2	Current Issues in Organizational Behavior	human resource management; organizational cultures; innovation; information technology; leadership

CASE SUMMARY

This case profiles the Panera Bread Company, the highly successful leader in the United States "quick casual" restaurant market niche. Recent financial and marketing successes, which are documented in the case, indicate that Panera has created value for its stockholders through aggressive growth and for its customers through marketing expertise. However, maintaining this position as a high-performance organization may require some changes to remain competitive.

Because this organization prides itself on providing customers with high quality service, Panera may be tending to ignore the needs and quality of work life of its employees who interact most directly with the customers. In the long term this can lead to customer dissatisfaction and open up opportunities for competitors.

RELATED WEB SITES

Description of Site	Web Site Address
Panera Bread Company	http://www.panera.com

QUESTIONS AND SUGGESTED ANSWERS

Note

Because on the surface Panera Bread looks like the perfect high-performance organization, students should analyze this case in terms of what changes this organization needs to make to maintain its success. Currently, this "quick casual" restaurant concept is still in a growth phase. As this segment of the service market matures, there will be more innovative competition for customers and employees and slimmer profit margins — exactly what already has happened to the traditional fast food restaurants. One way to start off the discussion on this case would be to ask students to perform a SWOT analysis of Panera Bread. This will force students to analyze the actions an organization must take to continue as a learning organization. Possible answers in a SWOT analysis are provided below.

Strengths (internal): include a well-defined corporate mission; financial and marketing expertise; profitable, high level of customer satisfaction with the products; strong corporate leadership; well defined target market; innovative and quick to respond to environmental changes (low-carb diets, technology, etc.); strong product development; franchising ⅔ of the new restaurants allows Panera to finance expansion without incurring heavy debt; etc.

Weaknesses (internal): with an aggressive growth strategy, has high economic barriers of entry for new franchisees; relies heavily on transient low paid part-time employees to be the first line of interaction with the customers and this can lead to lower customer satisfaction with the level of service than with the products; no evidence that this organization values diversity; encouraging diners to linger may contribute to a longer wait for tables or require that the bakery-cafes rent more space; minimal advertising; etc.

Threats (external): popularity of low-carb diets and trend towards decreased bread consumption; increasing competition; being bought out like the Boston Market chain which was purchased by McDonalds; stock price has declined in the past year which could cause the company to rely more on expansion through franchising rather than company owned stores; competition spends much more on advertising; etc.

Opportunities (external): expansion into global markets; more focus on growing diverse customer markets in United States; continued high growth through acquisition or development of another chain, new products, services; etc.

1. Referring to Figure 2.1 from the textbook, the upside-down pyramid view of organizations and management, which one of these levels could be the most likely to undermine the continued success of this organization?

    Answer:

    Once a SWOT analysis is done, it becomes clear that this organization, like the fast-food industry, is highly dependent on its counter help and food preparation employees to satisfy customers' needs. The stakeholders who are the lowest paid and have the least attachment to the organization, have the highest level of customer contact and are often the most responsible for perceptions of value and customer satisfaction.

    To sustain this organization's high performance, management needs to pay more attention to its human capital, particularly in terms of lower-level employees' quality of work life issues such as: providing increased training, fostering personal growth and development, providing opportunities to move up in the organization and promoting teamwork.

2. Visit http://www.panerabread.com and http://www.panera.com. What conclusions might you draw about diversity at the Panera Bread Corporation from these Websites and from the case? What does this company appear to be missing in terms of diversity? What benefits could increased diversity offer this organization?

Answer:

Many Panera locations tend to be staffed with white young employees 18-35 years old. As of September 6, 2004 there isn't a single mention of diversity on either Website. This could indicate that this is not a priority or an important value in the Panera culture. After reviewing over forty articles and Websites and contacting the company, the case author was unable to find a single reference to diversity at Panera. Unfortunately, when companies are successful and have not had high-profile discrimination lawsuits brought against them, the benefits of having a more diverse workforce sometimes are not recognized.

Since the high financial barriers of entry may make it more difficult for many minorities and even some women to become franchisees (*i.e.*, in effect erecting a "glass ceiling"), Panera could develop a recruiting program to diversify the management of its company-owned locations. Another option would be to institute a diversity supplier program such as the highly successful ones at Johnson Controls and The Coca-Cola Company.

Because of the high growth rates of ethnic and non-white minorities in the United States, if Panera does not pay attention to diversity in the future, it may make recruiting employees, innovative product development, continued growth and expansion, and moving into more diverse markets more difficult. For example, it is not easy to hire and retain reliable part-time help. If Panera instituted a special program to hire mothers, older or physically challenged workers, it could tap into a pool of employees who are more available for early morning shifts, are not as apt to need costly benefits, and have less job turnover.

3. Since Panera Bread has an aggressive growth strategy, what are the implications for this organization if the corporate management decides to open restaurant-cafes in other countries?

    Answer:

    Currently Panera restaurant-cafés are targeted to appeal to a specific market: the more affluent, American, suburban customer. So, global expansion would require a willingness to study and to adapt the products and services and quite possibly the franchising requirements, to the needs of other cultures. For example, in many European countries, coffee and pastries are cheaper if consumed standing up. In many parts of the world, people already are quite used to the concept of lingering for a long time over their food and beverages. Having more diverse employees at the corporate level could help the organization to change and adapt to these market opportunities.

FIELD ASSIGNMENT

If there is a Panera restaurant-cafe in your area, go in alone as a customer. Order something and sit and observe the service, products and operations. Given Panera's success, what did you observe that surprised you? If you were a consultant, hired by Panera Bread to suggest improvements, what changes would you suggest on the basis of your visit? Why?

These answers will vary according to the location visited, time of day, and expectations of the individual student. The case author made several visits to Panera locations at different times of the day. As a result of these observations, the following learning occurred regarding these restaurant-cafés:

- There is no children's menu — half sandwiches, etc. Many parents were observed sharing their meals with young children. Panera does provide high chairs.

- Because of the wood floors and lack of sound absorbent material, the noise levels were quite high. This makes it more difficult to work, "chill out" or to conduct a business meeting — all activities encouraged by Panera. In addition, it was difficult to hear one's name being called when an order was ready. This should be addressed in the design of new stores.

- On <u>all</u> visits, counter employees were observed spending considerable time chatting among themselves. As a result, one clerk, socializing with her co-worker, gave the case author $10 too much in change. The clerk had to be convinced of her error! An inquiry about the training for new employees indicated that it appears to be quite informal.

- The box for the customer comment (feedback) cards was difficult to find and located in the back of the store.

- The congestion and queuing around the food preparation area could suggest that one has a long time to wait, which would discourage patrons from staying to order, when in fact food is prepared quite quickly.

CASE 3: CROSSING BORDERS

SUGGESTED CHAPTER		CROSS-REFERENCE AND INTEGRATION
3	Organizational Behavior Across Cultures	diversity and individual differences; perception and attribution; performance management; job design; communication; conflict; decision making

CASE SUMMARY

This case discusses the experiences of Angelica Garza, a woman of Mexican American heritage, who is working in the HR department of both a maquiladora plant in Tijuana, and an American facility in San Diego. The company that she works for is a multinational medical products company. In the case, issues associated with mixing cultures are highlighted, including some of the specific barriers that needed to be overcome in this situation. There are also some examples of resistance to change from the subordinate and management levels.

There are no Web sites that directly pertain to this case.

QUESTIONS AND SUGGESTED ANSWERS

1. What competencies are appropriate to ensure greater effectiveness of U.S. employees operating in a maquiladora or other non-U.S. organization?

Answer:

It should not be assumed that similarity in the heritage of managers would necessarily ease the transition of managing in another culture. The competencies of effectiveness in communication, efficient hiring methods, and interpersonal relations all need to be imparted to a manager operating in a non-U.S. organization.

2.   What are some of the costs of not understanding diversity? What could the organization have gained by approaching the plant with greater cultural understanding?

Answer:

Some of the key leanings about diversity and HR are:

- Never underestimate the impact of culture.
- Do not assume that someone's heritage will dictate his or her ability to assimilate and overcome culture differences. This may, in fact, be more of a disadvantage than an advantage.
- Strong communication skills, patience and understanding are the most important qualities to have for someone who will be immersed in a new culture.

The cost of not understanding diversity therefore can affect communication, perceptions, and ultimately, productivity. The organization could have saved itself time and money in addressing these issues at the outset.

3.   From the HR perspective, what were the unique challenges that Angelica faced at various points in her work for USMed?

Answer:

One of the largest challenges that Angelica needed to overcome was the stereotype that Mexican Nationals would accept her. She also had to overcome the fact that management expected her to have no trouble understanding and communicating with the Mexican employees. Maintaining a position on a certain issue without appearing to be biased to one side or the other was another challenge that Angelica faced. There was also a large resistance to changing existing processes and procedures. The changes were especially needed for the processing of new employees since there was a 25 percent per month employee turnover rate. Her final challenge would be gaining the respect of other employees including her boss, who did not accept the changes that USMed was trying to implement with respect to accounting procedures.

4.   Angelica worked in a plant outside the U.S. What do her experiences and perspectives tell us that applies to domestic operations?

Answer:

The domestic operations are obviously quite different from the maquiladora with respect to observing and implementing standard processes and procedures. The impact of culture differentiates two operations especially when it comes to the workers' attitudes toward women.

CASE 4: NEVER ON A SUNDAY

SUGGESTED CHAPTER		CROSS-REFERENCE AND INTEGRATION
4	Diversity and Individual Differences	ethics and diversity; organizational structure, design, and culture; decision making; organizational change

CASE SUMMARY

McCoy's is one of the nation's largest family-owned and -managed building supply companies. The business has been in operation for almost 70 years and has sales exceeding $400 million from approximately 10 million customers in six states. The company has a strong corporate culture that includes a strong belief in God and commitment to servicing customers. One of the main consequences of this is, as the title suggests, that all the stores are closed on Sunday. Finally, it is important to note that most managers are promoted from within and that there are some signs that this may begin to change.

RELATED WEB SITES

Description of Site	Web Site Address
McCoy's Building Supply Centers	http://www.mccoys.com

QUESTIONS AND SUGGESTED ANSWERS

1. How do the beliefs of the McCoy family form the culture of this company?

    Answer:

    The beliefs of the McCoy family form the culture of this company in the following ways:

    - Most promotions are made from within the company.
    - The store does not open on Sundays.
    - There is a strong corporate responsibility to the community.
    - Participation in the annual Red Ribbon campaign.

2. Can a retailer guided by such strong beliefs compete and survive in the era of gigantic retailers such as Home Depot? If so, how can this be done?

    Answer:

    The future ability of McCoys to compete depends on:

    - How loyal their customers are.
    - Whether the corporate culture affects McCoy's ability to meet their customers' needs.
    - If the customer appreciates value added as a result of these benefits.

3. Is such a strong commitment to social responsibility and ethical standards a help or a hindrance in managing a company?

Answer:

The commitment to social responsibility and ethical standards has helped to establish a good reputation for the business, a source of pride for the employees, and opportunities to expand the business. As a result, these standards have aided in managing the company.

4.   How does a family-owned and -managed company differ from companies managed by outside professionals?

Answer:

Family-owned and -managed companies tend to differ from professionally managed companies in the following ways:

- Family-owned businesses tend to enforce their own personal beliefs on the rest of their employees.
- There is typically a much stronger corporate culture and corporate identity.
- There is more of a human element in the decision-making process.
- Opportunities for outsiders to enter into the corporation and advance rapidly are unlikely.
- Employees tend to stay for longer periods of time in family-owned operations since they may be related.

CASE 5: MAGREC, INC.

SUGGESTED CHAPTER	CROSS-REFERENCE AND INTEGRATION
5 Perception and Attribution	ethics and diversity, organizational structure, design, and culture; decision making; organizational change

CASE SUMMARY

MagRec is a company that specializes in the manufacturing and distribution of magnetic recording heads. Dinah Coates discovers a memo that describes a manufacturing defect and shows it to her boss Pat. A remedy to resolve the problem is devised; unfortunately, the life of the head will be significantly reduced. After Dinah is told about this decision, she contacts the customer and informs the customer of the problem. This results in the customer requesting the opportunity to inspect the manufacturing facility, reducing their reliance on MagRec to 60 percent of production and receiving a price reduction. The price reduction becomes industry knowledge and over the next two quarters, sales drop off by 40 percent. The employees become disheartened by the situation and Pat's boss Fred asks him to fire Dinah. Pat decides not to and takes her out for lunch instead. Over lunch, Pat suggests to Dinah that she move to a different location for a while. Dinah responds to this by suggesting that Pat should have stood up for her and that he should just fire her if that's what he wants.

There are no Web sites that directly pertain to this case.

QUESTIONS AND SUGGESTED ANSWERS

1.   Place yourself in the role of the manager. What should you do now? After considering what happened, would you change any of your behaviors?

Answer:

As the manager it will be necessary to have another discussion with Dinah to decide what her future at the company will be. The situation is obviously not acceptable as it is; however, it is too late to change what has happened. The best thing that can happen now is that Pat learns from this situation so that it does not happen again. Now that he is the sales manager, he is going to have to make some decisions on his own. It will be important for him to establish or determine a method of dealing with these ethical issues. He should support Dinah, however; it is important to establish a method of dealing with issues that does not bring the customer into the matter until it has reached the resolution stage.

2.   Do you think Dinah was right? Why or why not? If you were she and you had to do it all over again, would you do anything differently? If so, what and why?

Answer:

Ethically, Dinah was right; unfortunately she should not have contacted the customer as she did. The customer should be notified by the organization through the proper channels. If Dinah thought the issue was not being handled properly, she should have made her feelings known internally and not externally to the customer.

3.   Using cognitive dissonance theory, explain the actions of Pat, Dinah, and Fred.

Answer:

Cognitive dissonance theory, as expounded upon by Leon Festinger, attempts to explain the relationship between values, attitudes and behavior. "Dissonance" means a lack of equilibrium in a person, which exists because of two or more conflicting values, attitudes, or behaviors. The individual will seek balance and try to reduce the dissonance. This can be accomplished by determining the importance of the elements responsible for the dissonance, which is in the control of the elements (degree of influence), and the corresponding rewards.

The elements are truly important to Dinah in the case, but perhaps not as important to Pat and Fred. Fred dismisses the quandary quite easily by indicating it was a long time ago and some of the people have left the company. Pat, being guided by Fred, seems to agree and abides by the rationalization. It is only after the disclosure to the customer by Dinah, that the elements take on a sense of urgency and importance.

Dinah had a number of alternatives. One, she could have changed her behavior by not being upset and seeing Fred's point of view. Two, she could have adjusted her attitude by rationalizing that "this is business and everybody is dishonest to a certain degree." Three, she could have minimized the dissonance by examining her financial situation and her need for this job. Or lastly, she could have searched for more consonant elements to overcome the dissonant ones, such as the benefits this company has produced for the industry and its workers. Pat and Fred's actions can go through a similar analysis.

CASE 6: IT ISN'T FAIR

SUGGESTED CHAPTER	CROSS-REFERENCE AND INTEGRATION
6 Motivation Theories	perception and attribution; performance management and rewards; communication; ethics and decision making

CASE SUMMARY

Mary Jones accepts a job with a salary of $25,000 per year. She is happy with this salary and during her first year of work spends a significant amount of time working extra hours after work, on the weekends, and while on assignment in Costa Rica. She received no extra money for working these hours; however, after one year she is rewarded with the highest performance evaluation that her manager has ever given. As a result, she receives a 10 percent increase in salary effective immediately. After her review she finds out that Sue (another employee with similar qualifications who has just been hired) is making $28,000 per year. She is obviously upset about this and responds by saying, "It isn't fair!"

There are no Web sites that directly pertain to this case.

QUESTIONS AND SUGGESTED ANSWERS

1.   Indicate Mary's attitude before and after meeting Sue. If there was a change, why?

   Answer:

   Before the meeting with Sue, Mary was totally satisfied with her job. She enjoyed the challenges and working with the people at Universal Products. The review process and the increase in salary provided Mary with positive feedback that would motivate her to continue working hard and to do a good job as before. After the meeting with Sue, the positive feedback that Mary had received from her manager certainly overshadowed by the fact that even with the 10 percent increase Sue (who had no experience) was still making more money than Mary.

2.   What do you think Mary will do now? Later?

   Answer:

   Mary will become less interested in working hard now that it has been demonstrated that she will not be fairly rewarded for the extra effort. If the situation really annoys her, she may approach her manager about the issue or even begin to look for a new job.

3.   What motivational theory applies best to this scenario? Explain.

Answer:

The motivational theory that best applies here is equity theory. Before the meeting Mary would have been happy to continue working hard as before. Unfortunately in this situation, the reward system lacked fairness and consistency.

CASE 7: PERFECT PIZZERIA

SUGGESTED CHAPTER		CROSS-REFERENCE AND INTEGRATION
7	Motivation and Job Design	organizational cultures; globalization; communication; decision making

CASE SUMMARY

The case describes a situation at Perfect Pizzeria that gets progressively worse. The basic gist of the case is that bonuses are paid to local store managers based on the store meeting certain percentage targets regarding food and beverage costs and profits. Employee consumption of food and drinks is counted against this percentage. The manager of one local outlet significantly altered the policy that entitled each employee was to a free pizza, salad, and all the soft drinks he or she could drink for every 6 hours of work. The manager doubled the time to every 12 hours of work because of problems that cut into the percentages and essentially eliminated the manager's bonus. In spite of the manager's initial punitive actions, the problems continued to occur. The manager took further punitive action as the situation progressively deteriorated.

This case provides an opportunity to examine the motivational tactics that, unfortunately, are all too common in the fast food industry. Rather than doing anything positive, the all too common course of action is to use punitive measures. These measures seldom work very well; instead, the result frequently is the promotion of unintended negative side-effects with little long-term positive change in work behaviors.

There are no Web sites that directly pertain to this case.

QUESTIONS AND SUGGESTED ANSWERS

1. Consider the situation where the manager changed the time period required to receive free food and drink from 6 to 12 hours of work. Try to apply each of the motivational approaches to explain what happened. Which of the approaches offers the most appropriate explanation? Why?

    Answer:

    The content theories of motivation can be applied most easily by focusing on lower-order needs versus higher-order needs. The jobs and compensation focused almost exclusively on addressing lower-order needs and did virtually nothing to address higher-order needs. Of course, students should recognize that this is very typical in the fast food industry. Many jobs in this industry have very little enrichment potential, so motivational factors usually focus on satisfying the lower-order needs. The pizzeria manager then intervened into the satisfaction of the employees' lower-order needs, having a negative impact with respect to individual and organizational consequences.

The motivational approaches that are most appropriate for analyzing this situation are expectancy theory, equity theory and reinforcement theory. The key to this analysis is contained in the following quote from the case: "Previously, each employee was entitled to a free pizza, salad, and all the soft drinks he or she could drink for every 6 hours of work. The manager raised this figure from 6 to 12 hours of work. However, the employees had received these 6-hour benefits for a long time."

Clearly, the employees had formed expectations regarding the outcomes they would receive as a result of working at Perfect Pizzeria. The free pizza, salad, and all the soft drinks the employee could drink for every six hours of work was an important supplement to the minimum wage compensation they received. From an expectancy theory perspective, the employees' expectancies and instrumentalities reflected their perceptions that each six hours of work effort would result in realizing valued outcomes. In other words, expectancy and instrumentality were high and the free food and beverages was a positively valenced outcome. Then the manager arbitrarily doubled the amount of time required to receive them, thereby diminishing the employees' expectancy and/or instrumentality perceptions. Consequently motivation declined. From an equity theory perspective the employees felt underpaid, and took essentially retaliatory coping actions in an attempt to restore equity. From a reinforcement theory view, the manager used punitive actions in an attempt to decrease the incidence of behaviors that contributed to a high percentage of food and beverage costs. Rather than achieving the results he desired, he promoted backlash and the typical negative side-effects of punishment.

2.   Repeat Question 1 for the situation where the manager worked beside the employees for a time and then later returned to his office.

Answer:

The factors that were cited in the answer to question 1 apply here as well. The key element in the situation where the manager worked beside the employees for a time and then later returned to his office, however, is found in reinforcement theory. Punitive action tends to work only when the punishment or punishing agent is present. Once the punishment or punishing agent is removed, behavior typically returns to its former unacceptable level, or perhaps worse. The manager working along side the employees was likely viewed as an additional punitive measure. While he was present, the unacceptable job behaviors declined; once he returned to the office, the behavior returned to previous levels.

3.   Repeat Question 1 for the situation as it exists at the end of the case.

Answer:

The end of the case is basically an extension of the manager's punitive approach to dealing with the employees. The response to question 2 can be applied here and intensified.

4.   Establish and justify a motivational program based on one or a combination of motivation theories to deal with the situation as it exists at the end of the case.

Answer:

The manager needs to focus on promoting desirable work behaviors through positive reinforcement or in combination with punishment rather than relying exclusively on punishment. By emphasizing positive reinforcement the manager can also positively influence the employees' perceptions of inequity and the violation of their expectations. The manager also needs to work vigorously at repairing relationships with the employees.

CASE 8: I'M NOT IN KANSAS ANYMORE

SUGGESTED CHAPTER		CROSS-REFERENCE AND INTEGRATION
8	Performance Management and Rewards	organizational design; motivation; performance management and rewards

CASE SUMMARY

The case deals with telecommuting in a very general way. It should provoke discussion among the students and make them think about pros and cons of telecommuting. Those students who already have worked in a virtual company should share their experiences.

There are no Web sites that directly pertain to this case.

QUESTIONS AND SUGGESTED ANSWERS

1. Is telecommuting the wave of the future, or does top management lose too much control when people are off site?

    Answer:

    Telecommuting is certainly a viable alternative to the traditional workplace setting. However, there is some doubt that many people can deal with the isolation that they encounter when telecommuting. The social factors of work, which can make work much more interesting, do not exist in this new setting. Perhaps only very autonomous people who do not really enjoy working directly with others will succeed in telecommuting.

    The loss of control over people who work off site is not a major problem. The telecommuter's work can be evaluated as well if not even easier by management; and if there is constant contact between manager and employees, the work process can be supervised without difficulties.

2. How would you like to be a telecommuter, as either a manager or one managed?

    Answer:

    Answers will probably include most of the following pros and cons:

    - Pros: flexibility, no commuting, no office space required.

- Cons: social factor at work is nonexistent, risk of becoming a workaholic, self-discipline and time management skills are critical.

3. Do you think telecommuting is effective for both the employee and the organization? Why, or why not?

Answer:

It can be effective as long as both the manager and the employee feel comfortable with the limited interaction possibilities telecommuting offers.

4. How might you modify telecommuting so as to overcome the problems covered above and maintain an effective team?

Answer:

Other than increasing the frequency of meetings in which all members of the team get together and having periodic social functions, individual isolation might be reduced while personalized communication might be increased through the use of Web casting and instant messaging. That would involve an investment in high-speed Internet connections and a Web cam for each of the employees.

CASE 9: THE FORGOTTEN GROUP MEMBER

SUGGESTED CHAPTER		CROSS-REFERENCE AND INTEGRATION
9	How Groups Work	teamwork; motivation; diversity and individual differences; perception and attributions; performance management and rewards; communication; conflict; leadership

CASE SUMMARY

This case presents issues of teamwork, group process, group norms, leadership, motivation, conflict, and conflict resolution.

Christine Spencer is concerned about her organizational behavior group work project. The allotted mark will be given to the team as a whole, and her group is experiencing difficulties with one of its members, Mike. During the initial group meeting, Mike appeared to get along with everyone, and seemed jovial and content. However, once the time came to begin meetings about the OB assignment, Mike frequently could not make meetings, saying he had to work and only sending brief rough notes along for his contribution. He avoided the group at times, but became angry and defensive when he thought that they were meeting without him. A week later, Mike had phoned Christine and explained that he had been having problems with his girlfriend, on top of the pressure of his course load and his job. Although Christine empathized with him, she was concerned about the group, the project and her mark, and wondered how to deal with the situation.

Christine should consider discussing this with the rest of the group, and then discuss the problem with Mike. This is part of the group process that does not appear to have happened yet. They cannot go to the instructor before attempting to address the situation themselves first. They need to figure out how to motivate Mike, despite his obvious pressures.

RELATED WEB SITES

Description of Site	Web Site Address
Center for the Study of Collaborative Organizations	http://www.workteams.unt.edu

QUESTIONS AND SUGGESTED ANSWERS

1.   How could an understanding of the stages of group development assist Christine in leadership situations such as this one?

Answer:

Groups pass through various stages of development and the nature of the problems faced by group members and leadership varies from stage to stage. In the first place, Christine should have used her leadership role to better prepare the group to work together. This means that more attention should have been given to the forming stage. Here and during the next stage of storming, the members could have been engaged in a process of sharing needs, goals, and talents. Then issues such as differing grade expectations and differing workload constraints could have been addressed more directly. As it is, these problems simply emerged during the course of the group's life, and they did so with negative consequences. It is unlikely that total integration could be achieved in a temporary workgroup like this. But with proper "front-end" management, the group could be enabled to operate in the norming and performing stages for reasonable success. The key lesson in this case is that it is much better to have everyone share their expectations and limitations in the beginning than to confront them after they start causing problems.

2.   What should Christine understand about individual membership in groups in order to build group processes that are supportive of her workgroup's performance?

Answer:

This answer relates to the prior one. The key point is that people have different needs and expectations when they join groups. In a course workgroup, for example, some people will want to get an "A" and will put in a lot of work; others may take any grade that they get and won't want to do much of anything. It is probably best to recognize these differences and make them public since it is unlikely that major changes in a person's commitments will be made during the short life of temporary workgroup. Rather than have capable group members spend valuable time complaining about and trying to influence a "loafer" or an uncooperative member, it may be better to accept their restricted involvement and get on with the important things. Of course, it is also legitimate for the group to assign final grades differentially based on the amount and quality of contributions from the various members. In this way, the different needs of members may be well served and without any feeling of inequity.

3.   Is Christine an effective group leader in this case? Why or why not?

Answer:

Christine is not really effective as the leader of the group in this case. She could increase her effectiveness in this group by holding a "confrontation" meeting to get the issues on out in the open and accomplish some of the sharing discussed in the prior two answers. However, in all likelihood her best opportunities lie in the future when she again chairs or leads other group activities. In these cases, she can put her learning to work and do a better job of preparing her groups for high performance by spending more time managing the forming and storming stages of group development.

CASE 10: NASCAR'S RACING TEAMS

	SUGGESTED CHAPTER	CROSS-REFERENCE AND INTEGRATION
10	Teamwork and Team Performance	organizational cultures; leadership; motivation and reinforcement; communication

CASE SUMMARY

This case begins with a brief history of NASCAR and recent statistics on the popularity of stock car racing. Stock car racing is now the fastest growing American team sports. The balance of the case focuses on two of the most successful and visible personalities in NASCAR, racecar driver Jeff Gordon and his crew chief Ray Evernham, who left in September 1999. Jeff Gordon has reached superstar status with his charming personality and history of wins in high profile NASCAR races. Gordon attributes his success to his strong family upbringing and marriage to Brooke Sealy, a marriage that ended with a filing for divorce in March 2002. The case pays special tribute to Ray Evernham, Gordon's crew chief and the person that many people believe is the premier crew chief in the business. Evernham's views on teamwork and other attributes of success are discussed. Evernham left the team and the case points out the challenge of changing leadership, the initial losses, and the team's ultimate success.

RELATED WEB SITES

Description of Site	Web Site Address
NASCAR Homepage	http://www.nascar.com/
Jeff Gordon's Official Homepage	http://www.jeffgordon.com/
Ray Evernham's Interview in Fast Company	http://www.fastcompany.com/online/18/fastlane.html

QUESTIONS AND SUGGESTED ANSWERS

1. Evaluate Jeff Gordon's race team on dimensions covered in the text's discussion of characteristics of high-performance teams.

   Answer:

   The textbook identifies four characteristics of high-performance teams: (1) strong core values, (2) a general sense of purpose that is translated into specific performance objectives, (3) members have the right mix of skills, and (4) the teams possess creativity.

Strong core values provide the guidance of attitudes and behaviors consistent with the team's purpose. Hendricks Motorsports appears to exhibit the values of professionalism, winning, and creativity necessary to provide control over the team's actions. The selection of and training provided to the Rainbow Warriors is a good example of inculcating team members with the core values of the organization. The group reward system also enhances a shared value system that works to create homogeneity.

Specific performance objectives provide another source of direction to the team. The Winston Cup Series provides a tangible, overt set of objectives to the Gordon race team. Winning individual races in addition to earning Winston Cup points that lead to an overall series champion provides clear objectives that set obvious standards by which to measure results. The Rainbow Warriors take pride in regularly conducting pit stops in under 17 seconds and being recognized as an outstanding pit crew.

The right mix of skills among team members is critical in supporting the high-performance outcomes necessary to compete in NASCAR. The mechanics' technical skills provide the correct set-up for the car in order to allow the 200+ mile-per-hour speeds necessary to win Winston Cup races. Evernham provides the decision making skills necessary to solve problems including tire changes, gas choices, when to pass, when to draft cars ahead, and making adjustments in the aerodynamics of the car itself. All these skills combine to provide a winning recipe for the Gordon race team.

Creativity may be a particular strength to the Gordon team. Evernham is recognized as one of the best if not the best crew chiefs in NASCAR. His prime advantage is his experience, as both a driver and a crew chief. He is not afraid to try new ideas and methods to provide his driver with even the smallest edge over his competitors. The Gordon team exemplifies the meaning of constant improvement — continuously looking for small, incremental changes that over time add up to significant improvements.

2. Discuss Jeff Gordon's race team on dimensions covered in the text's discussion of methods to increase group cohesiveness.

Answer:

High-performance groups represent the dual characteristics of positive group norms and high group cohesiveness. The textbook recommends increasing group cohesiveness based on eight criteria: goals, membership, interactions, size, competition, rewards, location, and duration. By improving the conditions of each of these dimensions, group cohesiveness improves and positively impacts performance.

Goal agreement is high among the race-team members of Jeff Gordon's team. Winning races and scoring Winston Cup points, with the eventual goal of becoming Winston Cup champion, provides the team with highly visible and measurable goals. Group membership is highly homogeneous, as the team is largely young males under the age of 40 who are interested in racing cars.

Enhancing interactions within the group is another method to increase cohesiveness. When the Rainbow Warriors meet, they always put their chairs in a circle as a way a saying that they're stronger as a team than as individuals. The pit crew is both specialized and stays largely intact from one race to another. While the overall team supporting

Gordon's racecar is fairly large, they tend to be broken into smaller groups that interact together. Examples include the chassis and engine teams.

Competition is focused on competitor racing teams that are vying for Winston Cup points. Evernham's insistence on group rewards reinforces the group identity of team members. The extreme identity of the group, with the matching uniforms and logos provides a sense of isolation from other groups. Finally, the stability of the team provides the duration of membership suggested by the framework.

3.   Compare Gordon's race team on the methods of team building. Which one most applies to this situation?

Answer:

The text identifies three team-building methods: the formal retreat approach, the continuous improvement approach, and the outdoor experience approach. Gordon's racing team relies heavily on the continuous improvement approach, as evidenced by their painstaking preparation, egoless teamwork, thoroughly original strategizing, emphasis on team performance over individual performance, and pushing for perfection but accepting imperfection.

4.   What are the potential pros and cons when a successful team leader such as Evernham leaves and is replaced by someone else?

Answer:

A successful leader can become unsuccessful by doings things in a way that created success in the past and failing to adapt to new realities. New leadership involves "new blood" and possibly some creative approaches not previously used in the organization. On the other hand, it may also mean that the new leader will be living in the shadow of the predecessor:

- If success continues in the organization, the predecessor will be given credit for creating the successful organization and the predecessor may view the new leader as a caretaker who has benefited.
- If success does not continue, the new leader will be viewed in the unfavorable light of comparison to the predecessor.
- If the new leader tries to do things differently, the organization may lack confidence in what the leader is doing because the predecessor had an established track record and the new person does not — therefore, the employees' lack of confidence produces a lack of wholehearted effort and their doubts become self-fulfilling prophecies.

As it turned out, there was a transition period in which Jeff Gordon lost races for six months. The underlying strength of the team had been built over time. The ability of the new crew chief to adapt to the organizational culture and take charge, and the continued presence of Jeff Gordon's charismatic style enabled the team to go on to achieve new records.

CASE 11: PEROT SYSTEMS: CAN A HIGH-PERFORMANCE COMPANY HAVE A HUMAN SIDE?

SUGGESTED CHAPTER		CROSS-REFERENCE AND INTEGRATION
11	Leadership	organizational cultures; group dynamics and teamwork; motivation and reinforcement

CASE SUMMARY

This case focuses on the evolution of Perot Systems since the company was founded in 1988. The case provides a brief history of Ross Perot, the colorful founder of EDS and later Perot systems. Many students will remember Mr. Perot from his presidential campaigns in 1992 and 1996. Mr. Perot started EDS in 1962 and built the company into an economy powerhouse through an autocratic management system. GM eventually bought out EDS.

In 1988, Ross Perot started Perot Systems, an information technology company similar to EDS. During the early and mid 1990s, Mort Meyerson, who had worked for Ross Perot at EDS, ran Perot Systems. Reflecting back on his days at EDS, Mr. Meyerson concluded that the command and control atmosphere that Ross Perot had used to build EDS had significant downsides in terms of its personal impact on employees, and vowed to make Perot Systems a more humane place to work. The company struggled through Mr. Meyerson's leadership in terms of cost containment and earnings. Ross Perot has now resumed day-to-day management of Perot Systems, and is changing the company's culture to more command and control similar to what he did at EDS. The jury is still out with regard to whether Mr. Perot's leadership style can turn Perot Systems into a major force in the information technology field.

RELATED WEB SITES

Description of Site	Web Site Address
Mort Meyerson's Interview in Fast Company	http://www.fastcompany.com/online/02/meyerson.html

QUESTIONS AND SUGGESTED ANSWERS

1. Compare Mr. Meyerson's leadership style versus Mr. Perot's based on the Michigan and Ohio State behavioral theories of leadership.

   Answer:

   The Michigan studies looked at high- and low-performing leadership situations to identify the most effective styles. Mr. Meyerson's approach can best be described as an employee-centered style, where leaders place a strong emphasis on the welfare of their subordinates. His insistence on focusing on both organizational and individual concerns recognizes his change in attitude since his tenure as President of EDS. His concern for organizational outcomes is tempered with an equal concern for his employees' well being.

   Mr. Perot can best be described as production-centered or task-oriented in nature. Mr. Perot focuses on the bottom line, with an insistence on hard work and personal sacrifice on the part of his managers. r. Perot represents the more traditional "command and control" approach to management, requiring that his employees consent to a defined code of conduct.

The Michigan studies argue that leaders are high on one dimension or the other. The situation at Perot Systems seems to support this conceptualization of leader behaviors existing on a continuum, with leaders unable to switch styles. When Mr. Perot arrived, over one-third of the upper management at Perot Systems left rather than submit to Mr. Perot's style.

Similarly, the Ohio State studies found two different leader behaviors. Mr. Meyerson represents the consideration style, with a high concern for his subordinates' well being. He is sensitive to his followers' feelings and is interested in creating a pleasant work environment for them. Mr. Perot represents an initiating structure approach to leadership, given his concern with spelling out task requirements and clarifying other aspects of the work agenda.

The Ohio State studies fundamentally differ from the Michigan studies in that they assume that managers should be high on both consideration and initiating structure behaviors in order to promote high performing organizations. The situation at Perot Systems provides a good example of how difficult being high on both dimensions can be. Few individuals are flexible enough to move between both dimensions as conditions change. Both leaders believed their respective behaviors would encourage high performance at Perot Systems.

2. Utilizing Fiedler's Contingency Theory of Leadership, explain how either Meyerson's or Perot's style might be most appropriate based on specific characteristics of the situation at Perot Systems.

Answer:

Fiedler's Contingency Theory of leadership looks at how leader's behaviors interact with situational characteristics to determine the effectiveness of outcomes. The theory depends on the dual behaviors of task- or relationship-orientation of leaders. The three situational attributes included in the theory are: (1) leader-member relations, (2) task structure, and (3) position power of the leader. Based on the information provided in the case, it may be possible to anticipate that Meyerson would score higher on the Least-Preferred Co-worker scale and Perot much lower, representing their propensity for relationship or task leadership styles.

The situational variables determine whether a situation is high, moderate, or low control in nature. Task-oriented leaders do best in high control situations (*i.e.*, the positive nature of the situation allows the leader to ignore improving the relationship and concentrate on the task) and low control situations (*i.e.*, the relationship between leader and followers is so bad there is no sense in attempting to improve it, so the emphasis is on concentrating on the task). Relationship leaders do better in moderate control situations that emphasize improving the relationship in order to elicit better performance from the group.

Fiedler originally suggested that in conditions where the situation/leader arrangement does not match, the leader had to leave. More recently, he suggests that it is possible for leaders to change the situational variables in order to obtain a match. It is not possible to categorize the situation at Perot Systems without more information, but any mismatch between situation and leader could complicate the goal of a high-performance organization. Ross Perot, through his desire to remold the firm in his preferred military style, may unconsciously be creating a situation where his task-oriented style may be most appropriate.

3.　Evaluate Ross Perot, Jr.'s style of leadership from the viewpoint of transformational leadership.

Answer:

According to the text, transformational leaders broaden and elevate their followers' interests, generate awareness and acceptance of the group's purposes and mission, and stir their followers to look beyond their own self-interests to the good of others. The key elements of transformational leadership include charisma, inspiration, intellectual stimulation, and individualized consideration.

Two statements from the case indicate that Ross Perot, Jr. exhibits the attributes of transformational leadership. One of these is his formulation of the following values statement for the company: "Our company is built around tightly-fixed core values which are at the heart of who we are and a climate is fostered to support and instill them in every aspect of our organization. All associates operate in an honest and ethical manner with consistently high standards of integrity in all relationships with clients, governments, the general public and each other,"

The other statement comes from the company's Web site. It says: "Our culture encourages initiative and creative approaches to problem solving, yet always within the framework of close teamwork and accountability. Our business and professional ethics set the standard for the industry. Perot Systems has a flexible and dynamic operating structure, enabling our associates to respond to new opportunities and tailor their approach to the issues at hand. We see our company as a web, not a bureaucratic tower."

4.　Evaluate the situation at Perot Systems from the point of view of the discussion on New Leadership.

Answer:

The New Leadership is comprised of approaches emphasizing charismatic, transformational, and visionary aspects important to changing and transforming individuals and organizations. According to Robert House's charismatic approach, both Mort Meyerson and Ross Perot represent high needs for power, high feelings of self-efficacy, and a moral rightness in their beliefs. Both individuals rely heavily on symbolism to relay their vision to the organization.

The textbook's discussion comparing distant versus close-up charismatics fits well in the Perot Systems situation. Meyerson represents a close-up charismatic, with his reliance on sociability, dynamism, and articulation of his vision. Conversely, Perot represents the distant charismatic with his examples of courage and persistence, his emphasis on social courage (expressing opinions, not conforming to pressure), and his ideological orientation. Both share the behaviors of self-confidence, honesty, authoritativeness, and sacrifice.

Another comparison can be made based on transactional versus transformational leadership. Meyerson represented the transformational nature of leadership with his desire to elevate the interests of his followers, generate awareness and acceptance of the purposes and mission of the group, and his attempt to stir his followers to look beyond their own self-interests for the good of others. Perot is closer to the transactional leader, with his emphasis on active management by exception and his concern for rules and regulations.

CASE 12: POWER OR EMPOWERMENT AT GM?

SUGGESTED CHAPTER		CROSS-REFERENCE AND INTEGRATION
12	Power and Politics	communication; conflict; decision making; organizational change; job design

CASE SUMMARY

GM's subsidiary in Parma, Ohio has faced serious changes over the past 10 years. When being threatened by a shutdown of the whole operation in the early 1980s, the management introduced a team-based approach to managing work groups. Representatives of the labor union and the management started working together for the good of the plant and its jobs. $40 million were spent on training the entire workforce in problem solving, group dynamics, and effective communication skills.

Recently another agreement with the United Auto Workers union was finalized. However, the relationship deteriorated significantly due to the unexpected introduction of over 600 demands by the new head of the union. Bob Lintz, the general manager, and other members of the top management team were concerned about the future of the plant in light of the recent developments. However , the plant did survive and Bob Lintz retired.

RELATED WEB SITES

Description of Site	Web Site Address
General Motors Homepage	http://www.gm.com/
United Auto Workers Union	http://www.uaw.org/

QUESTIONS AND SUGGESTED ANSWERS

1. How would you describe Parma's environment in terms of its levels of uncertainty and complexity?

    Answer:

    Uncertainty is high as a result of GM's declining market share and profitability and the competitiveness in the worldwide automobile industry. Complexity is high as a result of GM's large number of interested stakeholders.

2. How would you characterize Bob Lintz's approach to communication, decision-making and the exercise of power to create change at Parma?

Answer:

Lintz encourages open communication by creating a climate of trust and openness through his informal and highly participative management style, having an open door policy, and walking through the plant every day. Shared decision making is manifested through sharing power with others, creating of floor-based members; introducing bi-weekly joint meeting among Bob, management, the union shop committee chairman, the union local president, and the union shop committee; and letting hourly people have more say in their jobs. Lintz employs power to create change in several ways, including using first-line supervisors as a liaison between hourly employees and management, spending $40 million on training to implement the team concept, forging interorganizational alliances such as the relationship with Medina Blanking, and hiring a management team that believes in his philosophy

3. What are the most critical issues still facing Parma, and what should be done to address them?

Answer:

Cost, quality, and productivity pressures: Bob Lintz still feels that the company has too many people versus its competitors, and many managers believe that quality goals need to be articulated. A former controller believes that GM still has a mentality of not demanding enough performance from its employees for their level of pay. The employees are still dependent on overtime, which makes it difficult to convince people to improve processes and reduce costs, because they will result in decreased overtime.

White-collar employees' and supervisors' low morale: The white-collar employees have been left behind in Bob's efforts to make the plant more cooperative. The number of white-collar employees has dramatically decreased in proportion to blue-collar employees, which means that they are doing more with less, while also paying for their own health care costs (which union employees do not do).

Training: While Parma immersed itself in training during its transition to a more cooperative environment, the current training director is worried that it will be less of an issue as Parma moves on to other challenges. That worries him because of the continual influx of new employees into Parma who have not been socialized to the same extent in terms of training.

4. How can resistance to change be overcome utilizing the existing workforce?

Answer:

When the Team Concept Implementation Group (TCIG) wanted to change Parma, it looked for outside professional assistance without success. When the group described the mission of changing the existing culture of the plant with the existing personnel, no consultants wanted to participate. Consultants were certain that the only way to change the culture was to close the plant for two years and start all over again, or to copy Saturn, where an entirely new set of rules could be adopted. One consultant told them their chances for success were about two percent and told them that although he would love the challenge, he could not afford to be associated with something destined for failure. The TCIG ended up managing its own transition.

The leader, Bob Lintz, had to create a culture of trust so that the hourly workforce would understand that he would implement changes. By following through on his promises, they trusted him and accepted his vision for a better working environment, and therefore changed their own attitudes and work habits.

CASE 13: THE POORLY INFORMED WALRUS

SUGGESTED CHAPTER		CROSS REFERENCE AND INTEGRATION
13	Information and Communication	diversity and individual differences, perception and attribution

CASE SUMMARY

This is a quaint and readable case that focuses on the vagaries of miscommunication.

There are no Web sites that directly pertain to this case.

QUESTIONS AND SUGGESTED ANSWERS

1. What barriers to communication are evident in this fable?

   Answer:

   The major communication barrier in this short fable is the "status effect." There is a clear unwillingness of the smaller walruses to communicate an accurate picture and express their true feelings to the big walrus. This leaves him with a false sense of security and makes complacency all too comfortable — sitting in the sun so to speak. This seems to be compounded by his tendency to speak harshly and gruffly to the others, perhaps intimidating them and making them fearful of him.

   All of this makes it even less likely that they will be willing to pass along information that may upset him. From his perch on high, the big walrus got comfortable and increasingly isolated from his herd; he also became more self-centered and less inclined to reach out and try to understand the situations of others. Because his "status" got in the way of his interactions and relationships with the small walruses, he didn't use his leadership position to support them and their needs. After spotting another opportunity, they left him ... alone on his perch.

2. What communication "lessons" does this fable offer to those who are serious about careers in the new workplace?

   Answer:

   Listen — that is the primary learning from this case. In order to be an effective communicator you have to be a good listener. The first and last rules of communication are to listen. This means that any leader needs to spend time with followers and learning how things look to them, and from their positions in the organization.

The leader needs to develop relationships of trust and credibility, which makes followers willing to communicate frankly and honestly with him or her. The common concept of "management by wandering around" probably has a lot to offer in this sense. One must interact with others in order to increase their willingness to communicate; one must develop and maintain the trust of others in order to sustain their willingness to communicate accurately.

CASE 14: JOHNSON & JOHNSON: ONE LARGE COMPANY MADE OF MANY

SUGGESTED CHAPTER		CROSS-REFERENCE AND INTEGRATION
14	Decision Making	organizational structure, organizational cultures; change and innovation; group dynamics and teamwork; diversity and individual differences

CASE SUMMARY

This case focuses on Johnson & Johnson, and how a company as large as J&J can infuse its decision-making process with the energy of a small start-up company. The case begins by providing a historical perspective of the company. Along with strong ethics, an attribute that has sustained the company over the years, is the fact that J&J does not view itself as just a pharmaceutical firm but rather as a health care organization. J&J represents an autonomous collection of independent entities whose decentralized structure fosters an entrepreneurial culture.

The case summarizes the J&J approach to decision making, with a special emphasis on FrameworkS, which is a program that involves a series of focused dialogues between the company's managers and operating personnel. FrameworkS is a novel approach to decision making and strategic planning pioneered by J&J and explained in the case.

RELATED WEB SITES

Description of Site	Web Site Address
Johnson & Johnson Homepage	http://www.jnj.com/home.htm

QUESTIONS AND SUGGESTED ANSWERS

1. How is J&J able to demonstrate social responsibility for the global community in its sustainable growth?

    Answer:

    Chairman and CEO William Weldon describes the Johnson & Johnson Credo as: "Healthy People, Healthy Planet, and Healthy Future." This is a succinct but powerful statement about J&J's enduring commitment to corporate social responsibility in a global context. Given that the credo effectively guides all of J&J's ventures and activities, it becomes the foundation for the company's sustainable growth.

2. How does the management of J&J hope that FrameworkS will help with creativity within the organization?

    Answer:

    As mentioned in the case, J&J wished to increase both the number and quality of innovations within the firm. The textbook describes creativity as the development of unique and novel responses to problems and opportunities of the moment. Research shows that groups are often superior to individuals in developing creative solutions due to the increased diversity of ideas available to the members.

    By investigating processes at its three internal and three external organizations, J&J managers attempted to benchmark high performance activities. Participants are interested in identifying the new processes and implementing them throughout J&J. The program "What's New" was the focus of the largest management conference in the company's history. In 1997, a four-day meeting of J&J executives from 54 countries were challenged by a roster of presenters to let go of their deep assumptions and regard complacency as destructive.

    By mixing managers from different organizations within J&J, the executive board is hoping to manage knowledge in a manner that supports new ideas. A manager from one area may be able to shed considerable insight into the problems of a manager from another section of the company. Learning is increased by this free exchange of ideas.

3. How does J&J attempt to infuse ethics into its decision-making?

    Answer:

    J&J is very committed to ethical behavior on the part of its employees and managers. Its Credo, identified in the case, has a solid and fundamental meaning to all those involved with the firm. Its reaction to the Tylenol poisoning, with its emphasis on socially responsible behavior above immediate profits, was entirely consistent with its ethical code of placing the customer first and shareholder interests second.

    By constantly reinforcing its Credo at every opportunity, it serves as a fundamental value system that directs decision making at all levels. The culture of J&J is particularly influenced by the importance of ethical behavior. The stories of General Johnson, the Tylenol situation, and others serve to reinforce the central role that ethics serve in the decision making process at J&J.

    J&J's insistence on training and development in addition to their Work/Family Program is reflected in their Credo. The importance of this statement is represented by its persistent presence in many sections of the Web site for Johnson & Johnson. The Credo serves as a central statement of purpose that permeates every aspect of the corporation.

4. After reviewing the recent performances of sales and the responses to the challenges of making a profit, what would you recommend Johnson & Johnson do to sustain its leadership in the health care products industry?

Answer:

A key element in sustaining industry leadership is for J&J to continue capitalizing on its FrameworkS program for empowering employees and democratizing the strategic decision-making process. By incorporating managers from around the organization, FrameworkS provides a process that successfully incorporates knowledge from a wide variety of sources. Managers are able to bring a variety of perspectives and experiences to bear on the problem at hand. By challenging long-held assumptions, a better decision develops from the interaction of group members.

CASE 15: FACULTY EMPOWERMENT AND THE CHANGING UNIVERSITY ENVIRONMENT

SUGGESTED CHAPTER		CROSS-REFERENCE AND INTEGRATION
15	Conflict and Negotiation	Change, innovation, and stress; job designs; communication; power and politics

CASE SUMMARY

Using two fictional universities, Upstate University and Downstate University, this case explores two approaches to distance education. Both approaches rely heavily on the standardization of course content and instructional approach, with one being much more regimented than the other. Both universities have a large adult learner student population. The case explores how standardization usurps faculty empowerment and how adult learners are affected by the flexibility afforded by faculty empowerment.

There are no Web sites that directly pertain to this case.

QUESTIONS AND SUGGESTED ANSWERS

1. Would you rather be a student in a class that has been standardized or one in which the instructor has a high degree of empowerment? Why?

    Answer:

    Some students will argue that they prefer a class where the instructor has a high degree of empowerment; others will argue in favor of standardization. Those arguing in favor of empowerment may recognize the potential for substantial intellectual enrichment that accompanies professorial freedom to include or exclude topics and to use different instructional approaches. They may also be individuals who are willing to take risks and can tolerate reasonable uncertainty and ambiguity — all characteristics that would enable them to respond more positively to the greater uncertainty associated with the instructional flexibility provided by empowerment. Embracing empowerment also encourages the exploration of alternative viewpoints, which standardization does not.

    Those arguing in favor of standardization most likely want a high degree of certainty and predictability in their lives. They may believe that there is one best approach and one correct answer — and that standardization helps provide this. In some instance there is one best approach or one correct answer, but certainly there are many instances where multiple approaches or multiple correct answers are viable.

Of course, in discussing this question, students should also recognize that the subject matter of some courses lends itself more to standardization. Thus, some courses may be viable candidates for standardization. However, to indiscriminately go totally in one direction or the other is a misguided educational initiative.

2.   What issues involving power and politics are involved in moving from a setting that encouraged faculty empowerment to one that required much more standardization of instruction? How would you deal with those issues if you if you were involved in university administration?

Answer:

Standardization usurps the professors' expert power and information power. Since faculty are the core of any university — contrary to what some academic administrators might believe — any reasonable and progressive university administration should seek ways to capitalize on rather than suppress faculty talents and expertise. This is where the second tradition of organizational politics — the creative art of compromise — comes into play.

3.   In the specific case of adult learners and use of multiple instructors, is it possible to reach a compromise between standardization and empowerment so that the benefits of standardization can be obtained while still allowing for the flexibility that comes with empowerment? How can this apply to courses taught online versus face-to-face?

Answer:

A compromise between standardization and empowerment can be reached with both online course and face-to-face courses. There are two key elements that need to be considered if such a compromise is to work effectively. One element involves the professors; the other involves the students. The key from the professorial side is creativity in designing and executing the course and the willingness to commit the energy and time needed to make the compromise work. The key from the student side is that they need to be responsible, self-motivated individuals.

Adult learners are in a position to benefit from a compromise between standardization and empowerment because they are somewhat more likely than traditional students to be responsible, self-motivated individuals. Additionally, the flexibility provided by a compromise can serve to better meet the multiple and varied needs of adult learners.

CASE 16: THE NEW VICE PRESIDENT

	SUGGESTED CHAPTER	CROSS-REFERENCE AND INTEGRATION
16	Change, Innovation, and Stress	leadership; performance management and rewards; diversity and individual differences; communication; conflict and negotiation; power and influence

CASE SUMMARY (PART A)

This case deals with leadership and management styles, change and stress management, communication, conflict, and conflict resolution.

Jennifer Treeholm, Associate VP for Academic Affairs at Midwest U, is appointed interim VP. Her popularity, ten years experience as associate VP, devotion to the school, and her energy made her appear the natural choice. Jennifer's entire career had been at Midwest U, and she seemed to constantly be going out of her way to befriend everyone who needed support at the University. During her ten years as associate VP, she handled academic complaints, oversaw committees, wrote most letters and reports for the VP, and ran errands for the President.

There are no Web sites that directly pertain to this case.

QUESTIONS AND SUGGESTED ANSWERS (PART A)

1. At this point, what are your predictions about Jennifer as interim vice president?

    Answer:

    It appears, at first, that Jennifer will be quite successful in her new position, simply due to her obvious popularity and long-term involvement with the University. Upon further examination, however, one may begin to question Jennifer's ability to adapt to the changes required in taking on the new position, as she has been doing the same thing for so long. Also, it is a position of considerably more power than to what she is accustomed. Her desire to please everyone may cause problems in her role of Vice President as well.

2. What do you predict will be her management/leadership style?

    Answer:

    Jennifer's management/leadership style can be classified as participative, as she is high on the relationship axis, and low on the task axis.

3. What are her strengths? Her weaknesses? What is the basis for your assessment?

    Answer:

    Jennifer's strengths include the fact that she is efficient, competent, and confident in herself. She is obviously familiar with the duties of her position and can handle a great deal of responsibility. Jennifer also has many years of experience in the university atmosphere, and as a result, knows the ins and outs of the system very well. She is well liked and respected by her peers and colleagues, and is known for her high level of energy, dedication to the school, and desire and ability to help others.

    Jennifer's weaknesses include the fact that she seems to think that she can do anything and everything — which is quite different from being confident in oneself. Taking on too much responsibility can quickly result in burnout and lack of direction and focus. The fact that she has almost no experience outside of the university may be perceived as a weakness as it may contribute to a narrow perspective when addressing issues. Her ten-year position has given her a lot of experience, but it is primarily doing the same things. She has never had to test her flexibility or her ability to adapt to change.

CASE SUMMARY (PART B)

Although Jennifer was very popular, it was soon realized that she was not making things happen in her new position, nor was she doing well making tough decisions. She wanted to please everyone, making it hard to "choose sides" when a decision had to be made. She was seen as having trouble planning, organizing, and managing her time. She also did not understand her role in supporting the President unequivocally in his decisions; she did not feel comfortable doing his "dirty work," which sometimes involved firing people.

Jennifer also found the behaviors and decision-making styles of the rest of the senior staff to be quite different from her own. She felt excluded from their decision making process. Her friends advised her to "just stay out of trouble" which did nothing to help her inability to make decisions.

QUESTIONS AND SUGGESTED ANSWERS (PART B)

1.   What is the major problem facing Jennifer?

Answer:

Jennifer's major problem is that she was unable to make the transition from her old position and its responsibilities, to her new role as VP. This may result from a lack of clear definition of her role and duties, lack of direction and understanding from her colleagues, or perhaps it is simply her inability to adapt to change.

2.   What would you do if you were in her position?

Answer:

Jennifer should meet with the President to discuss her problems and concerns, and immediately work to resolve them. She has already lost the confidence and support of at least some of the senior staff, and must stop it before it goes any further. Once she is aware of the President's concerns, she needs to work to meet the demands of her position — she must organize, delegate, and support the President and his decisions.

3.   Would a man have the same experience as Jennifer?

Answer:

Although Jennifer is definitely the minority as a female, she is not the only female on the senior staff. A man may or may not have the same experience; this is not a gender issue so much as it is a personality issue — Jennifer has trouble making tough decisions, organizing her time, and delegating to others. These problems have not been labeled as "characteristically female," although, one perspective may be to consider the possibility that Jennifer is having these problems because she feels disadvantaged as a woman. So as a representative of her gender in a position of power, she may be unusually cautious about making the wrong decisions and giving away responsibility. She may believe that if she does make the wrong choices or delegates to others, some people may see this as a weakness or flaw that is attributable to her gender, as opposed to her personality.

4. Are any of your predictions about her management style holding up?

Answer:

Answers will vary depending on students' predictions.

CASE SUMMARY (PART C)

When a national search for the position of permanent VP concluded that all of the external candidates were unacceptable, it was recommended that Jennifer be hired only if she agreed to change her management style. Upon hiring her, the President made a "private" agreement stating that she will organize her office and staff, delegate more to others, fulfill her Number Two role in backing the President, and provide greater direction to the Deans reporting to her. Jennifer accepted the position.

QUESTIONS AND SUGGESTED ANSWERS (PART C)

1. If you were Jennifer, would you have accepted the job?

Answer:

It's quite apparent that she is not incredibly aware of the problems/weaknesses that others are seeing in her performance. Even if she has become aware of these problems through her discussion with the president, she should still accept the job, and make the necessary improvements — Jennifer has the potential to be very successful in her position if she could only make the transition into her new role.

2. What would you do as the new permanent vice president?

Answer:

As the new permanent vice president, a person should begin by following the directives of the president to reassure him that the job is being done properly. A meeting should be held with the senior staff to discuss any issues that were awaiting a decision, make a list of issues, prioritize them, and proceed to decide on them one by one. It is vital at this moment that the staff and the president see that things are beginning to happen. The person should also make a list of personal task responsibilities, and begin delegating — even if it is only the least important tasks at first, it would show people that progress is being made.

3. Will Jennifer change her management style? If so, in what ways?

Answer:

Jennifer does not seem to know any management style other than that which has provided her with success to this point. It has also been demonstrated that she is not very good at adapting to change, and has stayed with her present style throughout her three years as interim vice president. She may be able to fulfill her role in backing and supporting the president, but she will likely have trouble delegating and making tough decisions, as her popularity for wanting to help everyone who needed it is what allowed her to get this far.

4. What are your predictions for the future?

Answer:

Most likely, Jennifer will continue to have problems. Even if she attempts to change her management style, which would be very difficult for her to do, a certain amount of her credibility has already been lost, and at senior levels, it's difficult to regain.

CASE SUMMARY (PART D)

Jennifer was now expected to take decisive action, and in fact, the problems got worse. In trying to do a thorough job and meet approval, things stopped moving once they hit her office as she dwelled on them, and her desire to make things better led her to do more herself, instead of delegating. Her social obligations as vice president left her exhausted as she continued to try to please everyone all the time. Some of the male Deans began making decisions without Jennifer's approval when they became tired of waiting for her direction. They felt that she always left room for negotiation — there was never a firm answer. People questioned her ability to lead.

QUESTIONS AND SUGGESTED ANSWERS (PART D)

1. If you were president, what would you do?

Answer:

The president should address the matter again with Jennifer, emphasizing the urgency of rectifying the problems outlined earlier. Jennifer needs to know that her job may be in jeopardy — perhaps that will be enough to motivate her to make the appropriate changes. The president should also hold a meeting with the rest of the senior staff to discuss the problems they each have had with Jennifer, and advise them that changes are being made.

There is obviously a huge lack of communication, or perhaps a problem with the quality of the communication between Jennifer and the senior staff, and perhaps between the senior staff and the president, and Jennifer and the president as well. If the communication was appropriate, one would assume that Jennifer would be aware of what was expected of her, as well as the problems people noticed in her performance. The communication issue must be addressed with all parties; the lines of communications as well as procedures and rules for communicating must be outlined and re-emphasized.

2. If you were Jennifer, what would you do?

Answer:

Jennifer should stop and assess what had been going on, and what has been going wrong. Jennifer needs to sit down with the president and the senior staff and openly discuss concerns: both theirs and her own. The communication issue needs to be clarified if any progress is to be made. Once she is truly aware of the situation and the changes that need to be made, she can accurately assess whether she is able/wants to make the transition. If not, she should quit, or look for another position within the university that better fits her management style.

EPILOGUE

The case focuses highly on communication, and the problems that occur when the lines of communication are not clear, or the level of communication is insufficient. It highlights the need for congruence between the demands of a position and the individual's leadership/management style, and makes readers sensitive to having the ability to recognize this immediately. It also demonstrates the importance of learning to know what management styles are appropriate and being flexible enough to learn/adopt those styles. The case also touches on issues related to the significance of performance management and feedback, direction, and conflict and negotiation.

CASE 17: FIRST COMMUNITY FINANCIAL

SUGGESTED CHAPTER		CROSS-REFERENCE AND INTEGRATION
17	Organizing for Performance	organizational structure, designs and culture; performance management and rewards

CASE SUMMARY

First Community Financial is an example of an organization that is structured to ensure productive communication as well as efficient workflow within its ranks. The officers in one department are aware of the needs within their area as well as the potential problems facing those who must deal with the clients whom they recruit. Thus, business development officers understand that clients must meet certain criteria for the credit administrators to approve their requests. The team is also a young, reasonably aggressive group in which there is not only communication, but also a large store of requisite enthusiasm.

There are no Web sites that directly pertain to this case.

QUESTIONS AND SUGGESTED ANSWERS

1. What coordinative mechanisms does First Community use to manage the potential conflict between its sales and finance/auditing functions?

   Answer:

   First Community management recognizes that there is an inherent conflict between marketing new accounts and selecting only those accounts that are the most financially secure. Using the informal coordination mechanisms backed by rewards work well in this small firm. Students should recognize the importance of informal coordinating mechanisms based on effective communication.

2. What qualities should First Community emphasize in hiring new staff to ensure that its functional organizational structure will not yield too many problems?

   Answer:

   Two sets of qualities are important. First, the new staff must be highly competent with regard to their functional technical expertise. Second, new staff members must be very competent with respect to interpersonal skills — effective interpersonal communication is especially important for minimizing problems emanating from the functional structure.

3.   What are the key types of information transfer that First Community needs to emphasize, and how is this transmitted throughout the firm?

Answer:

Understanding client needs, in the light of the financial risks to First Community is the most important information for this firm. Relaying client information to the technical staff and recycling this information from the technical staff to marketing can result in the proper understanding.

4.   Why might a small finance company have such a simple structure while a larger firm might find this structure inappropriate?

Answer:

This question is designed to help link the operations of small organizations with the concepts of organizational design. The student should recognize some of the basic design characteristics of smaller organizations break down when they are applied to much larger organizations.

CASE 18: MISSION MANAGEMENT AND TRUST

SUGGESTED CHAPTER		CROSS REFERENCE AND INTEGRATION
18	Organizational Design for Strategic Competency	organizational structure, designs and culture; performance management and rewards

CASE SUMMARY

Mission Management and Trust (MMT) is a very small, fairly young trust management company that targets individuals and organizations that are committed to socially conscious policies and want an investment strategy reflecting that commitment. MMT's goals include being a top quality trust company, promoting from within the company, increasing opportunities for minorities and women, and donating a portion of all revenues to charitable projects. Successfully following their mission statement, MMT has conquered an untapped market niche — trust management for religious institutions. MMT is a perfect example of a company servicing a small but profitable market niche. The recipe for its success is a strong corporate culture and clearly defined goals that are reflected in all strategic decisions made at MMT.

There are no Web sites that directly pertain to this case.

QUESTIONS AND SUGGESTED ANSWERS

1.   How do the mission elements of Mission Management differ from most firms?

Answer:

Firms within a capitalistic society normally have as their prime directive, the posting of as large a profit as possible. While Mission strives for this and, in fact, needs to be profitable to continue, as well as to impress potential investors, this is not its overriding goal. Mission differs from many firms because of its pervasive societal awareness.

2.   Does donating to charity before the firm is fully established mean that Mission is not demonstrating financial prudence?

Answer:

Donating to charity before maturity in the eyes of the businessmen and women does not necessarily imply financial imprudence. Because of the singular and different objective of maintaining a social conscience, Mission may in fact be shoring up its present and future business because of the kind of appeal this outlook would have for existing clients and clients-to-be.

3.   Could Mission's unique mission contribute to effective coordination as well as adjustment to the market?

Answer:

Given that Missions wants to be close to clients, it is ensuring that it keeps in touch with the world of its own niche market. The proximity to clients requires internal, effective communication and a responsive organizational structure. These realities allow Mission to keep its house in order as well as affording the means to be aware of and responsive to the market.

4.   Would Mission's unique mission still yield success with more traditional investors?

Answer:

Mission will, in all likelihood, not enjoy the same degree of success with more traditional investors. Many firms focus on the bottom line of profit margins, and tend to eschew societal awareness. It needs to be stressed that Mission caters to a niche market and so would generally not appeal to a broad spectrum of business interests.

CASE 19: MOTOROLA: SEEKING DIRECTION

SUGGESTED CHAPTER		CROSS-REFERENCE AND INTEGRATION
19	Organizational Culture and Development	innovation; conflict and negotiation; leadership; change and stress

CASE SUMMARY

This case focuses on Motorola, world famous for its Six Sigma quality control program and an early success story in the computer/electronics industry. Through much of its history Motorola was thought to be an extremely progressive company with excellent quality standards and employee relations. Its cellular phone and pager products were identified among the very best in the early 1990s. However, increased competition, the Asian economic crisis, and its failure to fully embrace the digital revolution have severely tarnished its operating image. The case illustrates the idea that organizations need cultures that are both strong and response to external forces.

RELATED WEB SITES

Description of Site	Web Site Address
Motorola Homepage	http://www.motorola.com/seamless_mobility/

QUESTIONS AND SUGGESTED ANSWERS

1. Discuss Motorola's relative success at the functions of organizational culture presented in the case.

   Answer:

   Organizational culture represents the "system of shared actions, values, and beliefs that develops within an organization and guides the behavior of its members." The two components that organizational culture must address in order to insure the long-term survival of any organization are (1) internal integration and (2) external adaptation.

   Internal integration involves the collective identity of an organization's members that encourages working and living together. Motorola appears to have an extremely strong presence in this area. Motorola has a strong culture that emphasizes quality, teamwork, people, ethics, and integrity. All of these features also contributed to the company's high performance into the 1990s. According to the case, these features may have contributed to Motorola's inability to adjust to changing external conditions as the 1990s unfolded.

   Motorola appears to do less well with the second component of organizational culture — external adaptation, which involves reaching goals and dealing with outside influences. The failure to recognize the importance of digital technology is directly related to this factor. Motorola remained the dominant supplier of a declining market product (*i.e.*, analog devices). In addition, its IRIDIUM system failed to address a number of cellular phone realities, including declining prices and miniaturization.

   The most important result of external adaptation — coping with reality — appears to have been a fundamental problem with Motorola. Difficulties in three areas of the business — semiconductors, cell phones, and pagers — represented a combination of deteriorating markets and significant missteps on the part of Motorola. The company clearly lost its market-leader position to other companies (Nokia and Erickson). Motorola appeared to want to blame market forces, rather than to question its internal culture.

2. How did Motorola lose its leading position in the electronics technology industry?

Answer:

Motorola lost its leading position for a number of reasons, some of which reflect a failure of external adaptation and others a failure of internal integration. The failure of external adaptation was mostly clearly evident in Motorola's failure to respond to market needs. In particular, the company failed to respond in a timely fashion to AT&T's need for digital handsets. Instead, Motorola developed an analog handset that was out of touch with the market. Another failure of external adaptation was the company's IRIDIUM satellite system. The system was very expensive and did not function well in conjunction with Motorola's cell phones — an unobstructed view of the sky presented operational difficulties for cell phones. Obviously, the heavy use of cell phones would be in cities with architectural obstructions. A decline in demand for semiconductors due to the Asian economic crisis also affected Motorola's external adaptability. Failure of internal integration was evident in Motorola's difficulty in restructuring its internal operations to cut costs and to be more responsive to external factors in the rapidly changing high-technology fields. Chris Galvin (CEO) was also viewed as an impediment.

3. Discuss the various options Motorola managers might use in attempting to change the culture at Motorola.

Answer:

As the textbook notes, changing an organization's culture is extremely difficult. This may be particularly true at Motorola, where the culture has historical significance to so many employees. Strong cultures are by their very nature difficult to change.

One benefit for Motorola is the institutional infrastructure elements available to it, including Motorola University and the various teams at Motorola. They provide valuable vehicles by which to educate employees and communicate to them that change is necessary. Strong statements from senior managers, including new CEO Ed Zander, can act to signal to the lower ranks that change is necessary and in fact productive for the company.

However, it has been shown at many other organizations that change often necessitates changes in management, both middle and upper. When Ross Perot returned to Perot Systems to manage day-to-day events, one-third of the upper management quit. A similar situation occurred when Eckhard Pfeiffer took over at Compaq. These leaders' desire to change something as fundamental as culture required that they bring in new managers who shared their vision.

However, many firms in the past have failed to overcome an older, out-of-date culture that no longer served the long-term interests of the organization. Having once been an industry leader, Motorola may find it necessary to make dramatic changes in how it conducts business. Cost-cutting and layoffs are not business as usual at Motorola.

As long as a strong culture remains productive, it is a valuable asset for any firm. However, if the culture becomes anti-productive, it can become a huge liability for a company. Motorola's situation highlights the opportunity or threat that a strong culture can exhibit.

4.   How do you think employees at Motorola will react to the efforts of Ed Zander to bring the company back to a leader?

Answer:

This question requires students to speculate about what they think will happen. In discussing these speculative musings, make sure that the students consider their ideas within the context of external adaptation and internal integration.

The OB Skills Workbook
CROSS-FUNCTIONAL
INTEGRATIVE CASE —
TRILOGY SOFTWARE: HIGH-PERFORMANCE COMPANY
OF THE FUTURE?

See companion Web site for online version: http://www.wiley.com/college/schermerhorn

CASE SUMMARY

The case focuses on the launch and development of a highly innovative software company in a highly competitive environment. Founder Joe Liemandt develops a sales configuration software program and builds Trilogy Software, Inc., to over 1,000 employees. The firm relies on a talented and motivated workforce whose members own shares in the company. Trilogy must maintain worker enthusiasm and commitment while growing and changing further to meet the challenges of competition and evolving technologies. The goal of being a high-performance organization is pursued relentlessly.

RELATED WEB SITE

Description of Site	Web Site Address
Trilogy Software Homepage	http://www.trilogy.com/

QUESTIONS AND SUGGESTED ANSWERS

1. Analyze Trilogy Software based on Robert Reich's Six "Social Glues." How does Trilogy stack up?

   Answer:

   Robert Reich's six "Social Glues" for 21st century companies are: (1) money makes it mutual, (2) mission makes a difference, (3) learning makes you grow, (4) fun makes it fresh, (5) pride makes it special, and (6) balance makes it sustainable. Reich believes that firms that exhibit these characteristics will be successful in the new economy.

   <u>Money makes it mutual.</u> Trilogy understands the importance of aligning the goals of its employees to match the goals of the firm. To do this, it not only pays an attractive salary, it also includes stock options with almost every new hire. It includes an impressive benefits package that includes a large number of interesting "perks" (ski boat, trips to Las Vegas). Trilogy is intent on a significant "pay-for-performance" component in its reward package.

Mission makes a difference. Trilogy, primarily through Joe Liemandt, has a very clear and concise mission for the firm. Trilogy's Web page makes it clear: "Trilogy's corporate mission is to empower companies to be more competitive and efficient in the sale of their products and services. Although Sales and Marketing comprises forty percent of most organizations' operational budgets and is the greatest total cost to the enterprise, the average technological investment in this area is a mere ten percent. Trilogy has recognized the value in transforming previously profit-draining and inefficient processes into sources of high profit and competitive advantage."

Trilogy only looks for people willing to share in this vision. In addition, it makes every effort to reinforce its mission in everything the company does. From the Parties on the Patio to the hiring process itself, Trilogy represents a near religious zeal for its sales configuration software. Joe Liemandt is able to transfer his energy and attitude throughout the organization.

Learning makes you grow. Trilogy University is perhaps the strongest evidence of Trilogy Software's commitment to learning. As the company Web site states: "Trilogy University is intense work and intense play — think of it like your freshman dorm, your hardest classes, your semester abroad and your favorite summer camp experience all rolled into one. From minute one, you take on more responsibility than you ever imagined, and learn an insane mount in an extremely short period of time. You will use your capability to its limits and then push it beyond those limits."

For the first two months at Trilogy, TUers spend almost every waking moment learning, working, and playing together. The main responsibility of the new TU class is to identify and create the new direction in which Trilogy must go to make us the next great software company. The greatest privilege for each member of the new TU class is total freedom to make his or her ideas happen. The most rewarding part of TU for many people is the teamwork, bonding, friendship and fun that begins the moment you meet your new class.

Trilogy puts huge pressure on new recruits coming up to speed in a hurry. The company expects results immediately upon arrival at the firm. Additionally, TU is the method by which new hires learn the unique culture of the organization. The firm puts responsibility for new products firmly on the new hires. As Liemandt states, the company is only as smart as their most recent hires.

Fun makes it fresh. This may be one of the most interesting facets to Trilogy, with its obvious insistence on having fun. As they say, work hard and play hard. There are times it's hard to tell which is which at Trilogy. Joe Liemandt is not afraid to mix the two together, as evidenced by his trips to Las Vegas and his legendary parties.

Pride makes it special. With its emphasis on "stars," Trilogy takes special pride in high performance. Trilogy has been careful to develop its reputation on major university campuses in order to attract the best candidates. In addition, Liemandt appears to be working hard to sustain the entrepreneurial culture that proved so successful to the firm in the past. With his recent spin-offs, he hopes to continue the energy and enthusiasm so vital to the organization. Trilogy employees are proud to be identified as such.

Balance makes it sustainable. Trilogy is sensitive to its employees' needs to balance work and family time. As Trilogy employee Chris Hyams states, "Trilogy is one of the rare companies that honestly cares about doing whatever it takes (within reason) to keep people happy." The firm supports commuting, flextime, working from home, and a large variety of additional employee-friendly work rules.

2.   What type of leadership style does Joe Liemandt appear to be exhibiting, based on (1) House's path-goal theory and (2) Hershey and Blanchard's situational leadership theory?

Answer:

House's theory espouses four leadership behaviors: directive, supportive, participative, and achievement-oriented. The correct leader behavior is associated with adjustment on the part of the leader to various work setting contingency factors and subordinate characteristics.

Joe Liemandt appears to be using an achievement-oriented approach to leadership at Trilogy. This approach emphasizes setting challenging goals, stressing excellence in performance, and showing confidence in group members' abilities to achieve high standards of performance. It is particularly appropriate for situations with ambiguous, nonrepetitive tasks such as those at Trilogy.

With Trilogy's expressed goal of hiring only the most qualified applicants, Liemandt's approach appears to be effective. "Stars" are the most successful of Trilogy's employees, and therefore have the most latitude in their work situations. Liemandt wants the most out of his employees, and recognizes that allowing them to determine the most appropriate means to reach their goals is healthy and productive to the organization.

Hershey and Blanchard offer a similar approach to leadership, focusing primarily on the situational contingency of maturity or readiness of followers. Liemandt appears to utilize the participating approach during the Trilogy University phase, when new hires are learning the culture of the firm. As new hires reach a higher state of maturity, he utilizes a delegating approach, turning over responsibility for decisions to others.

Telling would be totally inappropriate given the nature of the hiring process at Trilogy. The firm only attracts the most talented and well-trained candidates in the country. A telling leadership approach would defeat the purpose of the recruitment process. During the Trilogy University experience, Liemandt seems to use the project situation to actually separate the low and high performers. He appears to be looking for those individuals who react best to an achievement-oriented leadership approach.

3.   Trilogy appears to be leveraging its recruitment process through the development of CollegeHire.com. Do you think the unique approach can be duplicated on a wider scale?

Answer:

Trilogy's recruiting process is recognized as one of the most innovative in the high technology industry. Its emphasis on a highly personal process, with frequent contacts and numerous company visits is expensive, but highly successful. The question becomes, can Trilogy leverage this competitive advantage to a new enterprise (CollegeHire.com)?

CollegeHire attempts to pair the art of personal recruiting and Internet technology to find and place high technology recruits. They announce their core competence as "total personal attention." The approach is modeled entirely off of Trilogy's successful program. CollegeHire is interested in making the appropriate firm/recruit match that maximizes the potential for each party to benefit.

CollegeHire is targeting the medium to smaller technology firms that have trouble creating an effective campus recruiting program. By outsourcing the hiring process to CollegeHire, firms have a more cost effective means to reach college graduates. However, at 20 to 30 percent of a recruit's first-year salary, the process is not inexpensive.

CollegeHire goes beyond a mere collection of résumés by including surveys of prospective hires in order to provide a higher level of evaluation of each applicant's qualifications. It states that its purpose is not to replace a firm's recruiting department, but more so to supplement it.

As long as CollegeHire remains focused on a particular subsection of applicants, then it may be able to deliver services not easily duplicated by other recruiting services. If it branches out too far, companies may not be interested in outsourcing more sensitive recruiting processes in fear of losing proprietary information to other firms. In addition, will behaviors appropriate to Trilogy Software prove valuable to other high technology firms?

The OB Skills Workbook
EXPERIENTIAL EXERCISES

EXERCISE 1: MY BEST MANAGER

SUGGESTED CHAPTER	CROSS-REFERENCE AND INTEGRATION
1 Introducing Organizational Behavior	leadership

INSTRUCTOR'S NOTES

This exercise is designed as a class "ice-breaker" and as a tool for prompting students to think about the attributes of a "good" manager. The exercise can be done informally in a small class (with groups of four or five as suggested in the exercise), or can be slightly modified and assigned as a take-home assignment in a class that has permanent student teams. In a large lecture, it is recommended that you avoid using small group discussions, and instead have all students answer question #1 at their seats. Then, you can ask for volunteers or randomly select students from the class to create a master list. This approach typically results in lively class discussion. As an extension of this exercise you might also want to ask your students what the most "undesirable" attributes of managers are. This approach also results in interesting and lively class discussion.

The following is a report from one instructor's experience with the exercise. Students were assigned into four groups to work on the exercise. Rather than follow exact exercise procedures, the students were asked to list ten characteristics that described the best managers for whom group members have worked. The group part of the exercise worked very well and took approximately 15 minutes to complete. At the conclusion of the group brainstorming stage, spokespersons were asked to report on each group's list. The meaning of each item was discussed as it was being presented. A total of eight items was obtained from the four groups in approximately 20 minutes.

EXERCISE 2: GRAFFITI NEEDS ASSESSMENT

SUGGESTED CHAPTER	CROSS-REFERENCE AND INTEGRATION
1 Introducing Organizational Behavior	human resource management; communication

INSTRUCTOR'S NOTES

This exercise is intended to be an "ice breaker" that helps students to relax and become comfortable with talking in class. The exercise also helps students to start thinking about many of the issues that will be covered during the semester (or term). In your class discussion, be sure to pay careful attention to the similarities and differences among various students' answers. Point out to your students that the study of organizational behavior reflects both (1) the search for consensus in organizations, and (2) an appreciation of the differences that people have in their opinions and preferences.

This exercise should be administered very early in the semester (even the first class period, if possible). The exercise is designed to be somewhat lighthearted in nature, and should help students feel at ease in the classroom.

EXERCISE 3: MY BEST JOB

SUGGESTED CHAPTER		CROSS-REFERENCE AND INTEGRATION
2	Current Issues in Organizational Behavior	motivation; job design; organizational cultures

INSTRUCTOR'S NOTES

The purpose of this exercise is twofold. First, the exercise prompts students to think about the characteristics of "good" or "ideal" jobs. These ideas are then given a "reality check" by the assessments that are made relative to the likelihood that the goals (or ideal job characteristics) can be achieved. The second purpose of the exercise is to introduce students to the notion that some organizations are more likely to be able to deliver on "ideal job characteristics" than are others.

At the conclusion of the exercise, talk about some of the attributes of high-performance organizations. If your students believe that high-performance organizations are more likely to be able to deliver on ideal job characteristics than lower-performance organizations, ask them the following penetrating questions: "Do you believe that high-performing organizations are able to offer more attractive job characteristics than lower-performance organizations because they are high-performing organizations?" "Or, do you believe that high-performance organizations are high-performance organizations because they offer more attractive job characteristics?"

EXERCISE 4: WHAT DO YOU VALUE IN WORK?

SUGGESTED CHAPTER		CROSS-REFERENCE AND INTEGRATION
2	Current Issues in Organizational Behavior	diversity and individual differences, performance management and rewards; motivation; job design; decision making

INSTRUCTOR'S NOTES

This exercise should stimulate considerable interest among your students. The exercise not only highlights the differences in work-related values between men and women, but it also illustrates potential misconceptions that one gender may have about the other. Caution your students at the beginning of the exercise that there are no "right answers" to the questions and that the point of the exercise is not to be judgmental regarding what one gender prefers over another. Instead, the point of the exercise is to illustrate gender-based differences and how "misperceptions" often represent reality until we stop and listen to what people really feel is important to them and what they value.

Also, during or after the exercise, you might consider asking students to volunteer to share their feelings about why certain work-related outcomes are important to them. Often, the importance of a particular job-related outcome to a person hinges on his or her past experiences. For example, if a person was in a job that provided very little job security and that made the individual feel insecure, then the variable "job security" will probably be very salient to the person and rank high in his or her categorization of desirable job outcomes.

The experience of many instructors is that men tend to underestimate the importance of intrinsic rewards for women and are often wrong about their top-rated dimensions. This exercise is most involving when you emphasize gender-role issues. However, you may choose to play down this aspect in order to focus more clearly on the issue of motivation.

You may wish to conclude the exercise by posing the following thought-provoking questions to the class:

- Where do we get our ideas of what people want from work?
- Why is it important for managers to know what people want from work?
- To what extent do our personal expectations enter into our managerial decision-making?

In addition, after the exercise in concluded you might want to share the following information with your students. The table shown below reports the results of a study conducted by Beutell and Brenner (1986). In the study, men and women agreed on the most important characteristics of work; however, the biggest difference for the five highest-ranked dimensions occurred in the "high income" dimension, with men ranking it higher.

Results of the Beutell and Brenner (1986) Study (1 is the strongest ranking)

Item	Men (rank)	Women (rank)
Provides job security	2.5	2.0
Provides the opportunity to earn a high income	2.5	5.0
Permits advancement/responsibility	4.0	6.5
Is respected by other people	5.5	3.0
Provides comfortable working conditions	7.0	4.0
Rewards good performance with recognition	5.5	8.5
Encourages continued development/skills	8.0	6.5
Is intellectually stimulating	9.0	8.5

EXERCISE 5: MY ASSET BASE

SUGGESTED CHAPTER		CROSS-REFERENCE AND INTEGRATION
2	Current Issues in Organizational Behavior	perception and attribution; diversity and individual differences; groups and teamwork; decision making

INSTRUCTOR'S NOTES

Some students may find it difficult to draw out their strengths and abilities, or even point out their own accomplishments. It is sometimes hard to determine that something is a strength or ability, if we do it so often, and so well, that it's simply second nature. It may be helpful at this point to get input from other people, as it is often easier to highlight the qualities and experiences we are looking for from an objective viewpoint. It is also important to remember that strengths, abilities, and accomplishments may vary considerably, and what one person considers a strength or accomplishment may not be a big deal to another person who views things differently.

The discussion following the exercise should highlight the fact that people tend to develop preconceived opinions about other people based on very incomplete information. As they receive more information — in this case strengths and accomplishments — people's perceptions begin to change and evolve into something more accurate and complete. They realize the narrow view they previously held of an individual. Interestingly, people can develop such two-dimensional views about others and are surprised when they realize that there are so many more dimensions to the individual than they originally believed.

The exercise should also emphasize to students the fact that getting to know and care about a person is a long and involved process, and that an individual's perceptions, feelings and attitudes about others will change as you continue to get to know them.

EXERCISE 6: EXPATRIATE ASSIGNMENTS

SUGGESTED CHAPTER		CROSS-REFERENCE AND INTEGRATION
3	Organizational Behavior Across Cultures	perception and attribution; diversity and individual differences; decision making

INSTRUCTOR'S NOTES

This is a very innovative exercise that can be insightful, thoughtful, and fun. Asking students to adopt the perspectives of different "family members" can lead to some interesting insights. For example, how might an eight-year-old boy, or a 12-year-old girl, or a 16-year old high school student feel about moving overseas? What if the family has an elderly parent living with them? It is easy to say that an executive should consider his or her family's feelings when making a decision to relocate overseas. But we rarely gain insight into how actual family members might feel about the decision. Although this exercise is only a role play, some strong feelings may emerge that provide insight into why expatriate decisions are so difficult to make.

To help stimulate classroom discussion or to help a particular group get its discussion underway, the following are questions family members often ask when considering an overseas assignment:

- What is the cost of living?
- Is the standard of living similar to that in the United States?
- Is the language in the target country difficult to learn?
- How much will we miss our extended family and friends?
- Is the target country politically stable?
- Is the target country economically stable?

- Will it be difficult to move about in a normal way?
- Is the country safe?
- Are there other Americans in the target country that my family can visit and be friends with?
- What is the health system like in the target country? What happens if one of us gets really sick?
- Will we be accepted by the new culture, or are most people in the target country unfriendly to foreigners?
- Are there English-speaking schools available in the city in which we will be located?
- What type of entertainment is available? What will we do with our free time?
- How much does it cost to travel between the target country and the United States?
- Will it be difficult for our extended families to visit us in the target country?
- What is the weather like in the target country? What about shopping? What kind of clothing will we be expected to wear?

EXERCISE 7: CULTURAL CUES

SUGGESTED CHAPTER		CROSS-REFERENCE AND INTEGRATION
3	Organizational Behavior Across Cultures	perception and attribution; diversity and individual differences; decision making; communication; conflict; groups and teamwork

INSTRUCTOR'S NOTES

This is an innovative exercise that gives students a chance to feel what's it's like to try to quickly assimilate oneself into another culture. Many students have never been to a country outside the United States. As a result, they may not have an appreciation for what it feels like to be the "outsider" in a group of people who are all similar in terms of their cultural norms and behaviors. From a pragmatic standpoint, the goal of the exercise is also to strengthen your students' sensitivity to cultural cues and indicators. By visiting other "cultures" in the course of the exercise, students learn to pick up on cultural cues and the importance of assimilating their behavior to the culture they are in.

Debriefing (25-30 minutes)

Begin by asking the yellow group to report what cultural attributes it determined about the blue group. Have the blue group respond as to the accuracy of the yellow group's report. If there were any misperceptions, ask what they were and why they may have occurred. Do the same with the blue group.

Next, ask what methods were used to determine the cultural attributes of the foreign culture. Participants will say things such as "trial and error," "observation," "looking for signs of approval/disapproval of one's own culturally based behaviors."

Ask participants to describe how they felt in the presence of the foreign culture. How did they know when they had made a mistake within the context of the foreign culture? How did this make them feel? At this point, try to bring out the feelings of uncertainty, bewilderment, and disorientation that are common to such experiences.

In addition, ask your students to reflect on the exercise and then address the following questions:

- What advice would you give to someone who is about to interact with a foreign culture?
- Based on your understanding of how it feels to be new to a culture, what could you do as a member of the prevailing or home culture to help a foreigner adjust to your culture?

As an optional extension of this exercise, you might also want to point out to your students that individuals often encounter "different" or foreign cultures within their own countries or communities. Ask participants to name some of the cultures they interact with at home and how difficult it is to quickly assimilate into these cultures. Examples include:

- Ethnic groups/neighborhoods.
- Regional differences in customs and dialect.
- Gender differences.
- Social class distinctions (for example, would a student feel uncomfortable at a dinner party with the top executives of local firms?).
- New work environments.
- In-laws.
- Adjusting to a new living environment, such as a dormitory, apartment, or a fraternity/sorority.

This exercise has been used with undergraduates, graduate students, and management professionals. Participants have been enthusiastic about their experiences. Those who have traveled to foreign countries have observed that this simple exercise evokes many of the same feelings they experienced as "foreigners" when encountering new cultures. Most of the participants have expressed an increased awareness of cultural diversity issues and an interest in developing the skills to be more effective in dealing with people from other cultures.

This exercise is always a high point of the courses in which it is used. The participants enjoy the exercise and use the experience as a reference in subsequent class discussions.

EXERCISE 8: PREJUDICE IN OUR LIVES

SUGGESTED CHAPTER		CROSS-REFERENCE AND INTEGRATION
4	Diversity and Individual Differences	perception and attribution; decision making; conflict; groups and teamwork

INSTRUCTOR'S NOTES

This exercise can help students appreciate the broad base of individuals in our society who are subject to prejudice and stereotyping. It can also help students appreciate what it feels like to be the subject of stereotyping. There may be students in your class who have never thought of themselves as part of a group that is subject to prejudice and stereotyping. However, if your students generate a fairly extensive list of the groups that are the target of potential prejudice and stereotyping, everyone in the class will probably be able to relate to one or more of the groups.

Some of the groups that students may suggest are targets of prejudice and stereotyping include the following:

•	Women	•	Men	•	The elderly
•	Working women	•	Students	•	Economically disadvantaged
•	The wealthy	•	Union workers	•	Teenagers
•	Born again Christians	•	Asians	•	High school students
•	Native Americans	•	Overweight people	•	Polish people
•	Italians	•	British	•	Blue-collar workers
•	Mentally challenged	•	African Americans	•	Handicapped people
•	College professors	•	Blondes	•	Eastern Europeans
•	White-collar workers	•	Jewish people	•	Athletes
•	Immigrants	•	Government workers	•	Truck drivers

At the end of the exercise, remind your students that stereotypes in the workplace create self-imposed boundaries, which prevent people from thinking "outside of the box." Before most people meet someone, their stereotypes often dictate how they think and feel about the person, regardless of the person's individual qualities and merits. These kinds of boundaries limit a person's objective judgment of an individual. These boundaries also limit a person's willingness to solicit inputs from people of varying backgrounds.

EXERCISE 9: HOW WE VIEW DIFFERENCES

SUGGESTED CHAPTER	**CROSS-REFERENCE AND INTEGRATION**
5 Perception and Attribution	culture; international; diversity and individual differences; decision making; communication; conflict; groups and teamwork

INSTRUCTOR'S NOTES

This exercise is designed to reveal stereotyping, and how stereotypes often miss the mark. For example, when the country music groups hears the words that the other groups have come up with to describe them, the members will often be shocked (and perhaps somewhat offended) at the words that are used. The point is that you cannot judge someone on one criterion alone. Maybe some people who listen to classical music are "stuffy" or "aloof" but certainty not all of them are. This exercise helps drive this important point home.

The following are suggestions for guiding the discussion regarding the questions in part 3 of the exercise:

a) Help your students fully appreciate the value of the exercise, as described above.

b) Expect surprises, and expect lively class discussion. Encourage your students to develop what they believe are common stereotypes for the four groups. Even common stereotypes, when carefully considered, often sound foolish.

c) Answers will vary to this question.

d) Stereotyping.

e) Some of the potential consequences of stereotyping include: (1) unnecessarily hurting someone's feelings; (2) losing a good employee or job candidate as a result of making a judgment based on a stereotype rather than objective criteria; (3) defensiveness on the part of a person who is part of a group that is often the subject of negative stereotypes; and (4) failure to solicit diverse views that may be helpful in decision making.

f) The perceptual processes here relate to other kinds of intergroup differences in that people often make generalizations about everyone of a certain race, gender, culture, age, etc. based on their experiences with only one member of the group.

g) The exercise illustrates that intergroup stereotypes are formed with considerable ease.

h) First, recognize that stereotyping exists. Most people tend to believe that they personally don't engage stereotyping, while in reality most people do. Increasing awareness of the damaging side affects of stereotyping is the first step. Organizations may also help set aside stereotypes by putting together diverse work teams, so people can see that individuals of all colors, backgrounds, shapes and sizes are potentially valuable and can make significant contributions.

EXERCISE 10: ALLIGATOR RIVER STORY

SUGGESTED CHAPTER	CROSS-REFERENCE AND INTEGRATION
5 Perception and Attribution	diversity and individual differences; decision making; communication; conflict; groups and teamwork

INSTRUCTOR'S NOTES

This is a somewhat odd exercise, but does generate a high degree of interest among students. It also seems to be an exercise that can be an extremely powerful learning device. The exercise deals primarily with values, attitudes, and perceptions. It helps integrate the material on values and attitudes with perceptions treated elsewhere in the text.

One way of administering this exercise is as follows (this suggestion covers two class periods, but it could be condensed to one).

The First Class Session

During the first period of the two-class sequence, students are asked to read the "Alligator River Story" together with instructions on how to proceed.

The processes detailed in step 3 are a vital part of the exercise since they bring out several issues and controversies in the attitudinal, value, and perceptual differences of the group members. While the groups are discussing and debating the rankings, the instructor moves from one group to another, noticing some of the members' struggles with their own, and other members' values, attitudes, and perceptions. The instructor may choose discretely to reflect these back to the class later during the debriefing session.

After the class reassembles, the instructor tabulates on the chalkboard each group's rankings of the five characters in the story. Where there is an absence of group consensus, the subgroups' rankings are posted. By the time the rankings are tabulated, the students are struck with amazement (and dismay) at the divergence in their perceptions. It is not unusual to see that one group's first ranking is another's last, with each story character ranked all over the possible range of rankings.

A brief explanation of each group's rankings follows. Usually, a very interesting, and sometimes emotional, exchange of students' values, attitudes, and perceptions takes place before the class period is terminated.

This exercise seems to help in two ways. First, students begin to realize that there is not only a value difference between generations, but even among members of their own generation there is a difference in values, attitudes, and perceptions concerning what their own life styles and moral codes ought to be. Second, by the time students come to the next class session, it would seem that they have tried to analyze the reasons for the differences in the values, attitudes, and perceptions and pinned them down, at least partially, to the differences in their background and socialization processes. The nature and quality of their contributions to the class discussion during the next lecture/discussion session lends support to this interpretation.

The Second Class Session

The second class period in this sequence is devoted to a general lecture and discussion on values, attitudes, and perceptions. The values and attitudes discussion in the text and the text material covering perception can serve as the instructional base for this class session. Students are asked to read this material before they come to class. Begin this session by recapitulating the previous session's debriefing on the Alligator River exercise, being sure to project and explain to the students why it is so essential to understand more about individuals' values, attitudes, and perceptions, especially in organizational settings. These concepts, their interrelationships, and their relationship to the socialization processes are then discussed. Having gone through a personally meaningful exercise (*i.e.*, the Alligator River Story), students seem to add richness to the discussions that take place during this session. The instructor then gives several examples of potential areas in organizations where an understanding of these concepts could be usefully applied. Thus, students also are prepared to think about the organizational applications of these concepts.

EXERCISE 11: TEAMWORK AND MOTIVATION

SUGGESTED CHAPTER	CROSS-REFERENCE AND INTEGRATION
6	Motivation Theories	performance management and rewards; groups and teamwork

INSTRUCTOR'S NOTES

This exercise can provide your students with an opportunity to enter into a very substantive discussion on employee motivation and job satisfaction. Encourage your students to bring their textbooks with them the day you administer the exercise. Then ask your students to turn to the chapter on motivation during the administration of the exercise. Ask your students to discuss the various theories of motivation, and select the ones that have the best chances of succeeding in this situation. In a debriefing session after the exercise is completed, ask your students if they were "surprised" at how difficult it is to build a motivational plan.

Answers will vary in terms of how the "worksheet" is completed. Most completed worksheets, however, will resemble the following:

Worksheet

Individual Worker	Team Member
Talks	Discusses
Me oriented	Team (or group) oriented
Department focus	Company focus
Competitive	Collaborative
Logical	Holistic
Written message	Spoken message
Image	View
Secrecy	Openness
Short-term sighted	Long-term sighted
Immediate results	Longer-term results
Critical	Supportive
Tenure	Sharing

EXERCISE 12: THE DOWNSIDE OF PUNISHMENT

SUGGESTED CHAPTER		CROSS-REFERENCE AND INTEGRATION
6	Motivation Theories	motivation; perception and attribution; performance management and rewards

INSTRUCTOR'S NOTES

This is a fairly straightforward exercise that is designed to encourage your students to think deeply about the effects of punishment as a form of behavior management. Although punishment is a legitimate form of behavior management, it is typically a form of last resort and has to be administered carefully and appropriately to be effective. As your students address the eight questions in the exercise, ask them to think holistically about their answers, rather than just putting down the first thing that comes to mind. Also encourage your students to be mindful of alternative forms of behavior management as they address the questions.

EXERCISE 13: TINKERTOYS

SUGGESTED CHAPTER		CROSS-REFERENCE AND INTEGRATION
7	Motivation and Job Design	organizational structure; design and culture; groups and teamwork

INSTRUCTOR'S NOTES

This exercise tests the students' team abilities and skills. It identifies to each group how they approach problems, and how they analyze situations. Organization, and identification and fulfillment of team roles, are of extreme importance in this task. Discussion should emphasize conflict management in a team setting, as well as the importance of defining the objective or mission of the task (in this case, building the tallest tower), and staying focused on it throughout the process.

Have the students count off one to four to divide into four teams or temporary organizations. The mission of these organizations is to build in 60 seconds the tallest freestanding Tinkertoy tower possible. Using bonus points can enhance motivation. For example, give one bonus point to the winning team for each inch over the closest competitor. All members of the team, builders, consultants, and observers receive the points. You may want to limit the maximum number of points to five. Some groups may outperform their nearest competitor by as much as 26 inches.

After the planning period is over and the toys are back in the boxes, give the signal to begin building. After 60 seconds, call time and take measurements to determine the winning organization and the number of bonus points to be awarded.

Class discussion begins with reports from the observers. Record on the board all comments made related to planning, organizing, leading and controlling (which are generally considered to be the "four functions" of management).

LESSONS ILLUSTRATED

Planning

Mission statement. This exercise easily demonstrates that organizations exist to carry out some mission. Many learned that their organization failed to win because they focused on building the sturdiest tower, not the tallest as required. They learned that the mission should guide their efforts. It did not matter if their tower was the prettiest, the most colorful, and the most creative — only height counted.

Planning involves uncertainty. Students can readily see that organizational planning is no guarantee of success. Even well thought out plans can encounter problems during implementation. Teams that believe they have the "perfect plan" often groan when they see their towers fall or come up short. This is a valuable lesson. It reveals the necessity of backup plans and alternative strategies.

Organizational espionage. Occasionally during the exercise some individuals (usually consultants to the group) stroll around the room during the 15-minute planning period and observe other groups. They carry the other groups' ideas back to their own group for consideration. This illustrates the fact that organizations frequently get ideas from observing their closest competitors.

Laws and regulations bound organizational decision-making. This exercise shows that environmental factors may restrict options available to the organization. This lesson is apparent because the exercise has its own explicit rules.

Organizing

Division of labor. It is a rare group that does not divide the construction task into subtasks. The students already appreciate the fact that division of labor is an important strategy during competition. Specialization of jobs helps to speed up the process. Frederick Taylor's principles of using standard procedures and assigning tasks to those best suited can be illustrated here.

Job assignments. With a division of labor, students can see that some jobs are more interesting than others are, but someone has to do the dull work. For example, the task of strictly sorting colors and shapes or the task of putting two pieces together is not as exciting as building the base or directing the construction. The lessons learned can include the importance of personality-job fit and the necessity of motivating employees doing repetitive tasks.

Leading

Motivation through extrinsic and intrinsic rewards. When asked about their motivation, some students expressed their desire for the bonus points. Others insisted that the bonus points were nice, but they stressed that they simply wanted to win the competition. Others perhaps wanted to impress the professor or look competent in front of their peers. The various sources of motivation (intrinsic versus extrinsic) are the lesson here.

Teamwork. Students experience the joys and frustrations of working in teams. It may be difficult to be heard or to have your ideas taken seriously by the group. Students come to realize that cooperation is the best strategy.

Group leadership. Some students may attempt to dominate the group by striving for the leadership position. This can be positive if the individual possesses special skills or talents such as Tinkertoys expert or the ability to pull people together. Or, it can be negative if the individual is argumentative and disruptive. The debriefing can include an assessment of leadership as a requirement of success. For example, did the winning team have strong or weak leadership?

Controlling

Control is important in organizations. The most successful groups — realizing that they need input along the way — usually select one of the consultants to be timekeeper. This proves to be a valuable strategy in monitoring the progress of construction.

Importance of backup plans. The most successful groups often have a backup plan if it becomes necessary to change the original plan during the implementations phase. It is easy to then tie the control function back to planning.

EXERCISE 14: JOB DESIGN PREFERENCES

SUGGESTED CHAPTER		CROSS-REFERENCE AND INTEGRATION
7	Motivation and Job Design	motivation; job design; organizational design; change

INSTRUCTOR'S NOTES

This is an interesting exercise that should elicit a high degree of interest among your students. The point of the exercise is that people have different preferences with regard to the nature of the jobs they enjoy and find fulfilling. It is important that managers recognize this. A person is typically most committed to a job that fits with his or her personality and personal preferences. If a manager can put people in the jobs that they are most suited for, an increase in organizational commitment and a decrease in turnover will typically result.

In your class discussion following the completion of the exercise, run down the list of job characteristics (starting with variety of tasks, performance feedback, and so on), and ask for a show of hands of students that ranked each characteristics as 1 or "the most important." Among the hands that are raised, ask for volunteers to share with the class why that particular characteristic is so important to them. Also, when the hands are raised, notice if the rankings are consistent by gender or some other easily recognizable characteristic. If so, ask your students for an explanation for that finding.

EXERCISE 15: MY FANTASY JOB

SUGGESTED CHAPTER	CROSS-REFERENCE AND INTEGRATION
7	Motivation and Job Design	motivation; individual differences; organizational design; change

INSTRUCTOR'S NOTES

This is an appealing exercise that should elicit a high degree of student interest. It also illustrates that any job (regardless of industry or rank) can be measured against the five core job characteristics of skill variety, task identity, task significance, autonomy, and job feedback.

As your students complete this exercise, ask them to take some time and really think through the core job characteristics as they pertain to their fantasy job. Students are often surprised by how "much" or "little" their fantasy job lends itself to a particular characteristic. Also, when the students describe their fantasy jobs to the class, provide an opportunity for class members to agree or disagree with the assessment being provided (in a positive sort of way). This approach illustrates that the positive characteristics of a job are often in the mind of the jobholder. For example, one student may say that his fantasy job is to be a NBA basketball player and rank task significance very high (meaning that the job contributes a lot to the organization or society). Another student may say, "basketball players are just athletes, and contribute very little to society." The point is that a person's perception of the value of his or her job is often a function of his or her personal viewpoint.

EXERCISE 16: Motivation by Job Enrichment

SUGGESTED CHAPTER	CROSS-REFERENCE AND INTEGRATION
7	Motivation and Job Design	motivation; job design; perception; diversity and individual differences; change

INSTRUCTOR'S NOTES

Each group of five to seven members develops a job description for one of the following jobs: bank teller, retail sales clerk, manager of a fast food restaurant, wait person, receptionist, restaurant manager, clerical worker (or bookkeeper), or janitor. Each group focuses on a different job and develops a brief description of the duties for that job. Each group then analyzes its list in light of core job characteristics theory and develops a new list of job duties that attempts to incorporate the insights provided by job characteristics theory.

EXERCISE 17: ANNUAL PAY RAISES

SUGGESTED CHAPTER		CROSS-REFERENCE AND INTEGRATION
8	Performance Management and Rewards	motivation; learning and reinforcement perception and attribution; decision making; groups and teamwork

INSTRUCTOR'S NOTES

This exercise is a good role play for students to acquaint them with some of the difficult tasks that managers and human resource specialists confront on the job. Managers frequently have a fixed pool of money to work with when determining the annual raise for a work group, and often the decisions that are made are "close calls" and involve both subjective and objective considerations.

Challenge your students to establish a clear rational for each raise decision. To do this, the students will have to establish a set of criteria on which to base their decisions. Various criteria can be used, including job performance, effort, seniority, salience of money to the employee, etc. Also discuss equity issues with your students. Can you give a higher raise to one person opposed to another just because the first person "needs" the money more? What about the employee who is in the position that is "hard to fill?" Should you give this employee additional money just to keep him? If so, how will the other employees feel about that?

At the conclusion of the exercise, ask your students for a show of hands in response to the question: "Were the raise decisions harder to make than you thought that they would be?" In addition, ask your students: "Do you now have a better appreciation of why managers often labor over salary decisions?" You should get a good show of hands in response to each of these questions. As a result, this exercise can be a real "eye opener" for students in regard to the challenges involved in human resource management decisions.

EXERCISE 18: SERVING ON THE BOUNDARY

SUGGESTED CHAPTER		CROSS-REFERENCE AND INTEGRATION
9	How Groups Work	intergroup dynamics; group dynamics; roles; communication; conflict; stress

INSTRUCTOR'S NOTES

This is a structured exercise in which several groups are formed to solve a problem regarding international geography. Each group determines which one of its members is the "most competent" or knowledgeable with respect to international geography. These "experts" are formed into another group but still retain their membership in their respective home groups. This procedure enables the experts to be boundary persons between the expert group and their home groups. The expert group and the other groups are given the problem to solve, and a relatively structured interaction approach between the experts and the home teams is followed. After solving the problem, there is a class discussion of the nature and implications of the boundary person role.

EXERCISE 19: EGGSPERIENTAL EXERCISE

SUGGESTED CHAPTER		CROSS-REFERENCE AND INTEGRATION
9	How Groups Work	group dynamics and teamwork; diversity and individual differences; communication

INSTRUCTOR'S NOTES

This is a teamwork exercise, testing and strengthening the group process, and members' ability to work together under time constraints, and with limited resources. The goal is to get participants to utilize their creative abilities, increase their creativity and motivation by feeding off of the energy of other members, and learn to "think outside the box." The exercise also demonstrates the importance of group cohesiveness.

EXERCISE 20: SCAVENGER HUNT — TEAM BUILDING

SUGGESTED CHAPTER		CROSS-REFERENCE AND INTEGRATION
10	Teamwork and Team Performance	groups; leadership; diversity and individual differences; communication

INSTRUCTOR'S NOTES

This exercise provides students the opportunity to work in a team setting and exercise some of the positive and negative attributes of teamwork. Teamwork tends to work in many organizations because the old adage that "two heads are better than one" is generally true. While working through this exercise, students will find that one member of the team will know exactly where to go to find a particular item and another member of the team will know exactly who to talk to get another item. The point is that by working as a team, the members can find the items faster and easier than if each student tried to find all of the items together. Of course, the frustrations of teamwork are also illustrated through the exercise. There may be one or two students on each team who don't contribute at all to the team's overall effort. Point out to your students that sad as it may be, this also happens on occasion in the real world (this is called the "free rider" problem, meaning that one or more team members do little or no work but still benefit from the end result produced by the team).

This exercise results in teams performing at high levels regardless of prior experience and abilities. The building of effective work teams is exciting and fun for the students while building surprisingly high levels of cohesion and commitment in a short period of time. For a class session of 2½ hours, a 1½-hour search for the 20 items listed in the example below is recommended. This allows the remainder of the class session to be used for a discussion focused on the characteristics of effective teams. For shorter class sessions, modify the number of items in the search. For a 75-minute class, we recommend a search for 10 items in 45 minutes allowing for a 30-minute class discussion.

The underlying principles usually identified from the exercise include Larson and Lafasto's (1989) eight characteristics of how and why effective teams develop, which are listed below.

1.	There is a clear, elevating goal.
2.	The structure of the exercise is results-driven.
3.	Team members are all competent in some area.
4.	The exercise promotes a collaborative climate.
5.	The exercise builds commitment to the team.
6.	Standards of excellence are established.
7.	External recognition is given.
8.	An opportunity exists for team leadership to emerge.

EXERCISE 21: WORK TEAM DYNAMICS

SUGGESTED CHAPTER		CROSS-REFERENCE AND INTEGRATION
10	Teamwork and Team Performance	groups; motivation; decision making; conflict; communication

INSTRUCTOR'S NOTES

This exercise can be extremely useful at providing work teams with valuable insights into the dynamics of their groups. It should be especially useful if you use work groups in your class, since the members are more likely to have considerable insight into their teams' processes. Moreover, by examining the items for which the biggest differences of opinion arise, team members should be able to quickly pinpoint and discuss problem areas for the group. Finally, by creating action plans for improving group processes, the stage can be set for improving the effectiveness of these groups. In essence, this exercise can serve to facilitate the data gathering, data analysis and diagnosis, and action planning steps of the team building process for the work teams in your class.

EXERCISE 22: IDENTIFYING GROUP NORMS

SUGGESTED CHAPTER		CROSS-REFERENCE AND INTEGRATION
10	Teamwork and Team Performance	groups; communication; perception and attribution

INSTRUCTOR'S NOTES

Among other things, this exercise measures the cohesiveness of the organization under study, as well as its organizational values and cultural characteristics. The responses to the questionnaire highlight the strengths and weaknesses of the organization and its culture. It is important for participants to keep in mind that this is based only on their own perceptions and assumptions of the employee's reactions to the listed behaviors. It is not to say that their perceptions are inaccurate, but it is important to realize that another individual may have had very different experiences with or information about that particular organization.

EXERCISE 23: WORKGROUP CULTURE

SUGGESTED CHAPTER		CROSS-REFERENCE AND INTEGRATION
10	Teamwork and Team Performance	groups; communication; perception and attribution; job design; organizational culture

INSTRUCTOR'S NOTES

This exercise is useful from a variety of perspectives. It is important to the functionality and productivity of a group to understand the members' perceptions of it. The members' feelings and attitudes toward the group will help to indicate the extent and quality of each member's performance, as well as their degree of commitment to it.

In using the exercise to determine how the group is performing now, and how it should be performing, the group can identify the gaps between the two, analyze the root of the problem, and work toward improving it, thereby increasing the effectiveness of the team process. The assessment promotes discussion of feelings about the group, and may uncover problems or potential problems not yet evident.

Having outsiders evaluate the group on these criteria will allow a comparison with self evaluations, thus providing an objective "third party" perception of the group process and offering information and considerations that may have been overlooked by the group members.

EXERCISE 24: THE HOT SEAT

SUGGESTED CHAPTER		CROSS-REFERENCE AND INTEGRATION
10	Teamwork and Team Performance	groups; communication; conflict and negotiation; power and politics

INSTRUCTOR'S NOTES

This is an interesting exercise that your students should enjoy and from which they can learn. Seating arrangements are often overlooked when examining group dynamics and communications. They are important for both the researcher and the manager, because they have an impact on people's feelings and reactions. Just ask your students about their brother or sister sitting in their usual seat at the dinner table. This case demonstrates the importance of being conscious of appropriate seating to aid group effectiveness.

Here are suggested answers to the questions posed by the exercise.

1.   Which seat did Professor Stevens select and why?

   Answer:

   This question really asks about the effectiveness of each seat. Seats 1 and 2 are not very good since Professor Stevens would not want to be controlled by the Chair. Seats 6, 7, and 8 are also not effective since Professor Stevens is too far away from the group and gives the impression of that he is just there to "fishbowl" or observe the meeting. Seats 4, 5, 9, and 10 are too isolated with empty chairs surrounding them and off to the side. The two most effective seats are 3 and 11. But which one is better? Although 3 gives direct contact with the Chair and allies Professor Stevens with a +, it has two drawbacks. First, it permits the two **Xs** across the table to enter freely in the discussion and creates a strategic power bloc for the Chair. Second, influencing the swing votes or **?s** is more difficult when they are at the end of the table rather than in direct eye contact. The most effective seat is 11. This seat allows for direct contact with the Chair, direct eye contact with the **?s**, nullifies the influence of the two **Xs** by creating a "sandwich effect" with the + on the same side, and permits overt agreement with his statements by having an ally across the table and close to the **?s**.

2.   What is the likely pattern of communication and interaction in this group?

   Answer:

   There are obviously two and perhaps three subgroups at work. The **Xs**, **+s**, and perhaps the **?s** are blatant subgroups. Only two are competing, the **Xs** and **+s**. Therefore, some counteracting groups exist, which probably will cause a restrictive communication network. Blockage of the group's progress is imminent and the group probably will regress to the storming stage. Unless a consensus can be reached by the **?s** choosing a side, the group will be deadlocked and their performance will dwindle considerably.

3.   What can be done to get the group to work harmoniously?

   Answer:

   This question is intended to stimulate classroom discussion.

EXERCISE 25: INTERVIEW A LEADER

SUGGESTED CHAPTER		CROSS-REFERENCE AND INTEGRATION
11	Leadership	performance management and rewards; group and teamwork; new workplace; organizational change and stress

INSTRUCTOR'S NOTES

This exercise allows the students to acquire first-hand insight into leadership. A discussion comparing leading and managing may clarify the purpose, as it gives students something to on which to focus. The common characteristics of being a leader need to be emphasized, as well as factors that differentiate between leaders (*e.g.*, type of organization, type of group, personal characteristics, industry, business environment, culture, purpose or mandate, etc.). A comparison of the student's findings to the characteristics of well-known leaders may prove valuable.

EXERCISE 26: LEADERSHIP SKILLS INVENTORIES

SUGGESTED CHAPTER		CROSS-REFERENCE AND INTEGRATION
11	Leadership	individual differences; perception and attribution; decision making.

INSTRUCTOR'S NOTES

Students usually find self-assessments interesting. This particular self-assessment can benefit your students in several ways. First, some students may have never thought of certain qualities as "skills." For an example, a student may know that he or she is excellent at helping people resolve conflict, but may have never thought of this as a skill that might be useful on a job. Second, as the students take their self-assessments back to their groups, group members may be surprised to find that some of them may have certain skills that the group has not been utilizing. Finally, the exercise may prompt students to put more effort into the skill areas that are designated as "needs improvement."

EXERCISE 27: LEADERSHIP AND PARTICIPATION IN DECISION MAKING

SUGGESTED CHAPTER		CROSS-REFERENCE AND INTEGRATION
11	Leadership	decision making; communication; motivation; groups; teamwork

INSTRUCTOR'S NOTES

This exercise is intended to demonstrate the different approaches that people take in trying to solve (or cope with) the same problem. When going through each of the 10 decision situations, urge your students to consider each situation carefully before making a judgment regarding decision style. You may even ask your students to jot down a brief justification for each of their choices. Then, in the group setting, ask your students to be candid about their choices.

The group portion of the exercise should demonstrate two important points. First, people vary in the way they handle the same problem. Second, one approach may in fact be preferable to another. This can be determined by sorting through the different alternatives in the group discussions. This portion of the exercise may be a real eye opener to some students.

EXERCISE 28: MY BEST MANAGER: REVISITED

SUGGESTED CHAPTER		CROSS-REFERENCE AND INTEGRATION
12	Power and Politics	diversity and individual differences; perception and attribution

INSTRUCTOR'S NOTES

The earlier "My Best Manager" exercise (Exercise 1) allowed your students to reflect on their own definitions of what traits typify top-notch managers. This exercise is an extension of the original assignment, and brings a gender dimension into the discussion. Specifically, the exercise allows students to compare the perceived prevalence of certain managerial traits by gender. It also allows students to compare societal responses for managerial traits to student responses.

EXERCISE 29: ACTIVE LISTENING

SUGGESTED CHAPTER		CROSS-REFERENCE AND INTEGRATION
13	Information and Communication	group dynamics and teamwork; perception and attribution

INSTRUCTOR'S NOTES

This exercise provides participants with an effective and entertaining method of improving their communication skills. By allowing students to assume all three roles, they can view communication from each perspective, providing feedback to each other on strengths and weaknesses. Seeing certain characteristics in others will make individuals aware of them, so they can adopt them if they are positive characteristics, or look to avoid them if they are weaknesses.

The importance of listening skills is highlighted through this exercise. Point out to your students that a disproportionate amount of attention is typically placed on the verbal end of communication, without enough attention paid to effective listening. Both participants in a verbal communication, the speaker and the listener, must be equal participants for communication to function effectively. An effective listener can also contribute to the quality of the speaker: when a speaker knows that he or she is being attentively listened to, the speaker will likely be more enthusiastic about the subject and will be more dedicated to making it interesting, effective, and precise for the listener.

EXERCISE 30: UPWARD APPRAISAL

SUGGESTED CHAPTER		CROSS-REFERENCE AND INTEGRATION
13	Information and Communication	perception and attribution; performance management and rewards

INSTRUCTOR'S NOTES

This exercise accentuates the sensitive and often volatile nature of the feedback process. It must be carried out in a very non-threatening and constructive manner. It allows students to participate and at the same time observe the feedback process. Discussion should include feelings about how the feedback sessions should be structured, strengths and weaknesses observed, etc.

EXERCISE 31: 360-DEGREE FEEDBACK

SUGGESTED CHAPTER		CROSS REFERENCE AND INTEGRATION
14	Decision Making	communication; perception and attribution; performance management and rewards

INSTRUCTOR'S NOTES

There are several important tips that help this exercise work effectively. The tips are listed below.

1. Emphasize that students are to read the guidelines for feedback ahead of time and to make notes to themselves to prepare to discuss their perceptions of the course and instructor. The usefulness of the exercise will be limited if students come in "cold" and try to "wing it."

2. Instructors should avoid eavesdropping on groups of students while they are engaged in discussions. Lingering around students as they discuss the course and instructor evaluation typically inhibits candor.

3. To increase the learning effect of this exercise (and to model appropriate behaviors), it is highly desirable to have the instructor take notes and respond with only clarifying comments. It is particularly important not to be defensive or make comments that could be construed as rebuttals, back-peddling, or negative remarks that respond to students' observations.

4. It is important to recognize the team building effects of this exercise. That is, it will have less impact if it is perceived as "just" a contrived exercise that demonstrates effective feedback. On the other hand, if instructors use the exercise with a genuine interest in how to improve the classroom learning culture, students perceive it as a highly credible experience. Many students empathize with the instructor's openness and willingness to truly hear their concerns and feedback. A typical comment is, "I can't believe you put yourself through this."

5. Two related points merit comment. First, this exercise seems to work best if administered near the middle of the quarter or term. Second, the instructor must be willing to commit to change some things based on the feedback from the students. If he or she does not, it will lessen the impact of the feedback experience since it will likely be seen as an artificial experience that has little return to the students for the risk that they are taking in giving honest feedback to the instructor. This, incidentally, is an excellent opportunity to draw parallels to the reality of how many managers operate. That is, "participation" is often a superficial and glib concept that has a low likelihood of changing things for the better unless the manager (read instructor) is willing to act on the input that she or he receives.

6. Don't miss the opportunity to have the larger class provide feedback to the group representatives who give feedback to the instructor. In fact, it's appropriate to instruct the rest of the class (who may not actually be giving the feedback) that they are to look for the presence of effective feedback behaviors (*e.g.*, using descriptive language).

7. Instructors can vary the instructions by allowing students in the larger classroom audience (*i.e.*, those who are not chosen as representatives to provide feedback) to join in the discussion after 10-15 minutes. Sometimes students can feel stifled if they want to say something but were not chosen as their group's representative.

8. To provide closure to the exercise, it is especially important to draw generalizations about the experience. Though there are many to consider, these three seem to be particularly salient to students:

   • Feedback, when given and received from a high integrity perspective, is an important building block of effective relationships. It implies some risks, but also has a powerful potential to cement relationships. Especially in hierarchical environments (*e.g.*, many businesses and classrooms), it promotes a climate of openness and trust. It contributes to subordinates' perception that the manager (or instructor) is more "human."

   • The exercise is not a blanket endorsement of open feedback in all business environments. Indeed, many organizational cultures do not welcome or even permit high levels of openness and trust. Indiscriminate openness is, in fact, fairly risky (and potentially politically naive) behavior.

   • Students need to develop behavioral flexibility so that they have the skills to provide effective feedback when and where appropriate.

EXERCISE 32: ROLE ANALYSIS NEGOTIAITON

SUGGESTED CHAPTER		CROSS-REFERENCE AND INTEGRATION
14	Decision Making	communication; group dynamics and teamwork; perception and attribution; communication; decision making

INSTRUCTOR'S NOTES

On way of administering this exercise is as follows:

1. In small group, complete the instructions provided in the exercise. Create a list of questions for the instructor.

2. With the instructor at the chalkboard, "live board," etc., the class as a whole will identify, list, and discuss specific duties and requirements of the course until the group reaches agreement. The syllabus requirements provide the boundaries for the agreement. The final list is recorded.

3. The students, as a group, list their requirements of the instructor, particularly as the instructor's behavior affects the performance of the students. Again, the list needs to be agreed upon and the final list must be recorded.

4. The instructor then lists his or her expectations and desired behavior of the student role. Again, these expectations are discussed, modified, and agreed on. The list is recorded.

5. Individually, or with a small group of students, the instructor prepares a written summary of the two roles for later (next class meeting) distribution to the class. An effective way to prepare this summary is to list each of the course requirements and, next to each one, list the agreed upon behaviors (*i.e.*, activities, obligations, expectations) of the students and the instructor. This written role profile is distributed to all students.

EXERCISE 33: LOST AT SEA

SUGGESTED CHAPTER		CROSS-REFERENCE AND INTEGRATION
14	Decision Making	communication; group dynamics and teamwork; conflict and negotiation

INSTRUCTOR'S NOTES

According to the "experts," the basic supplies needed when a person is stranded in mid-ocean are articles to attract attention and articles to aid survival *until rescuers arrive*. Articles for navigation are of little importance — even if a small life raft were capable of reaching land, it would be impossible to store enough food and water to subsist during that period of time. Therefore, of primary importance are the shaving mirror and the two-gallon can of oil-gas mixture. These items could be used for signaling air-sea rescue. Of secondary importance are items such as water and food (*e.g.*, the survival meal). The experts' rankings are provided below.

Rank

Sextant	15
Shaving mirror	1
5 gallons of water	3
Mosquito netting	14
One survival meal	4
Maps of Pacific Ocean	13
Floatable seat cushion	9
2 gallons of oil-gas mix	2
Small transistor radio	12
Shark repellent	10
20 square feet of black plastic	5
One quart of 20-proof rum	11
15 feet of nylon rope	8
24 chocolate bars	6
Fishing kit	7

A brief rationale is provided for the ranking of each item. These brief explanations obviously do not represent all of the potential uses for the specified items but, rather, the primary importance of each.

1 — Shaving mirror.
>   Critical for signaling air-sea rescue.

2 —Two-gallons of oil-gas mix.
>   Critical for signaling — the oil-gas mixture will float on the water and could be ignited with a dollar bill and a match (obviously, outside the raft).

3 — Five gallons of water.
>   Necessary to replenish moisture loss by perspiring, etc.

4 — One survival meal.
>   Provides basic food intake.

5 — Twenty square feet of black plastic.
>   Utilized to collect rainwater, provide shelter from the elements.

6 — Twenty-four chocolate bars.
>   A reserve food supply.

7 — Fishing kit.
>   Ranked lower than the candy bars because "one bird in the hand is worth two in the bush." There is no assurance that you will catch any fish.

8 — Fifteen feet of nylon rope.
>   May be used to lash equipment together to prevent it from falling overboard.

10 — Shark repellent.
>   Obvious.

11 — One quart of 20-proof rum.
>   Contains alcohol — enough to use as a potential antiseptic for any injuries incurred; of little value otherwise; will cause dehydration if ingested.

12 — Small transistor radio.
>   Of little value since there is no transmitter (unfortunately, you are out of range of your favorite AM radio stations).

13 — Maps of the Pacific Ocean.
>   Worthless without additional navigational equipment — it does not really matter where you are but where the rescuers are.

14 — Mosquito netting.
>   There are no mosquitoes in the mid-Pacific.

15 — Sextant.
>   Without tables and a chronometer, relatively useless.

The basic rationale for ranking signaling devices above life-sustaining items (food and water) is that without signaling devices there is almost no chance of being spotted and rescued. Furthermore, most rescues occur during the first thirty-six hours, and one can survive without food and water during this period.

This exercise can be extremely useful at illustrating the importance of creativity in both individual and group decision making. As part of your discussion of this exercise, ask students to score their individual and group responses by summing their personal and group absolute deviations from the experts' rankings. Next instruct them to calculate the mean for the individual group members' responses. Typically, "the best individual" score will be superior to the group score; nevertheless, the group score is normally superior to the mean of the individual scores. These tendencies provide two important lessons. First, a creative individual, who may or may not have some relevant expertise, can often outperform a group on a problem-solving task. Second, the group will typically obtain a superior solution than will *most* individuals. Thus, while some people are capable of outperforming a group on a task, the capability of groups to share information and varied perspectives typically results in some improvement in the quality of solutions generated by most individuals. As such, there are clearly benefits of both individual decision-making (for creative or expert persons) and group decision-making.

EXERCISE 34: ENTERING THE UNKNOWN

SUGGESTED CHAPTER		CROSS-REFERENCE AND INTEGRATION
14	Decision Making	communication; group dynamics and teamwork; perception and attribution

INSTRUCTOR'S NOTES

Introduction

Professionals are frequently required to enter into new or unknown situations: a salesperson walks into a meeting with a prospective new client; a manager represents her company at a convention luncheon; a new employee faces his first day in a new job. Likewise, professors and students walk into a classroom on the first day of each new term to face a group of people who may mostly be total strangers. Uncertainty is often the most salient feature of these situations. Many questions go through one's mind upon entering a new social situation: "What will these people be like? Will I enjoy this situation? Will I learn anything interesting? Will I develop friends here?" (Schein, 1988).

We are accustomed to modifying our behavior to cope with various settings and cultures. At a football game, we are loud and boisterous. At grandma's house, we are witty and conventional. In a departmental meeting, we are aggressive and logical. But in an uncertain situation, it is not clear what type of behavior should be employed to achieve our goals. Norms, status, agendas, values, and procedures — the things that help us customize our behavior in a known environment — all may be unspecified at the outset.

Several common strategies can be identified for dealing with self-presentation under uncertainty (Goffman, 1959; 1969). Some people plunge in and begin introducing themselves to everyone, or some seek out others who appear for whatever reason to have high status. Others try to initiate structure for everyone. Many people withdraw and wait for someone else to initiate contact or to set a group agenda. Most of us tend to rely on a characteristic pre-programmed behavior (or persona) with which we are comfortable and familiar, or which we thus believe to be "safe" (Jung, 1942). However, these "canned" approaches often prove to be generally inefficient, slow, or even counter-productive ways to build constructive relationships with others (Bowen, 1986). Sometimes the first impression we leave is even misleading to others, who are trying to figure out what it will be like to be around us. Only gradually do we peel away the layers of social veneer and figure out who others really are, what they want, and how we can get our needs fulfilled through them.

More context-sensitive and genuine alternatives to these habitual entry strategies exist. To find them, we need to get to know whom we are and what we want to have happen in a given situation. Then we must seek to establish our true image to others (Egan, 1977). This involves, of course, a certain amount of risk. We have to accept that not everyone will like us, and that we won't necessarily like everyone also (Argyris and Schon, 1978). This risk need not prevent a civil, honest, and even useful level of relationship. However, to reach an honest level of exchange more quickly, we must achieve genuine behavior more quickly.

The purposes of the entry behavior exercise are to:

- Help students identify their current style of entering new and somewhat ambiguous situations and give them an opportunity to receive feedback on their entry style.
- Help students consider the extent to which their current style helps them achieve their goals.
- Allow students to develop insights into behaving in more genuine ways from the very early stages of a new social situation.

Thus, the aim of the exercise is to help students avoid an unnecessary restriction in range of behaviors available to them in entry situations, and to move from cautious or trite behavior to more genuine interactions.

The Exercise

In this exercise, students work in groups of four or five to get to know the other members of their group. The goal is for students to become more aware of their entry behaviors and to act in ways that can help them achieve comfortable behaviors with their group at a very early stage in an exchange. Typically, the process begins with the professor describing the importance of the first class session in establishing the climate for the rest of the course or semester. The professor explains that when individuals enter new situations there is a dynamic of uncertainty. This exercise helps students and the professor to make the most of the energy that is tied to this uncertainty and to capture the learning that is available from this situation. The point of the exercise is to move as quickly as possible to those behaviors we typically exhibit when we no longer feel uncertain or tense.

Experiences with the Exercise

This exercise is designed to promote an exchange of thought and feelings that are not typically shared until students become much more familiar with each other. It generally creates a climate of open expression, which helps students bond more quickly and respond more comfortably in future entry behavior situations. The exercise is designed to take approximately two hours. However, alternative designs, which can be conducted in shorter or longer periods of time, have been developed.

A short version of this exercise requires only about 35-40 minutes of class time. The procedure is to assign students to groups and instruct them to get to know one another for a few minutes. After about 15 to 20 minutes, interrupt the groups and give them an overview of entry behavior.

Invite the students to think back on how they have presented themselves over the past 15 to 20 minutes and consider what they have been trying to project. Then put them back into their groups to discuss this with the other group members as well as to seek feedback on how well their approach is working.

In addition to the full-scale exercise, an optional closing exercise can be employed. This additional exercise helps to facilitate the development of permanent groups (*e.g.*, established groups that will work together for an entire course). It also helps to underscore the learnings of the entry behavior exercise.

This additional closing exercise is conducted by asking groups to develop a way to introduce themselves to the rest of the class. Give each group approximately 15 minutes to form a method for introducing themselves as a group to the entire class. The objective here is to have individuals and groups identify ways to make initial connections more easily and successfully. Each group then is asked to share their introduction with the class.

Processing the Exercise

Begin the debriefing with a discussion of the Entry Behavior exercise by reminding students that behaviors are a result of both content (what) and process (how). Ask them to focus on the topics their group discussed (content). Then ask the students to think about the approaches they and their group members followed during the task (process). Encourage them to think about how they came across to others and how they felt about the approach they took and the behaviors they exhibited. This discussion helps students become more aware of and to understand their entry behaviors.

After identifying their own entry behaviors, it is valuable for students to obtain feedback on their entry style. Ask groups to discuss their perceptions of each other. What behaviors did they like or find useful? What, if anything, did they dislike? What reactions did they have to others?

Follow the above discussion questions with some information on entry behaviors (see Entry Behavior exhibit below). There are three kinds of behaviors that one brings to any situation: entry, present, and avoidance.

- *Entry behaviors* are how we act when we enter new, uncertain or anxious situations. We typically restrict our range of behaviors to leading or following — seeking information or listening, but seldom both.
- *Present behaviors* generally include a much broader range of actions. The term "present" denotes an active attention to the here-and-now of the interpersonal situation at hand. Present behaviors are those used when we feel comfortable or natural. We more freely express a broad range of emotions, such as being supportive, resolute, vulnerable, carefree, serious, sad, etc.
- *Avoidance behaviors* are when we withdraw from the situation. These behaviors may include sleeping, drinking alcohol, procrastinating, watching television, leaving the situation, thinking only about yourself, etc.

Student Reaction to The Exercise

Students and seminar participants report that this exercise helps them to quickly be open with others about the anxiety of a new situation. Very early in their relationships, they discuss their intentions, perceptions, and reactions. Variations of this exercise have been used very successfully in a variety of graduate and undergraduate organizational behavior courses as well as management training seminars.

EXERCISE 35: VACATION PUZZLE

SUGGESTED CHAPTER		CROSS-REFERENCE AND INTEGRATION
15	Conflict and Negotiation	conflict and negotiation; communication; power; leadership

INSTRUCTOR'S NOTES

This exercise provides a challenge to students' to test their problem-solving skills, ability to process information, and strategic and tactical abilities in deciding how to tackle a problem. The use of the chart is a good start to solving the puzzle, and provides the students with a tool to organize their work.

The solution of the puzzle is as follows:

1. No one vacationed in June or July.

2. According to (c) and (d), Quintaro did not vacation in January, March, April, August or December.

3. Because of (b), Quintaro could not have vacationed in September either; this leaves only October or November for her second week. According to (e), Middleton took her second week after Quintaro, so Middleton must have vacationed in November or December. But also according to (e), Middleton took her second week before McCain so Middleton must have vacationed in November, and McCain must have vacationed in December; this means Quintaro must have vacationed in October.

4. And because of (a), Porter must have vacationed in August, and Khalili must have vacationed in September.

5. Perhaps the key to this puzzle is noting that just because McCain took her first week before Khalili, who took hers before Porter (and the reverse for their second week), doesn't mean they took them in *consecutive* order.

6. Because of (b), Khalili must have vacationed in March.

7. According to (d), neither Porter nor McCain vacationed in January; this leaves only Middleton for that month.

8. So (a) places McCain in February.

9. And as Quintaro didn't vacation in April, she must have vacationed in May; this leaves only Porter for April.

10. Sure enough, according to (a), he fits there nicely.

11. So, the vacations looked like this:

January: Middleton	July: no one
February: McCain	August: Porter
March: Khalili	September: Khalili
April: Porter	October: Quintaro
May: Quintaro	November: Middleton
June: no one	December: McCain

EXERCISE 36: THE UGLI ORANGE

SUGGESTED CHAPTER		CROSS-REFERENCE AND INTEGRATION
15	Conflict and Negotiation	communication; decision making

INSTRUCTOR'S NOTES

Objectives of the Exercise

1. To explore the dynamics of two-person bargaining (negotiation).
2. To demonstrate the effects of low trust on information disclosure.
3. To demonstrate the need to diagnose whether goals are incompatible or whether information is not being adequately shared, before acting cooperatively or competitively.
4. Option 2: To compare the differences between interpersonal and intergroup negotiation.

What to Expect

The major benefits are that this exercise packs a lot of process points about cooperation and competition into a very short time period. Participants find the Ugli orange situation intriguing, and discussion is lively.

As the total class group gets larger (say, over 40) it becomes very time-consuming to have each group report back to the rest of the class. A variation is called for, which will be described later.

Advance Preparation

Prepare copies of the role descriptions as handouts.

Operating Procedure, Hints, and Cautions

The *key element* in this case is that Roland and Jones need *different parts* of the Ugli orange. Roland needs the *rind,* and Jones needs *the juice.* If each person discloses enough information to let him or her realize that their goals are compatible, they are likely to develop more trust and arrive at a satisfactory solution. If they withhold too much information and mistrust each other, they go on thinking that they each need the entire orange (an incompatible goal) and engage in competitive behavior but don't meet their needs.

To run this exercise, you can simply divide the class in half and then pair them up in a somewhat random manner or you can systematically use observers (in which case, the class should be divided into trios). You should coach the observers while those playing Drs. Roland and Jones are preparing their role information. Privately instruct the observers to look for the following:

- How much disclosure is there on each side about (a) how many oranges they want, and (b) what they want to use the oranges for?
- Do the parties trust each other (the role play materials clearly encourage mistrust and suspicion)?
- How creative or complex is their "solution" (if they arrive at one)? Even pairs which learn that they need different parts of the orange still distrust one another sufficiently that they have to work out very complex agreements for transporting and sharing the oranges with each other!

Instruct the pairs that if they reach some agreement to keep it to themselves, to not let other groups overhear it! Often, when they discover that they need different parts of the orange, their enthusiasm leads them to clue in other pairs.

Stop the exercise after about 10 minutes. Usually at this point about 50 percent of the groups have reached a solution. In the discussion, focus first on those groups that have NOT solved the problem (try to keep the groups which have under control — they will be very enthusiastic about sharing their settlement publicly!)

You will find that all groups will reach agreement pretty quickly (15 or 20 minutes) if you let them. People realize they need different parts of the orange even faster than that. However, you will still see evidence of low trust behavior — extremely elaborate "holding companies" which will receive the oranges and use tight security procedures to ensure that each company gets its part of the oranges. On the other hand, high trust groups may simply agree to offer Mr. Cardoza the market price for ordinary oranges and have the oranges shipped first to Dr. Jones' company, where the juice will be removed. In other words, the game is not over if people discover they need different parts of the orange.

When the groups have finished negotiating (or when you have stopped them), post the information from each group under the following headings:

- Solution.
- Was there full disclosure? (What information was shared?)
- Did you trust each other? (Ask the members and observer.)
- Would you work with each other again? (How satisfied were you?)
- How creative (or complex) was the solution?

There is often an inverse relationship between trust and the creativity (or complexity) of the solution. The solution is often very creative (complex, wild, weird) when trust is low.

Alternatives and Variations

Check to see if this phenomenon occurs in your groups.

1. With the "group option" (Option 2), you will find that all of the dynamics described above are magnified. Because negotiators are bargaining in front of their "constituencies," they feel more pressure to be competitive, tough, unyielding, and not give in under pressure. As a result, they are much less likely to share relevant information, and much less likely to make

concessions which might gain an agreement but make them look weak to their team. One excellent variation to magnify this effect is to divide the class into both dyads and small groups — approximately half and half. The outcomes of the dyads can then be compared to the outcomes of the small groups, and inferences drawn for the impact of groups on negotiator behavior and cooperative outcomes.

2. In large groups (more than 35), you may not have the time for each group to individually report back to the total class. One option is for only some of the groups to report. Ask for volunteers to describe what happened in their groups, and solicit feedback from as many groups for which you have time. (If the group feedback takes too long, the rest of the class will get bored.)

3. Another option for large classes is to take a poll of the class with a show of hands for each issue. First ask a few observers to describe what happened in their group and use these descriptions as examples of high or low trust behavior and high or low disclosure. You might get at this by asking, "Did anyone see behavior indicating high trust in his group?" (hands will go up). "Can someone describe that high trust behavior?" Then ask for examples of low trust, then of high and low disclosure.

Next, fill out the following table by asking for a show of hands for the various cells. Start by asking how many groups had high or low disclosure. Then ask how many of the high disclosure groups had high trust, then how many would want to work together again or not, then how many had complex or simple solutions. Then ask how many of the low-disclosure groups experienced each of the other conditions. After all the numbers are posted, ask what conclusions people can draw from the table. Usually with high disclosure you will find high trust, high satisfaction, and low complexity.

Disclosure	Trust	Working Together Again?	Working Together Again?
High =	High =	Yes =	High =
High =	Low =	No =	Low =
Low =	High =	Yes =	High =
Low =	Low =	No =	Low =

Concluding the Exercise

A number of conflict models can be used to explain the different patterns of results achieved by pairs and groups. For example, Massengill (1979) has suggested that a two-dimensional model of distributive-integrative bargaining can be used to describe different levels of conflict. Another one is related to the five different types of conflict management proposed by Killman and Thomas (Thomas, 1976) — collaborative, competitive, compromising, avoiding and accommodating. Collaborative solutions would be ones in which the parties agreed to buy 3,000 and split the rinds to one party and the juice to the other. Compromising solutions would be ones in which they each agreed to take 1,500 oranges. Competitive-accommodating solutions would be ones in which one party got 2,000 and the other got 1,000 oranges, while competitive-competitive solutions would be no agreement on how to divide the oranges at all.

Specific concluding points regarding the discussion questions are as follows:

1. What is the relationship between trust and the disclosure of information? There is a mutual interaction between open disclosure of information and trust. Each can stimulate the other, just as closedness can stimulate mistrust. Thus, in many situations, as in this exercise, it is possible to observe trust cycles in which the trust level steadily increases or decreases.

2. In a bargaining situation such as this, before competing or collaborating with the other person, what should you do first? It is important to identify whether goals are compatible before deciding whether competition or cooperation is appropriate. We often tend to assume competition exists when it may not be appropriate.

3. How does mistrust affect the creativity or complexity of bargained agreements? Where trust is low, bargained agreements tend to be very complex, with elaborate controls, checks, and balances to ensure good faith and compliance. Under conditions of mistrust, dreaming up ingenious strategies to take advantage of the other person or to avoid being taken advantage of wastes much creative energy.

The Role for Dr. Jones

This is a negotiation simulation. In this simulation, you will play the role of Dr. Jones, representing your company in the negotiations. Your opponent will play the role of Dr. Roland, representing his company in the negotiations.

The session leader will play the role of Mr. Cardoza. Once you have read these instructions, he will give you further information.

You are Dr. J.W. Jones, a biological research scientist employed by a pharmaceutical firm. You have recently developed a synthetic chemical useful for curing and preventing Rudosen. Rudosen is a disease contracted by pregnant women. If not caught in the first four weeks of pregnancy, the disease causes serious brain, eye, and ear damage to the unborn child. Recently there has been an outbreak of Rudosen in your state, and several thousand women have contracted the disease. You have found, with volunteer patients, that your recently developed synthetic serum cures Rudosen in its early stages. Unfortunately, the serum is made from the Ugli orange, which is a very rare fruit. Only a small quantity (approximately 4,000) of these oranges were produced last season. No additional Ugli oranges will be available until next season, which will be too late to cure the present Rudosen victims.

You've demonstrated that your synthetic serum is in no way harmful to pregnant women. Consequently, there are no side effects. The Food and Drug Administration has approved of the production and distribution as a cure for Rudosen. Unfortunately the present outbreak was unexpected, and your firm had not planned on having the compound serum available for six months. Your firm holds the patent on the synthetic serum, and it is expected to be a highly profitable product when it is generally available to the public.

You have recently been informed on good evidence that Mr. R.H. Cardoza, a South American fruit exporter, is in possession of 3,000 Ugli oranges in good condition. You can provide sufficient inoculation for the remaining pregnant women in the state. No other state currently has a Rudosen threat.

You have recently been informed that Dr. P.W. Roland is also urgently seeking Ugli oranges and is also aware of Mr. Cardoza's possession of the 3,000 available. A competing pharmaceutical firm employs Dr. Roland. He has been working on biological warfare research for the past several years. There is a great deal of industrial espionage in the pharmaceutical industry. Over the past several years, Dr. Roland's firm and yours have sued each other several times for infringement of patent rights and espionage law violations.

You've been authorized by your firm to approach Mr. Cardoza to purchase 3,000 Ugli oranges. You have been told he will sell them to the highest bidder. Your firm has authorized you to bid as high as $250,000 to obtain the 3,000 available oranges.

Your instructor (Mr. Cardoza) will give you information on the amount of time you have to meet with the other. By the end of this meeting, you should be prepared to do one of the following:

- Submit an individual bid to Mr. Cardoza for the number of oranges you wish to buy, and the price you are willing to pay.
- Submit a joint bid with the other party specifying the number of oranges you wish to buy, the amount you are willing to pay, and how the fruit is to be delivered.

The Role for Dr. Roland

This is a negotiation simulation, in this simulation, you will play the role of Dr. Roland, representing your company in the negotiations. Your opponent will play the role of Dr. Jones, representing his company in the negotiations.

The session leader will play the role of Mr. Cardoza. Once you have read these instructions, he will give you further information.

You are Dr. P. W. Roland. You work as a research biologist for a pharmaceutical firm. The firm is under contract with the government to do research on methods to combat enemy uses of biological warfare.

Recently several World War II experimental nerve gas bombs were moved from the United States to a small island just off the U.S. coast in the Pacific. In the process of transporting them, two of the bombs developed a leak. Government scientists who believe that the gas will permeate the bomb chambers within two weeks presently control the leak. They know of no method of preventing the gas from getting into the atmosphere and spreading to other islands and very likely to the West Coast as well. If this occurs, it is likely that several thousand people will incur serious brain damage or die.

You've developed a synthetic vapor that will neutralize the nerve gas if it is injected into the bomb chamber before the gas leaks out. The vapor is made with a chemical taken from the Ugli orange, a very rare fruit. Unfortunately, only 4,000 of these oranges were produced this season.

You've been informed on good evidence that a Mr. R. H. Cardoza, a fruit exporter in South America, is in possession of 3,000 Ugli oranges. The chemicals from the rinds of all 3,000 oranges would be sufficient to neutralize the gas if the vapor is developed and injected efficiently. You have also been informed that these oranges are in good condition.

You have also been informed that Dr. J. W. Jones is also urgently seeking purchase of Ugli oranges, and he is aware of Mr. Cardoza's possession of the 3,000 available. Dr. Jones works for a firm with which your firm is highly competitive. There is a great deal of industrial espionage in the pharmaceutical industry. Over the years, your firm and Dr. Jones's have sued each other several times for violations of industrial espionage laws and infringement of parent rights. Litigation on two suits is still in process.

The federal government has asked your firm for assistance. You've been authorized by your firm to approach Mr. Cardoza to purchase 3,000 Ugli oranges. You have been told he will sell them to the highest bidder. Your firm has authorized you to bid as high as $250,000 to obtain the oranges.

Before approaching Mr. Cardoza, you have decided to talk to Dr. Jones to influence him so that he will not prevent you from purchasing the oranges.

Your instructor (Mr. Cardoza) will give you information on the amount of time you have to meet with the other. By the end of this meeting, you should be prepared to do one of the following:

- Submit an individual bid to Mr. Cardoza for the number of oranges you wish to buy, and the price you are willing to pay.
- Submit a joint bid with the other party, specifying the number of oranges you wish to buy, the amount you are willing to pay, and how the fruit is to be delivered.

EXERCISE 37: CONFLICT DIALOGUES

SUGGESTED CHAPTER		CROSS-REFERENCE AND INTEGRATION
15	Conflict and Innovation	conflict; communication; feedback; perception; stress

INSTRUCTOR'S NOTES

This exercise requires participants to recreate a portion of the dialogue from a conflict situation they experienced at work or at school and then to engage in a role play of the dialogue, with another group member playing the role of the other party to the conflict. The entire group then analyzes the dynamics of the conflict situation.

EXERCISE 38: FORCE-FIELD ANALYSIS

SUGGESTED CHAPTER		CROSS-REFERENCE AND INTEGRATION
16	Change, Innovation, and Stress	decision making; organizational structures, designs, cultures

INSTRUCTOR'S NOTES

This exercise is designed to help students improve their analytical skills for addressing complex situations and show them how force-field analysis can aid the understanding of change. It allows them to take a current problem or solution and reflect upon how it can be changed.

This exercise can be done in its entirety in class, or steps 1 through 5 inclusive can be assigned as homework and steps 6 and 7 can be done in class. In a large class, you may wish to choose a problem or situation and do the exercise with the class as a whole. Encourage students to brainstorm driving forces, thus bringing in other course concepts to this exercise.

EXERCISE 39: ORGANIZATIONS ALIVE!

SUGGESTED CHAPTER		CROSS-REFERENCE AND INTEGRATION
17	Organizing for Performance	organizational design and culture; performance management and rewards

INSTRUCTOR'S NOTES

This is a useful exercise to demonstrate to students that businesses are not always run in an ideal fashion. For example, although mission statements are very valuable, some organizations do not have a formal mission statement. Other organizations, large and small, spend considerable time formulating a mission statement and updating it periodically. Encourage your students to consider both for profit and not-for-profit organizations in collecting their material. Your students may be surprised to find out that many not-for-profit organizations maintain very well thought out mission statements, codes of ethics, organizational charts, and job descriptions.

One way to approach this exercise is to have the students turn in these management items as the concepts appear in the text. Class attendance improves on the days a managerial item is due.

This exercise has the advantage of drawing on the students' current employment and bringing the issues of management and organizational behavior close to home.

EXERCISE 40: FAST-FOOD TECHNOLOGY

SUGGESTED CHAPTER		CROSS-REFERENCE AND INTEGRATION
18	Organizational Design for Strategic Competency	organizational design; organizational culture; job design

INSTRUCTOR'S NOTES

This is a very rich exercise that provides students with the opportunity to integrate the knowledge that they have learned throughout this course, along with their other business courses. This should be administered near the end of the course. It might also be suitable as a group assignment that is graded.

As your students approach this exercise, encourage them to think in a holistic and integrative fashion. There are typically a number of variables that influence employee motivation and other aspects of organizational performance. Ask your students to attempt to evaluate each restaurant on several dimensions, including job design, organizational culture, employee motivation, information technology, and so on. Ask your students to carefully observe the behavior of each restaurant's employees. The final assessment that each group makes should be based on several factors, rather than just one or two. Be sure to emphasize to your students that in real organizations, effective managers typically adopt a similar integrative and holistic perspective.

EXERCISE 41: ALIEN INVASION

SUGGESTED CHAPTER		CROSS-REFERENCE AND INTEGRATION
19	Organizational Culture and Development	organizational structure and design; international; diversity and individual differences; perception and attribution

INSTRUCTOR'S NOTES

This is an innovative and fun exercise. Its main intention is to illustrate to your students the salience of organizational culture. Students may not have thought about organizational culture a lot. Through this exercise, you are able to drive home the point that people behave in certain ways because they are a part of a culture that has established norms, routines, and standards with regard to acceptable and unacceptable behavior.

It's fun to step back and consider: "What would a Martian think if the Martian had a chance to observe humans?" "How would a Martian characterize our behavior?" "Would we seem sensible in the way we go about our daily lives, or would we seem odd, confused, or unusual?" After your students have completed the exercise and pondered some of these questions, ask them if they now feel they are better prepared to assess the culture of an organization with which they are familiar.

EXERCISE 42: POWER CIRCLES EXERCISE

SUGGESTED CHAPTER		CROSS-REFERENCE AND INTEGRATION
19	Organizational Culture and Development	influence; power; leadership; change management

INSTRUCTOR'S NOTES

In this exercise, students assess the extent to which their instructor uses position power, expert power, and referent power in the classroom by allocating 100 percent among the three power options. The students also do this power allocation with respect to several special situations that might be encountered in the classroom, including changing the format of the final exam, adding a additional group assignment or course requirement, etc. The professor also does a self-assessment of his/her power usage. The students' and the professor's assessments are then shared and discussed.

The OB Skills Workbook
SELF-ASSESSMENT INVENTORIES

ASSESSMENT 1: MANAGERIAL ASSUMPTIONS

SUGGESTED CHAPTER	CROSS-REFERENCE AND INTEGRATION
1	Introducing Organizational Behavior	leadership

INSTRUCTOR'S NOTES

The key to this assessment is for students to recognize the implications of their scores, particularly with respect to their behavior toward subordinates. You may want to provide students with an opportunity to discuss their scores with the classmate sitting next to them or in groups, before opening the discussion up to the class as a whole. Either way, it's a good idea to tell students that their scores are for their own benefit and it is not necessary to divulge them unless they want to do so. For those students who do wish to share their scores, however, be sure to ask them why they answered as they did. What kind of experiences have they had which lead to their assumptions about people? How might their scores affect them in their roles as group members? Leaders? What would it take to change their assumptions?

Some students are likely to report mixed scores. These students will probably argue that their assumptions vary depending on the types of people they would be managing. This provides you with a good opportunity to discuss the contingency approach to management. In other words, you might argue that the validity of Theory X and Theory Y assumptions, and the consequent ability of this manager to delegate, depends upon the subordinates and the situation.

ASSESSMENT 2: A TWENTY-FIRST-CENTURY MANAGER

SUGGESTED CHAPTER	CROSS-REFERENCE AND INTEGRATION
1	Introducing Organizational Behavior	leadership; decision making; globalization
2	Current Issues in Organizational Behavior	

INSTRUCTOR'S NOTES

This is an excellent self-assessment instrument for students. It can be used effectively at any point during the semester (or term), but is perhaps the most effective during the early portion of the class. Urge each of your students to ask someone who knows them to complete the instrument based on their perceptions of the respective student. Students will be amazed at how much their self-perceptions differ from how other people view them. This might help students understand how managers can seem insensitive at times, without appearing like they even know it. The fact is, they might not know it. For example, an individual manager may believe that he or she is very caring, but the manager's employees may feel the opposite. This is an important reason why candid communication in an organization is so important.

ASSESSMENT 3: TURBULENCE TOLERANCE TEST

SUGGESTED CHAPTER		CROSS-REFERENCE AND INTEGRATION
1	Introducing Organizational Behavior	perception; individual differences;
2	Current Issues in Organizational Behavior	organizational change and stress

INSTRUCTOR'S NOTES

This is an interesting self-assessment. With the exception of item 7, most of your students will see all of these job characteristics as undesirable. What the assessment accomplishes is illustrating to your students the characteristics of a really stressful and turbulent job. Point out to your students that some people thrive in this type of setting. Most people, however, would burn out quite quickly and look for another job within the organization or a different company.

As an option, consider putting your students in teams to discuss their individual assessments. The teams could then appoint one student to report back to the class on their group discussion.

ASSESSMENT 4: GLOBAL READINESS INDEX

SUGGESTED CHAPTER		CROSS-REFERENCE AND INTEGRATION
3	Organizational Behavior Across Cultures	diversity; culture; leading; perception; management skills; career readiness

INSTRUCTOR'S NOTES

Through this self-assessment, students can reflect on their readiness to interact and work with persons from other cultures. A high score would suggest that they deem themselves to be well prepared for intercultural relations; a low score would reveal a need to better prepare themselves for the global workplace. Such insights can be very useful for students as they consider their preparedness for their careers, and identify areas for self-improvement.

ASSESSMENT 5: PERSONAL VALUES

SUGGESTED CHAPTER		CROSS-REFERENCE AND INTEGRATION
4	Diversity and Individual Differences	perception; diversity and individual differences; leadership

INSTRUCTOR'S NOTES

This assessment provides students with the opportunity to be introspective and reflect on the values that are most important to them. Stress to your students that at times, it is helpful for all of us to "step back" and examine whether our lives are being lived in a manner that is consistent with our personal values. Often, in our busy everyday lives, we lose sight of this "big picture." This assessment is designed to help a person bring into focus the values that are most important to him or her.

Remind your students that these types of assessments are particularly important when an individual is making an important decision in his or her life. For example, if a person is thinking about changing jobs, it might be helpful to complete this assessment based on the person's perception of what his or her life would be like after the job change. Self-assessments at these key times in a person's life can be an eye opener. For example, the new job may require a person to work 60 hours per week opposed to the current job that requires a standard 40 hours per week. The jump to 60 hours per week may not be a problem for someone who places a high value on professional and financial rewards. In contrast, the jump to 60 hours per week may be particularly worrisome to a person who places high value on family and social activities.

ASSESSMENT 6: INTOLERENCE FOR AMBIGUITY

SUGGESTED CHAPTER		CROSS-REFERENCE AND INTEGRATION
5	Perception and Attribution	perception; leadership

INSTRUCTOR'S NOTES

This is a straightforward assessment that is designed to help individuals determine their tolerance for ambiguity. Ask your students to follow the directions carefully, and rate every item. Tell your students to take their time and think through each question before making a rating. The students can then figure their tolerance for ambiguity score as described in the assessment.

This assessment provides an ideal springboard for talking about the important of maintaining a high tolerance for ambiguity in today's hectic business world.

ASSESSMENT 7: TWO-FACTOR PROFILE

SUGGESTED CHAPTER		CROSS-REFERENCE AND INTEGRATION
6	Motivation Theories	job design; perception; culture; human resource management

INSTRUCTOR'S NOTES

This is a straightforward assessment that should elicit a high degree of interest among your students. Administer the assessment before you talk about Herzberg's two-factor theory of motivation in class. Ask your students to hold on to their scores because you will be referring to them later. Discuss Herzberg's theory and then return to the self-assessment. Students may be surprised when they look over their assessments for a second time. Most of us are naturally predisposed to think that "motivator" factors are much more important to us than "hygiene" factors. Many students, however, may score high on the hygiene factor dimension. Ask your students to comment on the results of their self-assessments. Then discuss whether they think Herzberg's theory is valid.

ASSESSMENT 8: ARE YOU COSMOPOLITAN?

SUGGESTED CHAPTER		CROSS-REFERENCE AND INTEGRATION
7	Motivation and Job Design	diversity and individual differences; organizational culture
8	Performance Management and Rewards	

INSTRUCTOR'S NOTES

This is a somewhat esoteric, yet interesting self-assessment. The assessment is designed to help an individual determine the extent to which he or she is a "cosmopolitan" in terms of career orientation. *Webster's* defines a cosmopolitan as someone who "belongs to all parts of the world; having no local or national attachments." In an organizational setting, a cosmopolitan tends to be someone who has a stronger attachment to his or her profession, rather than the single organization that he or she works for.

ASSESSMENT 9: GROUP EFFECTIVENESS

SUGGESTED CHAPTER		CROSS-REFERENCE AND INTEGRATION
9	How Groups Work	organizational designs and cultures; leadership
10	Teamwork and Team Performance	

INSTRUCTOR'S NOTES

This is an excellent self-assessment for the members of an ongoing team or group. It is appropriate to use in an actual work setting or in the classroom if students are assigned to groups to complete exercises or other projects. Stress to your students that "group work" or "teamwork" is a growing trend in business organizations and one of the major management challenges of the future will be how to help employees function effectively in groups (or teams). Recommend to your students that they keep a copy of this assessment instrument, and use it throughout their careers to assess the effectiveness of the various groups in which they participate.

ASSESSMENT 10: LEAST PERFERRED COWORKER SCALE

SUGGESTED CHAPTER		CROSS-REFERENCE AND INTEGRATION
11	Leadership	diversity and individual differences; perception; group dynamics and teamwork

INSTRUCTOR'S NOTES

To conserve class time, consider assigning the LPC Scale as homework prior to the period in which you intend to discuss Fiedler's leadership theory. During your lecture on the theory, ask for a show of hands of students who scored as relationship-oriented, task-oriented, or somewhere in between. You may also want to ask students if they feel the LPC accurately measured their respective leadership styles. While many will believe that it has, at least a few will usually think otherwise. At this juncture, you can point out that critics of Fiedler's theory share the skepticism of these students. These critics contend that one's score on the LPC Scale is not necessarily indicative of leadership style. It is also important to note, however, that Fiedler has obtained empirical support for his theory. You can then present the following propositions regarding the situations in which Fiedler asserts that task- and relationships-oriented leaders are most effective.

Proposition No. 1	A task-oriented leader will be most successful in either very favorable (high control) or very unfavorable (low control) situations.
Proposition No. 2	A relationship-oriented leader will be most successful in situations of moderate control.

Based on these conclusions, Fiedler recommends that prospective leaders should actively seek situations that *match* their respective leadership styles. When a *mismatch* occurs, he asserts that leaders should first engage in *situational engineering;* this involves changing the situational characteristics to better match one's leadership style. Only as a last resort should they *change their leadership style* to match the situation; Fiedler believes this would be difficult because leadership style is strongly tied to personality factors that are hard to change.

ASSESSMENT 11: LEADERSHIP STYLE

SUGGESTED CHAPTER		**CROSS-REFERENCE AND INTEGRATION**
11	Leadership	diversity and individual differences; perception; group dynamics and teamwork

INSTRUCTOR'S NOTES

This is a fascinating self-assessment that helps individuals know whether their leadership style is more task oriented or people oriented. It is important that leaders have a keen awareness of their respective leadership styles. Individuals who have a keen awareness of their leadership style can self-select themselves out of situations where that leadership style may not be optimal, and can place themselves in situations where that leadership style would be ideal.

ASSESSMENT 12: "TT" LEADERSHIP STYLE

SUGGESTED CHAPTER		**CROSS-REFERENCE AND INTEGRATION**
11	Leadership	diversity and individual differences;
13	Information and Communication	perception; group dynamics and teamwork

INSTRUCTOR'S NOTES

This assessment can be used for two primary purposes. First, it illustrates one way of measuring the transactional and transformational styles of leadership. Accordingly, you could ask students to assess the instrument's accuracy in measuring their leadership style. Some students will undoubtedly report that they consider the results to be inaccurate. Follow up on these remarks by asking students why they think this inaccuracy occurred. You can then ask them to identify some of the challenges and limitations inherent in designing an instrument to measure leadership style. While it is important to address some attention to these issues, be careful not to give students the impression that leader style cannot be measured. Most of the class will probably agree with the results. Make sure that these persons express this agreement. You can then stress that while no measurement instrument is perfect and all are susceptible to certain biases, well designed measures can provide a good indication of leader style for most of the people, most of the time.

Once the limitations of the instrument are apparent, this assessment can be used for a second purpose — to provide students with some potential insights into their leadership style and its implications for their managerial careers. For persons who score as having transactional leadership tendencies, the major implications are that they may have a tendency to emphasize exchange relationships with others. That is, they may tend to view leadership as a process of providing rewards and desired outcomes to others in exchange for certain behaviors and levels of performance. Given this perspective, such leaders look for followers to uphold their end of the bargain; that is, to provide a level of contributions commensurate with the rewards they receive. They would not, however, ask followers to provide more than this level since there would be an imbalance in the exchange. Because of their vested interests, familiarity and comfort with the status quo, transactional leaders see their role in organizations as one of maintaining the system at a high level of efficiency and effectiveness. It is important to emphasize that persons with these tendencies are an important component of organizations. Indeed, one could view these leaders as the "backbone" of our social institutions.

Transformational leaders are a rather rare breed; they are charismatic individuals who possess vision and the ability to inspire others to contribute above and beyond the level at which they are expected to give. In essence, these leaders transform followers who in turn transform the organization into something new, and hopefully better, than it was before. A recent example of such an individual would be Lee Iacocca (the former CEO of Chrysler). Students who have tendencies toward transformational leadership may be highly successful at changing the status quo and eliciting unusually high levels of performance from followers. Such individuals should seriously consider pursuing careers that enable them to tap this potential.

Before leaving this exercise, you may want to again assure students that there is no right or wrong style; both are critical to organizational success. Transformational leadership may be more glamorous and unusual, but transactional leaders are a key component of any organization's long-term success.

ASSESSMENT 13: EMPOWERING OTHERS

SUGGESTED CHAPTER		CROSS-REFERENCE AND INTEGRATION
12	Power and Politics	leadership; perception and attribution
13	Information and Communication	

INSTRUCTOR'S NOTES

This assessment can serve as a useful tool for providing students with insight into their willingness to delegate, and hence their capability or tendency to empower others. Since delegation and empowerment are becoming increasingly important in the modern workplace, students who score as being reluctant to delegate should be made aware of the potential adverse consequences of such reluctance. To provide such students with some suggestions of overcoming their reluctance to delegate, share with them the following *guidelines on how to empower others:*

- Get others involved in selecting work assignments and the methods for accomplishing tasks.
- Create an environment of cooperation, information sharing, discussion, and shared ownership of goals.
- Encourage others to take initiative, make decisions, and use their knowledge.
- When problem arise, find out what others think and let them help design the solution.
- Stay out of the way; let others put their ideas and solutions into practice.
- Maintain high morale and confidence by recognizing successes and encouraging high performance.

ASSESSMENT 14: MACHIAVELLANISM

SUGGESTED CHAPTER		CROSS-REFERENCE AND INTEGRATION
12	Power and Politics	leadership; diversity and individual differences

INSTRUCTOR'S NOTES

This is a straightforward assessment that computes a person's Machiavellianism score. Remember, a high Machiavellianism personality is pragmatic, maintains emotional distance from others, and believes that the ends justify the means. Ask your students to complete the self-assessment and then compare it against their own self-perception of their Machiavellianism tendencies.

ASSESSMENT 15: PERSONAL POWER PROFILE

SUGGESTED CHAPTER		CROSS-REFERENCE AND INTEGRATION
12	Power and Politics	leadership; diversity and individual differences

INSTRUCTOR'S NOTES

This assessment provides a straightforward assessment of an individual's power profile. Most of us probably do not have a good sense of our personal power profile. As a result, this assessment can be very useful in helping individuals assess the type of power they prefer to employ.

Stress to your students that leaders typically need to modify their power strategies based on the situation at hand. As a result, if a person strongly favors a particular type of power, such as coercive power, he or she may inadvertently use this type of power in situations that do not lend themselves to the use of coercive power. Good managers, then, should try to recognize the type of power an individual situation calls for and, to the extent possible, make the appropriate adjustments.

ASSESSMENT 16: YOUR INTUITIVE ABILITY

SUGGESTED CHAPTER	CROSS-REFERENCE AND INTEGRATION
14	Decision Making	diversity and individual differences

INSTRUCTOR'S NOTES

According to Agor, students with high *intuitive scores* have the ability to base their decisions on unknowns and possibilities. They are capable of applying ingenuity to problems to see how best to prepare for the future, and can tackle difficulties with zest. They are also more likely to prefer management situations that are unstructured, fluid, and spontaneous. Indeed, they have the potential ability to function best in occupations that are characterized by crisis or rapid change and where they are asked to chart new, emerging trends from data including unknowns. Finally, they prefer to solve new and different problems versus the same or similar problems time after time.

Optional Questions for Class Discussion

1. Can intuition be developed? Explain.

2. What are the limitations of intuition? How can they be overcome?

3. What types of professions would best suit someone scoring high on intuition? Low?

ASSESSMENT 17: DECISION-MAKING BIASES

SUGGESTED CHAPTER	CROSS-REFERENCE AND INTEGRATION
14	Decision Making	teams and teamwork; communication; perception

INSTRUCTOR'S NOTES

There is no better way to teach students about judgmental heuristics than through experiential activities such as those provided in this assessment. Students can readily understand these biases when they witness themselves exhibiting them.

Question 1 deals with bias that derives from the availability heuristic. Many students will choose "b," believing that airplane travel is riskier. In fact, driving has the poorer safety record. The choice of flying is often tied to the way airplane crashes are sensationally reported in the media. Events, like airplane crashes, that are more vivid and easily remembered, make them more "available" in our memory. They tend to influence decision making through the availability bias.

Question 2 also deals with the <u>availability heuristic</u>. Most people will choose "a – words that begin with an 'r'." It is incorrect. The bias results as people try to solve the problem by remembering words — those that start with "r" — such as "rich," and those whose third letters are "r"— such as "first." Because it is easier to remember or list words that begin with "r" (with our minds sorting much as we do when reading a dictionary) this becomes the choice. Wrongly, we assume that because these words are more "available" in our memory they must be the most frequent in the language.

Question 3 deals with the <u>representativeness heuristic</u>. The tendency is to consider how "representative" the impression of Mark is vis-à-vis people who would typically be associated with careers in each field. Because there is information offered that Mark is a musician this tends to dominate the impression. Factually, MBAs tend toward management consulting work as job choices. The likelihood is that Mark, as an MBA graduate, would do the same. Unless theses data are considered and adequate consideration given to the "MBA" degree choice Mark had made, the apparent representativeness of his musical interests and an arts job will dominate the choice.

Question 4 also deals with the <u>representativeness heuristic</u>. In this example the issue is misconception of chance, with the first four events being misconstrued as "representative" of the fifth. The correct logic in the situation is "b" — "incorrect." The records of the first four sales directors have no impact on the performance record of the fifth. This is true even though our intuition would suggest otherwise. Many people will think that because there were "four bad ones in a row" that the chances of getting a "fifth bad one" are very low. This intuitive judgment is wrong, since the performance of the fifth is independent of the preceding records.

Question 5 deals with the anchoring and <u>adjustment heuristic</u>. Most people's answers to the question will be influenced by the chemist's estimate. This provides an "anchor" from which their individual judgments will be developed. The tendency is to adjust up or down from information already provided, even though that information may have little or no credibility. Decision bias tends to link estimates in such situations to the original "anchor," with moves from the anchor point often marginal rather than substantial

Reference: See Max H. Bazerman, *Judgment in Managerial Decision Making*, Second Edition (New York: John Wiley & Sons, 1990); see also, Fifth Edition (2002) for other examples and an expanded discussion of these judgmental heuristics.

ASSESSMENT 18: CONFLICT MANAGEMENT STYLES

SUGGESTED CHAPTER		CROSS-REFERENCE AND INTEGRATION
15	Conflict and Negotiation	diversity and individual differences; communication

INSTRUCTOR'S NOTES

You may want to supplement your discussion of conflict management styles with the following information on the circumstances under which each tends to be useful.

Competing is useful:

a.	When quick, decisive action is vital — *e.g.*, emergencies.
b.	On important issues where unpopular courses of action need implementing — *e.g.*, cost cutting, enforcing unpopular rules, discipline.
c.	On issues vital to company welfare when you know you're right.
d.	To protect yourself against people who take advantage of noncompetitive behavior.

Collaborating is useful:

a.	To find an integrative solution when both sets of concerns are too important to be compromised.
b.	When your objective is to learn — *e.g.*, testing your own assumptions, understanding the views of others.
c.	To merge insights from people with different perspectives on a problem.
d.	To gain commitment by incorporating others' concerns into a consensual decision.
e.	To work through hard feelings which have been interfering with an interpersonal relationship.

Compromising is useful:

a.	When goals are moderately important, but not worth the effort or potential disruption of more assertive modes.
b.	When two opponents with equal power are strongly committed to mutually exclusive goals — *e.g.*, labor-management bargaining.
c.	To achieve temporary settlements to complex issues.
d.	To arrive a expedient solution under time pressure.
e.	As a backup mode when collaboration or competition fails to be successful.

Avoiding is useful:

a.	When an issue is trivial, of only passing importance, or when other more important issues are pressing.
b.	When you perceive no chance of satisfying your concerns — *e.g.*, when you have low power or you are frustrated by something that would be very difficult to change (national policies, someone's personality structure, etc.).
c.	When the potential damage of confronting a conflict outweighs the benefits of its resolution.
d.	To let people cool down — to reduce tensions to a productive level and to regain perspective and composure.
e.	When gathering more information outweighs the advantages of an immediate decision.
f.	When others can resolve the conflict more effectively.
g.	When the issue seems tangential or symptomatic of another more basic issue.

Accommodating is useful:

a.	When you realize that you are wrong — to allow a better position to be heard, to learn from others, and to show that you are reasonable.
b.	When the issue is much more important to the other person than to yourself — to satisfy the needs of others, and as a goodwill gesture to help maintain a cooperative relationship.
c.	To build up social credits for later issues that are important to you.
d.	When continued competition would only damage your cause — when you are outmatched and losing.
e.	When preserving harmony and avoiding disruption are especially important.
f.	To aid in the managerial development of subordinates by allowing them to experiment and learn from their own mistakes.

ASSESSMENT 19: YOUR PERSONALITY TYPE

SUGGESTED CHAPTER		CROSS-REFERENCE AND INTEGRATION
16	Change, Innovation, and Stress	diversity and individual differences; job design

INSTRUCTOR'S NOTES

This assessment is designed to identify whether an individual has a Type A or a Type B personality profile (or a balanced mix of Type A or Type B). Ask your students to complete this self-assessment just prior to the class period where you intend to discuss personality types.

It is helpful for students to be introspective at times and get a good handle on their own personality makeup. This assessment can be very helpful in that regard.

ASSESSMENT 20: TIME MANAGEMENT PROFILE

SUGGESTED CHAPTER		CROSS-REFERENCE AND INTEGRATION
16	Change, Innovation, and Stress	diversity and individual differences

INSTRUCTOR'S NOTES

This assessment is intended to draw attention to the topic of time management, and help students determine if they manage their time in an effective manner. Suggest that your students study their answers compared to the optimal ones and to "try" manipulating their time management habits to conform to the optimal ones for one week to see if it improves their effectiveness.

Mention to your students that many managers engage in self-improvement activities. The activities are typically designed to improve efficiency and effectiveness. Self-assessment techniques like the one shown above are the first step in determining areas for improvement.

ASSESSMENT 21: ORGANIZATIONAL DESIGN PREFERENCE

SUGGESTED CHAPTER		CROSS-REFERENCE AND INTEGRATION
17	Organizing for Performance	job design; diversity and individual differences
18	Organizational Design for Strategic Competency	

INSTRUCTOR'S NOTES

By providing students with some personal insights into their organizational design preferences, this assessment can make the discussion of mechanistic and organic designs more relevant to them. Students, who have strong and definite preferences for one type of design or another, should probably not take a job in an organization with an opposite design. Instead, they should look for an organization where they will "fit" in better.

1.	What kinds of experiences are individuals with preferences for organic designs likely to have in mechanistic organizations? Can they be successful in this setting? If so, how? If not, why not?
2.	What kinds of experiences are individuals with preferences for mechanistic designs likely to have in organic firms? Can they be successful in this setting? If so, how? If not, why not?
3.	What, if anything, can organizations with mechanistic or organic designs do to help people with preferences for the alternative design configuration adjust to their job and work environment?

ASSESSMENT 22: WHICH CULTURE FITS YOU?

SUGGESTED CHAPTER		CROSS REFERENCE AND INTEGRATION
19	Organizational Culture and Development	perception; diversity and individual differences

INSTRUCTOR'S NOTES

This assessment illustrates the importance of person-culture fit. Often, people find themselves in jobs that "rub them the wrong way" because there is a lack of congruence between their personal values and norms and the organization's values and norms. Use this assessment to drive home the point to your students that person-culture fit is an extremely important issue. This issue is something that students should be thinking about when they select an employer. You may want to provide students with the following more detailed set of descriptions of the four organizational cultures.

1.	*Baseball teams* — which are entrepreneurial, place a high premium on talent and performance, and reward people very well financially when they produce. Commitment isn't as important as daily performance, and job-hopping from one "baseball team" to the next is fairly common. They are common in such areas as advertising, software development, and consulting.
2.	*Clubs* — which are driven by seniority, loyalty, commitment, and working for the good of the group. Moving quickly up the ladder doesn't happen; in the "club" you're supposed to work your way up. Who you know counts, and people are concerned about "fitting in." Career progress often means becoming more of a generalist by working across functions in different jobs.
3.	*Fortresses* — in which corporate survival is an overriding concern. These firms are struggling in competitive markets and can't promise much job security. What they do offer is the chance to participate in a "turn-around" and experience the sense of really making a difference.
4.	*Academies* — in which new hires are carefully moved through a series of training programs and a series of well-defined and specialized jobs. IBM is an "academy" that requires all managers to attend management training each year and carefully grooms fast trackers to become functional experts.

These descriptions provide some indication of the types of career experiences that students could expect after joining an organization with these cultures. The key thing, of course, is to try and achieve a good fit between individual desires and capabilities and what the culture may expect of the newcomer. Then, too, it should be remembered that cultures can and do change over time.

SAMPLE COURSE OUTLINES

SAMPLE WEEKLY SCHEDULE: ORGANIZATIONAL BEHAVIOR
Based on 15 Week Semester (Class Meets Twice a Week)

Date	Topic	Assigned Reading
Week 1 — Class 1	Course Introduction/Introducing Organizational Behavior	Chapter 1
Week 1 — Class 2	Introducing Organizational Behavior	Chapter 1
Week 2 — Class 1	Current Issues in Organizational Behavior	Chapter 2
Week 2 — Class 2	Organizational Behavior Across Cultures	Chapter 3
Week 3 — Class 1	Diversity and Individual Differences	Chapter 4
Week 3 — Class 2	Diversity and Individual Differences	Chapter 4
Week 4 — Class 1	Perception and Attribution	Chapter 5
Week 4 — Class 2	Perception and Attribution	Chapter 5
Week 5 — Class 1	Motivation Theories	Chapter 6
Week 5 — Class 2	Motivation Theories	Chapter 6
Week 6 — Class 1	Individual Exam 1	Chapters 1-6
Week 6 — Class 2	Motivation and Job Design	Chapter 7
Week 7 — Class 1	Performance Management and Rewards	Chapter 8
Week 7 — Class 2	Performance Management and Rewards	Chapter 8
Week 8 — Class 1	How Groups Work	Chapter 9
Week 8 — Class 2	Teamwork and Team Performance	Chapter 10
Week 9 — Class 1	Teamwork and Team Performance	Chapter 10
Week 9 — Class 2	Leadership	Chapter 11
Week 10 — Class 1	Leadership	Chapter 11
Week 10 — Class 2	Power and Politics	Chapter 12
Week 11 — Class 1	Individual Exam 2	Chapters 7-12
Week 11 — Class 2	Information and Communication	Chapter 13
Week 12 — Class 1	Decision Making	Chapter 14
Week 12 — Class 2	Decision Making	Chapter 14
Week 13 — Class 1	Conflict and Negotiation	Chapter 15
Week 13 — Class 2	Change, Innovation, and Stress	Chapter 16
Week 14 — Class 1	Organizing for Performance	Chapter 17
Week 14 — Class 2	Organizational Design for Strategic Competency	Chapter 18
Week 15 — Class 1	Organizational Design for Strategic Competency	Chapter 18
Week 15 — Class 2	Organizational Culture and Development	Chapter 19
Final Exam	Administered During Finals Week	Chapters 13-19 or comprehensive

SAMPLE WEEKLY SCHEDULE: ORGANIZATIONAL BEHAVIOR
Based on 15 Week Semester (Class Meets Once a Week)

Date	Topic	Assigned Reading
Week 1	Course Introduction/Introducing Organizational Behavior	Chapter 1
Week 2	Current Issues in Organizational Behavior Organizational Behavior Across Cultures	Chapter 2 Chapter 3
Week 3	Diversity and Individual Differences	Chapter 4
Week 4	Perception and Attribution	Chapter 5
Week 5	Motivation Theories	Chapter 6
Week 6	Individual Exam 1 Motivation and Job Design	Chapters 1-6 Chapter 7
Week 7	Performance Management and Rewards	Chapter 8
Week 8	How Groups Work Teamwork and Team Performance	Chapter 9 Chapter 10
Week 9	Teamwork and Team Performance Leadership	Chapter 10 Chapter 11
Week 10	Leadership Power and Politics	Chapter 11 Chapter 12
Week 11	Individual Exam 2 Information and Communication	Chapters 7-12 Chapter 13
Week 12	Decision Making	Chapter 14
Week 13	Conflict and Negotiation Change, Innovation, and Stress	Chapter 15 Chapter 16
Week 14	Organizing for Performance Organizational Design for Strategic Competency	Chapter 17 Chapter 18
Week 15	Organizational Design for Strategic Competency Organizational Culture and Development	Chapter 18 Chapter 19
Final Exam	Administered During Finals Week	Chapters 13-19 or comprehensive

STUDENT AND INSTRUCTOR RESOURCES

This portion of the *Instructor's Resource Guide* (*IRG*) contains resources that may be helpful to you and your students throughout the course of the semester (term). You can reproduce these resources directly from the IRG or modify them to fit your individual circumstances.

STUDENT RESOURCES

The student resources includes three lists of resources that will be helpful to students as they study organizational behavior. These resources include the following:

- List of Useful Periodicals.

- Company Information.

- Career Resources of Interest to Business Students.

LIST OF USEFUL PERIODICALS

Trade Journals

These are oriented primarily toward practitioners.

> Academy of Management Executive
> Across the Board
> Advanced Management Journal
> American Management Association Research Reports
> Business Horizons
> Business and Society Review
> California Management Review
> Canadian Business
> Columbia Journal of World Business
> Dun's Review
> Fortune
> Futurist
> Harvard Business Review
> Industry Week
> Journal of Contemporary Business
> Journal of Long Range Planning
> Management International Review
> Management Record
> Management Review

Managerial Planning
Monthly Labor Review
Nation's Business
Organizational Dynamics
Personnel
Personnel Administrator
Personnel Journal
Personnel Series
Production and Inventory Management
Psychology Today
Public Administration Review
Public Personnel Management
SAM Advanced Management Journal
Sloan Management Review
Social Science Reporter
Supervision
Supervisory Management
Training and Development Journal

Scholarly Journals

These are oriented primarily towards the academician or specialist.

Academy of Management Journal
Academy of Management Review
Administrative Science Quarterly
American Journal of Sociology
American Political Science Review
American Sociological Review
Behavioral Science
Decision Sciences
Group and Organization Management
Human Organization
Human Relations
Human Resource Management
Industrial and Labor Relations Review
Industrial Relations
International Studies of Management and Organization
Journal of Applied Behavioral Sciences
Journal of Applied Psychology
Journal of Applied Social Psychology
Journal of Business
Journal of Business Ethics
Journal of Business Research
Journal of Business Strategy
Journal of Conflict Resolution
Journal of Management Studies
Journal of Small Business Management
Journal of Vocational Behavior
Management Science
Occupation Psychology
Operational Research Quarterly
Operating Research
Organization and Administrative Sciences

Personnel Management
Personnel Psychology
Psychological Bulletin
Public Administration Review
Sociology
Sociometry
Strategic Management Journal

Abstracting Services

These are useful for finding relevant material in journals and books.

Business Periodicals Index
Employment Relations Abstracts
Management Abstracts
Management Research
Personnel Management Abstracts
Psychological Abstracts
Sociological Abstracts
Wall Street Journal Index

COMPANY INFORMATION

Web Site	Web Site Address
Annual Reports Online	http://www.zpub.com/sf/arl/arl-www.html
Annual Reprint Service	http://www.annualreportservice.com/
BRINT — BizTech Network	http://www.brint.com/
Business Wire	http://www.businesswire.com/
PR Newswire	http://www.prnewswire.com/
Web 100: Big Businesses on the Web	http://www.metamoney.com/w100/

CAREER RESOURCES OF INTEREST TO BUSINESS STUDENTS

Career Builder	http://careerbuilder.com
Career Magazine	http://www.careermag.com/
Career Shop	http://www.careershop.com/
Career Site	http://www.careersite.com/
Employment Guide	http://www.employmentguide.com
Job Bank USA	http://www.jobbankusa.com/
Monster	http://www.monster.com
National Job Network	http://www.nationjob.com/

INSTRUCTOR RESOURCES

This section includes several different sample forms that may be useful with respect to administering different student assignments. Each form is on a separate page so that it can easily be photocopied and duplicated. On the following pages you will find:

- Sample Peer Evaluation Form: Option 1.

- Sample Peer Evaluation Form: Option 2.

- Sample Project Approval Form.

- Sample Library Term Paper Assignment Requirements.

- Sample Term Paper Grading Sheet: Option 1.

- Sample Term Paper Grading Sheet: Option 2.

- Sample Case Study Assignment Form.

- Sample Case Study Grading Sheet.

SAMPLE PEER EVALUATION FORM: OPTION 1

Peer Evaluation

Course Number _____

Semester and Year _____

Name _____

Group Number _____

Peer evaluations provide you an opportunity to assess the individual performance of your team members. Your peer evaluations should be based upon an assessment of each team members' contribution to the overall effectiveness of the team. You <u>do not</u> provide an assessment of your own performance.

Instructions:

Please provide the information requested below and rate each of your team members. You are to provide each team member points ranging from 0 to 10 (0 = low and 10 = high).

Names of Team Members: Score (out of 10)   Points out of 10

_____   _____

_____   _____

_____   _____

_____   _____

_____   _____

_____   _____

SAMPLE PEER EVALUATION FORM: OPTION 2

Peer Evaluation

Course Number _____

Semester and Year _____

Group Number _____

Rank order each of the members of your group except yourself on each of the items below (1 is best, 2 is next best, etc.).

Evaluation Attributes	Group Members					
	A	B	C	D	E	F
Quality of contribution to group discussions.						
Quality of contribution to writing the assignments.						
Quality of contribution to organizing assignments.						
Quality of initiative when things needed to be done.						
Reliability in completing assigned responsibilities.						
Amount of effort put forth.						
Commitment to the group.						
Leadership, inspiration provided to the group.						
Emphasis on task functions.						
Emphasis on relationship functions.						
Would want to work with again.						

Group Members: A _____

B _____

C _____

D _____

E _____

F _____

SAMPLE PROJECT APPROVAL FORM

Project Approval Form

Title of Project _____

Your Name _____

I. In about one-half page, summarize the major direction that you plan to take in the project. If it is a case briefly, summarize the problem(s) and give an idea of important background material. If the project is a term paper or research paper, indicate as specifically as possible the topic area, direction, and importance of the topic to organizational behavior. Attach the completed approval to the final draft of your project when you turn it in to the instructor.

II. If the project is a term paper, list below (in correct form) at least six references representative of those you plan to use.

Instructor comments:

_____

_____

_____

_____

_____

_____

_____

_____

_____

_____

Instructor signature of approval _____

Date of approval _____

SAMPLE LIBRARY TERM PAPER ASSIGNMENT REQUIREMENTS

Library Term Paper Assignment

1.	The term paper should include: • A title page. • A statement of purpose page, including a description of the project and an assessment of its importance to managers. • The term paper itself, including a summary or conclusion that indicates possible solutions to the problem you are investigating. • A bibliography.
2.	The term paper itself should be as thorough as possible. You should not confine your search for information to the Internet, but should use material available in the library as well as the Internet. Be sure to cite Web sites consistent with APA guidelines. Your research should include academic journals along with practitioner journals.
3.	All papers are due by _____. Papers may be submitted any time prior to the due date. You must have the instructor's signed approval before proceeding with this paper. Submit the completed and signed "Project Approval Form" along with the paper on the due date.
4.	Your paper should be typewritten, double-spaced, and follow standard report writing procedures. Just as in the business world, spelling, grammar, and the general appearance of the paper count. Ask your instructor if you have any questions about the format of the paper.
5.	The "Term Paper Grading Sheet" should be turned in along with your paper on the due date. Complete the "my rating" column and Question 7, when the Option 1 form is used. The instructor will complete the rest and return it to you as feedback.

SAMPLE TERM PAPER GRADING SHEET: OPTION 1

TERM PAPER GRADING SHEET

Title of Paper:

Name:	**Group Number:**

Grade (A+ to F-)

	A+	A	A-	B+	B	B-	C+	C	C-	D+	D	D-	F+	F	F-
Points	97	93	90	87	83	80	77	73	70	67	63	60	57	53	50

RATING CRITERIA	MY RATING	INSTRUCTOR'S RATING
1. Adequacy of statement and development of the problem.		
2. Adequacy of discussion of managerial implications.		
3. Adequacy of conclusions concerning the problem.		
4. Adequacy of literature utilized.		

5. Following acceptable report writing procedures.
    Format _____
 	
    References _____		

6. Style: grammar, spelling, typing errors, etc.		
7. Overall, how willing would I be to turn this report in to my boss if this were a "real world" assignment?		

Extremely Extremely Likely Unlikely	Quite Likely	Slightly Likely	Slightly Unlikely	Quite Unlikely

Overall Grade:

GENERAL COMMENTS:

SAMPLE TERM PAPER GRADING SHEET: OPTION 2

TERM PAPER GRADING SHEET

Title of Paper:

Name: | **Group Number:**

Grade (A+ to F-)

	A+	A	A-	B+	B	B-	C+	C	C-	D+	D	D-	F+	F	F-
Points	97	93	90	87	83	80	77	73	70	67	63	60	57	53	50

	Low High				
1. Adequacy of statement and development of problem.	1	2	3	4	5
2. Adequacy of discussion of managerial implication.	1	2	3	4	5
3. Adequacy of conclusions concerning the problem.	1	2	3	4	5
4. Adequacy of literature utilized.	1	2	3	4	5
5. Following acceptable report writing procedures.	1	2	3	4	5
6. Style: grammar, spelling, typing errors, etc.	1	2	3	4	5

Overall Grade:

GENERAL COMMENTS:

SAMPLE CASE STUDY ASSIGNMENT FORM

**Case Study Assignment for
Cases from *The OB Skills Workbook***

1.	Select a case from the textbook. Clear your case with the instructor, either after class or via e-mail. Case selections are on a first-come/first-serve basis. No more than three students can have the same case.
2.	Read the case at least twice to absorb the relevant information.
3.	Write a 350-word summary of the case (which is approximately one full page, double-spaced and typewritten).
4.	Answer the review questions at the conclusion of the case. You should answer each question thoughtfully and completely.
5.	Write a short summary of what managers can learn from the case (approximately 350 words typewritten. Make the summary as substantive as possible.
6.	The paper is due on _____.
7.	Your paper should be typewritten, double-spaced, and follow standard report writing procedures. Just as in the business world, spelling, grammar, and the general appearance of the paper count. Ask your instructor if you have any questions about the format of the paper.

SAMPLE CASE STUDY GRADING SHEET

<table>
<tr><td colspan="6" align="center">**CASE STUDY GRADING SHEET**</td></tr>
<tr><td colspan="6">**Title of Case Study:**</td></tr>
<tr><td colspan="6">**Name:**</td></tr>
<tr><td colspan="6">

Grade (A+ to F-)

	A+	A	A-	B+	B	B-	C+	C	C-	D+	D	D-	F+	F	F-
Points	97	93	90	87	83	80	77	73	70	67	63	60	57	53	50

</td></tr>
<tr><td></td><td>*Low*
High</td><td></td><td></td><td></td><td></td></tr>
<tr><td>1. Summary of the case.</td><td>1</td><td>2</td><td>3</td><td>4</td><td>5</td></tr>
<tr><td>2. Answers to review questions.</td><td>1</td><td>2</td><td>3</td><td>4</td><td>5</td></tr>
<tr><td>3. Summary of what managers can learn from the case.</td><td>1</td><td>2</td><td>3</td><td>4</td><td>5</td></tr>
<tr><td>4. Style: grammar, spelling, typing errors, etc.</td><td>1</td><td>2</td><td>3</td><td>4</td><td>5</td></tr>
<tr><td colspan="6">**Overall Grade:**</td></tr>
<tr><td colspan="6">

GENERAL COMMENTS:

</td></tr>
</table>

ORGANIZATIONAL BEHAVIOR LECTURE LAUNCHER VIDEOS

Supplied by: Joan R. Rentsch

INTRODUCTION TO THE INSTRUCTOR

The video clips for the *Organizational Behavior Lecture Launcher Videos* were selected to complement the text. In these clips, real CEOs, professors, and workers offer their opinions, expertise, and perspectives on various topics within organizational behavior. The representation of organizations and individuals in the clips is international and diverse. For some chapters, a lecture/group activity is included. Typically, these activities are designed to give students an opportunity to discuss a topic from the chapter in a group setting enabling them to explore their own experiences with the topic. The discussion questions are aimed at encouraging students to think systemically about organizations. For the later chapters, the questions are aimed at giving students the opportunity to integrate what they have learned throughout the course.

For each chapter, an overview of the video clip is presented first, followed by the activity, and then the discussion questions. However, you may find it to be more effective to integrate these pieces into the lecture in a different order. In addition, you will likely find that many video clips will be useful in discussing more than one topic or chapter.

Joan R. Rentsch
Knoxville, Tennessee

PART 1: ORGANIZATIONAL BEHAVIOR TODAY

CHAPTER 1: INTRODUCING ORGANIZATIONAL BEHAVIOR

Clip Source

The View from the Top: Boeing Reinvents the Airplane

Clip Title

OB at Boeing

Video Clip Overview

Boeing's President, Philip Condit, discusses the importance of human resources, motivation, change, teamwork, and innovation in organizational performance. He focuses on the integration of people and functions (*e.g.*, organizational design) in building the Boeing 777. This clip provides a perspective that will help students to see why the topics to be discussed in an organizational behavior class are important to organizational functioning. This clip offers a nice example of how all topics in organizational behavior are interrelated, providing a good opportunity to discuss the systemic nature of organizations.

Lecture/Group Activity

Ask students to get together in groups to discuss their own experiences in work organizations (or with any organization, if they have not worked). They should focus on an organization that was functioning properly and/or one that was functioning improperly. Use their answers to direct a discussion around the systemic nature of organizations and to discuss how understanding organizational behavior is NOT obvious.

Discussion Questions

1. What are the major topics that Condit discussed? How are these topics related to organizational functioning and to each other?

2. How does the type of people hired affect how an organization can be designed or changed?

3. What are the relationships between teams, organizational design, selection, training, and leadership?

CHAPTER 2: CURRENT ISSUES IN ORGANIZATIONAL BEHAVIOR

Clip Source

Ethics in Corporate America

Clip Title

Business Ethics in America

Video Clip Overview

This clip provides an overview of the ethical problems in corporate America. It begins by showing business students at a "scared straight" lecture. Then, Barbara Toffler describes her perceptions of the ethical breaches of Arthur Andersen and of Stewart Leonard, Sr., owner of a discount dairy chain. This clip closes with the outrageous contrast of Leonard touting his pride in his own upstanding business behavior with the facts of his unethical business behavior and prison sentence. Love of money as the root of all evil is emphasized.

Lecture/Group Activity

Present a case study of Arthur Andersen, Enron, or of a company nearest you that has had an ethical breach. Alternatively, present a case of a company that has maintained high ethical standards and has seen the payoff of doing so. A positive example might aid students in avoiding any temptation they may encounter in the future.

Discussion Questions

1. What are some characteristics of business ethics?

2. How are business ethics the same or different from "regular" ethics?

3. How likely it is that most corporate executives would violate ethical codes, just because they could?

4. What would motivate someone to behave ethically in business?

5. Suppose you could acquire $35 million if you cheated your co-workers. If you thought you could get away with it, would you cheat your co-workers?

CHAPTER 3: ORGANIZATIONAL BEHAVIOR ACROSS CULTURES

Clip Source

Your Cultural Passport to International Business

Clip Title

Cultural Differences

Video Clip Overview

This clip provides several examples of differences in cultures across the globe. The examples focus on appropriate topics of conversation and the meaning of body language in different cultures. Two powerful messages are: "talk less and listen more," and "read beyond the words."

Discussion Questions

1. In what other areas might cultural differences exist (*e.g.*, food, clothing, greetings)?

2. How should one prepare for conducting international business?

3. Please explain any experiences you might have with cultural differences. What would have helped in the situation?

PART 2: INDIVIDUAL BEHAVIOR AND PERFORMANCE

CHAPTER 4: DIVERSITY AND INDIVIDUAL DIFFERENCES

Clip Source

Helping New Employees Feel Valued

Clip Title

Diversity in the Workplace

Video Clip Overview

The clip provides an example of ineffective appreciation of individual differences. Marty, a black woman, started a new job and did not receive assistance from her supervisor (white male) or her co-workers. In addition, her supervisor and co-worker questioned her competence. The clip also provides a positive example of how to help a new employee and how to be sensitive to individual differences.

Lecture/Group Activity

Have students give examples of when they were treated properly and/or improperly. Emphasize that the visible individual differences of race, age, and sex are not the only individual differences that are important. All people are individuals and should be treated as such.

Discussion Questions

1. What did the boss do correctly and what did he do incorrectly in dealing with Marty?

2. How can people in work organizations be more sensitive to each other's differences?

CHAPTER 5: PERCEPTION AND ATTRIBUTION

Clip Source

The Power of Honesty

Clip Title

Creating a Bad Impression

Video Clip Overview

The clip provides an example of creating a bad impression. A salesman is just about to make a sale, when he completely turns off the customer by giving her the impression that he is not honest.

Lecture/Group Activity

Have students analyze the clip to determine what the salesman did wrong. Engage them in a discussion of eye contact, stereotypes, impression management, and the perception process.

Discussion Questions

1. What are the keys to creating a good impression?

2. What can happen to cause people to be misperceived (*e.g.*, how can an honest person be perceived as dishonest)?

CHAPTER 6: MOTIVATION THEORIES

Clip Source

Betting on the Workers: Harman International

Clip Title

Motivation at Harman International

Video Clip Overview

Sidney Harman is the chairman of Harman International, which makes high tech, high quality audio systems such as JBL and Infinity Audio Systems. Sidney discusses worker motivation and commitment to workers. Specifically, he talks about offering workers high levels of job security, which he sees as leading to highly motivated and committed workers. He refers to this as a "good business deal." In the second portion of the clip, he describes what he refers to as his "cost-saving sharing" program in which workers are encouraged to offer ideas to cut company costs. As part of this program, any savings achieved by the company are shared with the employees (60 percent to the company and 40 percent to the workers). This clip provides a nice starting point for discussions on such motivation theories as equity, expectancy, need, and behavioral.

Lecture/Group Activity

Working in groups, have students address the following questions: How are you motivated? What do you do to get yourself to complete a difficult task? Discuss with the class as a whole how the students' personal experiences with motivation link to motivational theories.

Discussion Questions

1. What theory of motivation is Sidney Harman applying?

2. Is it cheaper to pay workers more or to pay them less? What are the advantages of each strategy in terms of motivation theories?

3. How would you motivate workers? (Smart workers, motivated workers, lazy workers?)

4. How do you know what motivates someone?

CHAPTER 7: MOTIVATION AND JOB DESIGN

Clip Sources

BMW Portrait of a Business Giant
The View from the Top: An Obsession with Quality

Clip Title

Motivation and Job Design at BMW and Motorola

Video Clip Overview

This clip contains two sections. In the first section, executives and workers of BMW describe one method for utilizing the maximum capacity of a new factory. Specifically, in order to run the factory as much as possible workers work six or four days per week. Two workers react to their new schedules indicating both positive and negative effects of the schedules on their lives. In addition, BMW Chairman, Bernd Pischetssrieder, describes how all employees' jobs are changing in such a way as to require everyone at BMW to take on more responsibility. In the second section, George M.C. Fisher, CEO of Eastman Kodak, talks about his experience as CEO at Motorola (1990-1993) and his focus on quality. He speaks of employees striving to be the best, and how using what he calls "reach out goals" can help people to achieve.

Lecture/Group Activity

Have groups of students: (1) describe jobs they most liked/enjoyed and jobs they disliked; (2) create a list of descriptors of both types of jobs; and (3) narrow their list to the top five features of good jobs. Then lead a discussion of job characteristics and job design.

Discussion Questions

1. What are the implications for selection and training when companies change the level of responsibility required by jobs?

2. What difference does it make how many and which hours employees work?

3. Are all people motivated to be "the best"? If not, what can a manager do to motivate those who do not wish to be the best?

4. What are the psychological consequences of reaching or of not reaching a goal? Can goals have a negative effect on workers

CHAPTER 8: PERFORMANCE MANAGEMENT AND REWARDS

Clip Source

The View from the Top: An Obsession with Quality

Clip Title

Managing Performance at Motorola

Video Clip Overview

George M.C. Fisher, CEO of Eastman Kodak, talks about his experience as CEO at Motorola (1990-1993) and his focus on employees as assets. Indeed, he refers to employees as cherished assets who are with the company for a very long time. He notes that they must be retrained throughout their careers. He claims that training is one of Motorola's competitive edges. He cites training as an investment and a tool to change the culture of the organization. In the last portion of the clip, Fisher discusses the need to train basic skills, which costs the organization approximately $200 million in training development and time. He views this as an investment rather than as a cost.

Lecture/Group Activity

Let students get into groups to discuss how they intend to maintain their competitive advantage in the workplace. How do they intend to continuously improve their skill sets? Do they expect that they can count on a company to help them? What if they cannot count on their company to train them?

Discussion Questions

1. Is training a reward? Why or why not?

2. How does a company justify the enormous expense of training? Should training be evaluated?

3. In addition to teaching workers basic skills, what other benefits might an organization reap from developing high quality training programs?

PART 3: GROUP DYNAMICS AND TEAMWORK

CHAPTER 9: HOW GROUPS WORK
CHAPTER 10: TEAMWORK AND TEAM PERFORMANCE

Clip Source

All for One: Team Building in Action

Clip Title

Team Building

Video Clip Overview

A company is trying to build teams into its organizational structure. The team approach is very new for the organization. Fortunately, team members are eager to learn how to work together as a team. An expert provides an overview of team building to organizational members. For example, he suggests that the process of teambuilding requires: a shared vision, passing work around, allowing each other enough time, depending on one another, and sharing the glory. He urges team members to keep in mind that: all members have equal input, each member is entitled to free expression, each member must take a role in leadership, the team must reach consensus without being forced, trust is essential to good team building, and, above all, team members should be flexible. One of the most important points made is that team building is a *process* and should be expected to take time.

Lecture/Group Activity

Have students think about a time when they worked (or played) on a team, but the experience was not a good one. Ask the students to list some of the problems with that team. Put the students into groups so that they can share their negative experiences and discuss what could have been done to make the experience positive.

Discussion Questions

1. What is a group? What is a team? Describe the characteristics of different types of teams. Why is it important to be aware of these characteristics?

2. What should a team know?

3. Is it a waste of time for team members to spend time talking about team building? (Think about what was presented in the video.)

PART 4: LEADERSHIP AND ORGANIZATION DYNAMICS

CHAPTER 11: LEADERSHIP

Clip Source

A Report from Harvard Business School: Leadership

Clip Title

Leadership

Video Clip Overview

John Kotter, Harvard Business School Professor, discusses his perspective on leadership. He emphasizes the notion that organizations need leadership through all levels of the organization and that work through a common vision. In his opinion, the essence of leadership is to strategize, inspire, and motivate. Kotter describes Matsushita, Jack Welsh, and Sam Walton as excellent leaders. Each of them had the profound ability to create vision and to inspire followers. In addition, Kotter provides pointers for how individuals may engage in leadership behaviors by learning to think ahead and to have vision for their areas of work responsibility. Overall, Kotter's perspective will aid in a discussion of the systemic nature of organizations by highlighting linkages between such topics as leadership, organizational structure, organization change, motivation, and selection.

Lecture/Group Activity

Let students works in groups to discover what they believe are the most difficult leadership skills to develop. Have them list the top three skills.

Discussion Questions

1. What is leadership?

2. Who are leaders that you respect? What characteristics cause you to respect them?

3. What can you do to become a better leader in your current job?

CHAPTER 12: POWER AND POLITICS

Clip Source

Labor's Man on the Board

Clip Title

Power and Politics at Northwest Airlines

Video Clip Overview

Duane Woerth is the Director of Northwest Airlines and he represents labor at Northwest. He describes how he (and labor, in general) has gained power. At a time when Northwest experienced financial difficulty, Woerth, a pilot, worked with the labor leaders to negotiate a deal with the airline in which labor offered the company $900 million in concessions in exchange, in part, for 30 percent of the company and three board seats. Woerth states that without the board seats, labor would not have the power it needed. He discusses the issue of potential ethical and political conflicts associated with representing labor while simultaneously performing his role as a board member. For example, he participates in negotiations related to his boss's (John Dasburg, CEO) salary and vice versa (the CEO, John Dasburg is involved in negotiations about Woerth's salary.)

Lecture/Group Activity

Have the class generate specific ethical conflicts that Woerth and Dasburg may encounter and how they should address the ethical conflicts.

Discussion Questions

1. How did the employees at Northwest Airlines change their position power? What effect did this change have on the organization?

2. What are the ethical issues associated with the new alignment of power?

3. What are the keys of employee power at Northwest Airlines? At other organizations?

CHAPTER 13: INFORMATION AND COMMUNICATION

Clip Source

Communication Skills

Clip Title

Developing Communication Skills

Video Clip Overview

This clip gives students reasons for wanting to learn about communication. A diverse group of individuals describes why communication is important to their jobs and to their credibility. The effect of good communication in organizations is described. The issue of time and the need to recognize individual differences is emphasized.

Lecture/Group Activity

Have the students describe a time when they were working with someone who was an exceptionally effective communicator. How did the effective communication affect the situation? What was good about the communication? How did they feel in this situation?

Discussion Questions

1. What are the features of effective communication?

2. What are some barriers to communication?

3. Given earlier discussions regarding individual differences, leadership, power, and teams, describe how communication is relevant to these topics?

CHAPTER 14: DECISION MAKING

Clip Source

Achieving Competitive Advantage: Managing for Organizational Effectiveness
The Deep Dive: One Company's Secret Weapon for Innovation

Clip Title

Decision Making in Organizations

Video Clip Overview

This clip contains two sections. In the first section, Michael Useem, a professor of management and sociology at The Wharton School, suggests a number of mechanisms that enable decision makers (and therefore organizations) to process enormous amounts of information in order to make effective decisions. Using the Apollo 13 episode to illustrate his points, Useem discusses autocratic decision making, group problem solving, decentralization, and empowerment. In the second section, IDEO's "deep dive" process for group problem solving and innovation is demonstrated. The group is tasked with redesigning a shopping cart in five days. IDEO's decision-making process leads to innovation. he process involves team decision making and autocratic decision making.

Lecture/Group Activity

Have groups decide whether the class should be required to take the next exam in groups or as individuals. Discuss their conclusions by focusing on the how they framed the examination (as an information overload problem, as a difficult problem to solved using several individual's perspectives) and the process by which they reached their conclusions.

Discussion Questions

1.   When is it more reasonable to make an autocratic decision rather than a group decision?

2.   When is it more reasonable to make a group decision rather than an autocratic decision?

3.   What are the characteristics of effective decisions?

CHAPTER 15: CONFLICT AND NEGOTIATION

Clip Source

Conflict Resolution

Clip Title

Resolving Conflict

Video Clip Overview

This clip helps students learn the keys to collaboration as a means of resolving conflict. Several people describe their experiences in dealing with conflict. Follow-up, etiquette, and emotional control are emphasized.

Lecture/Group Activity

Let students work in groups to discuss times when they were in conflict situations and they and/or the other party were extremely effective in initiating a constructive or collaborative solution. What did they learn from the experiences that will help them to resolve conflicts in the workplace?

Discussion Questions

1. When is conflict dysfunctional and when it is functional?

2. What are the steps to using collaboration to resolve conflict?

3. What is the most important element in dealing with conflict?

CHAPTER 16: CHANGE, INNOVATION, AND STRESS

Clip Source

The Deep Dive: One Company's Secret Weapon for Innovation

Clip Title

Innovation at IDEO

Video Clip Overview

IDEO is tasked with redesigning a shopping cart in five days. The clip shows the process by which the design team creates an innovative solution. IDEO's decision-making process leads to innovation. The team is diverse in its membership, its members have no titles and no permanent assignments, and all members work together. The team collects information regarding shopping carts in the field and takes it back to the workroom (rather than an office) to discuss the information. The last segment of the clip shows the redesigned shopping cart, which is highly innovative. This clip sets up the possibility of discussions on many topics including teams, individual differences, leadership, organizational structure, job design, and motivation.

Lecture/Group Activity

Have groups of students discuss how IDEO's process of innovation could be applied to: organizations in which they are employed, the university student center, or their class projects.

Discussion Questions

1. Are individuals as creative and innovative as groups?

2. What role, if any, does conflict have in creating innovation?

3. What are the implications of promoting innovation in organizations for motivation, selection, decision making, leadership, teams, and individual differences?

PART 5: ORGANIZATIONAL STRUCTURE AND DESIGN

CHAPTER 17: ORGANIZING FOR PERFORMANCE

Clip Source

Achieving Competitive Advantage: Managing for Organizational Effectiveness

Clip Title

Organizing for Performance at Xerox

Video Clip Overview

Paul Allayer, Chairman and CEO of Xerox Corporation, describes how it was necessary for Xerox to redesign its organizational structure in order to be able to meet its strategic goals. Xerox and many other companies in the United States of America are restructuring units around different classes of customers. These units, called SBUs or strategic business units, are made to be relatively independent. This type of structure increases the company's ability to be flexible. Michael Useem, a professor of management and sociology at The Wharton School, comments on the idea of structuring the organization to meet the strategic goals.

Lecture/Group Activity

Divide the class into three groups. Assign one group to identify the advantages and disadvantages of a mechanistic structure. hey should also identify an organizational goal that would be supported by a mechanistic structure. Another group should complete the assignment for an organic structure, and the third group should address a hybrid structure. Discuss the results with the entire class.

Discussion Questions

1. What are the factors that executives should consider when designing an organization?

2. Considering the description of Xerox's corporate structure in the video clip, is this a mechanistic, organic, or hybrid structure?

3. How can a company designed like Xerox maintain quality control?

CHAPTER 18: ORGANIZATIONAL DESIGN FOR STRATEGIC COMPETENCY

Clip Source

Technological Change

Clip Title

Technology at the Airport

Video Clip Overview

Information technology (IT) is increasing the efficiency of organizations. In this clip, the impact of IT on Hong Kong's airline industry is explored. The potential of IT includes increased transparency, cost savings, flexibility, and efficiency for organizations. Duplication of effort is reduced among the workers, which increases cost savings. Examples are shown from the kitchen, baggage handling, security, staff training, and customer service areas.

Lecture/Activity

Have the class brainstorm ideas about how IT could improve the efficiency of a local pizza establishment. They need not take into account cost constraints, but they should consider the impact of IT on organizational behavior.

Discussion Questions

1. What impact will technology have on organizations? Employees? Customers?

2. How will IT change how leaders and teams function?

3. What effect might technology have on reward systems within organizations?

CHAPTER 19: ORGANIZATIONAL CULTURE AND DEVELOPMENT

Clip Source

Achieving Competitive Advantage: Managing for Organizational Effectiveness

Clip Title

Organizational Culture as a Competitive Advantage

Video Clip Overview

Michael Useem, a professor of management and sociology at The Wharton School, presents his perspective on organizational culture as a competitive advantage. He discusses the importance of matching reward systems to strategy in creating an organizational culture. Xerox's SBU (strategic business unit) structure and its associated reward system provide an illustrative example. In this clip, the emphasis is placed on making incentives contingent upon performance. Discussing compensation plans, Useem presents the notion of rewarding A while hoping for B. In addition, Southwest Airlines provides an example of a company using selection and training to create an organizational culture that gives the company a competitive advantage. Cross-training is also presented as a way to build teams and as a means of creating empowerment within a culture.

Lecture/Group Activity

Have groups of students outline how they would create an organization culture that is characterized by one of the following values: competition, cooperation, autocratic leadership, participative leadership, individual achievement, or team achievement. They should identify how the role of leadership, teamwork, performance management, and decision making could support the organizational culture. Compare and contrast the group's approaches to highlight the systemic nature of organizations.

Discussion Questions

1. What is organizational culture?

2. Organizational leaders should not waste time thinking about organizational culture, because it will naturally develop on its own. True or False? Why?

3. Organizational culture is easy to develop if you just … what?